Law, Governance and Technology Series

Volume 60

The *Law, Governance and Technology Series* is intended to attract manuscripts arising from an interdisciplinary approach in law, artificial intelligence and information technologies. The idea is to bridge the gap between research in IT law and IT-applications for lawyers developing a unifying techno-legal perspective. The series will welcome proposals that have a fairly specific focus on problems or projects that will lead to innovative research charting the course for new interdisciplinary developments in law, legal theory, and law and society research as well as in computer technologies, artificial intelligence and cognitive sciences. In broad strokes, manuscripts for this series may be mainly located in the fields of the Internet law (data protection, intellectual property, Internet rights, etc.), Computational models of the legal contents and legal reasoning, Legal Information Retrieval, Electronic Data Discovery, Collaborative Tools (e.g. Online Dispute Resolution platforms), Metadata and XML Technologies (for Semantic Web Services), Technologies in Courtrooms and Judicial Offices (E-Court), Technologies for Governments and Administrations (E-Government), Legal Multimedia, and Legal Electronic Institutions (Multi-Agent Systems and Artificial Societies).

Francisco António Carneiro Pacheco de Andrade •
Pedro Miguel Fernandes Freitas •
Joana Rita de Sousa Covelo de Abreu
Editors

Legal Developments on Cybersecurity and Related Fields

Springer

Editors
Francisco António Carneiro Pacheco de Andrade
School of Law
University of Minho
Braga, Portugal

Pedro Miguel Fernandes Freitas
Faculty of Law Oporto
Catholic University of Portugal
Porto, Portugal

Joana Rita de Sousa Covelo de Abreu
School of Law
University of Minho
Braga, Portugal

ISSN 2352-1902 ISSN 2352-1910 (electronic)
Law, Governance and Technology Series
ISBN 978-3-031-41819-8 ISBN 978-3-031-41820-4 (eBook)
https://doi.org/10.1007/978-3-031-41820-4

This Springer imprint is published by the registered company Springer Nature Switzerland AG
The registered company address is: Gewerbestrasse 11, 6330 Cham, Switzerland

Paper in this product is recyclable.

Contents

Legal Developments on Cybersecurity and Related Fields: Introductory Notes and Presentation

Francisco António Carneiro Pacheco de Andrade, Pedro Miguel Freitas, and Joana Rita de Sousa Covelo de Abreu

This book presents an innovative approach to cybersecurity issues, aiming not only to analyse the legal landscape of the European Union and its Member States, but to do it in an interdisciplinary way. Its interdisciplinary style is based on the need to understand cybersecurity demands on wider terms, approaching not only traditional matters but also emerging topics. Cybersecurity cannot be solely equated in the light of cybercrime and/or cyber defence; it also has to be thought through the lens of specific approaches, related to different legal fields, without forgetting ethical demands and fundamental rights protection, particularly, personal data protection. Only by doing so is it possible to understand its importance and role in the exercise of public power, the essential role it can play in fundamental values of Member States and of the European Union (such us the rule of law) and in providing trust, transparency and effectiveness to market relations and public administration interactions.

Furthermore, the book relies on the expertise of the authors to introduce insights on ICT components and technologies as their holistic understanding is relevant to perceive each and every "cyber" phenomenon.

Insofar, the Joint Communication of the European Commission and the High Representative of the Union for Foreign Affairs and Security Policy establishing "The EU's Cybersecurity Strategy for the Digital Decade" [JOIN(2020) 18 final], understand cybersecurity as "an integral part of Europeans' security" and it is "therefore essential for building a resilient, green and digital Europe". As these European entities perceive it, there are very strong "cross-sector interdependences"

F. A. Carneiro Pacheco de Andrade (✉) · J. R. de Sousa Covelo de Abreu
School of Law, University of Minho, Braga, Portugal
e-mail: fandrade@direito.uminho.pt; jabreu@direito.uminho.pt

P. M. Freitas
Porto Faculty of Law, Universidade Católica Portuguesa, Porto, Portugal
e-mail: pfreitas@ucp.pt

F. A. Carneiro Pacheco de Andrade et al. (eds.), *Legal Developments on Cybersecurity and Related Fields*, Law, Governance and Technology Series 60,
https://doi.org/10.1007/978-3-031-41820-4_1

since "[t]ransport, energy and health, telecommunications, finance, security, democratic processes, space and defence are heavily reliant on network and information systems that are increasingly interconnected", which lead to deeper security issues that demand new legal and technical approaches.

In this sense, as presented in the European Commission's Communication "2030 Digital Compass: the European way for the Digital Decade" [COM(2021) 118 final], cybersecurity demands the deepening of digital literacy, especially concerning specialists in this key area, and gender balancing on ICT specialists' sphere.

Furthermore, "digital infrastructure serving citizens, SMEs, the public sector and large companies require high performance computing and comprehensive data infrastructures" but "data produced in Europe is generally stored and processed outside Europe, and its value is also extracted outside Europe", which "can bring risks in terms of cybersecurity" even if business models based on generating and exploiting data must retain their free choice.

This led to the need of a Declaration of rights and principles to the Digital Decade of 2021–2030, where transparency, reliability, data protection and security gain a relevant focus.

In fact, threats to cybersecurity usually have a cross-border expression: in the European Union, it was understood that a cyberattack on critical facilities of one Member State can impact the Union as a whole. In this sense, Member States must rely on governmental bodies that can promote cybersecurity demands and are able to articulate with their counterparts of other Member States. This includes sharing useful information and good practices. The NIS Directive was created to foster cooperation between national governmental bodies while NIS2 Directive, which entered into force on January 16th, 2023, seeks the adoption of a set of measures for a high common level of cybersecurity across the European Union. Member States will have until October 18th, 2024 to transpose its terms into their own national legal orders.

Therefore, if the NIS Directive intended to enhance Union's "cyber resilience" (recital 2 of Directive nr. 2022/2555), the fact is that cybersecurity requirements posed to different operators are quite variable among Member States when it comes to "their level of detail and the method of supervision" which led to "additional costs and [. . .] difficulties for entities that offer goods and services across borders" (recital 4 of Directive nr. 2022/2555). These differences "entail a fragmentation of the internal market and [. . .] its functioning, affecting in particular the cross-border provision of services" which could enhance some Member States' vulnerabilities to cyber threats, "with potential spill-over effects across the Union" (recital 5 of the mentioned Directive).

The NIS2 Directive establishes out minimum rules regarding the functioning of a coordinated regulatory framework with a wide range of entities foreseen in its scope of application which enhances its effectiveness and achieves its main goal of improving the cybersecurity environment in the European Union.

An interdisciplinary approach was needed since cybersecurity must be applicable in heterogenous contexts and technological changes and developments make it inviable to solely implement stable and uniform ethical guidelines. Therefore, the intervention of the legislator and the action of control authorities, both national and supranational, is necessary.

This book consists of three major parts:

- Part 1, under the topic "Cybersecurity, cyberdefence and law", aims at addressing new cybersecurity demands where legal orders are called upon to present new regulatory solutions while also revaluating cybersecurity traditional domains in a new light;
- Part 2, "Cybersecurity and law: specific topics", focuses on emerging and old cybersecurity issues and how they can be addressed now and in the future;
- Part 3, "Cybersecurity, ethics and fundamental rights", brings contributions on current fundamental rights' framework and the ethical demands that might model new regulatory solutions that do not undermine fundamental values while promoting market freedom. In other words, this part examines the ethical and legal considerations, specifically those at the European Union level, and, particularly, issues such as profiling, evidence value and anonymization.

Part 1 is opened by the contribution of Ian Walden and Johan David Michaels, with the topic "Getting critical. Making sense of the EU security framework for cloud providers". In their contribution, these authors try to unravel how the EU cybersecurity regulatory framework impacts cloud computing services' providers in order to perceive if this legal setting can enhance the Union's digital economy and if cloud services can be seen as a critical infrastructure within the new legal approaches on the matter.

Bruno Reynaud de Sousa authored the chapter addressing the topic "Cyber operations targeting space systems. Legal questions and the context of privatisation". In this chapter, the author aims at exposing how cybersecurity issues can arise as space is more and more perceived as "the future frontier of the global economy and society", especially in regards to outer space, earth observation and remote sensing experiences benefiting from private sector innovation.

The following chapter—"A legal assessment of the concept of risk in reversible operations through cyber and electronic means"—is authored by Giulia Pavesi. The objective of this chapter is to deepen legal assessment of the concept of risk, particularly that pertaining to space infrastructures, and the need for legal obligations upon States from an International Public Law and International Space Law perspective.

João Manuel Assis Barbas authored the following chapter under the theme of "Knowledge management and continuous improvement in cyberspace". In this contribution, the author aims to prove "the synergetic correlation between cyberspace, knowledge management and continuous improvement" without undermining the importance of cybersecurity issues, and draw relevant conclusions.

Henrique Santos, Teresa Pereira and André Oliveira, authoring the chapter entitled "Information security metrics: challenges and models in an all-digital world", explore the subject of information security metrics and its role in monitoring, preventing and early detection of threats and the endeavour of an agile approach to cybersecurity.

Part 1 is concluded with a chapter authored by Pedro Miguel Freitas entitled "Cyberterrorism and the Portuguese counter-terrorism act". This chapter considers the international doctrine on the conceptualisation of cyber-terrorism and the Portuguese approach to the subject.

Part 2, which is dedicated to the theme "Cybersecurity and law: specific topics", begins with a chapter authored by Arno Lodder and Joeri Toet, dealing with the following theme: "Towards cybersecurity regulation of software in the European Union". The authors discuss the European legal framework applicable to software, not only equating legislative initiatives but also how principles and legal regime stemming from the GDPR can be useful in finding suitable solutions.

The following contribution, authored by Almudena Valiño Ces, is titled "The importance of the computer undercover agent as an investigative measure against cybercrime: a special reference to child pornography crimes". Based on the sensitivity that "[t]he Internet is a scenario in which a wide range of criminal activities can be carried out", the author understands that it also poses new challenges since it is very difficult to identify those committing crimes – the ones known as "cybercriminals". In this sense, the author aims to know if an undercover computer agent can play a vital role in combating crimes associated with child pornography crimes as "it represents a specific measure of technological investigation".

Marta Otero Crespo addresses the topic "*Post-Mortem* data protection and succession in digital assets under Spanish law". Here, the author aims to clarify the interaction amongst data protection, contract law and inheritance law, from the Spanish legal standpoint.

Pedro Dias Venâncio contributed to the book with a chapter titled "The suitability of the regime of technological measures for copyright protection in the face of modern cybersecurity risks". In this chapter, the author evaluates the need to equate new ways of digitally protecting copyright and related rights before economic exploitation in the digital market where technological protection measures (TPM) gain relevance. These measures are analysed from a legal standpoint, mobilising international, European and national standards to understand their feasibility and adequacy in the current era of digitalization.

Francisco C. P. Andrade and José Carlos Bacelar de Almeida wrote an interdisciplinary chapter on "Digital signatures and quantum computing". The chapter explores the threats of quantum computing for the services of electronic identification, in accordance with Regulation 910/2014, and the particular risks related to digital signatures.

Finally, Ana Rodríguez Álvarez presents the chapter "No words needed? Emojis as evidence in judicial proceedings". Being aware that emojis are a part of our daily communications as a complement to what their user feels, thinks or even wanted to express in words without success, the author analyses the potential of emojis as evidence before courts, highlighting the doubts and challenges they might pose to judicial action in the present and future.

Part 3, which is dedicated to "Cybersecurity, ethics and fundamental rights", begins with the contribution of João Paulo Magalhães, titled "Bug bounties: ethical and legal aspects". The author discusses the role of bug bounty programs in organisations, particularly when the number of vulnerabilities and the cost of detecting them becomes lower, which poses economic, ethical and legal issues, and requires the attention of national and international cybersecurity authorities.

In the next chapter, "Profiling and cybersecurity: a perspective from fundamental rights' protection in the EU", Alessandra Silveira examines the relationship between data protection and AI systems, focusing on GDPR's legal solutions for defending individuals against certain AI applications, such as profiling and automated decisions. The author assesses whether legal remedies are available to challenge automated inferences that are not reasonably justified, considering the fundamental referral stemming from Article 8 of the Charter of Fundamental Rights of the European Union.

The third chapter—"Legal developments on smart public governance and fundamental rights in the digital age"–, is authored by Isabel Celeste Fonseca and Joel Alves. They reflect on the obligation of public administration to explore digital solutions for "smartification of public governance" while still strictly respecting citizens' fundamental rights and freedoms.

Francisco C.P. Andrade, Ana Silva and Ricardo Guimarães analyse "Biometric signatures in the context of Regulation (EU) nr. 920/2014 and the general data protection regulation: the evidential value and anonymization of biometric data". This approach combines the analyses of two important EU regulations, the General Data Protection Regulation and the eIDAS Regulation, and explores the topics of evidence and anonymization.

The book concludes with Joana Covelo de Abreu's chapter on "Cybersecurity issues in electronic communications and some insights on digital literacy and technological infrastructures' demands – anticipations of the European Digital Decade through the lens of a Declaration on digital rights and principles". The author examines the digital divide in the European Union and its impact on cybersecurity demands, which has prompted political policymakers in the European Union to adopt two major goals in the digital decade: to enhance digital literacy and skills, and to establish secure and high-performing sustainable digital infrastructures. This chapter explores whether these goals can be achieved and if the European Declaration on digital rights and principles can "deploy and foster this digital decade".

This book owes its existence to its authors and their invaluable contributions. Since the very beginning they demonstrated full availability to meet rigorous deadlines and cooperate intensively with the Scientific Editors. Such dedication warrants special recognition.

Special mention should also be given to JusGov—Research Centre on Justice and Governance, as it provided a platform for the Scientific Editors to convene and engage in discussions on new and disruptive scenarios concerning cybersecurity. In this sense, Patrícia Jerónimo—former Director of JusGov—played a vital role to this book's debut.

Finally, the Scientific Editors would like to express their gratitude to Springer for its unwavering support, which has helped them to turn this book into a reality.

Francisco António Carneiro Pacheco de Andrade holds a PhD in Law (Legal Privatistic Sciences) from University of Minho and a MSc in Electronic Information Management from the University of Sheffield (United Kingdom). He is auxiliary professor at Universidade do Minho Law School and he has been, for 11 years, the Director of the Master Course in Law and Informatics. He is also lecturer in the same Master in the Units of "Cryptography, Electronic Identification and Documents", "Privacy and Data Protection", "Electronic Commerce and Electronic Contracting". He is an integrated member of JUSGOV—Research Center on Justice and Governation at University of Minho Law School.

Pedro Miguel Freitas holds a PhD in Public Legal Sciences (Criminal Sciences branch) from the Law School of the University of Minho, Portugal. Lecturer and researcher in the areas of Criminal Law and Procedure, Cybercrime and Criminology at the Universidade Católica Portuguesa (Portugal). He is a founding member of the Lusophone Institute of Criminal Justice and a member of the Secure Platform for Accredited Cybercrime Experts. Participated in teaching courses organized by the University of Massachusetts Lowell (USA), the University of Turin (Italy), the Polytechnic University of Valencia (Spain), and the Jean Piaget University (Angola), among others. Currently coordinates the Postgraduate Course on Law and Technology at the Universidade Católica Portuguesa, Portugal.

Joana Rita de Sousa Covelo de Abreu is a Professor of European Union law at the University of Minho – School of Law, Portugal. She acts within the European Union Law, namely devoting her attention to EU Procedure, Data Transfer and Interoperability within European e-Government and e-Justice paradigms. She is the Coordinator of the Jean Monnet Module eUjust—"EU Procedure and credits' claims: approaching electronic solutions under e-Justice paradigm". She was an appointed expert to the modernization of judicial cooperation in civil matters (DG Justice and Consumers—European Commission), in 2018, namely concerning discussing Commission's proposals on taking of evidence and service of documents' Regulations. Editor of UNIO—EU Law Journal and its official blog "Thinking & Debating Europe – The official blog of UNIO".

Part I
Cybersecurity, Cyberdefence and Law

Getting Critical: Making Sense of the EU Cybersecurity Framework for Cloud Providers

Ian Walden and Johan David Michels

Abstract In this chapter, we review how the EU cybersecurity regulatory framework impacts providers of cloud computing services. We examine the evolving regulatory treatment of cloud services as an enabler of the EU's digital economy and question whether all cloud services should be treated as critical infrastructure. Further, we look at how the safeguarding and incident notification obligations under the General Data Protection Regulation ('GDPR') and the Network and Information Systems Directive ('NISD') apply to cloud providers. We also consider how these obligations will develop under the NIS 2 Directive ('NIS2') and look at what newly developed voluntary assurance mechanisms mean for cloud providers, including codes of conduct and certification schemes. We conclude that, since cloud providers are typically subject to both NISD and GDPR and to jurisdiction from multiple regulators, they face divergent regulatory approaches, which can lead to unintended outcomes and high compliance costs.

1 Introduction

The EU cybersecurity regulatory framework has developed rapidly over recent years, both in terms of breadth and depth. In 2018, the General Data Protection Regulation ('GDPR')[1] and the Network and Information Systems Directive

[1]Regulation (EU) 2016/679 on the protection of natural persons with regard to the processing of personal data and on the free movement of such data (2016) OJ L 119 ('GDPR').

I. Walden (✉) · J. D. Michels
Centre for Commercial Law Studies, Queen Mary University of London, London, UK
e-mail: i.n.walden@qmul.ac.uk; d.michels@qmul.ac.uk

F. A. Carneiro Pacheco de Andrade et al. (eds.), *Legal Developments on Cybersecurity and Related Fields*, Law, Governance and Technology Series 60,
https://doi.org/10.1007/978-3-031-41820-4_2

('NISD')[2] came into force. In 2019, the EU Cybersecurity Act followed.[3] In 2023, the Network and Information Systems 2 Directive ('NIS2') came into force, which replaces the NISD.[4] In this chapter, we review what these developments mean for providers of cloud computing services ('cloud providers'). We start by examining the evolving treatment of cloud computing services as an enabler of the EU's digital economy and as critical infrastructure. Then, we review the two core components of the EU cybersecurity framework, namely: (i) safeguarding obligations (including voluntary schemes of assurance), and (ii) incident notification obligations. Finally, we consider issues of jurisdiction, oversight, and enforcement. Throughout, we reflect critically on the evolving regulatory framework and highlight strengths and shortcomings.

Our focus is on the security requirements the GPDR and NISD impose on cloud *providers* directly and generally. We do not cover EU legislation that imposes security requirements on cloud *customers* and so might impact cloud providers indirectly, as part of the supply chain, through contract negotiations. Nor do we examine sectoral requirements, such as the Regulation on Digital Operational Resilience in the financial sector ('DORA'), which applies both to financial entities and to designated cloud providers directly as critical third-party ICT service providers to the financial sector.[5] Finally, we do not cover the Directive on Critical Entities' Resilience ('CERD'), which replaces the European Critical Infrastructure Directive.[6] Cloud providers are covered directly by the CERD as 'critical entities'. This means Member States can identify them as critical providers and include them in their risk assessments and strategies.[7] However, the CERD does not impose cybersecurity obligations on cloud providers directly, since their physical security is already regulated as part of cybersecurity under the NISD.[8] Other elements of the

[2]Directive (EU) 2016/1148 concerning measures for a high common level of security of network and information systems across the Union [2016] OJ L 194/1 ('NISD').

[3]Regulation (EU) 2019/881 of 17 April 2019 on ENISA (the European Union Agency for Cybersecurity) and on information and communications technology cybersecurity certification and repealing Regulation (EU) No 526/2013 ('Cybersecurity Act'), OJ L 151.

[4]Directive (EU) 2022/2555 of 14 December 2022 on measures for a high common level of cybersecurity across the Union, amending Regulation (EU) No 910/2014 and Directive (EU) 2018/1972, and repealing Directive (EU) 2016/1148 ('NIS2'), OJ L 333. Member States have until October 2024 to transpose NIS2 into national law (Art. 41).

[5]Art. 2(u), 31, Recitals 20, 63 Regulation (EU) 2022/2554 of 14 December 2022 on digital operational resilience for the financial sector ('DORA'), OJ L 333. DORA entered into force in 2023. Regulated entities need to comply with it from January 2025.

[6]Directive (EU) 2022/2557 of 14 December 2022 on the resilience of critical entities and repealing Council Directive 2008/114/EC ('CERD'), OJ L 333.

[7]Art.4-6, Recital 20, and Annex under (8) CERD.

[8]Art.1(2), 8 and Recital 9, 20 CERD. See also EU Commission, 'Proposal for a Directive on the resilience of critical entities', 16 December 2020, COM(2020) 829 final, p. 3.

EU cybersecurity framework beyond the scope of this chapter include strengthening and harmonizing criminal law,[9] and the provision of trust services.[10]

2 Scope: Cloud as a Regulated Activity

In a little over 10 years, cloud computing has become the dominant paradigm for data processing. Survey evidence indicates that, as of 2020, 90% of companies used cloud services, running half of their workload and storing half of their data in the public cloud.[11] As a result, the market for public cloud services grew to $270bn in 2020.[12] As cloud computing spread, it raised challenges for applying existing laws and regulations, not least with respect to data protection laws.[13] However, until recently, cloud computing was not a distinct regulated activity, separate from other models for processing data, such as outsourcing. With the NISD, that changed. In 2018, the provision of cloud services became the subject of separate regulatory treatment in the context of cybersecurity.

Cloud computing offers data processing capacity in a flexible, efficient, and readily-accessible manner.[14] Accessing remote computing resources depends on connectivity over communications networks such as the public internet. As examined below, this communications network infrastructure is treated as a separate regulated activity from the networking that comprises part of a cloud computing service. Cloud computing is typically distinguished into three service types: infrastructure-as-a-service ('IaaS'), platform-as-a-service ('PaaS') and software-as-a-service ('SaaS').[15] The deployment of cloud computing can also be divided into different categories, such as public cloud, private cloud, community schemes, and hybrid implementations.[16] While these distinctions do not fully reflect the reality of this large and diverse sector, they can aid legal and policy analysis by highlighting different technical and market conditions.

[9] E.g. Directive 2013/40/EU on attacks against information systems (L 218/8, 14.8.2013).

[10] Regulation (EU) 2014/910 on electronic identification and trust services for electronic transactions in the internal market (L 257/73, 28.8.2014).

[11] Flexera, 'State of the Cloud Report 2020', (2020), https://info.flexera.com/SLO-CM-REPORT-State-of-the-Cloud-2020; Ponemon Institute, 'Protecting Data in the Cloud' (2019), <https://safenet.gemalto.com/cloud-security-research/> Accessed 10 March 2020.

[12] Gartner, 'Gartner Forecasts Worldwide Public Cloud End-User Spending to Grow 23% in 2021', 21 April 2021, https://www.gartner.com/en/newsroom/press-releases/2021-04-21-gartner-forecasts-worldwide-public-cloud-end-user-spending-to-grow-23-percent-in-2021.

[13] See generally Chapters 8–11 in Millard (2021).

[14] National Institute of Standards and Technology, U.S. Department of Commerce, 'Evaluation of Cloud Computing Services Based on NIST SP 800-145, Special Publication 500-322' (2018).

[15] See, for example, ISO/IEC 17788:2014 *Cloud Computing – Overview and Vocabulary.*

[16] National Institute of Standards and Technology, U.S. Department of Commerce, 'Evaluation of Cloud Computing Services Based on NIST SP 800-145, Special Publication 500-322' (2018).

The NISD imposes obligations specifically on providers of cloud computing services, while the GDPR is of general application, but creates complex issues when applied to some cloud providers. This section critically examines this twin-track regulatory approach. Given the prevalence of cloud computing, we question whether it is useful to distinguish between the regulation of cloud services specifically on the one hand, and generic behaviours, such as processing personal data, on the other. This approach can create a regulatory mess that obscures rather than clarifies cybersecurity obligations and imposes unnecessary additional compliance burdens.

2.1 Cloud Providers as Regulated Providers of Critical Infrastructure

Under the NISD, the term 'networks' is shorthand for electronic communication networks,[17] as defined under the New Regulatory Framework,[18] although public electronic communications network (*read:* external service providers) are excluded from the NISD regime.[19] By contrast, the notion of 'information systems' encompasses both on-premises devices for 'processing digital data', as well as the external provision of processing capacity in the form of services such as cloud computing.[20] Cloud computing services primarily fall under the concept of information society services, regulated under the eCommerce Directive.[21] This covers services provided by electronic means, at a distance, and at the request of the service recipient. These services are also referred to as 'OTT', since they are provided 'over-the-top' of the underlying electronic communications networks.

Telecoms networks typically had monopolistic origins and a utility-like nature. As a result, security (in terms of confidentiality, integrity and availability) has always been a key element of the EU regulatory framework. It was traditionally described as an 'essential requirement', embodying the 'general public interest'.[22] However, until 2009, the regulator was tasked with ensuring security,[23] through instruments such as

[17] Art. 4(1)(a) NISD.

[18] Directive 2002/21/EC on a common regulatory framework for electronic communications networks and services, OJ L 108/33, 24.4.2002 ('Framework Directive'), as amended.

[19] Art. 1(3) NISD.

[20] Art. 4(1)(b) NISD. The definition is taken from Directive 2013/40/EU 'on attacks against information systems' OJ L 218/8/, 14.8.2103.

[21] Directive 2000/31/EC on certain legal aspects of information society services, in particular electronic commerce, in the Internal Market, OJ L 178/1, 17.7.2000.

[22] See Walden (2018) at 4.4.2.

[23] Art. 8(4)(f) Framework Directive: "ensuring that the integrity and security of public communications networks are maintained".

prior authorisation.[24] This changed with the 2009 reform, which imposed safeguarding and incident notification obligations directly on operators.[25] In addition, sectoral data protection rules added another layer of security obligations upon providers of 'publicly available electronic communication services'.[26]

In contrast, the regulation of information society services started from the opposite end of the spectrum. In the early 2000s, these newly emerging services were subjected to a light-touch regulatory approach, designed primarily to facilitate their development. At the height of the first dot.com boom, security was not considered a key regulatory need, because the marketplace for these emerging services was characterised by diversity, innovation, and consumer choice.

The regulation of information society services has changed with the NISD and the reform of telecommunications law. First, the NISD imposed safeguarding and notification obligations on digital services providers (or 'DSPs'), which included cloud computing services. Second, the European Electronic Communications Code extended the scope of what constitutes an 'electronic communications service', and as a consequence the safeguarding and notification obligations, to encompass operators of 'interpersonal communication services', which includes cloud-based messaging services.[27] These developments therefore represented a fundamental regulatory shift for cloud services, aligning their regulatory obligations more closely with those of telecoms network operators. The marketplace of information society services has also fundamentally changed over the past two decades, with increased uptake of cloud services, as well as the development of complex supply chains and ever more nuanced service differentiation.

This raises the question: should all cloud service be treated as akin to critical infrastructure? The Commission's original proposal for an NISD listed six types of market operators:

1. e-commerce platforms;
2. internet payment gateways;
3. social networks;
4. search engines;
5. cloud computing services; and,
6. application stores.[28]

---

[24]Directive 2002/20/EC on the authorization of electronic communications networks and services OJ L 108/21, 24.4.2002, Annex, A.16: "Security of public networks against unauthorised access".

[25]The Framework Directive was amended in 2009 by Directive 2009/140/EC, which inserted Chapter IIIa: Security and Integrity of Networks and Services.

[26]Art. 4 Directive 02/58/EC concerning the processing of personal data and the protection of privacy in the electronic communications sector, OJ L 201/37, 31.7.2002, as amended.

[27]Chapter V Directive (EU) 2018/1972 establishing the European Electronic Communications Code (OJ L 321/36, 17.12.2018).

[28]EU Commission, 'Proposal for a Directive concerning measures to ensure a high common level of network and information security across the Union' COM(2013) 48 final, 7.2.2013 ('Proposal'), at Annex II.

This list was intended to be non-exhaustive, meaning that the measures could extend to other types of service providers.[29] According to the Commission, the distinguishing criterion was information society services that "enable the provision of other information services", meaning services which "underpin downstream information society services or on-line activities".[30] The Proposal explicitly excluded "software developers and hardware manufacturers", a distinction that remains in the final version.[31] In the final version of the NISD, the list of DSPs became exhaustive and was trimmed down from six to three. Yet the NISD rationale for the inclusion of the listed categories of DSPs became even more vague. The limitation to supply chains for the provision of other information society services disappeared, since all types of persons and entities rely on DSP services. Instead, the NISD stated that such services "*could be* an important resource for their users" and therefore reliance may be a source of vulnerability as "users *might not always* have alternatives available" [emphasis added]. Further, "many businesses in the Union increasingly rely" on DSPs "for the smooth functioning" of their businesses. As a result, disruption of DSP services could impact "key economic and societal activities in the Union". [32]

At face value, this seems a remarkably weak basis upon which to justify the imposition of a regulatory regime, with no evidence data proffered to support it. The stated rationale suggests two possible underlying factors: (i) widespread uptake and reliance; and (ii) limited alternative suppliers. As noted above, survey evidence certainly indicates that the use of cloud services is widespread. However, the degree to which users rely on such services "for the smooth functioning of their business" would seem to differ per service, depending on its functionality. SaaS services in particular support a wide range of different operational functions, from advertising on social media to backing-up files. Not all of these functions are equally 'critical'.

In terms of available 'alternatives', this could be as a result of market concentration and/or vendor lock-in, due to high switching costs. While a full market assessment lies beyond the scope of this paper, it could be argued that there is significant market concentration in the IaaS sector, particularly in the form of the hyperscale providers AWS, Microsoft Azure and Google Cloud.[33] Similar to telecoms networks, the IaaS market features high sunk costs and therefore may tend towards oligopoly. However, market conditions appear to differ at the PaaS and SaaS layers, although some have expressed concerns that market power at the IaaS layer might enable hyperscale providers to influence the markets for PaaS and

[29] Art. 3(8)(a) Proposal.

[30] Recital 24 Proposal.

[31] Recital 50 NISD.

[32] Recital 48 NISD.

[33] These hyperscale IaaS providers do face increasing competition from Chinese providers such as Alibaba and Tencent.

SaaS.[34] However, a competition-led rationale would seem difficult to justify given the current scale and diversity of the market, especially at the SaaS layer. The imposition of additional cybersecurity obligations could also have the counterproductive effect of entrenching market concentration by increasing regulatory costs that are borne most easily by larger operators. [35]

In terms of vendor lock-in, the ease of switching between cloud providers would depend on service type, as well as the applications deployed and the amount and format of data stored in the cloud. The on-demand, self-service nature of cloud services certainly provides customers with flexibility that should support switching, although, in practice, migrating applications and large data sets can be technically challenging, costly and time-consuming. Nonetheless, regulation has been introduced to facilitate porting of data between service providers, designed to lower switching costs.[36] Further, in February 2022, the Commission proposed a new regulation referred to as the 'Data Act'.[37] This imposes obligations on "providers of data processing services" to remove obstacles to porting data, as well as obligations on IaaS-providers specifically to support switching.[38] Second, there is a greater potential capability of cloud users to self-provision some or all of the facilities received 'as-a-service'. This distinguishes cloud from other 'critical' infrastructures that are not generally replicable in-house. Third, in terms of security, where a business completely relies on a single cloud provider for its "smooth functioning", such 'single-sourcing' would itself seem to be a poor security practice – and potentially an issue of corporate governance in terms of meeting obligations to ensure business continuity.[39] In sum, the argument for treating *all* cloud services as critical infrastructure, akin to telecoms networks, appears under-developed, at best, and weak, at worst.

Finally, the NISD distinction between software offered 'as-a-product' and 'as-a-service' also seems problematic, as well as being an age-old debate with the field of computer law. [40] The only justification proffered for excluding hardware manufacturers and software developers from the regime is that they are "already subject to

[34] See e.g. https://www.forbes.com/sites/peterbendorsamuel/2020/03/02/hyperscale-cloud-providers-shaping-the-platform-marketplace/?sh=7f031956103d.

[35] A similar argument can, and has, been made in respect of the GDPR.

[36] With respect to measures designed to facilitate the porting of data between service providers, see Art. 6 Regulation (EU) 2018/1807 'on a framework for the free flow of non-personal data in the European Union' (OJ L303/59, 28.11.2018). See also the Art. 20 GDPR.

[37] European Commission, "Proposal for a Regulation of the European Parliament and of the Council on harmonised rules on fair access to and use of data (Data Act)", (2022), COM(2022) 68 final ('Proposed Data Act').

[38] Art. 23, 26 Proposed Data Act.

[39] See, for example, the US Securities and Exchange Commission, 17 CFR Parts 229 and 249 (Release Nos. 33-10459; 34-82746), *Commission Statement and Guidance on Public Company Cybersecurity Disclosures* (18 February 2018). See also UK consultation on 'Restoring trust in audit and corporate governance' with regard to resilience statements (March 2021).

[40] See e.g. Samuelson (1993), p. 21; Pinkney (2002), pp. 62–82.

existing rules on product liability".[41] Although liability incentives are one element of a comprehensive policy response to enhancing security, they are more complex and convoluted tools for signalling and facilitating behavioural change than the imposition of direct compliance obligations. This is even more true in respect of product liability, where the regime has largely fallen into disuse.[42] Further action is needed in this space and has begun. In 2022, the Commission adopted a measure on the cybersecurity of radio equipment;[43] while the UK enacted the Product Security and Telecommunications Infrastructure Act 2022, which requires manufacturers, importers or distributors of 'relevant connectable products', such as IoT devices, to implement certain security requirements.[44]

The NIS2 promotes providers of cloud computing services to 'essential entities' (the new 'higher' category that replaces operators of essential services or 'OES'), together with data centre providers and content delivery network ('CDN') providers. Cloud, data centre, and CDN providers fall in the 'digital infrastructure' category of essential entities. alongside Internet Exchange Point ('IXP') providers, Domain Name System ('DNS') service providers, and Top Level Domain ('TLD') registries (which are all currently regulated as OES under the NISD). In addition, the NIS2 introduces "ICT service management" as a new category of essential entity, which includes managed service providers. By contrast, online marketplaces and online search engines remain merely 'important entities' (the new 'lower' category that replaces DSPs), together with newly regulated social networking service platforms. [45] In its proposal, the Commission had stated that the recategorization took into account both "the level of criticality of the sector or of the type of service, as well as the level of dependency of other sectors or types of service". Unfortunately, the Commission failed to provide analysis or evidence to indicate how these factors have been measured and assessed.[46] Treating all cloud services as essential (as opposed to merely important) is particularly problematic since, as we have argued above, the argument for treating all cloud services as critical is itself under-developed.

Further, the NIS2 also alters the definition of cloud computing in three respects. First, it is unclear whether the current definition under NISD covers private cloud, which arguably does not involve 'shareable' resources, since it typically entails

---

[41] Recital 48 NISD.

[42] Noto La Diega and Walden (2016).

[43] Commission Delegated Regulation (EU) 2022/30 of 29 October 2021 supplementing Directive 2014/53/EU of the European Parliament and of the Council with regard to the application of the essential requirements referred to in Article 3(3), points (d), (e) and (f), of that Directive, OJ L 7.

[44] Product Security and Telecommunications Infrastructure Act 2022.

[45] Art. 3 and Annexes, NIS2. This applies to all cloud providers who do not qualify as micro, small and medium-sized enterprises ('SMEs') under Art. 2(1) of the Annex to Recommendation 2003/361/EC Commission Recommendation of 6 May 2003 concerning the definition of micro, small and medium-sized enterprises. SMEs employ fewer than 250 persons and have an annual turnover not exceeding EUR 50 million, and/or an annual balance sheet total not exceeding EUR 43 million.

[46] EU Commission, 'Proposal for a Directive on measures for a high common level of cybersecurity across the Union, repealing Directive (EU) 2016/1148'(2020) COM(2020) 823 final, Recital 11.

physically separated hardware for each customer.[47] We have previously argued that private cloud *should* be considered critical, since disruption of private cloud could equally have far-reaching effects on key economic and societal activities, given the widespread adoption of corporate hybrid cloud strategies.[48] The new definition under NIS2 explicitly includes all deployment models, including private cloud. That said, private cloud deployments might not involve access to an "elastic pool of shareable" resource (defined as different users being served "from the same underlying equipment"), which remains part of the NIS2 definition of cloud.[49] The definition therefore seems internally inconsistent. Second, cloud services should enable "on-demand administration", which is described as the capability for a "user to unilaterally self-provision".[50] While part of the standard NIST definition, [51] it is not immediately obvious why this characteristic is a necessary part of the new legal definition, unless the implication is that self-provision generates greater security risks. Third, it must involve *remote* access to resources. This could be interpreted as excluding on-premises private cloud services, [52] although the use of on-premises resources can be viewed either as a security risk or a mitigation measure. The amended definition of cloud still contains ambiguities, that might make it more difficult for service providers to determine whether they fall within the regulation's scope.[53]

2.2 Cloud Providers as Regulated Processors of Personal Data

The GDPR applies generally to the processing of personal data. Under the GDPR, security is a critical component of the compliance regime. Controllers have an obligation to comply with, and be able to demonstrate compliance with, the 'integrity and confidentiality' principle, by which they should ensure that any personal data is processed with 'appropriate security'.[54] This principle is then elaborated into specific obligations on both controller and processor to implement 'appropriate technical and organisational measures'; which are examined further below in Sect.

[47] See Michels and Walden (2021), pp. 396–397.

[48] Michels and Walden (2021), p. 397.

[49] Art. 6(30), Recital 33 NIS2.

[50] Art. 6(30), Recital 33 NIS2.

[51] National Institute of Standards and Technology, U.S. Department of Commerce, Eric Simmon 'Evaluation of Cloud Computing Services Based on NIST SP 800-145, Special Publication 500-322' (2018), 3 <https://nvlpubs.nist.gov/nistpubs/SpecialPublications/NIST.SP.500-322.pdf> accessed 5 December 2019 (hereafter NIST, 'Special Publication 500-322').

[52] E.g. AWS Outposts.

[53] See further Michels and Walden (2021), pp. 396–398.

[54] Art. 5(1)(f) GDPR.

3. While controllers and processors share certain obligations, the compliance burden sits more heavily with the controller than the processor. It is therefore important to consider the different roles of cloud computing providers under the GDPR regime, as controller, joint controller, processor and/or sub-processor.[55]

With respect to personal data placed on a cloud service by a customer, cloud providers are normally viewed as processors or sub-processors, processing data on behalf of the customer as controller. This is likely to be more obviously the case the further down the cloud supply chain, with PaaS and IaaS providers exercising less control over the customer's processing activity than a SaaS provider, who may, depending on the nature of the processing activity and relationship with the customer, be considered a joint controller in respect of certain personal data.[56] Conversely, for personal data generated through use of the cloud service by the cloud customer and its users, as meta-data, the cloud provider will generally be acting as the controller. However, any determination of the regulatory status of a provider of cloud computing services will ultimately be based on their actual role in the particular circumstances, rather than any designation contained in contractual statements.[57]

While the GDPR operates on the presumption that the controller issues instructions to the processor, in the cloud market, the service provider as processor will generally determine the conditions under which the service is used and thereby the ability of the controller to meet its compliance obligations. Indeed, given the size of some of the market players, such as AWS and Google, we have seen the emergence of GDPR 'compliance-as-a-service' offerings, whereby service providers provide customers with the necessary assurances required by the customer as controller to meet their compliance obligations, including evidencing accountability, in terms of ensuring appropriate security.[58]

Finally, the GDPR does not apply to companies that merely develop hardware and software for processing personal data, but do not process personal data themselves. Instead, "producers of [. . .] products, services, and applications" are merely "encouraged to take into account the right to data protection".[59] As a result, software developers who offer software 'as a product' are covered neither by the NISD, nor by the GDPR. In contrast, a company that offers the same software 'as a service' would be covered as a cloud provider under the NISD and a processor under the GDPR. The omission of hardware and software developers from the scope of the EU cybersecurity regulatory framework leaves a hole that product liability rules alone are unfit to fill.[60]

---

[55] See further Kamarinou et al. (2021).

[56] See C-40/17, Fashion ID GmbH & Co KG v Verbraucherzentrale NRW eV [2020] 1 C.M.L.R. 16; Millard et al. (2019).

[57] EDPB, Guidelines 07/2020 on the concepts of controller and processor in the GDPR, at para. 12.

[58] See Kamarinou et al. (2018).

[59] Recital 78 GDPR.

[60] See Fuster and Jasmontaite (2020), pp. 109–110; Wolters (2017), pp. 171–172.

3 Substance: Cybersecurity Obligations for Cloud Providers

The EU cybersecurity regulatory framework imposes two categories of obligation:

1. safeguarding obligations; and,
2. incident notification obligations.

Broadly speaking, the first category requires cloud providers to take measures to prevent, and mitigate damages from, security incidents. The second is triggered after a provider has suffered a security incident and imposes obligations to notify certain parties. Below, we address each component in turn.

3.1 Safeguarding Obligations

Regulations typically oblige entities to put in place *appropriate* and *proportionate* security measures. For example, under the NISD, DSPs must take "appropriate and proportionate technical and organisational measures" to manage the risks posed to the security of the IT systems they use and ensure a level of security appropriate to the risk posed.[61] Under the GDPR, controllers are responsible for "appropriate security" as a principle of personal data processing;[62] while controllers and processors are required to "implement appropriate technical and organisational measures to ensure a level of security appropriate to the risks" posed to the rights and freedoms of natural persons.[63] On top of this overarching, principles-based safeguarding obligation, the NISD layers more specific security objectives addressed to cloud providers. DSPs must aim for "ensuring the continuity of their services".[64] The Commission's Implementing Regulation further lists required "security elements", including physical security, security of critical supplies, and controls on physical and logical access.[65] The GDPR also spells out specific security objectives for controllers and processors, to ensure the CIA of processing systems and the ability to restore access to personal data.[66] It further mentions pseudonymisation and

[61] Art. 16(1)-(2) NISD.

[62] Art. 5(1)(f) GDPR.

[63] Art. 32 GDPR.

[64] Art. 16(1) NISD.

[65] Commission Implementing Regulation (EU) 2018/151 laying down rules for application of Directive (EU) 2016/1148 as regards further specification of the elements to be taken into account by digital service providers, OJ L 26, Art. 2 (hereafter 'Commission NIS Implementing Regulation').

[66] Art. 32(1)(b) and (c) GDPR.

encryption as measures for protecting personal data, as well as a process for regularly testing and evaluating security measures.[67]

These obligations do not require cloud providers to put in place specific security measures (such as cryptography or two-factor-authentication for access control) or assurance methods (such as external on-site audits or penetration testing). Instead, they require cloud providers to engage in risk management: the ongoing process of identifying, assessing, and responding to risk.[68] As the European Commission put it, the NISD "promotes a risk management culture".[69] The NIS2 maintains this risk-management-based approach.[70] The regulations *do* guide cloud providers' risk management by listing factors they should consider. For example, both the NISD and the GDPR require the provider to consider the 'state of the art' and the cost of implementation.[71] Thus, cloud providers must keep abreast of technological developments, but need only adopt cost-effective measures.[72] In effect, safeguarding obligations are more about process than about outcomes. In other words, they are "an obligation of means".[73] To comply, a provider must follow a defined risk management process, analyse relevant information, and make a good-faith determination on how to respond.[74] As Banasiński and Rojszczak put it: because "information security is a process rather than a state", the prevailing regulatory approach is "based on assessing the maturity of the process of ensuring security".[75] To prove compliance, an entity must document its risk management carefully and comprehensively. For example, under NISD, DSPs must have adequate documentation to enable the competent authority to verify compliance with security requirements.[76] Under the GDPR, being able to demonstrate compliance is part of the accountability principle.[77]

---

[67] Art. 32(1) GDPR.

[68] See National Institute of Standards and Technology ('NIST'), "NIST Framework for improving critical infrastructure cybersecurity v. 1.1", (2018), p. 4.

[69] European Commission, 'Report assessing the consistency of the approaches taken by Member States in the identification of operators of essential services in accordance with Art. 23(1) of Directive 2016/1148/EU on security of network and information systems', (2019) COM(2019) 546 final.

[70] Art. 21 NIS2.

[71] Art. 32(1) GDPR; Art. 16(1) NISD. The Art. 16(1) NISD reference to 'proportionate' measures suggests the cost of measures is a relevant factor, particularly since the Directive aims to avoid imposing disproportionate financial or administrative burdens on the regulated entities. See further NIS Cooperation Group, "Reference Document on security measures for Operators of Essential Services", CG Publication 01/2018, p. 9.

[72] Kamarinou et al. (2021), p. 318.

[73] Wolters (2017), p. 171.

[74] Michels and Walden (2021), pp. 409–412.

[75] Banasiński and Rojszczak (2021), p. 10.

[76] Art. 2(6) Commission NIS Implementing Regulation.

[77] Art. 5(2) GDPR.

Such open, principles-based safeguarding obligations can lead to legal uncertainty, since different courts and regulators might interpret them differently. [78] Regulators and other official bodies can reduce this uncertainty somewhat by issuing guidance on how to interpret and implement risk management in practice. For example, in 2016, ENISA published technical guidelines for DSPs under NISD. The guidelines define "common baseline security objectives" and describe measures that DSPs can implement to meet these objectives, with reference to common industry standards such as by the International Organisation for Standardisation ('ISO'). [79] National regulators also publish guidance. For example, the Commission Nationale Informatique et Libertés ('CNIL') (the French supervisory authority), has published a guide on securing personal data under the GDPR.[80] Such guidance can be helpful, although it is generally non-binding. However, if different national regulators publish different guidance under GDPR, this can complicate compliance for cloud providers, who are often subject to concurrent territorial jurisdiction, as discussed below in Sect. 4.1.

In sum, as DSPs under NISD, cloud providers need to manage the risk that a service disruption would pose to broader societal and economic activities. To do so, they must consider, inter alia, the type of service they provide and their relevant market share. As controllers under the GDPR, cloud providers need to manage the risks to the rights and freedoms of data subjects, taking into account the type of data and the "nature, scope, context and purposes" of their processing activities.[81] What about cloud providers acting as processors? The GDPR imposes an independent obligation to ensure appropriate security on processors, which did not exist under the previous Data Protection Directive. [82] Yet there are limits to how cloud providers acting as processors can exercise the required risk management, in two respects: (i) control and (ii) knowledge. First, since cloud resources are often self-service, a cloud provider necessarily shares control over security aspects with its customers. [83] For example, while an IaaS provider controls security at the physical infrastructure and virtualisation layers, customers control the security of the software they install on virtual machines and configuration settings.[84] As a result, the cloud provider-as-processor's responsibility should be limited to security aspects within its control.

[78] Wolters (2017), p. 175; Calliess and Baumgarten (2020), pp. 1167–1168.

[79] ENISA, "Technical Guidelines for the implementation of minimum security measures for Digital Service Providers", (2016), p. 11. See also, ENISA, "Guidelines on assessing DSP and OES compliance to the NISD security requirements", (2018).

[80] CNIL, "Security of Personal Data", (2018), https://www.cnil.fr/sites/default/files/atoms/files/cnil_guide_securite_personnelle_gb_web.pdf.

[81] Art. 32(1) GDPR.

[82] Directive 95/46/EC of the European Parliament and of the Council of 24 October 1995 on the protection of individuals with regard to the processing of personal data and on the free movement of such data.

[83] ENISA, "Cloud Security for Healthcare Services", January 2021, p. 14.

[84] Kuan Hon et al. (2021a), pp. 28–29.

Second, a cloud provider might have limited knowledge of how its service is being used. Admittedly, in some cases, the nature of the service might indicate its use, such as with a SaaS-service for HR or payroll functions. Yet in other cases, the cloud provider cannot reasonably foresee customer use. For example, imagine IaaS provider 'A' with thousands of customers. A has no idea how each customer is using the self-service resources it makes available. Further, in case of 'cloud layering', provider 'B' might build a SaaS-service on top of A's IaaS service, which B's customer ('C') uses to process personal data. In that case, A would have no contact with or insight into C's processing. What's more, if either B or C encrypts data, A might technically be unable to determine what data is being stored, even if it tried.[85] So, how can a provider as (sub-)processor consider the "nature, scope, context and purposes" of processing? For A to engage in meaningful risk management, each customer would need to inform A of relevant factors such as the types of personal data they are processing. What's more, customers would need to update this information on an ongoing basis, as their cloud use develops. Finally, in case of layered cloud, this information would need to be passed down the supply chain to sub-processors. This is difficult to align with the passive provision of self-service resources on a one-to-many basis as practised by major public cloud providers.[86]

The GDPR tries to achieve such supply-chain transparency by requiring the controller to enter into a contract with the processor that details the "subject-matter and duration" and "nature and purpose" of processing, as well as "the type of personal data and categories of data subjects".[87] The processor is then obliged to pass the same information onto any sub-processor used to carry out processing on behalf of the controller.[88] However, in practice, cloud contracts are typically based on the provider's standard terms. These often describe types of data at a general level, by reference to whatever the customer chooses to upload to the cloud.[89] This generic description provides little input for a provider's risk assessment. This mismatch between processor risk management obligations, on the one hand, and a cloud provider's control and knowledge, on the other, can lead to significant legal uncertainty. In theory, a provider could take a cautious approach and apply the strictest security measures to all its services. However, this would increase the cost of cloud services for all customers, regardless of the risks posed by the relevant processing. That would not be in line with the regulations' requirement of "appropriate and proportionate" security. Instead, the cloud industry has responded by addressing this uncertainty through GDPR codes of conduct, which we review below.

---

[85] Kamarinou et al. (2021), p. 317.

[86] Kuan Hon et al. (2021a), p. 33.

[87] Art. 28(3) GDPR.

[88] Art. 28(4) GDPR.

[89] Kuan Hon (2021b), pp. 116–117.

3.1.1 Assurance Methods: Certification and Codes of Conduct

Assurance refers to a set of actions that bring some level of confidence that certain security requirements are met.[90] A cloud provider can provide assurance that it is fulfilling its safeguarding obligations through certification and/or adherence to a code of conduct. In 2021, ENISA proposed a draft certification scheme for cloud providers under the Cybersecurity Act,[91] and the EDPB issued positive opinions on two codes of conduct under the GDPR.[92] These assurance schemes are voluntary.[93] The GDPR explicitly states that controllers and processors can use adherence to an approved code of conduct to demonstrate compliance with security obligations.[94] The NISD does not explicitly mention certification. Nonetheless, certification under ENISA's scheme should help cloud providers demonstrate compliance with NISD. The NIS2 goes one step further: Member States and the Commission can *require* essential and important entities (including cloud providers) to certify ICT services under specific certification schemes to demonstrate compliance or to only use certified ICT services.[95] Cloud providers could, in future, face mandatory certification requirements under NIS2, while cloud *customers* who are regulated as essential or important entities could be required to only use certified cloud services. Below, we first review ENISA's draft certification scheme for cloud providers, before describing the sector-specific codes of conduct for GDPR.

The Cybersecurity Act tasks ENISA with setting up a certification framework for ICT services.[96] In December 2020, at the Commission's request, ENISA published a draft certification scheme for cloud services ('EUCS').[97] ENISA is also developing schemes for ICT products ('EUCC') and for 5G networks ('EU5G').[98] The EUCS builds on existing national schemes, such as C5 in Germany and SecNumCloud in

---

[90] ENISA, "Cybersecurity certification is a global trade and trust instrument", webinar slides, 11 January 2021, https://www.enisa.europa.eu/events/eventfiles/enisa-cybersecurity-certification-of-cloud-services-presentation p. 16.

[91] ENISA, "EUCS – Cloud Service Scheme", (2020).

[92] Opinion 17/2021 on the draft decision of the French Supervisory Authority regarding the European code of conduct submitted by the Cloud Infrastructure Service Providers (CISPE), adopted 19 May 2021 and Opinion 16/2021 on the draft decision of the Belgian Supervisory Authority regarding the "EU Data Protection Code of Conduct for Cloud Service Providers" submitted by Scope Europe. Both adopted on 19 May 2021.

[93] Art. 56(2), Recitals 91-92 Cybersecurity Act.

[94] Art. 32(3), 40, 42 GDPR. The GDPR also mentions 'approved certification mechanisms'. See, for example, the GDPR-CARPA certification scheme adopted in Luxembourg: https://cnpd.public.lu/en/actualites/national/2022/06/adpoption-gdpr-carpa.html.

[95] Art. 24 NIS2.

[96] Art. 8 Cybersecurity Act.

[97] European Commission, 'Towards a more secure and trusted cloud in Europe', 9 December 2019, https://ec.europa.eu/digital-single-market/en/news/towards-more-secure-and-trusted-cloud-europe; ENISA, "EUCS – Cloud Service Scheme", (2020), 49–50.

[98] See ENISA, 'Learn more about EU Cybersecurity Certification', https://www.enisa.europa.eu/topics/certification/eu-cybersecurity-certification-faq accessed 28 March 2023.

France.[99] Certification reflects that the cloud provider has met a number of listed security objectives to a certain level of assurance. There are three assurance levels. A *basic* level of assurance can be achieved through the assessment of technical documentation. A *substantial* level requires an additional review of known vulnerabilities and testing of through on-site audits. A *high* level of assurance requires an additional assessment of the system's resistance to skilled attackers, by means of penetration testing.[100] The EUCS contains a detailed 80-page list of security measures for each assurance level, such as two-factor authentication ('2FA') for access to non-public areas of physical sites; signature-based and behaviour-based malware protection tools; data backup at a remote location; and regular penetration tests. The EUCS further includes measures for identity and access management ('IAM'), such as account-specific privileges and encrypted storage of passwords, and encryption mechanisms and key management.[101] Despite this level of detail, the EUCS aims to be technology-neutral.[102] This leaves scope for provider discretion in implementation. For example, while the EUCS refers to 2FA, it doesn't require specific techniques (such as strong passwords). That leaves cloud providers free to experiment with effective alternatives, such as 'password-less' authentication based on biometrics. ENISA will publish further guidance on accepted techniques for fulfilling EUCS objectives.[103]

Further, as a sector-specific scheme, the EUCS accounts for the cloud-specific issues we identified above, such as shared responsibility and cloud layering. For example, it requires providers to explicitly and publicly document the allocation of responsibility for security between provider and customer.[104] Further, SaaS-providers who rely on an underlying IaaS-provider face a simplified certification process, if they use a certified sub-provider. Provided the split of responsibilities between the providers is defined, the SaaS-provider can rely on the underlying sub-provider's certification for relevant aspects of the system (such as access controls on physical sites).[105] Discussion of the draft EUCS was ongoing as of the time of writing, in April 2023.

Under the GDPR, national supervisory authorities can approve codes of conduct for processing activities in their territory. For processing activities in multiple Member States, the national supervisory authority shall first seek an opinion from

[99] ENISA, "Cybersecurity certification is a global trade and trust instrument", webinar slides, 11 January 2021, https://www.enisa.europa.eu/events/eventfiles/enisa-cybersecurity-certification-of-cloud-services-presentation pp. 24, 34–36.

[100] Art. 52(1), (6)-(7), 53(1) Cybersecurity Act; ENISA, "EUCS – Cloud Service Scheme", (2020), pp. 19–20, 24–26.

[101] ENISA, "EUCS – Cloud Service Scheme", (2020), pp. 81–159.

[102] ENISA, "EUCS – Cloud Service Scheme", (2020), p. 82.

[103] ENISA, "EUCS – Cloud Service Scheme", (2020), p. 82.

[104] ENISA, "EUCS – Cloud Service Scheme", (2020), p. 9.

[105] ENISA refers to this as 'composition' on a 'base cloud service', see ENISA, "EUCS – Cloud Service Scheme", (2020), pp. 74–75.

the European Data Protection Board ('EDPB').[106] The Commission can then decide that the approved code of conduct is valid across the EU.[107] In May 2021, the EDPB adopted favourable opinions on two codes of conduct for cloud services.[108] In June 2021, the CNIL approved the Cloud Infrastructure Service Providers in Europe Code ('CISPE').[109] CISPE is tailored specifically to IaaS providers acting as processors.[110] Its members include AWS and some 25 smaller providers.[111] Second, in May 2021, the Belgian Data Protection Authority ('SA') approved the EU Cloud Code of Conduct ('EUCoC').[112] The EUCoC covers all business-to-business cloud service types (i.e. IaaS, PaaS, and SaaS) where the provider acts as a processor.[113] Its members include Microsoft and Google Cloud, as well as others including Alibaba Cloud, Cisco, Dropbox, IBM, Oracle, Salesforce, and SAP.[114] Like the EUCS, the CISPE and EUCoC list security objectives that cover a range of topics including physical security, logical access management, encryption, vulnerability management, and logging and monitoring. The codes also provide examples of relevant security measures, with reference to relevant international standards, such as ISO.[115]

These sector-specific codes also account for cloud-specific issues. For example, the CISPE Code sets out a shared responsibility model for IaaS-providers that addresses the complications of knowledge and control we described above. Specifically, CISPE recognises that IaaS-providers "have no control" over whether customers use the service for processing personal data and, if so, for what purpose.[116] Only the customer knows its intended processing in sufficient detail to determine an appropriate level of security.[117] To address this, the CISPE Code allocates responsibilities between the IaaS provider and the customer. Broadly speaking, the provider is responsible for the physical infrastructure, the virtualisation layer, and any host operating software. We refer to this as the 'host system'. Conversely, the customer is

[106] Art. 40(6)-(7) GDPR.

[107] Art. 40(9) GDPR.

[108] EDPB, "EDPB adopts opinions on first transnational codes of conduct", 20 May 2021, https://edpb.europa.eu/news/news/2021/edpb-adopts-opinions-first-transnational-codes-conduct-statement-data-governance-act_en.

[109] CNIL, "The CNIL approves the first European code of conduct for cloud infrastructure service providers (IaaS)" (2021), https://www.cnil.fr/en/cnil-approves-first-european-code-conduct-cloud-infrastructure-service-providers-iaas.

[110] CISPE Code, 9 February 2021, available at https://cispe.cloud/, pp. 5–6.

[111] https://cispe.cloud/members/.

[112] Belgian Data Protection Authority, "Approval decision of the "Eu Data Protection Code of Conduct for Cloud Service Providers" (2021), Decision n° 05/2021 of 20 May 2021 https://www.dataprotectionauthority.be/publications/decision-n05-2021-of-20-may-2021.pdf.

[113] EUCoC, pp. 3–4.

[114] https://eucoc.cloud/en/home/.

[115] CISPE Code, Annex A, pp. 58-71; EUCoC, pp. 17-20, 24, Annex A, pp. 29–46.

[116] CISPE Code, p. 14.

[117] CISPE Code, p. 19.

responsible for software it installs on the host system.[118] We refer to this as 'guest software'. This distinction between responsibility for the host system and guest software resembles AWS's distinction between the provider's responsibility for security '*of* the cloud' and the customer's responsibility for security '*in* the cloud'.[119] Under the Code, the provider must implement a "baseline" of security measures for the host system and can offer additional "enhanced" measures for customers to select and apply.[120] As under the EUCS, the provider must clearly document its measures and the split of responsibilities. The customer has ultimate responsibility for ensuring that an appropriate overall level of security is in place for its processing activities.[121]

The EUCoC similarly implies a shared responsibility model. As under CISPE, the provider must provide a "baseline" of security and must transparently describe the security measures in place. The provider can offer further "security options", which customers can choose to apply.[122] The EUCoC further acknowledges the complications IaaS-providers face when acting as processors, by stating that providers must take account of their "knowledge (if any) of the sensitivity of the Customer Personal Data being processed", including by considering "the nature of the Cloud Service" and the impact of a data breach "insofar as this is known to the [provider]". By way of example, a provider might gain actual knowledge of sensitive personal data being processed through negotiations with the customer.[123] This implies that, in other situations, the provider might not have relevant knowledge at all.

In sum, the EUCS and GDPR Codes of Conduct provide welcome legal certainty in three respects. First, they provide a greater level of *specificity* as to the objectives and kinds of measures that constitute "appropriate and proportionate" security for cloud providers. This provides concrete guidelines as to how cloud providers can comply with the over-arching principles-based safeguarding obligations under NISD and GDPR. Second, the schemes provide a greater degree of *uniformity*, by applying a single set of guidelines across the EU. This matters since cloud providers can find themselves subject to multiple concurrent national jurisdictions under GDPR, as discussed below in Sect. 4.1. Third, the schemes account for *cloud-specific factors* that limit a provider's ability to manage risk, including a lack of knowledge and control. In particular, each scheme supports a shared responsibility model, that differentiates between the provider's host system and the customer's guest software and data. Under GDPR, the customer-as-controller remains responsible for deciding: (i) whether the provider's baseline security is sufficient for its processing, (ii) whether to use the provider's enhanced security options; or (iii) whether to

---

[118]CISPE Code, p. 18.

[119]AWS, "Shared Responsibility Model", https://aws.amazon.com/compliance/shared-responsibility-model/.

[120]CISPE Code, p. 18.

[121]CISPE Code, p. 9.

[122]EUCoC, pp. 4, 9, 17, 20.

[123]EUCoC, p. 17.

avoid using the cloud service at all. In other words, each scheme aims to support the customer's assessment of whether the provider's security measures meet the customer's security requirements.[124]

The approved Codes of Conduct have significant uptake, including from all three major IaaS providers. It remains to be seen whether the draft EUCS would see such widespread adoption. However, over time, EUCS certification could evolve into a *de facto* standard. For instance, organisations in the public sector and in regulated sectors, like operators of essential or financial services, might require certification to a high level as a prerequisite for their use of cloud services. Further, the EUCS might not, in practice, require major cloud providers to change much. Such providers typically already submit themselves to annual external audits and make audit reports (such as SOC 1 and 2) available to (potential) customers.[125] One main difference between these current practices and the EUCS would be that the audit will cover security objectives and controls, and will be done to a standard, publicly set by ENISA, instead of by the cloud provider. That might promote trust in the cloud. EUCS certification might generate more challenges for small cloud providers. That said, EUCS certification could equally simplify their risk management. Instead of weighing up 'appropriate and proportionate responses' to a range of possible risks, they need only determine whether their service presents a low, medium, or high risk and obtain certification accordingly.[126] The EUCS then provides ready-made security objectives and controls, while ENISA recommends accepted techniques.

3.2 *Incident Notification*

Both the NISD and the GDPR require entities to notify cybersecurity incidents. An incident refers to any set of circumstances that compromises cybersecurity.[127] The requirements differ in relation to: (i) who the entity must notify and (ii) what kind of incident triggers a notification obligation, which we refer to as a 'reporting threshold'. Under NISD, DSPs must notify the competent authority or the national Computer Security Incident Response Team ('CSIRT') of security incidents that have a substantial impact on the provision of its service.[128] Whether an impact is *substantial* depends on factors like the number of affected users, the incident's duration and geographic spread, and the extent of the service disruption.[129] The Commission has specified that DSPs must report an incident if: (i) its service is

[124] ENISA, "EUCS – Cloud Service Scheme", (2020), p. 9; CISPE Code, p. 9; EUCoC, p. 2.

[125] Kuan Hon et al. (2021b), pp. 127–132.

[126] Art. 52(1) Cybersecurity Act: "The assurance level shall be commensurate with the level of the risk associated with the intended use of the ICT service."

[127] Art. 4(7) NISD.

[128] Art. 16(3) NISD.

[129] Art. 16(4) NISD.

unavailable for more than 5 million user-hours; or the incident (ii) affected the CIA of data relating to more than 100,000 users; (iii) created a risk to public safety, security, or loss of life; or (iv) caused material damage of at least EUR 1m.[130] In some cases, cloud providers can face difficulties in assessing the impact of a service disruption. As noted above, an IaaS provider might have no idea how customers are using its service.[131] The NISD recognises this; incident notification requirements only apply when DSPs have access to the information needed to assess an incident's impact.[132] Further, under the GDPR, a controller must notify the relevant supervisory authority of a personal data breach that is likely to result in a risk to the rights and freedoms of natural persons.[133] In addition, the controller must notify the affected data subjects in case a personal data breach is likely to result in a *high* risk to the rights and freedoms of natural persons.[134] Conversely, a processor must notify a controller after becoming aware of any personal data breach (regardless of any risks posed).[135]

The NISD and GDPR therefore present three different incident reporting thresholds. First, the NISD features a quantifiable, outcome-based threshold (substantial impact). Second, the GDPR obligation for controllers has a risk-based threshold (a (high) risk to natural persons). Third, the GDPR obligation for processors applies to every incident that affects personal data, without any further reporting threshold.[136] This means that incidents that do not disrupt a cloud provider's service would not trigger NISD's notification. However, such non-disruptive incidents could still reveal serious shortcomings in the provider's security. For example, incidents of unauthorised access might impact confidentiality, without leading to service disruption. Further, a cloud provider might suffer a ransomware attack, but pay the ransom before it caused any disruption to its service. In such cases, regulators risk missing information about incidents that point to serious security failures.[137] Conversely, under GDPR, a cloud provider-as-processor would need to notify a customer-as-controller of any such incidents that involved personal data. The customer then assesses the risk posted to natural persons and decides whether to notify regulators and data subjects, as appropriate.[138] If the non-disruptive incident posed a risk to natural persons, for instance because of a confidentiality breach, the controller would need to notify. If not, the controller would at least need to consider the non-disruptive incident as part of its risk management process, including in determining whether the provider's security measures meet its requirements.

[130] Commission NIS Implementing Regulation, Art. 4.

[131] Michels and Walden (2021), pp. 397–399.

[132] Art. 16(4) NISD.

[133] Art. 33(1) GDPR.

[134] Art. 34(1) GDPR.

[135] Art. 33(2) GDPR.

[136] Art. 4(12) GDPR

[137] Michels and Walden (2021), pp. 412–414.

[138] Kamarinou et al. (2021), p. 323.

The NIS2 changes the incident notification threshold. It re-defines a *significant* impact as including an incident that "is capable of causing" severe operational disruption.[139] This would address the issue of non-disruptive incidents identified above. The rapporteur had criticised this change, arguing that reporting incidents which only have a 'potential impact' could lead to "[o]ver-reporting of potential incidents that have not happened", which could overwhelm regulators.[140] We disagree. In our view, the revised obligation only applies to *actual* security incidents of a serious nature, which could have caused widespread disruption, but did not do so for reasons other than the provider's security measures—as in the examples above. This can help alert regulators to serious security failures.

4 Enforcement: Overseeing Cloud Providers' Compliance

The institutional framework of EU cybersecurity oversight and enforcement is complicated. It involves multiple bodies across the Member State and EU level and can differ per sector. In addition, cloud providers who offer services in multiple Member States can be subject to the concurrent jurisdiction of several national regulators. In this section, we first look at territorial jurisdiction, before turning to oversight and remedies for non-compliance.

4.1 Territorial Jurisdiction

Under the NISD, a DSP is supervised by a single competent authority in the EU. A cloud provider falls under the jurisdiction of the Member State in which it has its *main establishment*, typically meaning its head office.[141] Consider a major cloud provider who offers services to customers across the EU, operates data centres in various Member States, and has its European headquarters in Dublin. It would fall under the jurisdiction of the Irish regulator: the National Cyber Security Centre ('NCSC'), which is part of the Irish Government Department of Communications.[142] Providers who are not established in the EU, but offer cloud services in the EU, must designate an EU representative in a Member State. It then falls under that Member

[139] Art. 23(3)(a) NIS2.

[140] Groothuis B, "Draft report on the proposal for a directive of the European Parliament and of the Council on measures for a high common level of cybersecurity across the Union", 3 May 2021, 2020/0359(COD), pp. 38–39.

[141] Recital 64 NISD provides that a DSP's main establishment "in principle corresponds to the place where the provider has its head office in the Union".

[142] European Commission, "Implementation of the NIS Directive in Ireland", https://digital-strategy.ec.europa.eu/en/policies/nis-directive-ireland.

State's jurisdiction.[143] As a result, cloud providers are subject to the exclusive jurisdiction of one NISD regulator. The NIS2 maintains this system.[144]

Jurisdiction is more complicated under the GDPR. In principle, each national supervisory authority is competent for processing activities that affect data subjects on its territory.[145] However, the GDPR establishes a 'one-stop-shop' ('OSS') mechanism for cross-border processing: the supervisory authority of the Member State where a cloud provider has its *main establishment* acts as the provider's *lead supervisory authority*.[146] In the above example of a major cloud provider headquartered Dublin, the lead authority is the Irish supervisory authority: the Data Protection Commission ('DPC').[147] The lead authority has primary responsibility for coordinating investigations and decisions on enforcement, while cooperating with "concerned" supervisory authorities in other Member States. The GDPR sets out a cooperation procedure, which involves sharing information and discussing draft decisions to try to reach consensus.[148]

However, the lead supervisory authority does not have exclusive jurisdiction for cloud providers, in four respects. First, the EDPB can adopt a binding decision that overrides a decision of the lead supervisory authority,[149] which it has done in relation to a decision of the DPC concerning WhatsApp Ireland.[150] Second, other supervisory authorities retain a residual competence to handle complaints from data subjects, if the subject matter substantially affects data subjects in one Member State only.[151] For example, a cloud provider headquartered in Dublin could experience a local cloud outage that only affects data subjects in France. The CNIL is then competent to consider related complaints from data subjects, although the DPC is the lead authority. Third, as noted above, a cloud provider will typically process personal data as a processor on behalf of customers who act as controllers and who are based in multiple Member States. Under Recital 36, "in cases involving both controller and processor", the lead supervisory authority is the *controller's* lead authority (*not* the processor's), which effectively means that the processor might

[143] Art. 18 NISD. Recital 65 clarifies that the mere accessibility of services in the EU is insufficient to determine whether a DSP is offering services in the EU, but that other factors, such as currency and language of the service or the mentioning of customers in the EU, are relevant.

[144] Art. 26 (1)(b), 2-3 and Recitals 113-116 NIS2.

[145] Recital 122 GDPR.

[146] Art. 56 GDPR.

[147] Data Protection Commission, https://www.dataprotection.ie/.

[148] Art. 60 GDPR.

[149] Art. 65(1)(a) GDPR.

[150] EDPB, Binding decision 1/2021 on the dispute arisen on the draft decision of the Irish Supervisory Authority regarding WhatsApp Ireland under Article 65(1)(a) GDPR (28 July 2021). See also Decision 1/2020 (9 November 2020) concerning a decision by the DPC regarding Twitter International, in which the DPC's decision was upheld.

[151] Art. 56(2) and (3) GDPR.

have to deal with multiple supervisory authorities.[152] Since cybersecurity is a shared responsibility between a cloud provider and its customers, an incident "involving both the controller and the processor"[153] is likely to be a common occurrence. As a result, cloud providers acting as processors can be subject to the jurisdiction of their customers' lead authorities. Fourth, cloud providers who are not established in the EU cannot benefit from the one-stop-shop mechanism; they are supervised by local supervisory authorities in every Member State.[154] It is less clear what happens when a cloud provider *is* established in a Member State, but acts as a processor for a controller who *is not* established in a Member State. Following the logic that (i) the non-EU controller does not benefit from the one-stop-shop mechanism and (ii) in cases involving both controller and processor, the processor is subject to the controller's competent authority, it would appear that (iii) the cloud provider is then also subject to the jurisdiction of supervisory authorities in every Member State.

In sum, territorial jurisdiction under both NISD and GDPR is based on the cloud provider's main establishment. However, while the NISD regulator's jurisdiction is exclusive, the GDPR lead authority only has primary responsibility. This effectively renders the GDPR's OSS mechanism meaningless for cloud providers in their role as processors, as predicting which supervisory authorities will exercise jurisdiction in the event of an incident is fraught with uncertainty. Given the self-service nature of cloud services, the cloud provider might not know where their customers' main establishment is. That can, in turn, complicate compliance with safeguarding obligations, particularly if different supervisory authorities each publish their own cybersecurity guidelines.

The draft EUCS and approved Codes of Conduct might help address this uncertainty, by providing uniform security requirements applicable across the EU.[155] While potentially simplifying compliance, the schemes add another layer of institutional complexity. For example, under the draft EUCS, three types of bodies are involved in issuing certificates and monitoring compliance: conformance assessment bodies ('CABs'), national accreditation bodies ('NABs') and the national cybersecurity certification authority ('NCCA'). Each Member State shall appoint a NAB[156] and an NCCA.[157] NABs accredit and monitor CABs who, in turn, issue certificates

---

[152] Article 29 Data Protection Working Party, "Guidelines for identifying a controller or processor's lead supervisory authority", WP244 rev.01 (2017), adopted by the EDPB on 25 May 2018, https://edpb.europa.eu/our-work-tools/our-documents/guidelines/guidelines-identifying-controller-or-processors-lead_en, p. 9 ('A29WP Guidelines for identifying lead supervisory authority').

[153] Recital 36 GDPR.

[154] A29WP Guidelines for identifying lead supervisory authority, p. 10.

[155] See e.g. Recital 95 Cybersecurity Act.

[156] Regulation (EC) No 765/2008 of 9 July 2008 setting out the requirements for accreditation and market surveillance relating to the marketing of products and repealing Regulation (EEC) No 339/93, Art. 4.

[157] Art. 58 Cybersecurity Act.

to cloud providers.[158] A cloud provider can choose to submit its application for certification to a CAB anywhere in the EU. Once issued, the certificate is valid across the EU.[159] The CAB who issued the certificate and the NCCA shall supervise and enforce compliance with the certification scheme rules and suspend or withdraw certificates where needed.[160] The NCCA shall have the power to request information from and audit certificate holders as required.[161]

The GDPR Codes of Conduct also introduce new oversight bodies. Under CISPE and EUCoC, a cloud provider can be confirmed as compliant by a Monitoring Body ('MB').[162] The CNIL accredits MBs under CISPE, while the Belgian SA accredits MBs under the EUCoC.[163] In 2021, the CNIL appointed EY Certifypoint as MB under CISPE, while the Belgian SA appointed Scope Europe as MB under EUCoC.[164] The provider can apply to an MB of their choice. [165] The provider is subject to an initial assessment and then annual review by the MB.[166] In case of non-compliance, the MB can issue warnings or reprimands, suspend the provider's declaration of adherence, or exclude the provider from the Code entirely.[167] In sum, should a cloud provider choose to certify under EUCS and adhere to a GDPR code of conduct, they would become subject to the supervision of three new authorities, namely: a CAB, an NCCA, and an MB.

4.2 Oversight and Enforcement

Under the NISD, regulators are expected to take a light-touch, reactive supervisory approach to DSPs. Instead of ongoing supervision, regulators should only act *ex post* when provided with evidence that a DSP is not taking appropriate measures.[168] When presented with such evidence, the regulator can investigate and, in case of

158 Art. 60, Recital 65 Cybersecurity Act; ENISA, "EUCS – Cloud Service Scheme", (2020), pp. 26, 29.

159 Recitals 73, 97 Cybersecurity Act.

160 ENISA, "EUCS – Cloud Service Scheme", (2020), pp. 39–48.

161 Art. 58(7)-(8) Cybersecurity Act.

162 CISPE Code, pp. 40–41; EUCoC, pp. 21–23.

163 CISPE Code, pp. 47–48; EUCoC, p. 21.

164 CNIL, "Code of conduct: CNIL grants first accreditation to a monitoring body", 16 July 2021, https://www.cnil.fr/en/code-conduct-cnil-grants-first-accreditation-monitoring-body; Belgian SA, "Accreditation of the "Scope Europe" for the monitoring of the "EU Cloud Code of Conduct"", Decision n° 06/2021 of 20 May 2021, https://www.dataprotectionauthority.be/publications/decision-n-06-2021-of-20-may-2021.pdf. For a list of CISPE accredited MBs, see https://www.codeofconduct.cloud/monitoring-bodies/ accessed 29 March 2023.

165 CISPE Code, pp. 48, 50.

166 CISPE Code, pp. 42–43; EUCoC, pp. 24–25, 27.

167 CISPE Code, pp. 52–54; EUCoC, pp. 28–29.

168 Art. 17 and Recital 60 NISD.

non-compliance, issue an administrative fine. The NISD does not specify the level of fines. It states only that Member States must provide for penalties that are effective, proportionate, and dissuasive.[169] This has led to divergent national implementations, with maximum fines under Member State law ranging from €5m to a mere €1400.[170] The NIS2 changes this supervisory and enforcement regime. Cloud providers instead become subject to ongoing, *ex ante* and *ex post* supervision as essential entities. [171] It also harmonises the level of fines for essential entities at €10m or 2% of annual turnover, whichever is highest. [172]

The NIS2 further introduces new obligations and remedies that target management personnel as *natural persons*, rather than cloud companies as *legal persons*. Member States must ensure that management bodies approve the risk management decisions taken to comply with the NIS2 safeguarding obligation, oversee their implementation, and can be held liable for non-compliance. They must also follow cybersecurity training.[173] Further, the regulator can request a temporary prohibition from exercising managerial functions against a CEO or legal representative, in case other enforcement measures prove ineffective. In addition, Member States shall ensure that natural persons who represent, exercise control of, or take decisions on behalf of, cloud providers can be "held liable for breach of their duties to ensure compliance" with the Directive. [174] The NIS2 does not specify the type of liability. This could, in theory, range from civil liability for damages to third parties; or personal liability to shareholders for failing in a fiduciary duty; to regulatory liability in the form of administrative fines; or possibly even criminal liability.[175] One possible implementation would be for Member States to provide in their national law that senior management can be subject to administrative fines imposed for their failure (under Art.20(1) NIS2) to ensure the cloud provider's compliance with its safeguarding obligations (under Art.21(1) NIS2).

The GDPR also features administrative fines. There are two levels of fines: the lower level of €10m or 2% of annual turnover and the higher level of €20m or 4% of annual turnover (in both cases, whichever is higher). [176] The applicable level of fines

---

[169] Art. 21 NISD.

[170] Commission, "Impact Assessment Report accompanying the document Proposal for a Directive of the European Parliament and of the Council on measures for a high common level of cybersecurity across the Union" Part 1 of 3, 16 December 2020, SWD(2020) 345 final, pp. 25–26 ('Commission Impact Assessment').

[171] Art. 32-33 and Recital 122 NIS2.

[172] Art. 34 NIS2.

[173] Art. 20 NIS2.

[174] Art.32(5)-(6) NIS2.

[175] The Commission did not address this point in detail. See e.g. Commission Impact Assessment Part 1, pp. 64–65. Recital 128 NIS2 states only that the Directive does not "require Member States to provide for criminal or civil liability with regard to natural persons with responsibility for ensuring that an entity complies with this Directive for damage suffered by third parties as a result of an infringement of this Directive."

[176] Art. 83(4)-(5) GDPR.

for non-compliance with cybersecurity requirements will depend on the circumstances of the case. The lower threshold applies to breaches of the safeguarding and notification duties under Articles 32–34; while the higher threshold applies to breaches of the security principle under Article 5(f). This implies that a cloud provider acting as a processor should only be liable to the lower threshold for failure to fulfil its independent obligation to ensure appropriate security under Article 32, as compliance with the principles under Article 5 is the controller's responsibility. However, whether regulators will in practice treat these cybersecurity obligations as distinct when determining penalties remains to be seen.

Finally, the draft EUCS and GDPR Codes of Conduct provide further oversight and enforcement. In both cases, non-compliance with security obligations can lead to withdrawal of certificates, which could lead to significant reputational damage. Further, the NCCA can also impose penalties under the draft EUCS.[177] The Cybersecurity Act further states that Member States shall put in place effective, proportionate, and dissuasive penalties for infringements of certification schemes.[178] Thus, in future, a certified cloud provider could be subject to administrative fines for cybersecurity under NISD, GDPR, and EUCS. In theory, these fines could relate to the same incident, although this raises concerns of the 'double jeopardy' or *ne bis in idem* principle, i.e. that a person should not be tried twice for the same offence. Cumulative fines might be justified however where the regulations "relate to different aspects of the wrongdoing and different impacts".[179] The NIS2 removes the risk of double fines under NISD and GDPR. Where a supervisory authority imposes a fine under GDPR, the NISD regulator shall not impose a fine for the same infringement.[180]

To date, the cybersecurity regulatory framework for cloud providers presents a mixed bag concerning enforcement. The Commission has characterised the NISD "supervision and enforcement regime" as "ineffective".[181] As of December 2020, the Commission was not aware of a single NISD penalty having been issued.[182] In contrast, GDPR supervisory authorities have issued fines for non-compliance with security obligations.[183] Nonetheless, some commentators have criticised perceived

[177] Art. 58(8) Cyberscurity Act.

[178] Art. 65 Cybersecurity Act.

[179] DCMS, 'Security of Network and Information Systems: Government response to the public consultation' (January 2018), p. 16. See also Cole and Schmitz-Berndt (2019), p. 18.

[180] Art. 35(2) NIS2.

[181] EU Commission, 'Proposal for a Directive on measures for a high common level of cybersecurity across the Union, repealing Directive (EU) 2016/1148'(2020) COM(2020) 823 final, p. 5.

[182] Commission Impact Assessment Part 1, p. 26.

[183] CNIL, "Credential stuffing: la CNIL sanctionne un responsable de traitement et son sous-traitant", 27 January 2021, https://www.cnil.fr/fr/credential-stuffing-la-cnil-sanctionne-un-responsable-de-traitement-et-son-sous-traitant. In the UK, in October 2020, the ICO fined British Airways £20m for data breach affecting more than 400,000 customers (see https://ico.org.uk/about-the-ico/news-and-events/news-and-blogs/2020/10/ico-fines-british-airways-20m-for-data-breach-affecting-more-than-400-000-customers); and Marriott International Inc. £18.4million for failing to

under-enforcement of the GDPR. For example, the Irish Council for Civil Liberties ('ICCL') argued in 2021 that the DPC has failed to take sufficient action as the lead authority for cross-border GDPR cases, thereby presenting an enforcement bottleneck. It argued that "enforcement against Big Tech is paralysed by Ireland's failure to deliver draft decisions on cross-border cases."[184]

The problem is not per se that regulators lack powers, but that they are not using them. This might be because regulators lack resources. In a survey of 46 NISD regulators conducted in September 2020, the most cited challenge to implementing NISD was "limited resources (staff and financial)".[185] Giving regulators new powers to target management personnel directly (as under NIS2) is unlikely to help, if regulators lack the resources to make use of their existing powers. What's more, if regulators are expected to engage in ongoing, proactive oversight of cloud providers under NIS2, this will place further strain on already limited resources. This raises a question: might a narrower objective of *ex post* enforcement, backed by sufficient resources and (the threat of) high fines, lead to better outcomes?

Hopefully, new oversight bodies under EUCS and the approved Codes of Conduct will provide new resources for oversight and enforcement. Cloud providers will pay CABs and MBs for initial review and ongoing oversight. However, Kamara *et al.* point out that such industry funding can undermine trust in the certification process, which:

> suffers from a fundamental ambiguity insofar as the applicant is also a client. The certification body is a service provider that must, at the same time, satisfy a paying client and scrutinise its procedures with impartiality. The certification body must thus constantly balance the need to ensure the quality of the certification process and the requirement to satisfy a client that is able to swap, at any time, from one provider to another.[186]

What's more, since certification by a single CAB or MB applies across the EU, there is a risk of forum-shopping, as cloud providers might look to certify with the most industry-friendly body. Nonetheless, given the above enforcement issues, additional oversight is welcome. Further, participation in the draft EUCS and Codes of Conduct only *demonstrates* compliance, it does not *guarantee* it. Only regulators and courts can determine compliance with NISD and GDPR.

---

keep customers' personal data secure (see https://ico.org.uk/about-the-ico/news-and-events/news-and-blogs/2020/10/ico-fines-marriott-international-inc-184million-for-failing-to-keep-customers-personal-data-secure/).

[184] ICCL, "Europe's enforcement paralysis" (2021), https://www.iccl.ie/wp-content/uploads/2021/09/Europes-enforcement-paralysis-2021-ICCL-report-on-GDPR-enforcement.pdf.

[185] Commission Impact Assessment, Part 3, pp. 5,12.

[186] Kamara et al. (2019), p. 141.

5 Concluding Remarks

In this chapter, we have examined how three of the main legislative instruments of the European cybersecurity regulatory framework (the NISD, the GDPR, and the Cybersecurity Act) impact the provision of cloud computing services. In terms of scope, the NISD can be said to adopt a structural approach to cybersecurity regulation; application of the regime being triggered by the role that the regulatee plays within a supply chain, as an 'enabling' service for its users. This is in contrast to the GDPR, which adopts a substantive approach, the regime being triggered by the regulatee's role in processing personal data. Cloud providers are typically subject to both NISD and GDPR. A key concern with the NISD approach is that the resulting regime is a blunt instrument that imposes asymmetric regulatory burdens on a vast range of market participants (especially the long tail of SaaS service providers) that are no more critical or enabling than other parts of the supply chain, such as hardware and software producers. Nonetheless, it is arguable that this is the best available regulatory approach, given the complexities of determining whether each individual cloud service is crucial enough for the businesses that rely on it that it should qualify as 'critical' infrastructure. Further, since the NISD imposes risk management obligations, cloud providers need only determine the level of security 'appropriate' to the risk which disruption of their service would pose, which should be lower for providers of less 'critical' cloud services. Although for those operating at the lower layers of the cloud stack, such as IaaS providers, such risk analysis is inherently speculative, since they might not know for which purposes customers are using the service.

In terms of substance, while the NISD and GDPR impose similarly-worded obligations, they comprise high level principles that inevitably require further elaboration in the form of further regulations, guidance, and codes, as well as assurance mechanisms, such as codes of conduct and certification schemes. Together with a multiplicity of regulatory authorities claiming jurisdiction, both at a domestic level and between Member States, such variety is likely to result in divergent regulatory approaches and unintended outcomes, as well as imposing unnecessary compliance costs on providers of cloud computing services.

In sum, the provision of cloud services has moved from being lightly regulated to being treated as critical infrastructure, triggering public interest concerns of which cybersecurity is but one dimension. More recently, the Commission has argued that the cloud is not just 'critical', but 'strategic' infrastructure, and therefore key to Europe's "digital strategic autonomy".[187] It has accordingly argued that "Europe

[187] European Commission, "A European strategy for data", (2020) 19.2.2020 COM(2020) 66 final; European Commission, "2030 Digital Compass: the European way for the Digital Decade", (2021) 9.3.2021 COM(2021) 118 final ('2030 Digital Compass'). See further ENISA, "Cybersecurity Research Directions for the EU's Digital Strategic Autonomy", April 2021; European Political Strategy Centre, "Rethinking Strategic Autonomy in the Digital Age", EPSC Strategic Notes, Issue 30, July 2019, https://op.europa.eu/en/publication-detail/-/publication/889dd7b7-0cde-11ea-8c1f-01aa75ed71a1/language-en.

needs to strengthen its own cloud infrastructure and capacities".[188] As of the time of writing in April 2023, it was unclear where such calls for 'European cloud sovereignty' would lead. For many years, security professionals have bemoaned the lack of attention policy makers and legislators paid to cybersecurity. Today, the EU's rush to regulate may prove as much of a gift as a curse for those trying to protect our systems, services, and data.

References

Banasiński C, Rojszczak M (2021) Cybersecurity of consumer products against the background of the EU model of cyberspace protection. J Cybersecur

Calliess C, Baumgarten A (2020) Cybersecurity in the EU the example of the financial sector: a legal perspective. German Law J

Cole M, Schmitz-Berndt S (2019) The Interplay between the NIS Directive and the GDPR in a Cybersecurity Threat Landscape. University of Luxembourg Law Working Paper Series Paper number 2019-017

Fuster GG, Jasmontaite L (2020) Cybersecurity regulation in the European Union: the digital, the critical and fundamental rights. In: Christen M, Gordijn B, Loi M (eds) The ethics of cybersecurity. Springer

Kamara I, Leenes R, Lachaud E, Stuurman K, van Lieshout M, Bodea G (2019) Data Protection Certification Mechanisms: Study on Articles 42 and 43 of the Regulation (EU) 2016/679, Report for European Commission

Kamarinou D, Millard C, Oldani I (2018) Compliance as a Service, Queen Mary School of Law Legal Studies Research Paper No. 287/2018

Kamarinou D, Millard C, Turton F (2021) Responsibilities of controllers and processors of personal data in clouds In: Millard C (ed) (2021) Cloud computing law 2nd edn. Oxford University Press

Kuan Hon W, Millard C, Singh J (2021a) Control, security, and risk in the cloud. In: Millard C (ed) Cloud computing law, 2nd edn. Oxford University Press

Kuan Hon W, Millard C, Walden I, Ward C (2021b) Negotiated contracts for cloud services. In: Millard C (ed) Cloud computing law, 2nd edn. Oxford University Press

Michels JD, Walden I (2021) Cybersecurity and critical infrastructure. In: Millard C (ed) Cloud computing law, 2nd edn. Oxford University Press

Millard C (ed) (2021) Cloud computing, 2nd edn. Oxford University Press

Millard C et al (2019) At this rate, everyone will be a [joint] controller of personal data! Int Data Priv Law 9(4)

Noto La Diega G, Walden I (2016) Contracting for the 'Internet of Things': looking into the nest. Eur J Law Technol 7(2)

Pinkney K (2002) Putting blame where blame is due: software manufacturer and customer liability for security-related software failure. Albany Law J Sci Technol 13

Samuelson P (1993) Liability for defective electronic information. Commun ACM

Walden I (2018) European Union communications law. In: Telecommunications law and regulation, 5th edn. Oxford University Press

Wolters P (2017) The security of personal data under the GDPR: a harmonized duty or a shared responsibility? Int Data Priv Law 7:3

[188]European Commission, "2030 Digital Compass", pp. 7–8. See further European Commission, "Updating the 2020 New Industrial Strategy: Building a stronger Single Market for Europe's recovery" (2021), 5.5.2021 COM(2021) 350 final.

Ian Walden is Professor of Information and Communications Law at the Centre for Commercial Law Studies, Queen Mary, University of London. His publications include *Media Law and Practice* (2009), *Free and Open Source Software* (2013), *Computer Crimes and Digital Investigations* (2nd ed., 2016) and *Telecommunications Law and Regulation* (5th ed., 2018). Ian has been a visiting professor at the universities of Texas, Melbourne and KU Leuven. Ian has been involved in law reform projects for the World Bank, European Commission, Council of Europe, Commonwealth and UNCTAD, as well as numerous individual states. Ian was an 'expert nationaux détaché' to the European Commission (1995–1996); Board Member and Trustee of the Internet Watch Foundation (2004–2009); on the Executive Board of the UK Council for Child Internet Safety (2010–2012); the Press Complaints Commission (2009–2014); a member of the RUSI Independent Surveillance Review (2014–2015); a member of the Code Adjudication Panel at the Phone-paid Services Authority (2016–2021); a member of the European Commission Expert Group to support the application of the GDPR (2017–2021), and is a Non-Executive Board Member of the Jersey Competition Regulatory Authority (2020-). Ian is a solicitor and Of Counsel to Baker McKenzie. Ian leads Queen Mary's qLegal initiative and is a principal investigator on the Cloud Legal Project and co-author of *Cloud Computing Law* (2nd edn., 2021).

Johan David Michels is a Researcher in the Microsoft-funded Cloud Legal Project, a PhD candidate at Queen Mary University of London (QMUL), and a guest teacher at the London School of Economics (LSE). He has over 10 years' experience working in law and policy, including at the communications regulator Ofcom and at the United Nations war crimes tribunal in The Hague. He has lectured and taught seminars at QMUL and LSE covering e-Commerce, IP, and information security and the law. He is a co-author of *Cloud Computing Law* (2nd edn., OUP, 2021) and has published articles on a range of technology law issues, including cloud contracts, copyright, crypto-currency, and cybersecurity. He holds LLMs from the LSE (with distinction, 2014) and from the University of Amsterdam (cum laude, 2009) and studied at Columbia Law School in New York (2008). His PhD looks at the legal protection of digital assets.

Cyber Operations Targeting Space Systems. Legal Questions and the Context of Privatisation

Bruno Reynaud de Sousa

Abstract The present chapter addresses how legal uncertainty creates an environment where the escalation of cyber operations targeting space systems may quickly occur. Overall, whereas during the four decades preceding the twenty-first century, the ability of States to project power in outer space was limited primarily to two space-faring nations, the number of players in the global space sector is now higher and more diverse. As 2022 demonstrates, private sector-driven innovation in space technologies has revolutionised space activities, changing their context dramatically. In February, the Russian invasion of Ukraine became the first conflict demonstrating the added value of private Earth observation capabilities and satellite communications. In April, the first-ever wholly private mission by Axiom Space launched on a SpaceX rocket inaugurated an era of private astronautics regarding crewed space flight. Thus, the present chapter posits that innovation increased the value of targeting space systems harnessing the non-kinetic nature of cyber-enabled attacks. Secondly, a discussion on legal uncertainty and the weaponisation of space in connection with the concept of cyber operations follows, highlighting that State and non-State actors recognise space as a key enabler for national security and economic prosperity. Finally, a set of conclusions is proposed premised on the idea that outer space must not become a domain where ascertaining, classifying and reacting to aggressive behaviours is governed exclusively by the "eye of the beholder" rule.

B. R. de Sousa (✉)
University of Minho (School of Law), Braga, Portugal

University of Oporto (Faculty of Arts and Humanities), Porto, Portugal
e-mail: breynaud@direito.uminho.pt

F. A. Carneiro Pacheco de Andrade et al. (eds.), *Legal Developments on Cybersecurity and Related Fields*, Law, Governance and Technology Series 60,
https://doi.org/10.1007/978-3-031-41820-4_3

1 Introduction

The fight against the Covid-19 pandemic signalled that national and individual security are increasingly interconnected. Crucially, the State no longer holds the national defence capabilities monopoly. Companies such as Palantir (data analytics) or Mandiant (cyber security) are leading examples of how private sector innovation outmatched state-owned capabilities in the cyber domain.

Concerning outer space, Earth observation and remote sensing are examples of technologies that have benefitted significantly from private-sector innovation. Amazingly, in 2022, there is one entity capable of imaging the whole Earth's landmass every 24 hours: a private company called Planet.[1] Moreover, other private companies like Space Exploration Technologies Corporation ("SpaceX"), Capella Space or BlackSky Global have deployed Earth observation and satellite-based telecommunication capabilities that rival those of historical space powers. Such capabilities are now accessible to non-space-faring States, further to international organisations, private companies and Non-Governmental Organizations.

Space is recognised as the "future frontier of the global economy and society".[2] During the past 5 years, the space sector has experienced momentous change as an increasing number of States have been developing a space economy and joining the international space community. Additionally, there is notable recognition that space activities are vital to confronting the many societal challenges creating uncertainty vis-à-vis human development in the post-COVID-19 economic recovery. [3] Significantly, the added value of space is recognised with reference to the Sustainable Development Goals (SDGs).[4]

The digitalisation of the global economy develops apace, and enhanced artificial intelligence looms on the cyber domain's horizon. Estimates are that in 2020 there were 12.4 billion Internet of Things (IoT) devices connected around the world, "a number expected to more than double to 26.4 billion by 2026 alone". [5] Countless IoT devices depend on space-based technology such as Global Navigation Satellite Systems (GNSS) for the most impactful operations. Whereas satellites are an essential enabler for the era of the Internet of Everything (IoE),[6] they are themselves just another thing connected to the IoT.[7]

The private sector has successfully leveraged digitalisation for innovation[8] and is remaking the space economy into one of the fastest and most promising economic

[1] Planet (2021).

[2] Group of Seven (2021), para 31.

[3] OECD (2021).

[4] U.N. (2015).

[5] DigitalEurope (2021).

[6] DeNardis (2020).

[7] Blount (2017).

[8] Pelton (2017).

sectors, bridging industry, science, and financial services.[9] Multinational corporations and thousands of start-up companies are emerging as key players in the space economy, leading a revolution in space technologies that have decisively changed space mission design. In brief, satellite operations have abandoned missions with single complex satellites for satellites of small dimensions deployed as part of large constellations or collocations that rely on launching services increasingly provided by private companies. Leading innovators such as SpaceX and Blue Origin achieved the most significant milestone with the development of very competitive launch technologies characterised by reusability.

Crucially, the digitalisation of the world economy is leading to societies worldwide becoming increasingly dependent on space-based services and technologies.[10] For example, in the European Union (E.U.), there are ca. 14 million jobs affected by space systems[11] and virtually all sectors of the European economy are highly dependent on space infrastructure either directly, indirectly (prime users), or peripherally (knock-on users).[12]

The importance of space for the European economy is further evidenced by E.U. law and policy developments.[13] Most recently, Regulation (E.U.) 2021/696 of 28 April 2021 (known as the E.U. Space Regulation) established the Union Space Program and created the European Union Agency for the Space Program (EUSPA), expanding the E.U.'s flagship programs being pursued in the 2021–2027 period.[14] In addition, the work by the recently created E.U. Commission Directorate-General Defense Industry and Space[15] signals an improved European ambition in the wake of previous E.U. Commission work, namely the 2011 Space Strategy[16] and the 2013 E.U. Space Industrial Policy.[17]

Rising digitalisation and deeper dependency on space systems blur the boundaries between national security, economics, and science.[18] If the current dynamic holds, the private sector will continue to expand existing business models in view of providing new types of space services that require a heavily data-driven environment. Such a dynamic will unquestionably lead to increased cyber security risks related to satellites and space systems.

Activities in cyberspace and outer space share at least three common characteristics. First, these are interconnected domains whose resources are extensively used by societies worldwide in everyday life. Second, both domains are built upon

---

[9] OECD (2021).

[10] U.N. (2021a).

[11] EU (2017).

[12] Ibid.

[13] European Space Agency (2021).

[14] EU (2011).

[15] EU (2021a).

[16] EU (2011).

[17] EU (2013).

[18] Robinson et al. (2018).

immaterial resources that remain unrestrained in the absence of any tailored-made form of world government. Lastly, State and non-State actors' interests are increasingly in competition in both domains, leading States to assert their sovereignty—most recently regarding outer space.[19]

The present chapter is premised on the fact that the development of space activities by State and non-State actors enabled by the cyber domain occurs in a context of consequential legal uncertainty encompassing the fields of private law and public law.[20] Firstly, a brief characterisation of private sector involvement in space activities will be provided to better understand the types of cyber security threats to satellites and related systems. Secondly, attention will focus on cyber operations and the weaponisation of space by States, providing a background to assess how legal uncertainty enables certain types of ambiguous space activities. Finally, a set of conclusions will be presented in support of the need for more effective legal instruments to address the challenges posed by the development of capabilities for cyber operations targeting space objects in orbit and related systems.

2 Privatisation and Increased Competition in Outer Space

Whereas in the 1960s, only six States possessed artificial satellites in orbit, presently, more than eighty States have launched or acquired satellites, mainly for telecommunications and remote sensing. Furthermore, at least fourteen States presently have the technology to build and place in orbit launch vehicles, namely the Russian Federation, the Peoples' Republic of China (PRC), the United Kingdom, France, Canada, Japan, India, Israel, Ukraine, the Islamic Republic of Iran, New Zealand and the US[21]—a number that is set to increase in the medium term.

Presently, no one disputes the fact that the signs of increased competition among State actors in outer space are disquieting and foreshadow a scenario of space warfare.[22] Firstly, the geopolitical tensions between the U.S., the Russian Federation, and the PRC have extended to outer space, connected with humankind's return to the Moon. Secondly, different space powers have been developing policy decisions in line with a recognition that conflict can originate in space or increasingly have a space dimension, such as the creation of dedicated branches of the armed forces.[23] Moreover, some States have undertaken direct actions displaying uses of force in outer space by targeting satellites and related systems with anti-satellite (ASAT) weapons.

[19] Steer and Hersch (2020).

[20] Delerue (2020).

[21] Dawson (2018), p. 13.

[22] Johnson-Freese (2017).

[23] Goswami and Garretson (2020).

In parallel, private companies such as SpaceX, Blue Origin (both US-based), and Rocket Labs (New Zealand-based) now have a higher number of successful launches than most G7 economies and emerging space-faring nations such as India.[24] Statistically,[25] between 2011 and 2020, 3968 spacecraft of variable mass were launched, totalling ca. 4000 metric tons. In 2020 alone, 1282 spacecraft were launched, totalling ca. 554 metric tons, 94% of which were small satellites (600 kg and under), corresponding to 43% of the total upmass.

Space is thus becoming more congested, contested and competitive.[26] Remarkably, 40% of all small satellites launched in the last ten years were launched in 2020, and Low Earth Orbit (LEO)—located at an altitude of 200–600 km—presently concentrates more than 4550 active satellites.[27] This trend is expected to continue for the next 5 years, as the number of active small satellites in LEO is set to increase exponentially: the US-based company SpaceX is seeking approval of 30,000 satellites to add to ca. 1700 composing the *Starlink* large constellation of satellites.[28] Other operators such as Boeing, Amazon.com Inc.'s Kuiper Systems LLC,[29] and Astra Space Inc. have requested licenses from the U.S. regulator (the U.S. Federal Communications Commission) for more than 35,000 satellites.[30]

In this context, the cybersecurity risks connected with space activities are heightened since, nowadays, the collection of data using space platforms is essential for (1) the global economy, (2) national security and defence,[31] and (3) the safety of space activities themselves. Focusing on national security and defence, remote sensing has progressively gained importance. The use of satellites to gather images, electronic signals and other data is essential for weather forecasting, responding to catastrophes and collecting information on remote locations inside the territory of States that are inaccessible by other means, such as aerial photography.

As explained above, the space market dynamic points to a rising number of States increasingly relying on private companies to provide high-quality and affordable remote sensing data for civilian and military purposes. In the context of the militarisation of space, Space Situational Awareness (SSA) capabilities (such as land-based radars, telescopes, and space-based sensors) will become essential enablers of State-owned ASAT capabilities as the efficiency of space weapons is correlated with the precision of the information on the exact location of orbiting satellites.[32] Consequently, as LEO becomes increasingly congested, building up

---

[24] BryceTech (2020).

[25] BryceTech (2021).

[26] Harrison (2013), pp. 26–49.

[27] Union of Concerned Scientists (2021).

[28] Masunaga (2019).

[29] Bloomberg (2021).

[30] Time (2021).

[31] Malik et al. (2020).

[32] See, for example, The French Ministry for the Armed Forces (2019).

SSA capabilities to detect and observe satellites in orbit will become critical and usher in new public-private partnerships.

3 The Weaponisation of Space and Cyber Operations Targeting Space Systems

Although the kinetic operations that characterise war have yet to move decisively to outer space, the same cannot be said of non-kinetic operations. Whereas the Gulf War of 1991 may be considered the first space war,[33] due to the crucial advantage afforded by space-based technology—namely, GNSS technology in the form of the US-made GPS—the ongoing Ukraine War demonstrates the fundamental shift in military space operations that occurred in the two following decades.

The Russian invasion of Ukraine on 24 February 2022 unleashed the ongoing conflict that will be recorded in history books as humanity's second space war. There is evidence that the conflict's proverbial "first shot" occurred in connection with outer space as the Russian invasion was preceded by a military cyber operation successfully targeting modems part of Viasat's European satellite network (KA-SAT), crippling the communications of Ukraine's military and other government agencies.[34] Conversely, it has become manifestly clear that the operational success achieved by Ukraine against a far more combat-experienced adversary largely rests on the continuous access to private space-based capabilities for telecommunications and Earth observation. Specifically, SpaceX's Starlink large constellation is widely recognised as a key enabler of data fusion propelling the Ukrainian armed forces to twenty-first-century-style, highly effective military operations.

There are at least three crucial concepts concerning the intersection of cyberspace with outer space. First, a cyber-attack is understood as being "an attack initiated from a computer against a Web site, network, or individual computer that compromises the confidentiality, integrity, or availability of that system or stored information.".[35] Secondly, cyber weapons are "programs, equipment, tactics, techniques, and procedures used for offensive cyber operations.".[36] Finally, cyber warfare is understood as "an extension of policy by actions taken in cyberspace by state actors (or by non-state actors with significant state direction or support) that constitute a serious threat to another state's security, or an action of the same nature taken in response to a serious threat to a state's security (actual or perceived)".[37]

---

[33] Borgen (2022).

[34] Nakashima (2022).

[35] Springer (2017).

[36] Ibid.

[37] Green (2015), p. 2.

All three concepts taken together clarify at least one fundamental difficulty: attribution. This much is exemplified by past cyber operations targeting Estonia (2007), Georgia (2008), the Islamic Republic of Iran (2010, 2019, 2021), Ukraine (2014), Germany (2014, 2015 and 2016), and the U.S. (2014, 2016). Additional complexity stems from the fact that cyber operations are primarily non-kinetic actions causing physical but possibly reversible consequences—as opposed to kinetic actions whereby physical damage is the single direct and irreversible consequence of the attack. Prospectively, non-kinetic actions may be refined to cause physical damage, as was allegedly the case concerning the catastrophic failure of an Iranian space program launch in 2019.[38]

For the purposes of the present chapter, we adopt the concept of cyber operations given it encompasses "any operation that uses a computer network".[39] Further to being a real and actual threat, cyber operations targeting space systems are quite possibly the main counter-space threat given the ratio between the cost, the vulnerabilities of multiple vectors (namely, the satellites and all related systems), and their non-kinetic nature.

Although the majority of incidents are attributed to State actors, there is open-source information pointing to terrorist organisations and individuals disposing of the capabilities to target satellites—some Linux-based solutions costing as low as seventy-five dollars (U.S.).[40] In fact, a non-state actor allegedly perpetrated the first known cyber-attack targeting a satellite. In 2007, the Liberation Tigers of Tamil Eelam (LTTE), a terrorist organisation fighting for the independence of a region in Sri Lanka, hacked an Intelsat communications feed.[41] In addition, publicly available data points to an event in 2014, when a British citizen was arrested for "hacking into a U.S. military satellite and stealing personnel and satellite phone data".[42]

Despite exceptionally few known examples, the actual number of cyber operations by individuals targeting satellites may be much higher. Satellite hacking is a topic discussed in cybersecurity conferences open to the general public, including live demonstrations, as was the case in 2015 when a telecommunications satellite part of the Iridium network was hacked in public.[43] In fact, in 2020 and 2021, the U.S. Space Force organised satellite hacking contests—named "Hack-A-Sat"—in the framework of which real hardware is placed at the disposal of hackers in a controlled environment.[44] For the 2021 edition, the staggering number of over one thousand teams registering worldwide was reduced to "eight teams from the United States, Poland, Germany, and Romania".[45] In 2022 the second edition of the

[38] Weeden and Samson (2021).

[39] Delerue (2020), p. 12.

[40] Ibid.

[41] Aerospace (2020), Space News (2007).

[42] Aerospace (2020), Farmer (2017).

[43] Aerospace (2020), Porup (2015).

[44] Barrett (2019).

[45] Waterman (2021).

"CYSAT" conference scheduled for April was advertising "Europe's first live satellite hacking demo" following the launch of an open call to ethical hackers.[46]

Unsurprisingly, the most significant number of cyber operations targeting satellites and related systems is perpetrated by State actors and publicly available information points to one State in particular: the Peoples Republic of China (PRC).[47] Public information dating back to 2007—the year when the first cyber-attack attributed to the PRC targeted a U.S. remote sensing satellite (Landsat-7)[48]—explicitly attributes at least seven other cyber operations to the PRC. The data details the successful hacking of U.S. government satellites, at instances taking control but not issuing any commands (2007, 2008, 2014),[49] and the hacking of server infrastructure that supports satellite command and control (2011).[50] In 2014 a cyber-attack attributed to the PRC targeted the U.S. National Oceanographic and Atmospheric Administration (NOAA), forcing it "to take down the system and stop transmitting satellite images to the [U.S.] National Weather Service for two days before the organisation was able to seal off the vital data".[51] Additionally, there is information dating back to 2014–2015 about Russian hackers successfully deploying malware to access commercial satellite data links and stealing data.[52] Lastly, further exemplifying the interconnection between cyberspace and space-related systems, Chinese hackers allegedly gained access to an Indian government video chat taking place via satellite in 2017.[53] Overall, in the context of the Covid-19 pandemic, the rise in the use of video conference and similar tools is an additional cause for concern and a source of heightened cybersecurity risks for the space industry as it also adopted remote working.[54]

Commercial space and military activities in outer space are inherently interconnected due to a defining characteristic of space technologies: they all have "dual-use" potential.[55] For example, the U.S.-operated Global Positioning System (GPS) is a strictly military GNSS programme universally accessible for civilian purposes. In contrast, the European-operated Galileo system is a civilian GNSS programme that provides military applications. Therefore, a disruption of the satellites providing positioning, navigational and timing (PNT) data would have critical repercussions for the day-to-day of some societies making it impossible either to operate commercial flights globally or to execute baking operations—at the same

[46] CYSAT (2021).

[47] Weeden and Samson (2021).

[48] Aerospace (2020), Chen (2017).

[49] Ibid.

[50] Aerospace (2020), NASA (2019).

[51] Aerospace (2020).

[52] Nakashima (2015), Symantec Security Response (2014).

[53] Aerospace (2020), New India Express (2017).

[54] Halpern (2020).

[55] Khan (2017).

time, the operation of the world's most advanced armed forces would be seriously hindered.[56]

Adding to this context, a few States are currently developing and testing new technologies to condition or deny the conduct of space activities and access to outer space.[57] These objectives may be accomplished by generating harmful interference with satellites or attacking the ground-based command and control infrastructure of space objects through cyber means.

The current scholarly debate focusing on the question of the weaponisation of outer space shows increasing concern with the deployment of new types of ASAT weapons by space powers, encompassing both missile technology and satellites with the ability to track, interfere with or even destroy other space objects.[58] Additionally, some of the most advanced armed forces in the world are expected to increasingly rely on the private sector for space operations capabilities as the market for sub-contractors and space security as a service continues to grow.[59]

Although the placement of weapons in outer space is a complex topic, this domain has long been a source of conventional and non-conventional threats. Historically, the perception of the threats originating in outer space began by emphasising nuclear weapons; contemporary discussions start from a distinction between kinetic and non-kinetic threats. Looking at a possible categorisation of ASAT weapons, a 2021 report by the Centre for Strategic and International Studies (CSIS) bases the analysis on a division between "kinetic physical weapons" (capable of striking a target directly via impact or detonation) and non-kinetic physical weapons (capable of producing physical effects on a target without making any physical contact).[60]

The first type of weapons encompasses direct-ascent ASAT weapons and co-orbital ASAT weapons. Both are used to cause irreversible damage instead of force in a direct attack targeting a ground station. Regarding kinetic ASAT weapons,[61] only a small group of States has a proven capability to destroy satellites by kinetic means from Earth, namely the U.S., the Peoples Republic of China, the Russian Federation and India.

Although the list of ASAT tests is much longer,[62] three main examples may be quoted chronologically. Starting in 2007, the PRC's widely criticised ASAT weapon test produced a substantial debris field. A second example was India's ASAT test in 2019, most recently followed by the Russian Federation's ASAT test in November 2021. All three events generated space debris that will stay in orbit for many decades, placing added stress on the SSA infrastructure tracking orbital debris and

[56] Dawson (2018), pp. 3–7.

[57] Ibid.

[58] Bowen (2019).

[59] Frankowski (2019), Rosello et al. (2022).

[60] Center for Strategic and International Studies (2021).

[61] Dawson (2018), pp. 12–32.

[62] Weeden and Samson (2021), pp. 10-1–10-5.

increasing the overall risk of space operations in LEO. The Russian direct-ascent ASAT missile test of 2021 drew wide condemnation with statements by the E,[63] the U.S. (through military and civilian agencies such as U.S. Space Command,[64] NASA,[65] and the U.S. Department of State[66]), Japan, and Australia.

This event, however, foretells the possible added value of public-private partnerships for the provision of space sector services. Astonishingly, the most accurate data on the Russian action itself was made available by a private company—Leo Labs—that resorted to social media to publicise what its space-based assets had gathered about the consequences of this dangerous action.[67]

The second type of weapons encompasses directed energy weapons, utilising either laser optics or radio-frequency waves to cause harmful interference, the effects of which may either be (1) reversible (e. g., temporarily impairing optical sensors of a satellite) or (2) permanent (e. g., permanently damaging components or destroying a satellite). Actions may, thus, encompass radio-frequency jamming, micro-wave broadcast, direct delivery of chemical substances, or direct tampering via mechanical action.[68]

In this regard, "space electronic warfare"[69] features prominently in the most recent literature focusing on the intersection of electronic warfare (E.W.) and satellites. Such actions target space objects by using satellites and related systems to cause harmful non-kinetic outcomes, at times by virtue of a specific type of space activity designated as remote proximity operations (RPO).[70] Starting in 2014, there have been verified observation data regarding Russian Federation satellites manoeuvring in proximity to governmental satellites owned by other States with unknown intents but at a distance close enough to conduct cyber-enabled attacks.[71]

Considering these developments, it is then no surprise that in 2019 the North Atlantic Treaty Organization (NATO) took the step of classifying space as the fifth operational domain,[72] and in 2021 recognising that "attacks to, from, or within space" could lead to the invocation of the mutual defence clause in Article 5 of the North Atlantic Treaty.[73] Interestingly, at the Warsaw Summit of 2016, cyberspace had been designated "as a domain of operations in which NATO must defend itself as effectively as it does in the air, on land, and at sea".[74] Unsurprisingly, a few States

---

[63] EU (2021b).

[64] U.S. Space Command (2021).

[65] NASA (2021).

[66] U.S. Department of State (2021).

[67] LeoLabs (2021).

[68] Weeden and Samson (2021).

[69] Adamy (2021).

[70] Johnson-Freese (2017).

[71] Weeden and Samson (2021), pp. 2–12.

[72] NATO (2019).

[73] NATO (2021a), para 33.

[74] NATO (2016).

have taken steps to reorganise the architecture of their armed forces, highlighting the importance of outer space for national defence, with the U.S. going as far as creating a dedicated sixth branch of the armed forces—the U.S. Space Force.[75]

Increased competition in outer space has been impacting State behaviour to the point that it may be more accurately described as a "new armaments race".[76] In this context, scholars and partitioners alike have called for a revision of the international law regime governing armaments control to encompass ASAT weapons.[77] It is worth noting that, in 1981, UNGA Resolution 36/97[78] called for a treaty prohibiting anti-satellite weapons and UNGA Resolution 36/99[79] called for a ban on the placement of any weapons in outer space. In the following decades, other proposals intending to frame military activities in outer space under international law, including uses of force, never bore fruit. Most recently, in 2020 and 2021, the U.N. General Assembly (UNGA) adopted two resolutions calling for measures to reduce space threats. Firstly, UNGA resolution 75/36 entitled "Reducing space threats through norms, rules and principles of responsible behaviours",[80] followed by UNGA resolution 76/22 on the "Prevention of an arms race in outer space"[81]—perhaps multilateralism could be spurred, however unlikely it may be in this day and age.

In truth, prominent space actors have renewed calls for a binding international legal instrument. The Sino-Russian initiative of a *Draft Treaty on the Prevention of the Placement of Weapons in Outer Space, the Threat or Use of Force against Outer Space Objects* (PPWT)[82] is worth noting, albeit rightly criticised.[83] In actual fact, Eastern calls against the placement of weapons in outer space date back to the 1980s, when USSR foreign minister Eduard Shevardnadze presented a Soviet Union proposal at the U.N. aimed at the "renunciation by states of the development, testing and deployment of space strike weapons".[84]

Regarding cyberspace, the mitigation of State-sponsored cyber operations is underlying the agenda of two U.N. working groups: the Group of Governmental Experts (established by UNGA Resolution 73/266, of 22 December, 2018); and, the Open-Ended Working Group, (established by UNGA Resolution 73/27, of 05 December, 2018). However, space is not one of the main issues discussed in either one.

---

[75] US (2019).

[76] Dawson (2018).

[77] Koplow (2018), pp. 12–32.

[78] UN (1981a).

[79] UN (1981b).

[80] U.N. (2020).

[81] U.N. (2021b).

[82] People's Republic of China (2008).

[83] Bowen (2019), pp. 273–275.

[84] New York Times (1985), p. 3.

Conversely, other contemporary attempts to address the legal uncertainty have taken the form of non-binding legal instruments[85] and the proposal of rules to regulate State conduct in cyberspace and outer space. The "Tallinn Manual on the International Law Applicable to Cyber Operations",[86] foresees rules specifically applicable to cyber-enabled space operations in line with the OST, acknowledging the "peaceful purposes" requirement and the need to respect the International Law limitations on the use of force.[87] Similarly, there are two other initiatives aimed at drafting rules to discipline the use of force in outer space—the Manual on International Law Applicable to Military Uses of Outer Space (MILAMOS)[88]; and the Woomera Manual on International Law of Military Space Operations[89]—the outcome of which is expected in the short-term.

4 Navigating Legal Uncertainty: Cyber-Enabled (Non-) Aggressive Space Operations with (Un)Peaceful Purposes?

The *corpus iuris spatialis* does not provide a satisfactory answer regarding the legality of conducting military operations in outer space. Legal uncertainty is sometimes associated with the use of vague albeit inspirational formulations that co-exist with precise treaty obligations.[90] Further to challenging international lawyers to ascertain the exact nature of the obligations thereof, such formulations lead to scholars questioning if all military activities in outer space are to be considered excluded or if only military activities of a hostile nature are prohibited thereunder.[91]

The 1967 Outer Space Treaty (henceforth, OST) begins by recognising "the common interest of all mankind in the progress of the exploration and use of outer space for peaceful purposes". Also, Article III of the OST determines that States "shall carry on activities in the exploration and use of outer space [. . .] in the interest of maintaining international peace and security and promoting international co-operation and understanding". Additionally, Article IV of the OST then states that the "Moon and other celestial bodies shall be used by all State Parties to the Treaty exclusively for peaceful purposes". Similar references to "peaceful purposes" may be found in other binding and non-binding international legal instruments.

In broader terms, however, it is clear from Article IV of the OST that the Moon and other celestial bodies cannot be used for military activities as the "establishment

[85] UN (2007, 2010, 2019), EU (2014).

[86] Schmitt and NATO Cooperative Cyber Defence Centre of Excellence (2013, 2017).

[87] Schmitt and NATO Cooperative Cyber Defence Centre of Excellence (2017), p. 273.

[88] McGuill (2016).

[89] University of Adelaide (2019).

[90] Blount (2020).

[91] Tronchetti (2015), Lyall and Larsen (2009), Remuss (2011).

of military bases, installations and fortifications, the testing of any type of weapons and the conduct of military manoeuvres on celestial bodies shall be forbidden". Furthermore, Article IX of the OST states that State Parties "shall conduct all their activities in outer space [...] with due regard to the corresponding interests of all other States Parties to the Treaty".

Taking into account the developments concerning the weaponisation of outer space and precisely the issue of cyber-enabled capabilities targeting satellites and related systems, one may certainly question in what way "the legal content of peaceful purposes has been gradually eroding towards a legal minimum of non-aggressive uses of outer space".[92]

One of the acute challenges is determining how current international law applies to actions that leverage cyberspace to target satellites and related systems, the complexity of which makes classifying them as hostile, offensive or aggressive highly debatable. The peculiarities of space-based technologies determine that, further to conventional weapons capable of causing kinetic interference with other space-based assets, it is currently possible to use technologies capable of non-kinetic outcomes to cause interference and/or damages. This circumstance builds on a degree of legal uncertainty creating a state of affairs where it is advantageous for States to adopt actions that may be both aggressive and non-kinetic, thereby remaining below the legal threshold and triggering the applicability of international law.

In essence, the intersection between cyberspace and outer space is being leveraged by State and non-State actors alike for hybrid warfare.[93] A dynamic has ensued whereby known vulnerabilities and legal uncertainty are leveraged to conduct cyber-enabled ASAT attacks.

A first scholarly effort to reflect this reality is the development of a concept of "space hybrid operations" defined by the Prague Security Studies Institute as: "intentional, temporary, mostly reversible, and often harmful space actions/activities specifically designed to exploit the links to other domains and conducted just below the threshold of requiring meaningful military or political retaliatory responses.".[94]

A further element of analysis comes from the abovementioned Tallinn Manual[95] developed by NATO's Cooperative Cyber Defence Centre of Excellence. This outcome of expert-led research on the international law applicable to cyber warfare distinguishes between "space-enabled cyber operations" and "cyber-enabled space operations".[96] Whereas the first type may be limited to the use of satellite communication links, the second type encompasses the use of "cyber means to affect the functionality of a space asset or its payload".[97]

[92] Blount (2019); Bowen (2019), pp. 271–272.

[93] Weissmann et al. (2021), McFarland (2021).

[94] Robinson et al. (2018), p. 3.

[95] Schmitt and NATO Cooperative Cyber Defence Centre of Excellence (2013, 2017).

[96] Schmitt and NATO Cooperative Cyber Defence Centre of Excellence (2017), p. 270.

[97] Ibid., p. 271.

Examples of cyber threats that leverage cyber tools and the cyber domain connected with space-based technologies are "GNSS Jamming" and "GNSS Spoofing". In essence, these actions are aimed at causing harmful interference by employing cyber means to either force the receiving GNSS equipment to display a false signal (GNSS Spoofing) or prevent the GNSS receiving equipment from detecting and processing the original GNSS signal (GNSS Jamming), both of which are using space-based technology providing PNT data. Specifically, information was made public by NATO of "frequent observations of loss and interference of [GNSS] onboard vessels and aircraft" occurring in the Central and Eastern Mediterranean since mid-2019.[98]

Ascertaining the terms in which a State may respond to a cyber-attack is highly debatable. This challenge extends to non-kinetic actions targeting satellites, as framing a cyberattack in the UN Charter remains complex and debated in scholarly doctrine. Briefly, it is difficult to frame non-physical methods of coercion as a use of force in the letter of Article 2 (4) of the UN Charter. However, one may question the consequences of harmful cyber operations in connection with a State's national sovereignty and political independence. State practice in this regard could develop towards governments equating a cyber-enabled non-kinetic attack targeting a governmental satellite to a violation of national sovereignty, therefore providing a semblance of justification for a measured response. France gives one example, having stated the principle that the country "reserves the right to take retaliatory measures against an unfriendly act in space".[99] Nonetheless, such a development would be highly questionable, namely given that Article 51 of the UN Charter sets the occurrence of an "armed attack" as a requirement for the legitimate use of force in self-defence.[100]

Crucially, in the present context, State practice may be said to be moving decisively away from strict adherence to the "peaceful purposes" obligation,[101] thereby elevating the threshold of tolerable space activities up to the level of aggressive behaviour entailing *de minimis,* a kinetic action producing a permanent outcome. This possibility brings into perspective: (1) the criteria of the means, scale and effects of the purported action in order to ascertain the international legal relevance thereof; and (2) the attribution of a cyber-enabled or non-kinetic-space-based attack in a context where there is a variety of cyber tools to strike at (a) physical distance, (b) invisibly, (c) without leaving a trace, (d) resorting to easy camouflage, (e) capable of differed effects, and (f) possessing similarities to cyber-espionage (as gathering information is not equal to an attack).

As cybersecurity threats increase and societies worldwide accommodate a lifestyle enabled by the IoE in a world without an "off switch"[102] in the face of a

---

[98] NATO (2021b).

[99] The French Ministry for the Armed Forces (2019), p. 26.

[100] Ruys (2010).

[101] Blount (2019), pp. 1–18.

[102] DeNardis (2020).

weaponised competition for space, one international law concept warrants consideration. As proposed previously,[103] value could perhaps come from attempting to devise a framework whereby non-kinetic cyber- and RPO-enabled actions targeting space objects would be qualified as an "act of piracy" in terms of the customary norm of the Law of the Sea—thereby construing cyber operations in accordance with a lower international law threshold for violence.

For the near future, the failure to address the legal uncertainty enabling (a) non-aggressive cyber-enabled non-kinetic actions, and (b) aggressive cyber-enabled non-kinetic actions will embolden ever riskier State behaviour in outer space, thus contributing categorically to further weaponisation. In due time, the conduct of space activities in such a "grey zone" circumstance—reminiscent of cyberspace deregulation—will likely be leveraged by non-State space actors for the provision of cyber-enabled ASAT harmful interference services.

5 Conclusion

As discussed in the present chapter, the innovation in the past decade regarding space technologies has decisively changed the context in which space activities now occur. Whereas during the four decades preceding the twenty-first century, the ability of States to project power in outer space was limited primarily to two space-faring nations, the number of players in the global space sector is now higher and more diverse.

Outer space is becoming an increasingly important part of a rising number of States' national security where aggression is in the eye of the beholder. As traditional space powers reaffirm purported claims, other States have become space-faring nations thanks to private companies—a dynamic making space into a congested, competitive, and contested domain. The entry barriers are low, and the vulnerabilities are high, with multiple vectors that can be exploited, unsurprisingly leading space to be categorised as a warfighting domain. By leveraging cyberspace, an increasing number of actors—State and non-State alike—is able to strike stealthily at a distance, causing temporary or permanent outcomes with virtually no international accountability. Hence, the weaponisation of space is perhaps proof that States are aware of the high dependency on space-based technologies that modern, digitalised societies benefiting from a globalised economy have.

Two main trends signal heightened cybersecurity risks for space systems. Firstly, States may be expected to increasingly turn to private companies to procure much-needed services based on space technology as the response to crises like the Covid-19 pandemic continues to pressure national budgets. Secondly, the growth of the new space economy continues to be led by the entry into the sector of many inexperienced start-up companies for which legal regulations and cybersecurity

[103] Sousa (2021).

requirements are hindering costs. Although the internet revolution was mainly enabled by low-demanding regulatory frameworks to safeguard innovation, the complexity of the cyber risks concerning space technologies will require States to engage with non-traditional stakeholders to devise a holistic approach.

The weaponisation of the cyber domain to target space systems challenges international lawyers to call upon old concepts to deal with new realities. Cyberspace and outer space are interlinked in the sense that the former is militarised and also weaponised through cyber capabilities, although the known incidents have stayed below International Law thresholds. On the one hand, the technology developments that allowed the placement in orbit of satellites and human space flight were entirely based on military technology. On the other hand, the degree of dependency of the world's armed forces vis-à-vis space technologies has increased due to the interoperability of armed forces and the use of specific capabilities such as remotely piloted aircraft (RPA) by States. The most advanced armed forces in the world currently cannot operate without resorting to the cyber domain, a key enabler of interoperability among different types of capabilities. In essence, so-called multi-domain operations where every system deployed at a given theatre of operations is interconnected are now wholly dependent on space-based technologies for a vast range of needs from intelligence collection to secure communications and data links.

The future of warfare will decisively leverage cyberspace, outer space, and artificial intelligence. Cyber operations targeting space systems are the medium-term counter-space threat, and the incentive is there for States and private companies to develop cyber-enabled space weapons. Foreseeably, as space operations shift to large constellations of connected satellites, the military scholarly thought will crystallise based on the premise that cyber operations are the most advantageous option to strike an entire network of satellites.

For international law, the legal uncertainty surrounding cyber operations risks fragmentation and hinders stability in international relations in the context of the known tensions between democracies and autocracies. Holding ever truer, the long-standing perception that the era of treaty-making ended decades ago is nowadays fuelled by the crisis that has befallen multilateralism and is preventing any initiatives under the auspices of UNCOPUOS from flourishing. Foreseeably, absent an international consensus toward a more effective legal framework to deter the development and deployment of capabilities in cyber operations targeting space systems, namely in-orbit, the slow march will continue toward a Hobbesian scenario of *bellium omnia contra omnes* encompassing both the cyber and the space domains.

References

Adamy D (2021) EW 105: space electronic warfare. Artech House, Boston

Aerospace (2020) Counterspace Timeline, 1959–2020. https://aerospace.csis.org/counterspace-timeline/?startYear=1962&endYear=2020&country=all&showStories=false&categories=Cyber&subcategories=IntrusionCyber. Accessed 31 Oct 2021

Barrett B (17 September 2019) The Air Force will let hackers try to hijack an orbiting satellite. Wired. Retrieved from https://www.wired.com/story/air-force-defcon-satellite-hacking/ Accessed 31 Oct 2021

Bloomberg (05 November 2021) Amazon Seeks Another 4,538 Satellites to Challenge Musk's SpaceX. https://www.bloomberg.com/news/articles/2021-11-05/amazon-seeks-to-add-4-538-satellites-to-challenge-musk-s-spacex. Accessed 31 Oct 2021

Blount PJ (2017) A satellite is just a thing on the internet of things. Air Space Law 42

Blount PJ (2019) The shifting sands of space security: the politics and law of the peaceful uses of outer space. Indonesian J Int Law 17(1):1–18

Blount PJ (2020) Peaceful purposes for the benefit of all mankind: the ethical foundations of space security. In: Steer C, Hersch MH (eds) War and peace in outer space: law, policy, and ethics. Oxford University Press, New York, pp 109–122

Borgen CJ (2022) The second space age. In: Waxman MC, Oakley TW (eds) The future law of armed conflict. Oxford University Press, New York, pp 155–179

Bowen B (2019) Space oddities: law, war and the proliferation of spacepower. In: Gow J, Dijxhoorn E, Kerr R, Verdirame G (eds) Routledge handbook of war, law and technology. Routledge, Abingdon, pp 265–279

BryceTech (2020) 2020 Orbital Launches Year in Review. https://brycetech.com/reports. Accessed 31 Oct 2021

BryceTech (2021) Smallsats by the numbers 2021. https://brycetech.com/reports. Accessed 31 Oct 2021

Center for Strategic and International Studies (CSIS) (2021) Report of the CSIS aerospace security project: space threat assessment 2021. CSIS, Washington DC

Chen DD (23 February 2017) Opening Statement of Mr. David Chen: Testimony before the U.S.-China Economic and Security Review Commission. Available at: https://www.uscc.gov/sites/default/files/transcripts/China%27s%20Advanced%20Weapons.pdf. Accessed 31 Oct 2021

CYSAT (2021) Hack Ops. https://hackopssat.cysat.eu/. Accessed 31 Oct 2021

Dawson L (2018) War in space: the science and technology behind our next theater of conflict' 1st space exploration. Springer International Publishing, Cham

Delerue F (2020) Cyber operations and international law. Cambridge University Press, New York

DeNardis L (2020) The internet in everything: freedom and security in a world with no off switch. Yale University Press, New Haven

DigitalEurope (2021) Setting the standard: how to secure the Internet of Things. Available at: https://www.digitaleurope.org/wp/wp-content/uploads/2021/09/DIGITALEUROPE_Setting-the-standard_How-to-secure-the-Internet-of-Things.pdf. Accessed 31 Oct 2021

EU (2011) Towards a space strategy for the European Union that benefits its citizens. 04 April. COM(2011) 152 final

EU (2013) Releasing the potential for economic growth in the space sector. 28 February. COM (2013) 108 final

EU (2014) International Code of Conduct for Outer Space Activities. Available at: https://eeas.europa.eu/archives/docs/non-proliferation-and-disarmament/pdf/space_code_conduct_draft_vers_31-march-2014_en.pdf. Accessed 31 Oct 2021

EU (2017) Dependence of the European Economy on Space Infrastructures. March. European Commission/PwC, Brussels

EU (2021a) Annual Activity Report 2020. 07 April. Directorate-General Defense Industry and Space. Available at: https://ec.europa.eu/info/sites/default/files/annual-activity-report-2020-defis_en.pdf. Accessed 31 Oct 2021

EU (2021b) Statement by the High Representative of the Union for Foreign Affairs and Security Policy on behalf of the E.U. on the Russian anti-satellite test on 15 November 2021. Press Release 878/21 (19/11/2021). Available at: https://www.consilium.europa.eu/en/press/press-releases/2021/11/19/statement-by-the-high-representative-of-the-union-for-foreign-affairs-and-security-policy-on-behalf-of-the-eu-on-the-russian-anti-satellite-test-on-15-november-2021/pdf. Accessed 16 Nov 2021

European Space Agency (2021) Dependence of the European Economy on Space Infrastructures. 19 November. ESA/C-M/CCCII/Res.1 (Final)

Farmer B (16 June 2017) British hacker admits stealing Pentagon satellite data. The Telegraph. Retrieved from https://www.telegraph.co.uk/news/2017/06/16/british-hacker-admits-stealing-pentagon-satellite-data/. Accessed 31 Oct 2021

Frankowski P (2019) Outer space and private companies: consequences for global security. In: Gow J, Dijxhoorn E, Kerr R, Verdirame G (eds) Routledge handbook of war, law and technology. Routledge, Abingdon, pp 280–304

Goswami N, Garretson PA (2020) Scramble for the skies: the great power competition to control the resources of outer space. Lexington Books, Lanham

Green JA (2015) Cyber warfare: a multidisciplinary analysis. Routledge, Abingdon

Group of Seven (2021) Carbis Bay G7 Summit Communiqué: Our Shared Agenda for Global Action to Build Back Better (11-13 June 2021)

Halpern S (05 July 2020) Is the future of space ops officeless? SpaceNews. Retrieved from https://spacenews.com/op-ed-is-the-future-of-space-ops-officeless/. Accessed 31 Oct 2021

Harrison RG (2013) Unpacking the three C's: congested, competitive, and contested space. Astropolitics 11(3):123–131. https://doi.org/10.1080/14777622.2013.838820

Johnson-Freese J (2017) Space warfare in the 21st century: arming the heavens. Routledge Taylor & Francis Group, London; New York

Khan AR (2017) Space wars: dual-use satellites. Rutgers J Law Public Policy 14(3):314–346

Koplow DA (2018) The fault is not in our stars: avoiding an arms race in outer space. Harv Int Law J 59(2):331–388

LeoLabs Analysis of the Cosmos 1408 Breakup. https://leolabs-space.medium.com/analysis-of-the-cosmos-1408-breakup-71b32de5641f. Accessed 31 Oct 2021

Lyall F, Larsen PB (2009) Space law: a treatise. Ashgate, Georgetown

Malik MI, McAteer IN, Hannay P, Ibrahim A, Baig Z, Zheng G (2020) Cyber security for network of things (NoTs) in military systems: challenges and countermeasures. In: Ahmed M, Ullah AB, Pathan A-SK (eds) Security analytics for the internet of everything. CRC Press, Florida, pp 231–249

Masunaga S (2019) SpaceX seeks permission to launch 30,000 more satellites. Los Angeles Times. Retrieved from https://www.latimes.com/business/story/2019-10-15/spacex-30000-starlink-satellites. Accessed 31 Oct 2021

McFarland D (2021) Understanding Hybrid Warfare: navigating the smoke and mirrors of international security. Independently published by David McFarland

McGuill University Manual on International Law Applicable to Military Uses of Outer Space (MILAMOS) (2016) Centre for Research in Air and Space Law. https://www.mcgill.ca/milamos/. Accessed 31 Oct 2021

Nakashima E (09 September 2015) Russian hacker group exploits satellites to steal data, hide tracks. Washington Post. Retrieved from https://www.washingtonpost.com/world/national-security/russian-hacker-group-exploits-satellites-to-steal-data-hide-tracks/2015/09/08/c59fa7cc5657-11e5-b8c9-944725fcd3b9_story.html?utm_term=.43d8b0ed4c7f. Accessed 31 Oct 2021

Nakashima E (24 March 2022) Russian military behind hack of satellite communication devices in Ukraine at war's outset, U.S. officials say. Washington Post. Retrieved from https://www.washingtonpost.com/national-security/2022/03/24/russian-military-behind-hack-satellite-communication-devices-ukraine-wars-outset-us-officials-say/. Accessed 26 March 2022

NASA (2019) NASA Office of the Inspector General, Cybersecurity Management and Oversight at the Jet Propulsion Laboratory Washington, DC. Available at: https://oig.nasa.gov/docs/IG-19-022.pdf. Accessed 31 Oct 2021

NASA (2021) NASA Administrator Statement on Russian ASAT Test. Available at: https://www.nasa.gov/press-release/nasa-administrator-statement-on-russian-asat-test. Accessed 25 Nov 2021

NATO (2016) Warsaw Summit Communiqué. Issued by the Heads of State and Government participating in the meeting of the North Atlantic Council in Warsaw 8-9 July 2016. 09 July. Available at: https://www.nato.int/cps/en/natohq/official_texts_133169.htm. Accessed 31 Oct 2021

NATO (2019) London Declaration. Issued by the Heads of State and Government participating in the meeting of the North Atlantic Council in London 3-4 December 2019. 04 December. Available at: https://www.nato.int/cps/en/natohq/official_texts_171584.htm. Accessed 31 Oct 2021

NATO (2021a) Brussels Summit Communiqué. Issued by the Heads of State and Government participating in the meeting of the North Atlantic Council in Brussels 14 June 2021. 14 June. Available at: https://www.nato.int/cps/en/natohq/news_185000.htm. Accessed 31 Oct 2021

NATO (2021b) Threat to commercial shipping in the Mediterranean 2021. https://shipping.nato.int/nsc/operations/news/2021/threat-to-commercial-shipping-in-the-mediterranean. Accessed 30 Nov 2021

New India Express (2017). https://www.newindianexpress.com/nation/2017/nov/19/hackers-from-china-break-into-secret-indian-government-video-chat-1705010.html Accessed 31 Oct 2021

New York Times (1985, 17 August). Soviet Proposes U.N. Space Talks. New York Times, p 3. Retrieved from https://www.nytimes.com/1985/08/17/world/soviet-proposes-un-space-talks.html. Accessed 31 Oct 2021

OECD (2021) Space Economy for People, Planet and Prosperity: OECD paper for the G20 Space Economy Leaders' Meeting, Rome, Italy 20-21 September 2021. Available at: https://www.oecd.org/sti/inno/space-forum/space-economy-for-people-planet-and-prosperity.pdf. Accessed 31 Oct 2021

Pelton JN (2017) The New Gold Rush: The Riches of Space Beckon! 1st edn. Springer International Publishing, Cham

People's Republic of China (2008) Draft Treaty on the Prevention of the Placement of Weapons in Outer Space, the Threat or Use of Force against Outer Space Objects. https://www.fmprc.gov.cn/mfa_eng/wjb_663304/zzjg_663340/jks_665232/kjfywj_665252/200802/t20080212_599554.html. Accessed 31 Oct 2021

Planet (2021). https://www.planet.com/our-constellations/ Accessed 31 Oct 2021

Porup JM (21 August 2015). It's surprisingly simple to hack a satellite. Motherboard. Retrieved from https://motherboard.vice.com/en_us/article/bmjq5a/its-surprisingly-simple-to-hack-a-satellite/. Accessed 31 Oct 2021

Remuss N-L (2011) Space and security. In: Brünner C, Soucek A (eds) Outer space in society, politics and law. Springer-Verlag, Vienna, New York, pp 519–568

Robinson J, Šmuclerová M, Innocenti LD, Perrichon L, Pražák J (2018) Europe's preparedness to respond to space hybrid operations. The Prague Security Studies Institute, Prague. Available at: https://www.pssi.cz/download//docs/8252_597-europe-s-preparedness-to-respond-to-space-hybrid-operations.pdf. Accessed 31 Oct 2021

Rosello AD, Mane M, Emslie P (2022) Assessing the readiness of contractor-provided space operations capabilities. RAND Corporation, Santa Monica

Ruys T (2010) "Armed attack" and Article 51 of the UN Charter: evolutions in customary law and practice. Cambridge University Press, New York

Schmitt MN, NATO Cooperative Cyber Defence Centre of Excellence (2013) Tallinn manual on the international law applicable to cyber warfare: prepared by the international group of experts at the invitation of the NATO Cooperative Cyber Defence Centre of Excellence. Cambridge University Press, Cambridge

Schmitt MN, NATO Cooperative Cyber Defence Centre of Excellence (2017) Tallinn manual 2.0 on the international law applicable to cyber operations. Cambridge University Press, Cambridge

Sousa BRD (2021, 08-10 November). Deterring 21st century privateers: hybrid actions in outer space as acts of piracy. Paper presented at the ESSCA Space Policy Workshop (Routledge Handbook on Space Politics. ESA ESRIN, Rome)

Space News (18 April 2007) Intelsat vows to stop piracy by Sri Lanka separatist group. http://spacenews.com/intelsat-vows-stop-piracy-sri-lanka-separatist-group/ Accessed 31 Oct 2021

Springer PJ (2017) Encyclopedia of cyber warfare. Abc-Clio, Llc: Santa Barbara, p 1 online resource

Steer C, Hersch MH (2020) War and peace in outer space: law, policy, and ethics. Oxford University Press, New York

Symantec Security Response (7 August 2014) Turla: Spying tool targets governments and diplomat. Retrieved from https://www.symantec.com/connect/blogs/turla-spying-tool-targets-governments-and-diplomats. Accessed 31 Oct 2021

The French Ministry for the Armed Forces (2019) Space Defence Strategy: Report of the "Space" working group. DICoD, Paris

Time (18 November 2021) Space Junk Is Spreading, Creating the Risk of No-Go Zones for Satellites. https://time.com/6121097/space-junk-satellites/. Accessed 30 Nov 2021

Tronchetti F (2015) Legal aspects of remote sensing. In: Dunk FGVD, Tronchetti F (eds) Handbook of space law. Edward Elgar Publishing, Cheltenham, pp 501–553

UN (1981a) UNGA Resolution 36/97 (A/RES/36/97) (09 December) part C

UN (1981b) UNGA Resolution 36/99 (A/RES/36/99) (09 December)

U.N. (2007) UNCOPUOS Space Debris Mitigation Guidelines. UN General-Assembly Resolution 62/217, doc. A/RES/62/217 of 22 December 2007

U.N. (2010) Voluntary Guidelines Proposed by the U.N. Group of Governmental Experts (GGE) on Transparency and Confidence-building Measures (TCBM) in Outer Space Activities. UN General-Assembly Resolution 65/68, doc. A/RES/65/68 of 08 December 2010

U.N. (2015) Transforming our world: the 2030 Agenda for Sustainable Development. A/RES/70/1. 21 October

U.N. (2019) UNCOPUOS Guidelines for the Long-term Sustainability of Outer Space Activities. U.N. doc. A/74/20, Report of the Committee on the Peaceful Uses of Outer Space, Sixty-second session (12-21 June 2019)

U.N. (2020) UNGA Resolution 75/36, Reducing space threats through norms, rules and principles of responsible behaviours, (A/RES/75/36), (16 December)

U.N. (2021a) Report of the Secretary-General: Reducing space threats through norms, rules and principles of responsible behaviours. 13 July. A/76/77

U.N. (2021b) UNGA resolution 76/22, Prevention of an arms race in outer space, (A/RES/76/22), (08 December)

Union of Concerned Scientists (2021) UCS Satellite Database. In-depth details on the 4,550 satellites currently orbiting Earth, including their country of origin, purpose, and other operational details. Available at: https://www.ucsusa.org/resources/satellite-database. Accessed 30 Dec 2021

University of Adelaide The Woomera Manual (2019). https://law.adelaide.edu.au/woomera/. Accessed 31 Oct 2021

U.S. (2019) Space Policy Directive-4: Establishment of the United States Space Force. https://trumpwhitehouse.archives.gov/presidential-actions/text-space-policy-directive-4-establishment-united-states-space-force/. Accessed 31 Oct 2021

U.S. Department of State (2021) Russia Conducts Destructive Anti-Satellite Missile Test. Press Statement by Antony J. Blinken, Secretary of State. Available at: https://www.state.gov/russia-conducts-destructive-anti-satellite-missile-test/. Accessed 20 Nov 2021

U.S. Space Command (2021) Russian direct-ascent anti-satellite missile test creates significant, long-lasting space debris. U.S. Space Command Public Affairs Office. Available at: https://www.spacecom.mil/News/Article-Display/Article/2842957/russian-direct-ascent-anti-satellite-missile-test-creates-significant-long-last/. Accessed 20 Nov 2021

Waterman S (16 August 2021) Space Force's Hack-A-Sat dips a toe in digital waters. Air Force Magazine. Retrieved from https://www.airforcemag.com/hack-a-sat-space-force-digital-waters/ . Accessed 20 Nov 2021

Weeden B, Samson V (2021) Global counterspace capabilities: an open source assessment. Secure World Foundation, Washington, DC

Weissmann M, Nilsson N, Palmertz B, Thunholm P (eds) (2021) Hybrid warfare: security and asymmetric conflict in international relations. I.B. Tauris, London

Bruno Reynaud de Sousa is a Guest Assistant Professor for International Law at the University of Minho (School of Law) and the University of Porto (Faculty of Arts and Humanities). He is a SUSI Scholar on US Foreign Policy (Fulbright Commission/US Department of State), full member of the International Institute of Space Law and a member of the European Centre for Space Law.

Legal Management of the Concept of Risk in Reversible Operations Against Space Assets

Giulia Pavesi

Abstract In recent years, the spectrum of risks to space infrastructures has broadened considerably, both in terms of heterogeneity and severity. Today, the security of space systems is constantly threatened not only by environmental instability, due to the proliferation of debris and natural phenomena, but also by the contestation of outer space through new operations capable of remotely incapacitating a satellite without the need to necessarily physically destroy it. These operations, mostly reversible and conducted through non-kinetic physical, cyber and electronic means, currently exploit gaps in international space law and pose a threat to the resilience of modern societies.

This chapter will analyse how to fill this gap not only by using the existing tools of international space law, but also by integrating technical research on critical infrastructures and critical infrastructure protection in an original way to assess the type of risk posed by these operations. Finally, a series of risk assessment methodologies will be proposed when conducting malicious reversible operations in space in order to prevent space actors from having, or exploiting, a different conception of risk, fostering misinterpretations and ultimately threatening international peace and security.

1 Introduction

Since the beginning of space exploration, with the launch of Sputnik I in 1957, space systems have gradually outgrown their usefulness as traditional strategic assets and political tools to drive development, becoming increasingly integrated into national security and defence activities as tools of force enhancement.

Today, space systems are deeply integrated into modern societies for both civil and economic as well as military purposes. This progressive change has led to them being perceived as possible targets of malicious operations and to an increased

G. Pavesi (✉)
Leuven Centre for Global Governance Studies, KU Leuven (GGS), Leuven, Belgium
e-mail: giulia.pavesi@kuleuven.be

F. A. Carneiro Pacheco de Andrade et al. (eds.), *Legal Developments on Cybersecurity and Related Fields*, Law, Governance and Technology Series 60,
https://doi.org/10.1007/978-3-031-41820-4_4

interest in research and development of technologies capable of denying access to space, as part of defensive strategies in space. Moreover, at a faster pace than nuclear security, space contestation has evolved from a bipolar to a multipolar environment, with medium and emerging powers developing counter-space capabilities.

This new pattern of contestation has also influenced the type of technology chosen, and the effects thereof, as well as the likeliwood of attributing an attack, with a clear shift towards malicious operations that could have some margin of reversibility, rather than traditional irreversible kinetic physical ASATs, now perceived and used primarily in terms of power projection.

Particularly, malicious reversible operations against space assets are gaining momentum due to the increased awareness of the space debris problem and the ability of kinetic physical ASATs to cause indiscriminate long-term damage, also endangering the attacker's interests, favoring a so called "neo-liberist" approach to space security dynamics.

The challenge through these reversible malicious operations and the technical and regulatory framework to assess and mitigate the risks arising from such operations are the focus of this, limited, contribution.

The chapter will first conceptually describe these operations.

It will then examine the potential implications of recognising specific space systems as critical infrastructures in order to effectively assess, manage and mitigate the risks arising from such operations.

Then, the legal mechanisms for protecting such infrastructures from reversible operations will be analysed, extracting from the current corpus iuris spatialis the primary obligation to prevent one state from endangering another state's freedom to use outer space when conducting reversible operations against space assets, along with an ancillary obligation of due diligence during the conduct of such operations.

Finally, in addition to the current risk assessment and management methods used in space operations, the author proposes to expand on traditional methodologies when it comes to addressing the risks associated with reversible operations against space assets, borrowing some considerations from the field of risk studies and in particular from the application of "global risk management" theory to these operations.

2 A Paradigm-Shift in Space Contestation

Today, outer space has become a contested domain, with more countries engaging in "space for security", i.e. using space assets and applications for force enhancement and national security, as well as "security in space", with a growing increase in the development of defensive counterspace capabilities meant to disrupt, deny, degrade or destroy space systems.[1]

[1] Samson and Weeden (2022) <https://swfound.org/media/207350/swf_global_counterspace_capabilities_2022_rev2.pdf> last accessed 24/06/2022.

In the past decades, contestation in outer space has essentially developed in four categories of counterspace: kinetic physical, non-kinetic physical, electronic and cyber[2].

The former consist of hit-to-kill ASATs meant to physically intercept and destroy the targeted satellite via explosions or direct impact, potentially resulting in massive pollution of the outer space environment. The latter consist of operations having physical effects on satellites without physical contact and include lasers, high-powered microwaves (HPM) and electromagnetic pulse (EMP).[3]

Finally, while jamming and spoofing are electronic operations able to respectively temporarily interfere or interrupt the signal or to transmit fake signals, cyber operations against space assets refer to operations which target the data itself or the system that uses, transmits or controls this data, potentially resulting in data loss, disruption or loss of the satellite, as well as control of the object.[4]

While kinetic physical ASATs are completely irreversible, non-kinetic physical, electronic and cyber operations against space assets usually allow some margin of reversibility, depending on the intensity of the attack and can represent malicious reversible operations against space assets.

In recent years, through technological development and increased awareness for the space debris issue, which could cause indiscriminate long-term damages, the development and testing of counterspace capabilities has progressively shifted from kinetic physical ASAT capabilities to the contestation of the space environment through the aforementioned "reversible" and non-kinetic operations, usually for limited periods of time.

In fact, although reversible, those operations present numerous advantages from a strategic perspective, being very precise, cost-effective, strategically favourable in terms of attribution and minor public awareness, as well as creating significant operational challenges for the targeted actors without necessarily triggering escalatory responses or falling above the threshold of use of force.

From a legal perspective, those operations currently exploit the grey zone of space law militarization, potentially resulting in critical asymmetry before confrontation, strategic advantage, as well as in severe consequences for the civilians without a clearer normative framework and in the absence of a conflict.

It becomes therefore essential for the purposes of this analysis to understand what are the limits to those operations in the current normative framework and clarify what type of risks those operations entail in relation to the role that space infrastructures play in today's society.

---

[2] Harrison et al. (2019).

[3] For the purposes of this contribution, the analysis will be limited only to reversible operations through cyber and electronic means, and will not encompass laser dazzling and rendez-vous and proximity operations.

[4] Harrison et al. (2022) <https://csis-website-prod.s3.amazonaws.com/s3fs-public/publication/220404_Harrison_SpaceThreatAssessment2022.pdf?K4A9o_D9NmYG2Gv98PxNigLxS4oYpHRa> last accessed 24/06/2022.

3 The Concept of Reversible Operations

3.1 Reversible Operations Against Space Assets in the ITU Regime

Although reversible operations are hostile, they do not automatically constitute a use of force and do not even reach the threshold of an armed attack, but in most cases constitute interference with the space activities of other states and are carried out in peacetime. The first regime governing unlawful satellite interferences not falling within the threshold of use of force under Article 2(4) of the UN Charter is the ITU regime.

Here, "harmful interference" is defined, and limited to "Interference which endangers the functioning of a radionavigation service or of other safety services or seriously degrades, obstructs, or repeatedly interrupts a radio communication service operating in accordance with Radio Regulations".[5]

Intentional interferences through jamming or spoofing constituting harmful interference not only are prohibited under Article 45 of the ITU Constitution,[6] but also violate Article 15 of the Constitution, constituting unnecessary transmission of power. When a harmful interference occurs, member states are obligated to ensure compliance with the ITU provisions and to cooperate to eliminate the disruption[7] while solving their disputes first through negotiations and, if these fail, through arbitration, or to seek dispute resolution.[8] However, in spite of the increasing number of radio-frequency interference events detected in the past years, none of these tools have ever been used to tackle these intentional or unintentional events.[9]

Moreover, according to Article 48 of the ITU Constitution, member states retain their entire freedom with regard to military radio installations, the expressions "entire freedom" and "so far as possible" only requiring military installations to exercise "due regard" and making the resolution of harmful interference incidents involving military actors problematic.[10]

Finally, despite calls by ITU member states and international organisations to eliminate jamming, compliance with ITU rules remains voluntary and accountability is often undermined by failure of the offender states to recognise the interference.[11]

[5] Article 1.169 of the ITU Radio Regulations (RR).

[6] According to Article 45 of the ITU Constitution: "All Stations, whatever their purpose, must be established and operated in such a manner as not to cause harmful interference to the radio services or communications of other Member States".

[7] Article 15.21 of the ITU Regulation.

[8] Article 56 of the ITU Constitution.

[9] ITU, Circular Letter CR/488, Prevention of harmful interference to Radio Navigation Satellite Service Receivers in the 1559–1610 MHz frequency band, 8 July 2022.

[10] Mountin (2014), p. 138.

[11] Jakhu and Singh (2009), pp. 79, 83–85.

Moreover, the lack of a mandatory international dispute settlement system within the ITU regime, the non-universal ratification of ITU rules and regulations, and the lack of enforcement mechanisms in the event of violation[12] have severely undermined the ITU's ability to deal with this phenomenon, which brings us back to the search for a satisfactory regime in the corpus iuris spatialis.

3.2 *Reversible Operations Against Space Assets in the Outer Space Treaty*

Instead of trying to fit reversible operations against space assets within one of the many definitions of space weapons elaborated by the academic[13] and international[14] community, the present contribution will adopt a behavioural and functional approach investigating whether those activities fall within the broader notion of "space activities".

The Outer Space Treaty (OST) applies to the space activities of states, individually or jointly led, to those of their nationals and to the activities of international organisations of which a state party to the OST may be a member.[15]

---

[12] Despite the procedure foreseen in Article 13.2 of the Radio Regulations and the amended Article 15.21 § 13 of the Radio Regulations expecting the intervention of national administrations in case of interference.

[13] See for instance: Krepon and Clary (2003), pp. 1–142.

See also: Boothby (2017), pp. 178–214 <https://archive.law.upenn.edu/live/files/7832-boothbyspcwpnslawintllawstdspdf> last accessed 24/06/2022.

[14] See, for instance, the joint initiative put forward by China and Russia on the 12th of February 2008 to the Conference of Disarmament, named Draft Treaty on the Prevention of the Placement of Weapons in Outer Space and of the Threat or Use of Force against Outer Space Objects, usually re-named Draft PPWT Treaty. Here a vague definition of space weapons is proposed in Article I(c): "The term "weapon in outer space" means any device placed in outer space, based on any physical principle, which has been specially produced or converted to destroy, damage or disrupt the normal functioning of objects in outer space, on the Earth or in the Earth's atmosphere, or to eliminate a population or components of the biosphere which are important to human existence or inflict damage on them".

[15] Article VI of the Outer Space Treaty (1967): "States Parties to the Treaty shall bear international responsibility for national activities in outer space, including the moon and other celestial bodies, whether such activities are carried on by governmental agencies or by non-governmental entities, and for assuring that national activities are carried out in conformity with the provisions set forth in the present Treaty. The activities of non-governmental entities in outer space, including the moon and other celestial bodies, shall require authorization and continuing supervision by the appropriate State Party to the Treaty. When activities are carried on in outer space, including the moon and other celestial bodies, by an international organization, responsibility for compliance with this Treaty shall be borne both by the international organization and by the States Parties to the Treaty participating in such organization."

However, as per many concepts addressed by the Outer Space Treaty, the drafters of this document did not provide a circumscribed and precise definition of what constitutes "activities in the exploration and use of outer space".[16]

Leveraging the views expressed by some delegations within the Legal subcommittee of the UN Committee on the Peaceful Uses of Outer Space (COPUOS), stressing a functional approach to the definition of outer space and a teleological one with regard to space activities,[17] and taking into consideration the inclusion within the category of reversible operations of a cyber component, the author suggests to borrow by analogy some observations from the law governing cyber operations.

Interestingly, here the Tallinn Manual distinguishes between space-enabled cyber operations, e.g. cyber communications between satellites or between a satellite and a ground station, and cyber-enabled space operations, e.g. the use of cyber means to affect the functionality or take control of a satellite.[18]

Specifically, on the basis of Article I of the OST, the authors of the Manual refer to "space activities" as a concept which deals with the use, exploration and investigation of outer space, claiming that most of cyber activities fall within the notion of "use". They then go even further encompassing in the legal category of space activities also those activities carried on from Earth and involving or producing effects in outer space, stressing the fact that most cyber operations have their origin on Earth.

This comparison does not entail that reversible operations against space assets are mere cyber operations in disguise, but interestingly it embraces the teleological approach, i.e. the purpose of the activity to produce effects in outer space.

In light of the objectives pursued through reversible operations, and instead of segmenting each type of non-kinetic and reversible counterspace in a single cathegory depending on the technology and technique used, it could be argued that those operations should be considered as a unicum and although they could be carried on both from the ground and from space, they qualify as space activities, renamed for the purposes of this contribution reversible operations against space assets.

4 The Relationship Between Critical Infrastructures and Critical Space Infrastructures for the Purposes of Risk Assessment and Management

Before investigating, and in order to do so, the limits to the lawfulness of reversible operations against space assets, an important step is to assess the impact of these operations on their target.

[16]In fact, for many years this element has also been part of agenda item 5 of the Legal-Subcommittee of the UN COPUOS 'Matters relating to the definition and/or delimitation of outer space activities'. See for instance: Report of the Legal-Subcommittee on the work of its eighteenth session (12 March-6 April 1979), A/AC.105/C.2/L.124/Add.6.

[17]Historical summary on the consideration of the question on the definition and delimitation of outer space, A/AC.105/769/Add.1, 3 February 2020.

[18]Schmitt (2017).

Since the very beginning of space exploration, space infrastructures have been integrated more and more within modern societies, both for military and civil applications, to the point that today some space systems, and particularly government-led global navigation satellite systems, remote sensing, communication systems and observation systems supporting states' activities and decision-making have become *essential* for the functioning of recognized critical infrastructures (CIs, such as energy supply, transportation, ICT, defence and national security).[19]

Moreover, in the past two decades and even more so with the advent of New Space and the space economy, the space sector has experienced an innovation paradigm-shift with enhanced focus on the market deriving from the exploitation of downstream space applications.[20] As a consequence, space infrastructures have evolved into sociotechnical systems intrinsically supporting modern economies.[21]

For this reason, and particularly the reliance of infrastructure systems-of-systems on space-based capabilities, part of the doctrine, and states' practice, has suggested to expand the scope of infrastructure systems up to include some space infrastructures as critical infrastructures (renamed by part of the technical doctrine CSI, critical space infrastructures) or as essential for critical infrastructures' functioning.[22]

While a shared universal definition of critical infrastructures does not exist, from national,[23] regional[24] and academic[25] approaches to CIs, the emerging common defining feature of this category is the increasing interdependence among infrastructure systems, where each infrastructure reciprocally affects the status of connected infrastructures.[26] This interdependency can display in many forms: physical, cyber, geographical, logical, policy and/or procedural, as well as societal.[27]

Therefore, the analysis of CIs, and the possible failures associated to them, requires a "system-of-systems" perspective.[28]

---

[19] Georgescu et al. (2019).

[20] Space economy encompasses 'the full range of activities and the use of resources that create and provide value and benefits to human beings in the course of exploring, understanding, managing and utilizing space'. OECD, The Space Economy in Figures: How Space Contributes to the Global Economy (OECD 2019) <https://www.oecd-ilibrary.org/science-and-technology/the-space-economy-in-figures_c5996201-en> last accessed 24/06/2022.

[21] Georgescu (2020), pp. 227–244 <https://doi.org/10.1007/978-3-030-23210-8_129> last accessed 24/06/2022.

[22] Georgescu (2020).

[23] See Section 1016 (e) for a definition by the United States. US Congress 'Uniting and strengthening America by providing appropriate tools required to intercept and obstruct terrorism (USA PATRIOT ACT)' No. 147 (2001) <http://www.gpo.gov/fdsys/pkg/PLAW-107publ56/content-detail.html> last accessed 24/06/2022.

[24] European Council 'Communication from the Commission to the Council and the European Parliament: Critical infrastructure protection in the fight against terrorism' (2004) <https://eur-lex.europa.eu/legal-content/EN/ALL/?uri=CELEX:52004DC0702> last accessed 24/06/2022.

[25] Zio (2016), pp. 97–114 <https://doi.org/10.1007/s41125-016-0004-2> last accessed 24/06/2022.

[26] Gheorghe and Schlapfer (2006), pp. 580–584.

[27] Georgescu (2020).

[28] Idem.

In this sense, most of the definitions describing CIs refer to vital systems whose incapacitation, degradation, disruption or destruction would significantly impact on other connected systems.

A key feature in CI identification and protection relates then to the effects linked to a potential disruption or destruction of the system. Here, failures can mainly display in cascading failures, where the failure of infrastructure *a* disturbs the functioning of infrastructure *b*; escalating failures, where the failure of *a* worsens an independent disturbance in *b*; and, common cause failures, where a common cause disrupts more infrastructures, in close proximity, at the same time.[29]

The designation of CIs is not a mere formality. Rather, it has substantial implications: it formalizes a duty on the part of the states to protect, through critical infrastructure protection (CIP), these infrastructures and creates a due diligence obligation to implement adequate safety and security measures. Moreover, the designation of an infrastructure as critical or as essential for critical infrastructures functioning impacts the assessment of the scale and effects resulting from the degradation, disruption or destruction of such infrastructure.

When analysing the failures associated with critical infrastructures in space or space-dependent CIs, it is evident that those are mainly cascading failures, where the disruption of a space system propagates across the entire system-of-systems to which it belongs, in the case of space infrastructures irrespective of the temporality or not of the incapacitation.[30]

Particularly, in comparison with terrestrial CIs, critical space infrastructures do not feature intermediate thresholds of functioning, which means that partial utility of the infrastructure is unlikely to be maintained in case the risk materializes, making these assets even more vulnerable.[31]

Here, the safety and security of space infrastructures would certainly benefit from the qualification of some systems as critical space infrastructures or as essential for critical infrastructure functioning and would entail the implementation at national and regional level of CIP obligations, pursued through a variety of mechanisms including legal frameworks and policies.

In fact, the concept of CIP is strictly related to the one of resilience, i.e. the capacity of the system (in space and on the ground) to recover after the risk materializes while minimizing the exposure to disruption or damage, aiming to maintain "the level of functioning of CSIs above a predefined threshold in case of the materialization of a threat and to minimize the casualties, material damage, and systemic impact on other CIs".[32]

While from a technical point of view, it is increasingly evident that the governance of this component shouldn't be legally managed exclusively at the national level, since a national CIP governance of space systems would lead to the fragmentation of standards and laws and jeopardize the overall safety and security of the

[29] Ibidem.

[30] Ibidem.

[31] Ibidem.

[32] Ibidem.

space environment, it is also true that legally and politically-wise the identification and designation of national infrastructures as "critical" currently is and will remain a national prerogative, implemented through different levels of classification based on national security interests.[33]

However, rather than pursuing an international or regional approach to CSIP, existing sources and obligations available in International Space Law, as lex specialis, and Public International Law, as its subsidiary body of law, could be leveraged while essentially considering some space infrastructures as critical infrastructures per se and/or as *enablers* for the functioning and resilience of other critical infrastructures.

5 Limits to Reversible Operations Against Space Assets in International (Space) Law

5.1 The Obligation to Prevent Harms Deriving from Reversible Operations

Article I of the Outer Space Treaty codifies the freedom of exploration and use of outer space by all states.

From Article I, two main precepts emerge: international law applies in outer space, which read in conjunction with Article III, translates in the applicability to space activities of the general principles of international law;[34] and, states are free to explore and use outer space, without discrimination on the basis of equality and in accordance with international law.

Moreover, from its joint interpretation with Article II[35] of the Treaty, a further consideration emerges: outer space should be qualified as *res communis omnium.*[36] This concept of roman origins does not entail the applicability of a sharing and caring mechanism; rather, it contains a negative obligation, that is states' duty to not

---

[33] See for instance: Policy Directive 21, Critical Infrastructure Security and Resilience (PPD-21), The White House (2013) https://obamawhitehouse.archives.gov/the-press-office/2013/02/12/presidential-policy-directive-critical-infrastructure-security-and-resil. See also: NIPP 2013, Partnering for Critical Infrastructure Security and Resilience (2013) https://www.cisa.gov/sites/default/files/publications/national-infrastructure-protection-plan-2013-508.pdf: last accessed 24/06/2022. See also: COUNCIL DIRECTIVE 2008/114/EC of 8 December 2008 on the identification and designation of European critical infrastructures and the assessment of the [2008] OJ 2 345/75.

[34] According to Article III of the Outer Space Treaty: "States Parties to the Treaty shall carry on activities in the exploration and use of outer space, including the moon and other celestial bodies, in accordance with international law, including the Charter of the United Nations, in the interest of maintaining international peace and security and promoting international co-operation and understanding."

[35] According to Article II of the Outer Space Treaty: "Outer space, including the moon and other celestial bodies, is not subject to national appropriation by claim of sovereignty, by means of use or occupation, or by any other means."

[36] Hobe (2009).

impede the use of outer space by other states, including space-based services provided by space infrastructures.[37]

Therefore the *res communis omnium* principle together with the *common interest* one ensured by Article I requires states to balance their interests in space with those of the international community. This can also be interpreted as a further implementation of the *sic utere tuo ut alienum non laedas* general principle of law, whose corollary will be that each state has to exercise its rights of use of the outer space, including the development of counterspace capabilities for defensive purposes, without prejudice for other states to benefit from space systems, reinforcing the existence of a generic obligation of non-interference in other states' activities.

This translates into a primary obligation for states not to jeopardise the freedom of other states in the use of outer space when conducting reversible operations against space assets.

The second provision supporting this preventive obligation is then Article IX of the OST which introduces the obligation of states parties to conduct all their activities in outer space with due regard to the corresponding interests of all other states parties.

Article IX complements the primary obligations set in Article I, paragraph 2, and in Article III of the Outer Space Treaty and introduces a due regard clause, imposing a standard of care when performing space activities,[38] including reversible counterspace.

In fact, similarly to other regimes dealing with the exploration and use of *res communes omnium*, this provision is inspired by considerations of equity, where states sharing a common resource have to balance their activities, including defensive and military ones, with protective measures aimed at attaining the optimum utilization of that resource.

In conclusion, when interpreted in conjunction with Article I, the principle of due regard does not simply recall the common interest and benefit clause.

Rather, it specifies the ways in which the freedom of use should be ensured and it creates an obligation for the states parties to avoid and prevent hazards deriving from reversible operations against space assets that may affect the present and future use of outer space by other states parties in support of their national or critical space-dependent infrastructures.

5.2 *Due Diligence Obligations When Performing SROs*

The primary obligation of prevention is then complemented by a procedural due diligence obligation through the consultation mechanism recalled in the second part of Article IX of the Outer Space Treaty.

---

[37] Pavesi (2017).

[38] Hobe (2009).

Regarding Article IX, it states:

> If a State Party to the Treaty has reason to believe that an activity or experiment planned by it or its nationals in outer space (...) would cause potentially harmful interference with activities of other States Parties in the peaceful exploration and use of outer space (...) it shall undertake appropriate international consultations before proceeding with any such activity or experiment.

This mechanism is designed to prevent potentially harmful interference in outer space and obliges a state which has reason to believe that its or its nationals' activities would cause potentially harmful interference to undertake appropriate consultations, before proceeding with such activity.

In this regard, as some authors argued, the consultation clause could be considered an "outgrowth" of the due regard and common interest clause, as well as a specification of the "appropriate measures", recalled in Sentence 1 of Article IX.[39]

Regardless of the effectiveness and enforceability of the consultation clause with respect to the strategic advantages and defensive purposes pursued through electronic and cyber counterspace, it is the expression "reason to believe", interpreted in conjunction with Articles I and IX, that establishes a certain level of fact-finding in determining whether the interference is harmful or not, especially since, contrary to the ITU regime, in the OST the concept of "harmful interference" is not defined.

The clause could imply that the state must already have some level of knowledge that its planned activity has the potential to harmfully interfere and, in the case of critical infrastructure, severely affect the activity of another state[40]. This could also help to set the threshold to distinguish mere harmful interference, that entails international responsibility, from a violation of Article 2(4) of the UN Charter, that engages instead the use of force.

Moreover, it could also translate into a procedural due diligence requirement for the state to preliminarily assess the risks associated with reversible operations against a specific space asset, if it supports or enables the operation of a dependent critical infrastructure or if the space asset can be considered a critical infrastructure per se.

This also seems to be confirmed by the subsequent requirement to make "appropriate" consultations (although not strategically feasible in the case of the operations under consideration), which, in the silence of the Treaty as to its meaning, can be interpreted as a counterbalance to the notion of "harmful", where the degree of appropriateness will be calibrated on the basis of the nature of the activity and the degree of hazard.

---

[39] Sztucki (1974).

[40] Mineiro (2008).

6 Risk Assessment Methodologies for Reversible Operations

Regarding the abovementioned "knowledge" held by the state of the risks associated to the performance of reversible operations in each and every case to space-dependent CIs, this contribution suggests various criteria for risk assessment, in addition to the traditional environmental one in line with the findings of the CIJ in the Pulp Mills case.

First, risk assessment in space operations shall be conducted from a technical perspective, through the implementation of ECSS and ISO Standards (e.g. the ECSS-M-ST-80C of the European Cooperation for Space Standardization).[41]

Second, the environmental component has to be considered through environmental impact assessment procedures (EIA). Indeed, although these operations have less impact in terms of debris generation than kinetic physical operations, debris may result from the incapacitation of the space asset through reversible operations.

While to this extent some primitive forms of EIA in space operations already exist as a pre-requisite in mission planning of many space agencies,[42] as well as national legislation,[43] usually providing debris mitigation, these are not sufficient to address reversible operations. Indeed, to take into account the environmental impact on the space ecosystem, EIA requires *actual* knowledge of the space environment in which the space object is to operate and implies a certain level of SSA capability, which not all countries possess.

Moreover, the risks associated with the disruption or destruction of space-dependent critical infrastructures through reversible counterspace also have a strong economic and social component, legitimising, as suggested by authoritative doctrine, not only an integrated approach to Space Situational Awareness systems, but also Strategic Environmental Assessments (SEAs),[44] aimed at including in the assessment also the potential socio-economic consequences of strategic initiatives in weighing the performance of reversible operations. To this end, in risk assessment procedures, the obvious cyber component must be evaluated, as space technologies are ultimately cyber-dependent as well, increasingly digitized and intertwined both at the level of the space systems themselves and in the environment in which they operate.

Finally, in assessing and managing the risks arising from these operations, this contribution suggests that developments in the field of risk studies and in particular

---

[41] ECSS standards https://ecss.nl/standard/ecss-m-st-80c-risk-management/: last accessed 24/06/2022.

[42] For an assessment of the mitigation standards adopted by states and international organizations, refer to the compendium developed by some COPUOS member states, in reference to agenda item 10 of the Legal Subcommittee https://www.unoosa.org/documents/pdf/spacelaw/sd/Space_Debris_Compendium_COPUOS_25_Feb_2019p.pdf: last accessed 24/06/2022.

[43] See for instance the French Space Operation Act. Loi n° 2008-518 du 3 juin 2008 relative aux opérations spatiales https://www.legifrance.gouv.fr/loda/id/JORFTEXT000018931380/: last accessed 24/06/2022.

[44] Gachechiladze-Bozhesku and Fischer (2012), pp. 22–30.

the application of "global risk management" theory to reversible operations against space assets should also be taken into account.

Scholars supporting, with different approaches, risk global management theory argue that society, as a result of emerging defensive technologies, witnessed a shift from traditional security management, where risks were perceived as calculable and manageable, to a reality where this is not anymore valid and where stability is based on the active management of risk vis-à-vis a constantly changing security environment.[45]

In particular, in recent warfare risk management, a "sociologically inspired risk analysis" has emerged, dependent not on a scientific or objective quantification of risk, but rather on what authoritative doctrine has dubbed the "social constructivist interpretation and political selection of risk", which in the case of reversible operations through cyber and electronic means could potentially translate into a risk calculus between action and inaction.[46]

In this case, while the reversibility and apparent low-scale effects of such operations could lead to their use as a risk management capability, able to create significant risk for the enemy while minimising that for the attacker, its potential on space-dependent critical infrastructures should not be underestimated. In particular because, by doing so, such operations could lead to a risk transfer (including in subsequent conflicts), where in fact the risk would increase for civilians indirectly affected through the incapacitation or destruction of critical, or dependent, (space) infrastructures, whether the operation is still reversible or not.[47]

7 Concluding Remarks

This paper has shown that in the current dynamics of space contestation there has been a shift in the type of technologies and approach used by modern space powers. Due in part to the increased awareness of the effects of kinetic counterspace technologies on both the attacker and the stability of the environment in which space actors operate, most space powers are currently developing counterspace methods aimed at exploiting the gray areas and gaps in international space law.

In this regard, during peacetime their strategies have turned out to be increasingly oriented toward integrated, multi-domain options and the minimization of physical contact with the targeted object.

However, the harmful effects of these operations on critical infrastructures safety will not be long in coming, especially in light of the significant growth of the satellite population and dependency of modern societies on space infrastructures.

Only through a more substantial effort on the part of the international and academic community to address these operations, through risk prevention,

---

[45] Petersen (2012), pp. 693–717

[46] Heng (2018), pp. 544–558.

[47] Idem.

mitigation, and management will it be possible to contain the effects of these operations on the dependent systems on which the civilian population relies.

This paper has shown that although reversible operations against space assets through cyber and electronic operations may indeed qualify as harmful interference under the ITU, this regime does not necessarily provide the appropriate tools to address the phenomenon.

Instead, a functional and teleological approach to the notion of "space activities" first allows for the qualification of such operations as space activities and for the extrapolation from international space law of a number of mechanisms to prevent, in part, the direct and indirect effects of such operations on critical or space-dependent infrastructures.

In addition, a thorough understanding of the interdependencies between space systems and dependent terrestrial infrastructure will be fundamental to assess the risks arising from such operations and to substantiate the content of any preventive and due diligence obligations.

Finally, the range of risk assessment methods in reversible operations should be expanded to include all the different interests worthy of protection, from environmental to economic and social.

References

Boothby B (2017) Space weapons and the law. Int Law Stud Ser US Naval War Col 93:178–214. https://archive.law.upenn.edu/live/files/7832-boothbyspcwpnslawintllawstdspdf

Gachechiladze-Bozhesku M, Fischer TB (2012) Benefits of and barriers to SEA follow-up — theory and practice. Environ Impact Assessment Rev 34:22–30

Georgescu A (2020) Critical space infrastructures. In: Schrogl KU (ed) Handbook of space security: policies, applications and programs, 2nd edn. Springer, pp 227–244. https://doi.org/10.1007/978-3-030-23210-8_129

Georgescu A, Gheorghe AV, Piso M-I, Polinpapilinho FK (2019) Critical space infrastructures: risk, resilience and complexity, 1st edn. Springer International Publishing

Gheorghe AV, Schlapfer M (2006) Ubiquity of digitalization and risks of interdependent critical infrastructures. In: Systems, man and cybernetics. IEEE International Conference, pp 580–584

Harrison T, Johnson K, Roberts TG (2019) Center for Strategic and International Studies (CSIS). Report of the CSIS Aerospace Security Project: Space Threat Assessment 2019. Washington DC, CSIS. https://aerospace.csis.org/wp-content/uploads/2019/04/SpaceThreatAssessment2019-compressed.pdf

Harrison T, Johnson K, Roberts TG, Way T, Young M (2022) Space Threat Assessment 2022 Center for Strategic and International Studies. https://csis-website-prod.s3.amazonaws.com/s3fs-public/publication/220404_Harrison_SpaceThreatAssessment2022.pdf?K4A9o_D9NmYG2Gv98PxNigLxS4oYpHRa

Heng Y-K (2018) The continuing resonance of the war as risk management perspective for understanding military interventions. Contemp Secur Policy 39:544–558

Hobe S (2009) Article I. In: Hobe S, Schmidt-Tedd B, Schrogl K-U, Meishan Goh G (eds) Cologne commentary on space law: outer space treaty. Heymanns, Köln

Jakhu R, Singh K (2009) Space security and competition for radio frequencies and geostationary slots. ZLW 58:79, 83–85

Krepon M, Clary C (2003) Space assurance or space weapons, The Henry L. Stimson Center, pp 1–142
Mineiro MC (2008) FY-1C and USA-193 ASAT intercepts: an assessment of legal obligations under Article IX of the outer space treaty. J Space Law 34
Mountin SM (2014) The legality and implications of intentional interference with commercial communication satellite signals. Int Law Stud 90(101):138
Pavesi G (2017) A sustainable elaboration of the outer space treaty. N Proc on L Outer Space 68
Petersen KL (2012) Risk analysis – a field within security studies? Eur J Int Relat 18(4):693–717
Samson V, Weeden B (2022) Global counterspace capabilities: an open source assessment. Secure World Foundation. https://swfound.org/media/207350/swf_global_counterspace_capabilities_2022_rev2.pdf
Schmitt MN (2017) Tallinn Manual 2.0 on the international law applicable to cyber operations, 2nd edn. Cambridge University Press, Cambridge
Sztucki J (1974) International consultations and space treaties, N. Colloquium L Outer Space 17
Zio E (2016) Critical infrastructures vulnerability and risk analysis. Eur J Secur Res 1:97–114. https://doi.org/10.1007/s41125-016-0004-2

Giulia Pavesi is a PhD researcher in International Space Law at the Leuven Centre for Global Governance Studies, at KU Leuven (GGS). Her fields of interest are space security and the law on the use of force, with a focus on the legal regime of the use of non-kinetic counterspace in space. She is involved as an expert in the EU JMCE on European Space Governance and provides expertise in multi-stakeholders projects on Space Traffic Management, European space policy and European space security. Giulia previously worked at GSA (now EUSPA) and ESPI. She is a member of the IISL and alumna cum laude of the Institute for Advanced Defence Studies (Italian Defence).

Knowledge Management and Continuous Improvement in Cyberspace

João Manuel Assis Barbas

Abstract This paper discusses the synergetic relationship between Cyberspace, Knowledge Management, and Continuous Improvement. Information Systems connected through Cyberspace establish the shared interaction context to support data processing and the information life-cycle required to create new knowledge assets and promote core competencies. The interdependence between Knowledge and Cyberspace and its weaknesses requires a more profound comprehension of Information Security and Cybersecurity concepts. We argue their differences are limited and related to a greater emphasis on business success, business continuity, and compliance for Information Security (InfoSec); and a broader technological focus on Cybersecurity (CySec). The InfoSec/CySec cross-functional domain addresses Cyberspace challenges to business cyber-resilience, requiring a new mindset and evolving corporate governance models and structures. To address Cyberspace threats that explore the vulnerabilities of information assets, we offer an overview of the ISO/IEC 27005 risk management process and highlight the IMF recommendation to integrate it into the corporate risk processes.

As it becomes apparent, the InfoSec/CySec domain also uses technologies and generates data that are corporate information assets requiring protection. Continuous improvement and lessons learned are paramount for InfoSec/CySec risk management and business continuity applying PDCA process, proving the relation with Cyberspace.

J. M. A. Barbas (✉)
National Defense Institute, IDN, Lisbon, Portugal
e-mail: joao.barbas@defesa.pt

F. A. Carneiro Pacheco de Andrade et al. (eds.), *Legal Developments on Cybersecurity and Related Fields*, Law, Governance and Technology Series 60,
https://doi.org/10.1007/978-3-031-41820-4_5

1 Introduction

This article tries to prove the correlation between Cyberspace, Knowledge Management, and Continuous Improvement. In line with that goal, it outlines arguments to questions that support the central thesis: How does Cyberspace impact organizations and citizens? When do Western societies become aware of the consequences of using Cyberspace by cyber threat actors? Is there any correlation between technological development and Cyberspace vulnerability? How do Information Systems influence individual and organizational knowledge creation? What additional security concerns result from creating and expanding the organizational knowledge base? What is the relationship between Cyberspace and core competencies? Are Information Security and Cybersecurity significantly distinct concepts? Is there any impact on organizations by the new InfoSec/CySec cross-functional domain? How can organizations deal with the necessity to protect their information assets? Why is continuous improvement mandatory for any successful InfoSec/CySec capability?

2 Cyberspace

The typical twenty-first century environment is uncertain, requiring flexible and innovative organizations where Knowledge is the only source of competitive advantage. (Nonaka and Toyama 2003) Their competitive advantage depends on intangible knowledge elements such as technological know-how, product design, marketing presentation, customer knowledge [profile], personal creativity and innovation, and other strategic intangibles such as culture, style, and commitment (Quinn 1992).

Knowledge caused or contributed to shifts in power and the rise of a new global system to create wealth based on intellectual capacity (Toffler 1990). Knowledge acquired through organizational learning is an essential source of competitive advantage since it cannot be traded and is extremely difficult to imitate (Nonaka et al. 2001).

Over the last 40 years, computing and communications have increasingly supported knowledge development, which expanded their performance, usability, and resilience through innovation, entrepreneurship, and standardization. Information Technologies have become an essential resource to the Government, public and private sectors, and citizens in all societies. Informational resources such as Information and Communication Technologies (ICT), information, and data are indispensable to individual and organizational Knowledge and must be secured continuously.

During that timeframe, public and private ICTs intertwined with Cyberspace[1] became imperative, a fundamental element of modern societies, and a goal for other communities. That virtual environment supported by a global, decentralized, and redundant network, the Internet, standards (e.g., TCP-IP), and techniques (e.g., packet-switching) achieved the desired resilience and further unforeseeable interoperability.

Cyberspace enhanced by mobile communications supports connectivity between persons and organizations anytime and anywhere, making geography less restrictive, regardless of their physical location or time zone. All the identified benefits had side effects such as less privacy, cyber criminality, cyber espionage, etc.

Markets, exploring Information Technologies and Cyberspace attributes, became digital and global. E-business platforms and social networks set new marketing channels besides traditional physical ones, reducing intermediaries, time-to-market, and transaction costs and improving product life cycle to offer products adjusted to global customers. This new economic environment led governments and multinational organizations (e.g., the European Union) to develop digital market policies.

From the early days of computers, Information Security (InfoSec) was concerned with confidentiality by user access control policies and systems availability due to virus propagation in single-manufacturer networks. The expansion of Cyberspace since the 1990s changed that focus.

The increased importance of the security of Cyberspace on Western countries' political agendas stemmed from three key events—the NATO military campaign in Kosovo in 1999, the cyber-attacks on Estonia in April 2007, and the importance of the cyber element in Russia's hybrid warfare tactics in the conflict between that country and Georgia in the summer of 2008.

The first cyber actions[2] known by the public occurred in March 1999 against NATO. As a result of the air campaign against Serbia, many hackers attacked NATO's Internet infrastructure. Later, following the U.S.'s accidental bombing of the Chinese embassy in Belgrade, a Distributed Denial of Service (DDoS) attack was launched by Chinese hackers. It flooded NATO's mail server with email messages and made unavailable the NATO website documenting the conflict in Kosovo. Simultaneously, the official websites of several NATO member countries were targeted by defacement attacks with anti-NATO messages.

This new conflict dimension affected NATO's strategic communication campaign and, for the first time, placed that issue on the concerns of political and military leaders, back then, only as a technical problem with limited potential damage (Hegenbart 2014).

[1]"Global domain within the information environment consisting of the interdependent network of information technology infrastructures, including the Internet, telecommunications networks, computer systems, and embedded processors and controllers." in DOD USA (2020). DOD Dictionary of Military and Associated Terms.

[2]Hegenbart (2014) Semantics Matter - NATO, Cyberspace and Future Threats. Available: https://www.ndc.nato.int/download/downloads.php?icode=416.

Estonia was one of the European countries with the highest penetration rate of digital services. For many years, the Internet was an essential communication infrastructure in banking transactions, access to the media, voting in local elections, etc. The extensive dependence on ICTs made the country highly vulnerable to possible cyberattacks. The 2007 cyber-attack on Estonia's critical infrastructures got the full attention of Western governments as a global security concern (Hegenbart 2014).

The conflict between Georgia and Russia in 2008 revealed the use of offensive cyber-attacks synchronized with military operations. It demonstrated the use of several cyber-warfare techniques, their limitations, and their impact on the population. The public nature of the conflict has induced additional concerns about the possibilities that cyber-attacks could have in the future (AFCEA 2012).

Cyberspace, in general, and the Internet, in particular, facilitate anonymity and have limited barriers to the entry of malicious actors, creating a space where offensive actions are usual and formidable to defend.

3 Information and Knowledge

Data, information, and Knowledge are diverse concepts sometimes indistinctively used. Data can be defined as observations or facts in digital format representing physical or virtual events before being arranged in an understandable form, and information as data organized into a shape understandable to humans (Laudon and Laudon 2018).

This characterization emphasizes data as the source of information and the significance and added value for humans granted by the given context (shape). The contexts that provide the indispensable environment for data are usually Information Systems. They include interdependent components that assure essential functions (retrieval, processing, storage, distribution, and destruction) for manipulating the information required to support organizations' decision-making and control (Laudon and Laudon 2018).

Information systems and their associated data and information are essential elements for any organization's primary and support activities.[3] That information crosses all functional and organizational levels (senior, middle, and operational management) to accomplish the mission and business objectives and is a source of individual and collective Knowledge.

Information Systems require connectivity to pursue their essential functions, internally and externally. Communication resources within Cyberspace, such as local area networks, corporate networks, or the Internet, grant that linkage.

There are many proposed definitions of Knowledge. We will consider it meaningful information correlated with other content promoting understanding. Bates

[3]Generic Value Chain model. Porter (1998).

(2005) That statement emphasizes the importance of information and the required human comprehension in individual or personal Knowledge.

Nonaka and Takeuchi (1995) explain the creation of organizational Knowledge as the capacity of an organization to create new Knowledge, propagate it throughout the organization, and integrate it into products, services, and systems.

Personal Knowledge becomes organizational through a two-dimensional evolutionary process—epistemological and ontological—related to the nature, validity, and level of social interaction.

In epistemological terms, there are two types of Knowledge: tacit and explicit.[4] Tacit Knowledge is closely linked to experience. It involves cognitive and technical elements and has a personal quality that hinders formalization.[5] The explicit or codified Knowledge can be transmitted in a formal and systematic language, shared in the form of data, and is relatively easy to process, transfer, and store, for example, through Information Systems. The epistemological dimension corresponds to the interactive conversion between Tacit and explicit Knowledge.

The ontological dimension concerns the individual in the value chain, crossing different levels of aggregation and expanding organizational boundaries. This dimension is fundamental because people are indispensable to creating Knowledge (Nonaka 1994). Knowledge creation is an organizational process that amplifies the Knowledge created individually by people.

The two dimensions of knowledge creation form a spiral with four patterns of interaction between Tacit and explicit Knowledge. Assuming that Knowledge is created through conversion or interaction between the two types of Knowledge, thus expanding its quality and quantity, Nonaka (1994) described four distinct forms of knowledge conversion: socialization, outsourcing, combination, and internalization (SECI).

In socialization, tacit Knowledge is created from exchanging experiences and requires interaction between people. Using language may not be necessary, such as developing skills by apprentices.

The combination is the most common form of knowledge acquisition. It involves social processes in converting various forms of explicit personal Knowledge into more complex and systematized forms of *explicit Knowledge*, allowing the creation and sharing of new Knowledge with other elements of the organization. The use of interaction mechanisms (e.g., information systems, communication networks, social networks, portals, etc.) facilitates the interaction.

When *tacit Knowledge* is made *explicit* through *externalization*, it can be shared and become a starting point for new Knowledge.[6]

The conversion of *explicit Knowledge* into *tacit Knowledge* is designated *internalization.* It has similarities to the traditional notion of learning through practice. Internalized Knowledge becomes *tacit Knowledge* of the individual and can give rise

---

[4]Polanyi (1996).

[5]Nonaka (1994), p. 24.

[6]Nonaka (1994), p. 24.

to a new spiral of Knowledge when shared with other individuals through socialization.[7]

Although all forms of conversion can create Knowledge independently, Nonaka (1994) argued that *organizational Knowledge* stems from its dynamic interaction and occurs when these forms are managed by organizations cyclically and continuously in a "spiral of knowledge."

Nonaka et al. (2000) expanded the SECI process with two additional elements:

- The shared context of knowledge creation: '*ba*'[8] (Japanese word for 'place');
- Knowledge assets or resources: inputs, outputs, and moderators of the knowledge creation process; [9]

The shared context is indispensable to producing Knowledge and facilitating the exchange of context and a common language between the participants. Nonaka et al. (2000) identified four types of shared context with two interaction dimensions: type of interaction (individual or collective) and media (face-to-face or virtual[10]). Each of the identified typologies provides a specific context for each stage of the knowledge-creation process. Therefore, creating, maintaining, and using shared contexts are extremely important for organizational Knowledge.

In generic terms, assets[11] are unique resources indispensable to the value chain[12] of each organisation. Nonaka et al. (2000) proposed four categories of knowledge assets:

- *Experiential knowledge* assets created from tacit Knowledge are shared through experience.
- *Conceptual knowledge* assets created from explicit Knowledge are expressed over images, symbols, and language.
- *Routine knowledge* assets created from tacit Knowledge are embedded into actions and standard practices.
- *Systemic knowledge* assets created from pre-arranged Explicit Knowledge.

*Bogner and Thomas (*1992*)* defined *core competencies* as firm-specific skills to achieve the highest viable customer satisfaction given their competitors, which promote future opportunities for organizations (Hamel and Prahalad 1994).

In any industry, the most valuable *core competencies* allow access to a vast diversity of markets. On the other hand, the lack of such leadership could inhibit a

[7]"*learning by doing*". Ibid.

[8]Nonaka and Konno (1998), p. 15.

[9]*Knowledge Assets. Nonaka (*2000*).*

[10]Examples: e-mail platforms, colaborarative portals, vídeo conference, etc.

[11]"Anything that has value to the organization" such as information, software, hardware, services, people and intangibles (reputation and image). International Standards Organization (ISO) (2009). ISO/IEC 27000:2009(en): Information technology — Security techniques — Information security management systems — Overview and vocabulary [Online]. Available: https://www.iso.org/obp/ui/#iso:std:iso-iec:27000:ed-1:v1:en: [Accessed].

[12]Porter (1998).

company from accessing a particularly competitive market and broader business opportunities. The difficulty of competitors in copying or acquiring it is the litmus test for a *core competence* (Rigby 2015).

Information Systems manipulate *data* to provide *information* for corporate use and provide indispensable capabilities for developing personal and collective Knowledge, which are fundamental to corporate *core competencies*. The interdependence of *Information Systems* from Cyberspace requires close attention to Information Security/Cybersecurity to protect the vital information assets that support *core competencies,* addressing its vulnerabilities and associated risks.

Cyberspace capabilities also significantly influence the virtual media context, either at the individual or collective type of interaction, and the conceptual and systemic knowledge assets that support knowledge development in organizations. That fact requires further consideration by corporate security policies.

4 Information Security

A former FBI Director[13] stated that companies have already been or would be hacked in the future and will be hacked again. This statement tells us that cyber-attacks are inevitable and in line with the Cyberspace weaknesses we know.

In Cyberspace, like in the physical world, it is impossible to avoid all threats and risks everywhere at all times. To deal with this fundamental limitation, organizations must prioritize actions and resources according to their context, such as the business value and vulnerability of the information assets,[14] risk profile, and the most plausible threats. Several concepts emerged to cope with this new business domain: Information Security, Information Assurance, Computer Security, Cybersecurity, etc. We will focus our attention on the two most used.

Information Security (InfoSec) and Cybersecurity are not identical concepts but are frequently used interchangeably. Some definitions differentiate them mainly on their targets: general information (analog and digital) or only digital information and IS/IT. The proposals of the International Standard Organization (ISO)[15] and the

[13] Robert and Mueller (2012).

[14] "Knowledge or data that has value to the organization". International Standards Organization (ISO). (2009). ISO/IEC 27000:2009(en): Information technology — Security techniques — Information security management systems — Overview and vocabulary [Online]. Available: https://www.iso.org/obp/ui/#iso:std:iso-iec:27000:ed-1:v1:en: [Accessed].

[15] "Information security ensures the confidentiality, availability and integrity of information. Information security involves the application and management of appropriate controls that involves consideration of a wide range of threats, with the aim of ensuring sustained business success and continuity and minimizing consequences of information security incidents. Information security is achieved through the implementation of an applicable set of controls, selected through the chosen risk management process and managed using an ISMS, including policies, processes, procedures, organizational structures, software and hardware to protect the identified information assets. These controls need to be specified, implemented, monitored, reviewed and improved where necessary, to

Table 1 Information security and cybersecurity

Topics	Information Security (InfoSec)	Cybersecurity (CySec)
Objectives	Confidentiality, Integrity, and Availability.	Confidentiality, Integrity, and Availability. (It may include authenticity and non-repudiation)
Aims	Ensuring business success and continuity and minimizing consequences of information security incidents	Attainment and maintenance of the security properties of the organization
Constraints	Wide range of threats	Relevant security risks in the cyber environment
Targets	Information assets	Organization and user's assets
What [Elements]	Controls are selected through risk management and managed using an ISMS, including policies, processes, procedures, organizational structures, software, and hardware.	Tools, policies, security concepts, security safeguards, guidelines, risk management approaches, actions, training, best practices, assurance, and technologies
Compliance	Controls need to be specified, implemented, monitored, reviewed and improved where necessary to ensure that the organization's specific information security and business objectives are met.	

Source: Compiled from (International Standards Organization 2018a) and (ITU)

International Telecommunications Union (ITU)[16] don't match that presumption (Table 1). The most significant differences between the two comprehensive definitions are the relevance given to business success and continuity (Aims) and compliance mechanisms of InfoSec, and eventually, a broader technological emphasis on Cybersecurity.

ensure that the specific information security and business objectives of the organization are met. Relevant information security controls are expected to be seamlessly integrated with an organization's business processes." International Standards Organization (2018a) ISO/IEC 27000:2018, Information security management systems: Overview and vocabulary.

[16]"Cybersecurity is the collection of tools, policies, security concepts, security safeguards, guidelines, risk management approaches, actions, training, best practices, assurance and technologies that can be used to protect the cyber environment and organization and user's assets. Organization and user's assets include connected computing devices, personnel, infrastructure, applications, services, telecommunications systems, and the totality of transmitted and/or stored information in the cyber environment. Cybersecurity strives to ensure the attainment and maintenance of the security properties of the organization and user's assets against relevant security risks in the cyber environment. The general security objectives comprise the following: Availability; Integrity, which may include authenticity and non-repudiation; Confidentiality. " ITU. *Cybersecurity* [Online]. Available: https://www.itu.int/en/ITU-T/studygroups/com17/Pages/cybersecurity.aspx [Accessed].

Table 2 ISO/IEC Standards for Information Security

27000: 2018	Information technology — Security techniques — Information security management systems — Overview and vocabulary
27001: 2022	Information security, cybersecurity, and privacy protection — Information security management systems — Requirements
27002: 2022	Information security, cybersecurity, and privacy protection — Information security controls
27003: 2017	Information technology — Security techniques — Information security management systems — Guidance
27004: 2016	Information technology — Security techniques — Information security management — Monitoring, measurement, analysis, and evaluation
27005: 2022	Information security, Cybersecurity, and privacy protection — Guidance on managing information security risks
27014: 2020	Information security, Cybersecurity, and privacy protection — Governance of information security
31000: 2018	Risk management: Guidelines
38500	Information technology — Governance of IT for the organization

Source: (International Standards Organization (ISO))

4.1 *Information Security in Business*

Managers often have difficulty understanding InfoSec/CySec cross-functional domain within their organizations, like in the past with Information Systems and Information Technologies (IS/IT). However, managers have learned how to use IS/IT strategically, embedding its capabilities to support existing businesses and promoting innovative solutions to create business value and distinctive core competencies. InfoSec/CySec domains requires the same learning process from management, users, and other stakeholders to secure strategic business autonomy and resilience.

To support this effort, several standardization institutions[17] developed norms for Information Security. ISO/IEC standards are a reference and are used complementary by others. Tables 2 and 3 display some of the most relevant ISO/IEC and NIST standards to support organizations in creating their own Information Security Management Systems (ISMS).[18]

Implementing an ISMS integrated into the organization requires institutional support from the Administration. A specific governance model and dedicated

[17] Such as International Standards Organization (ISO), National Institute of Standards and Technology (NIST) and Information Systems Audit and Control Association (ISACA).

[18] "An ISMS consists of the policies, procedures, guidelines, and associated resources and activities, collectively managed by an organization, in the pursuit of protecting its information assets. An ISMS is a systematic approach for establishing, implementing, operating, monitoring, reviewing, maintaining." International Standards Organization (2018a) ISO/IEC 27000:2018, Information security management systems: Overview and vocabulary.

Table 3 NIST Standards Applicable to Information Security

SP 800-53 Rev. 5	Security and Privacy Controls for Information Systems and Organizations
SP 800-18 Rev. 1	Guide for Developing Security Plans for Federal Information Systems
SP 800-30 Rev. 1	Guide for Conducting Risk Assessments
IR 7298 Rev. 2	Glossary of Key Information Security Terms
SP 800-34 Rev. 1	Contingency Planning Guide for Federal Information Systems
SP 800-100	Information Security

Source: (National Institute of Standards and Technology (NIST))

InfoSec/CySec structure should be established,[19] including an InfoSec/CySec manager[20] and coordination committee[21] roles to assure leadership and seamless coordination between all relevant stakeholders. Additionally, the criticality of InfoSec/CySec to business success requires a comprehensive understanding of all involved's internal and external business contexts.

4.2 *Risk Management*[22]

InfoSec/CySec capabilities, like other corporate resources, have economic value and therefore are limited, requiring risk prioritization of the vital information assets according to business criteria.[23] A risk treatment plan with controls[24] should be produced and approved at the end of the risk management process.

According to ISO/IEC standards 31000[25] and 27005,[26] the iterative risk management process involves establishing the context; risk assessment; risk treatment; risk acceptance; risk communicating and consultation; and risk monitoring and review.

In establishing the context, the organization must define the purpose and scope of the risk management activities, understand the internal and external contexts and identify and define the risk criteria.

The risk assessment stage consists of the following activities:

---

[19] See clause 6.1.1 Information Security Roles and Responsibilities. International Standards Organization (2013). ISO/IEC 27002:2013 - Information technology — Security techniques — Code of practice for information security controls.

[20] Examples: Chief Information Security Officer (CISO) or Cybersecurity Officer (CSO).

[21] Example: Information Security Steering Committee (ISSC).

[22] International Standards Organization (2018b).

[23] See Business Impact Analysis (3.2), National Institute of Standards and Technology (NIST) (2010). NIST Special Publication 800-34 Rev. 1 - Contingency Planning Guide for Federal Information Systems.

[24] *Vd* ISO/IEC 27002:2022 or NIST SP 800-5.

[25] International Standards Organization (ISO) (2018). ISO 31000:2018(en): Risk management — Guidelines.

[26] International Standards Organization (2018b). ISO/IEC 27005:2018 — Information technology — Security techniques — Information security risk management.

- *Risk Identification*. It involves the identification of assets, threats, existing controls, vulnerabilities, and consequences.
- *Risk Analysis*. A qualitative or quantitative risk analysis produces a list of the assessed consequences concerning the assets, the impact criteria, the likelihood of the incident scenarios, and a list of risks with the associated value level assigned.
- *Risk Evaluation*. It supports prioritization and risk treatment decision-making by comparing the ordered list of risks with the risk evaluation and acceptance criteria.

Risk treatment follows risk assessment and comprises selecting and implementing options (controls) to address risks for each chosen asset. Ultimately, a risk treatment plan and residual risks will be submitted to the Administration for endorsement. Risk treatment options are not mutually exclusive or relevant in all circumstances and are, in general:

- *Risk modification*. Risk is managed by introducing, removing, or changing controls[27] so that the residual risk can be accepted.
- *Risk-retention*. When the risk meets the acceptance criteria, it may be decided to retain (accept) the risk without further action.
- *Risk avoidance*. The condition does not meet the acceptance criteria, and the specific risk should be avoided.
- *Risk sharing*. When another party can better manage the identified risk, it can be shared or transferred (ex., outsourcing of InfoSec/CySec processes, infrastructures, or services).

Risk Acceptance follows the approval of the risk treatment plan and involves the acknowledgment by management of the residual risks involved according to the risk acceptance criteria.

Communication and consultation assist stakeholders in understanding risk and promote their awareness, facilitating the exchange of information to support decision-making.

The World Economic Forum recommended integrating cyber risk assessment into corporate risk management, budgeting, and resource allocation. In the same direction, ISO/IEC Risk Management Guidelines[28] also suggest risk treatment plans integration into corporate management processes.

Continuous monitoring and periodic review of the risk management process and outputs encompasses planning, collecting, and analyzing information, compiling results, and providing feedback. That information should be integrated into corporate performance management and reporting activities (International Standards Organization (ISO) 2018).

[27] Controls, safeguard or countermeasures include any process, policy, device, practice, or other actions which modify risk. International Standards Organization (2018a). ISO/IEC 27000:2018, Information security management systems: Overview and vocabulary.

[28] International Standards Organization (ISO) (2018). ISO 31000:2018(en): Risk management — Guidelines.

5 Continuous Improvement in Cyberspace

Continuous improvement origins back to business initiatives in the nineteenth century that, with the participation of employees, aimed to introduce organizational changes (Bhuiyan and Baghel 2005). At the beginning of the twentieth century, scientific methods were adopted to solve production optimization problems. During World War II, the U.S. government created the Training Within Industry[29] (TWI) program to improve industrial production, which included continuous improvement techniques, later adopted and expanded by the Japanese industry (e.g., *Kaisen*).[30]

Continuous improvement can be described as a planned, systematized, and organized process to modify existing practices and improve performance. (Boer et al. 2000) That may reflect a structured top-down approach, which is challenged by other authors who argue for the involvement of employees in implementing initiatives.

Continuous improvement is a type of change focused on increasing the effectiveness and efficiency to meet business objectives and reflects a culture to eliminate waste. (Bhuiyan and Baghel 2005) However, the focus of continuous improvement is not the change but the evaluation of the results of the alteration to allow a reasoned action that improves the process (Michela et al. 1996).[31]

The continuous improvement applies to the public and the private sectors, facing the need to do more with less. The need for continuous improvement in the private sector stems from the increasing competition and regulation of markets and the expectations of increasing the quality of products and services provided, while in the public sector results from the need to improve processes that progressively satisfy more citizens, to reduce costs and minimize errors (Fryer et al. 2007).

The possible benefits of continuous improvement are: Maximization of results and the possibility of achieving extensive changes following multiple small competing successes; Increased learning (individual and organizational) resulting from a greater acceptance of changes in which they participate; Promotion of Knowledge and learning through the dissemination of small successes in the organization (Cole 2001).

Experiences with adopting scientific management methods and the need to increase the scale of their implementation have fostered the development of several

---

[29]During World War II the Allies were confronted with a set of logistical, tactical and strategic problems of great complexity. To support its resolution through the scientific method, a group of scientists (mathematicians, physicists, and engineers) developed mathematical models that allowed them to understand the problems, test and evaluate hypotheses in order to find optimized solutions that supported the decision-making process. This new methodological body allowed the individualization of Operational Research (Operational *Research (UK) or Operations Research (USA)*. In the post-war period, some of the mathematical methods then developed for military application were progressively introduced into the industry, so in the US Operational Research is also known as Management *Science.*

[30]Japanese word for continuous improvement.

[31]Cit. by Fryer et al. (2007), pp. 497–517.

continuous improvement methodologies. One of them, the PDCA method, is common to the ISO, NIST, and ISACA standards.

The PDCA *or Deming cycle*[32] is an iterative management methodology for continuous improvement and control of processes and products based on the scientific method, developing critical thinking, and increasing efficiency and competitiveness. The essential stages of PDCA are as follows:

- (Plan). The objectives are defined for a given process/product for which improvement is to be obtained.
- (Do). Implements what was planned.
- (Check). Assess whether the objectives have been achieved and whether the improvement has been implemented.
- (Act). Identifies the factors of success or failure to influence a new planning process to define further improvement actions.

The PDCA cycle is an analytical approach that uses internal organization data for analysis and decision progress, the verification of which allows to confirm or reject the hypothesis raised by the research.

Another iterative methodology is the *Boyd cycle*[33] or OODA (*Observe—Orient—Decide—Act*). Although developed for military application, this method can also improve business or competitive situations and is subjacent to several Lessons Learned processes (e.g., United Nations, European Union, NATO).

The ISO standard for Business Continuity Management Systems,[34] which supports the implementation of an ISMS, declares that management review should consider, among other things, lessons learned and actions from near-misses and disruptions and opportunities for continual improvement.

6 Conclusions

Modern societies extensively depend on Information Systems and Cyberspace. The proliferation of cyber threat actors, the limited barriers to abusing the Internet, and the innovative alternatives to their malicious actions make the most technologically sophisticated societies more vulnerable to cyber-attacks.

Western countries only had the conscience of the dramatic changes in the balance of power caused by cyber threat actors after the disruptive events in Estonia (2007) and Georgia (2008). In European Union, the initial focus was the digital society for

[32] Released by Edwards Deming and based on the studies of Walter A. Shewart.

[33] Developed in the 1970s by Colonel John Boyd.

[34] International Standards Organization (2019). ISO 22301:2019(en) - Security and resilience — Business continuity management systems — Requirements.

greater economic competitiveness,[35] and the first Cybersecurity Strategy was published in 2013.[36]

NATO members recognized the need to strengthen defense capabilities against cyber-attacks at the Prague Summit in 2002. Since then, Cyber Defense has become an increasingly important focus of the Alliance.

The synergetic relationship between humans and Information Systems and their associated information favors knowledge creation's epistemological and ontological dimensions. That expands organizational boundaries in different interaction contexts, generating knowledge assets indispensable to corporate Knowledge.

Corporate and personal Knowledge are essential to organizations to create, maintain, and expand core competencies that promote business excellence and resilience. That requires protecting the corporate information, communications, and Information Technologies that assure individual and collective interaction contexts and knowledge assets.

Information Security and Cybersecurity are concepts frequently used interchangeably. The most significant differences between the definitions proposed by ISO and ITU are the relevance given to business success and continuity, the monitoring and review mechanisms of InfoSec, and, eventually, a broader technological emphasis on Cybersecurity.

The InfoSec/CySec cross-functional domain requires a new mindset and evolving traditional corporate governance models and structures to accommodate Cyberspace challenges and support business resilience.

Information Security standards are essential to implement resilient InfoSec/CySec environments where risk management is paramount. Risk management is an iterative process that addresses risk for each information asset with the Administration's commitment. Following the analysis of the organizational context promotes the identification of the information assets to protect, select, and implement controls according to the risk profile of the organization and treatment options.

The PDCA and Boyd are two continuous improvement models which are compatible and complementary. International standards (ISO, ISACA, and NIST) adopt PDCA to improve internal processes. The ISO/IEC standards for risk management (27005) and business continuity (22301) apply PDCA iterative and continuous improvement processes.

The continual monitoring and reviewing of risks (ISO/IEC 27005:2018) and performance evaluation (ISO/IEC 22301:2012) requires the application of the Boyd cycle in identifying lessons from collected information and implementing them (lessons learned).

In summary, the extensive use of Cyberspace capabilities to generate Knowledge, individual and collective (organizational) embedded into products and services creating wealth and well-being required by human societies demands the protection

[35] European Parliament (2011). A new Digital Agenda for Europe: 2015.eu.

[36] European Commission (2013). Cybersecurity Strategy of the European Union: An Open, Safe and Secure Cyberspace. EU Commission.

of fundamental information assets that creates additional data and information under indispensable continuous improvement processes.

References

AFCEA (2012) The Russo-Georgian War (2008): The Role of the cyber attacks in the conflict, in https://www.afcea.org/committees/cyber/documents/therusso-georgianwar2008.pdf

Bates M (2005) Information and knowledge: an evolutionary framework for information science. Information Research [Online], 10. https://files.eric.ed.gov/fulltext/EJ1082014.pdf

Bhuiyan N, Baghel A (2005) An overview of continuous improvement: from the past to the present. Manage Decis 43:761–771

Boer H, Berger A, Champna R, Gertsen F (2000) CI changes: from suggestion box to organisational learning. Continuous Improvement in Europe and Australia. Burlington, Vt., Ashgate, Aldershot

Bogner WC, Thomas H (1992) Core competence and competitive advantage: a model and illustrative evidence from the pharmaceutical industry

Cole R (2001) From continuous improvement to continuous innovation. Quality Manage J 8:7–20

DOD USA (2020) DOD Dictionary of Military and Associated Terms

European Commission (2013) Cybersecurity strategy of the European Union: an open, safe and secure cyberspace. EU Commission

European Parliament (2011) A new Digital Agenda for Europe: 2015.eu

Fryer K, Antony J, Douglas A (2007) Critical success factors of continuous improvement in the public sector: a literature review and some key findings. TQM Magazine 19:497–517

Hamel G, Prahalad CK (1994) Competing for the future. Harvard Business School Press, Boston

Hegenbart C (2014) Semantics Matter - NATO, Cyberspace and Future Threats, in https://www.ndc.nato.int/download/downloads.php?icode=416

International Standards Organization (2013) ISO/IEC 27002:2013 - Information technology — Security techniques — Code of practice for information security controls

International Standards Organization (2018a) ISO/IEC 27000:2018, Information security management systems: Overview and vocabulary

International Standards Organization (2018b) ISO/IEC 27005:2018 — Information technology — Security techniques — Information security risk management

International Standards Organization (2019) ISO 22301:2019(en) - Security and resilience — Business continuity management systems — Requirements

International Standards Organization (ISO) (2009) ISO/IEC 27000:2009(en): Information technology — Security techniques — Information security management systems — Overview and vocabulary [Online], in https://www.iso.org/obp/ui/#iso:std:iso-iec:27000:ed-1:v1:en:

International Standards Organization (ISO) (2018) ISO 31000:2018(en): Risk management — Guidelines

International Standards Organization (ISO). in www.iso.org

ITU. Cybersecurity [Online], in https://www.itu.int/en/ITU-T/studygroups/com17/Pages/cybersecurity.aspx

Laudon KC, Laudon JP (2018) Management information systems: managing the digital firm, 15th edn. Pearson Education

Michela JL, Noori H, Jha S (1996) The dynamics of continuous improvement. Int J Quality Sci 1: 19–47

Mueller RS (2012) Speech RSA Cyber Security Conference

National Institute Of Standards And Technology (NIST) (2010) NIST Special Publication 800-34 Rev. 1 - Contingency Planning Guide for Federal Information Systems

National Institute Of Standards And Technology (NIST). in www.nist.org

Nonaka I (1994) A dynamic theory of organizational knowledge creation. Org Sci 5:24
Nonaka I, Konno N (1998) The concept of "*Ba*": building a foundation for knowledge creation. Calif Manage Rev 40:15
Nonaka I, Takeuchi H (1995) The knowledge-creating company. Harvard business review classics. Harvard Business Press, Boston
Nonaka I, Toyama R (2003) The knowledge-creating theory revisited: knowledge creation as a synthesizing process. Knowl Manage Res Pract:2–10
Nonaka I, Toyama R, Konno N (2000) SECI, Ba and leadership: a unified model of dynamic knowledge creation. Long range planning. Pergamon
Nonaka I, Toyama R, Byosière P (2001) A theory of organizational knowledge creation: understanding the dynamic process of creating knowledge. In: Dierkes MEA (ed) Organizational learning and knowledge. Oxford University Press, New York
Polanyi M (1996) The Tacit dimension. Routledge & Kegan Paul, London
Porter ME (1998) Competitive advantage: creating and sustaining superior performance
Quinn JB (1992) Intelligent enterprise: a knowledge and service based paradigm for industry. Free Press, Maxwell Macmillan Canada, Maxwell Macmillan International, New York, Toronto
Rigby DK (2015) Management tools 2015: an executive's guide. Bain & Company, Inc, Boston
Toffler A (1990) Powershift: knowledge, wealth, and violence at the edge of the 21st century. Bantam Books, New York

João Manuel Assis Barbas (MBA) is Director of the National Defense Course and Advisor at IDN. He is a lecturer at the University and Polytechnic Higher Education and a researcher in the areas of Security and Information Technology. Over more than 40 years of military career he has held several positions related to ICT and Security.

Information Security Metrics: Challenges and Models in an All-Digital World

Henrique Santos, Teresa Pereira, and André Oliveira

Abstract The evolution of ICT and the accelerated adoption process in all sectors of activity have revealed immense cybersecurity threats, which can definitively compromise this evolution and with a heavy impact. The problem, the technological and human vulnerabilities, and the possible solutions have been intensely studied and standardised, and it is now widely recognised that cybersecurity is, in essence, a risk management activity. However, to manage something, it is necessary to have metrics, and only a few aspects of cybersecurity are easily and understandably measurable. This article presents a systematic approach to cybersecurity and risk management, emphasising how to obtain appropriate security metrics and focusing on the industrial sector. For this, we use the most well-known standards illustrated with examples extracted from a typical industrial environment. An outline of a taxonomy of metrics and a framework for their identification and application are presented. It also discusses a continuous certification model that derives from the metrics model and aligns with one of the emerging standards to address cybersecurity in industrial environments (ISA/IEC 62443). The article ends by discussing some of the challenges facing the adoption of a metrics program suitable for organisations' information security objectives.

1 Introduction

Information security is a topic attracting more and more interest from organisations and governmental agencies. The amount of digital data organisations have to deal with daily, the increasing number of online transactions, and the rising number of

H. Santos (✉) · T. Pereira
University of Minho, Department of Information Systems, Braga, Portugal
e-mail: hsantos@dsi.uminho.pt; tpereira@dsi.uminho.pt

A. Oliveira
University of Minho, ALGORITMI Centre, Braga, Portugal
e-mail: id9301@alunos.uminho.pt

F. A. Carneiro Pacheco de Andrade et al. (eds.), *Legal Developments on Cybersecurity and Related Fields*, Law, Governance and Technology Series 60,
https://doi.org/10.1007/978-3-031-41820-4_6

vulnerabilities, along with a lack of computer security awareness and a perceived low risk of being caught, are greater motivations not only to exploit software weaknesses but also to exploit human vulnerabilities Lu (2017). In general, users tend to accept new technologies with complete disregard of their security vulnerabilities and even the impact on their own privacy, if they get sufficient benefits from them. Fostering and continuously encouraging a security culture and recognising that people still are, and will always be the weakest link, will certainly assist organisations to achieve their adequate levels of security and thus become closer to their business goals Fielding (2020).

Moreover, prevention, monitoring, and early detection also play an important role, as it enables organisations and governmental agencies to handle threats more efficiently and react more quickly to events or incidents that are harder to find and understand, from the security management point of view. Rapid response to security events and establishing preventive actions to manage security are beginning to become competitive strategy for organisations. Such an endeavour requires an agile approach to Cybersecurity using simpler and more effective models and mechanisms Santos (2022).

But nowadays it is not enough to have an effective model and a robust set of security controls implemented, or even to reach a high maturity level with all the stakeholders. Threats, context, and technologies change too rapidly. Some studies involving CISOs and other Cybersecurity professionals reveal that most security strategies will probably be outdated in less than two years Olsen (2022). It is essential to have mechanisms that measure, in real-time, the security state of an Information System and the Security Controls' efficiency in place, continuously assessing compliance with established safety objectives, to respond to that dynamic. For that purpose, the investigation and selection of the right security metrics is fundamental. However, such a job is very demanding and far from simple Pendleton et al. (2016), Anu (2021), Houngbo et al. (2015).

Security metrics are derived from any measurable effect that is presumably linked to a security event or incident. Relevant effects can be observed through Cybersecurity tools, system logs, network traffic patterns, performance indicators, and a myriad of other sources. Cybersecurity tools provide them directly and in a meaningfully way, usually, but most of the other sources require a deep understanding of the effects and their semantic meaning in each context Santos (2022). We can find well-known standards addressing security metrics Chew et al. (2008); Aldya et al. (2019), along with some studies aiming to characterise generic properties of security metrics Zaber and Nair (2020). But most of the published works focus on specific domains, such as software Savola (2013), cloud-based architectures Casola et al. (2018), smart grids Leszczyna (2018), healthcare Ahmed et al. (2019), and more recently, addressing emerging technological challenges within IoT and industrial applications Setzler and Mountrouidou (2021); Santos et al. (2021). With much less relevance, but mainly due to the task's difficulty, security metrics can also contribute to forensic analysis and the construction of digital evidence. In Amran et al. (2009), the authors describe how it is possible to use security metrics to increase the credibility of evidence collected in network traffic.

In this chapter, we intend to contribute to the challenging task of defining and choosing security metrics to deliver actionable information to decision makers to manage their corporate assets and ensure their resilience. Although the approach seeks to be generic, the focus is on industrial environments. Due to the emerging IoT paradigm and the openness of Information Systems in what is referred to as Industry 4.0, security assessment and the need for a form of continuous certification are very evident da Silva Oliveira and Santos (2022). To address this problem, in Sect. 2, we will first synthesise a set of fundamental aspects and an implementation model of the security of the information system, which serve as pillars for the definition of security objectives and which are intended to be evaluated using appropriate metrics. Section 3 presents a general characterisation of security metrics, including a taxonomy. In Sect. 4, we describe a proposed model to implement a continuous certification scheme that uses the taxonomy previously described. Finally, in Sect. 5, we discuss some challenges facing the implementation of the proposed model and draw some conclusions and future work.

2 Cybersecurity Fundamentals

Before jumping into the metrics and their importance in the Cybersecurity context, we need to understand some fundamental concepts and models. We will follow the ISO/IEC 27001 standard, with some simplifications that help in the security objectives definition phase and the security controls selection. As already referred, these two phases are central to the security metrics definition and implementation. The main concepts to be retained are Santos (2022):

Information Security It is a process that aims to maintain a given set of properties or goals relevant to Information Security; more specifically, it aims at the "*preservation of confidentiality, integrity and availability of information*" (ISO/IEC 2016, p. 6):

- **Integrity**, to assure information **is not modified** or **created** in an uncontrolled way;
- **Confidentiality**, to ensure information **is available only** to legitimate subjects;
- **Availability**, to ensure information **is available** whenever we need it; and
- **Others**, which is a placeholder for all properties resulting from a refinement of the main three above, whenever an organisation feels necessary to focus on more specific ones; this is particularly critical with integrity and confidentiality since the concepts are too abstract (e.g., assuring ownership and authenticity is probably critical for healthcare information, and both are related to Integrity).

Threat—Anything we foresee **possible to cause damage** in one or more security properties. When analysing threats, it is possible to have no idea as to their origin, or how an accident might occur. The important thing is to recognise the existence of threats. For this reason, threats are usually strongly linked to security properties.

However, they can also arise from the perception of the existence of weaknesses in the Information System, or even dangerous subjects in the environment.

Attack—Any malicious action or group of actions, intentional or not, that will **offend one or more security properties**, causing some harm to the organisation's Information System. Attacks may be performed by external or internal agents. When analysing possible attacks, we usually start with a relevant threat and in all possible ways it can be accomplished. However, we can also start from a new announced attack, relating it to a threat and/or a vulnerability.

Vulnerability—Any **flaw** or **weakness** existing in the Information System, which can be explored by a possible attack.

Security Event—Any **identifiable change** in Information System state that clearly **violates a Security Policy**, shows a **failure in a Security Control**, or shows a **previously unknown situation** with security relevance.

Security Incident—Occurrence of one or more **unexpected** or **unwanted security events**, which have **significant probability of compromising the operation** of the organisation and threaten information security.

Resource—Any asset that has value to the organisation. Knowing the value of a resource is crucial to define its impact in case of a total or partial loss. With intangible resources, determining this value can be a very demanding challenge.

Risk—Result of **uncertainty on security objectives**, when the Information System faces deviations from the correct behaviour. Uncertainty is related to knowledge or information deficits about events, their consequences or likelihood. Given the nature and variety of the events, that deficit may be impossible to overcome.

Security Controls—All the measures we can take for **manage the risk**. It includes **policies, guidelines, procedures, and practises**. Their nature can be **administrative, technical, management, or legal**. Frequently, they are also referenced by safeguards or countermeasures. The ISO/IEC Standard 27001 ISO/IEC (2013) defines 14 security controls' classes, linked to 34 security objectives and a total of 124 specific controls. About half of those controls address technical issues, while the other group address organisational issues. Despite the relevance of this standard, there is no general consensus about the benefits of this framework. Frameworks like the SP 800-53 NA (2020), or the CIS Critical Security Controls (CIS Controls) (n.d.), among a few others usually promoted by specific companies selling security related services, are usually considered as alternatives. In Roy (2020) the authors discuss a high-level comparison between some of them.

Security Policy—A document that specifies in a clear, objective, and unambiguous way what is and what is not allowed with respect to resource operation and information handling. Penalties for noncompliance are also frequently included. Usually, organisations have a main document describing the general posture concerning Information Security (frequently referred to by 'The'Security Policy), linked to a set of sector policy documents, like network access policy, password policy, software installation policy, to name just a few.

The relationships between all these concepts are highlighted in Fig. 1. While the detailed analysis of this model is out of scope, it is important to highlight some details. The three elements related to hazards (threats, attacks, and vulnerabilities)

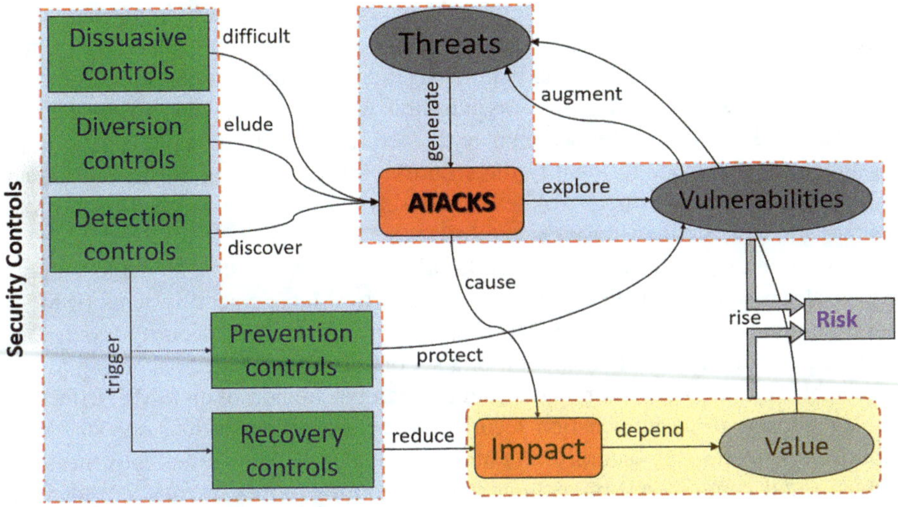

Fig. 1 Information security model

must allow us to understand the likelihood of any malicious action. Combining with the impact value of a given resource, we can determine the risk, which should be the basis to choose the proper security controls. However, the subjective nature of the above analysis and the lack of assertive ways to choose the most efficient control (or controls), or even the security objectives, forces the adoption of a continuous cycle aiming to improve the security function. This requirement points to the Information Security function as a **management process**. Furthermore, the classification of security controls suggested in Fig. 1 differs from the standard approach. It focusses on the purpose towards threats from five alternative perspectives: deterrence, illusion, detection, prevention and recovery. Each class exhibits a particular level of cost, efficacy and expectation, which impacts the required level of monitoring and the linked metrics.

2.1 Risk Management

The Information Security Management Systems (ISMS) is a concept introduced in the security standard ISO/IEC 27000 and promotes a model to establish, implement, operate, monitor, review, maintain and improve the protection of information assets, which has value and requires adequate protection against the loss of the information security properties (confidentiality, integrity and availability), to achieve business objectives based on a risk assessment and the risk acceptance levels of the organisation, designed to effectively deal with and manage risks ISO/IEC (2016).

Risk management is a central function of information security management activities, and it must be monitored and improved according to the involvement of the business and the technology adoption level. This is particularly important when organisations rely heavily on IT-based systems to operate daily. According to the ISO/IEC 27000 security standard, risk management comprises a set of coordinated activities to direct and control an organisation with regard to risk, referred to in ISO/IEC (2016). These activities involve the definition of an adequate plan, including time and resources, to identify the security vulnerabilities of all organisational critical assets, and by critical we mean the assets the organisation needs to normal operate and develop their business activity.

In this context, the security standard ISO/IEC 27001 suggests a model to support organisations to implement an Information Security Management Systems (ISMS). Furthermore, according to the same standard, information security goals are achieved through the implementation of a set of controls, selected according to the acceptable risk management process, and through the support of an ISMS. Effective implementation of an information security policy, according to the same standard, requires the following actions: (1) monitor and evaluate the effectiveness of implemented controls and procedures, which requires proper metrics; (2) identify emerging risks to be treated and evaluate critical assets; and (3) select, implement, and improve appropriate controls as needed ISO/IEC (2013). The ISMS reflects the organisation's approach to risk assessment and risk management, the level of information security risk to which the organisation is willing to be exposed, and the controls to be implemented. In practise, all these tasks resemble a typical management process.

Management involves the supervision and taking of the necessary decisions to achieve business objectives through the protection of organisation's information assets. The Plan-Do-Check-Act (PDCA) process model, adopted by the International Standard ISO/IEC 27001 supports the development and improvement of an organisation management system. Concerning information security, each task of the PDCA model can be described as follows:

Plan—establish security objectives, policies, processes and procedures, based on a risk management approach and improving information security to deliver results according to overall objectives and policies;

Do—implement plans, i.e. *do what was planned to do*; implement and operate the ISMS policy, controls, processes and procedures;

Check—measure results; this process/activity intends to measure/monitor the controls' working indicators, allowing to check when they meet the planned objectives and report the results to management review; and

Act—correct and improve the security policy, based on the results of the internal ISMS audit and management review or other relevant information, to achieve continual improvement of the ISMS. The principle consists in learning from mistakes in order to improve activities and thus achieve better results.

The PDCA model illustrated in Fig. 2, was designed to be used as an iterative four-step problem solving process, with each cycle flowing directly into the beginning of the next. The idea is to be a continual improvement process. The rationale of the PDCA model is that we cannot manage what we do nor control what it is not possible

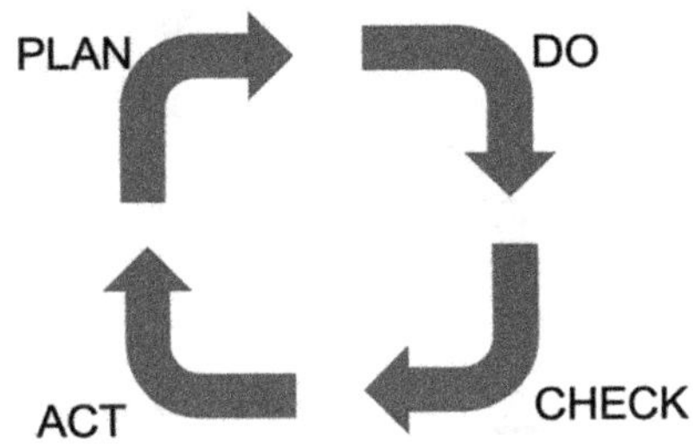

Fig. 2 PDCA Model

to measure or assess. The general nature of this model enables an organisation to align or integrate its ISMS with its management system requirements.

As stated above, central to the ISMS model is security risk management. According to the international standard ISO 31000 Risk Management - Guidelines, and as illustrated in Fig. 3 risk management process "*involves the systematic application of policies, procedures and practises to the activities of communicating and consulting, establishing the context and assessing, treating, monitoring, reviewing, recording and reporting risk*" (ISO/IEC 2018, Sec. 6.1).

The identification of the scope is the first activity to be performed, and involves the establishment of the basic criteria necessary for information security risk management to define the scope and boundaries, which mainly include the identification of the criticality of the information assets involved, in alignment with the organisational business objectives. The next activity is the risk assessment. This activity encompasses "*the overall process of risk identification, risk analysis and risk evaluation*" (ISO/IEC 2018, Sec 6.4.1). Risk identification comprises the activities of finding, recognising and describing the risks that can compromise the achievement of an organisational objectives. Risk analysis consists of the systematic use of information to identify risk sources, consequences, likelihood, events, scenarios, controls, and effectiveness. In fact, an adequate risk analysis will enable organisations to identify their needs regarding information security requirements providing input to risk evaluation, to support decisions regarding the risk needs to be treated and how, and on the most appropriate risk treatment strategy and methods. Lastly, risk evaluation relies on the process of comparing the risk analysis results against given risk criteria to determine the need of additional action ISO/IEC (2018). The likelihood of an attack exploiting a vulnerability to cause harm creates a risk and has an impact. An impact might be a loss of availability, integrity and confidentiality, and other possible losses (lost income, loss of real property, a penalty imposed by regulation, et cetera). If these activities provide sufficient information to effectively determine the actions required to mitigate the risks to an acceptable level, then the task is complete and it follows the risk treatment. However, if the information is not sufficient, another iteration of risk assessment with revised context (e.g. risk evaluation criteria, risk acceptance criteria or impact criteria) will be conducted. The effectiveness of the risk treatment depends on the results of the risk assessment. However, if the risk treatment does not conduct to an acceptable risk level, again another iteration of risk assessment needs to be performed with changed context

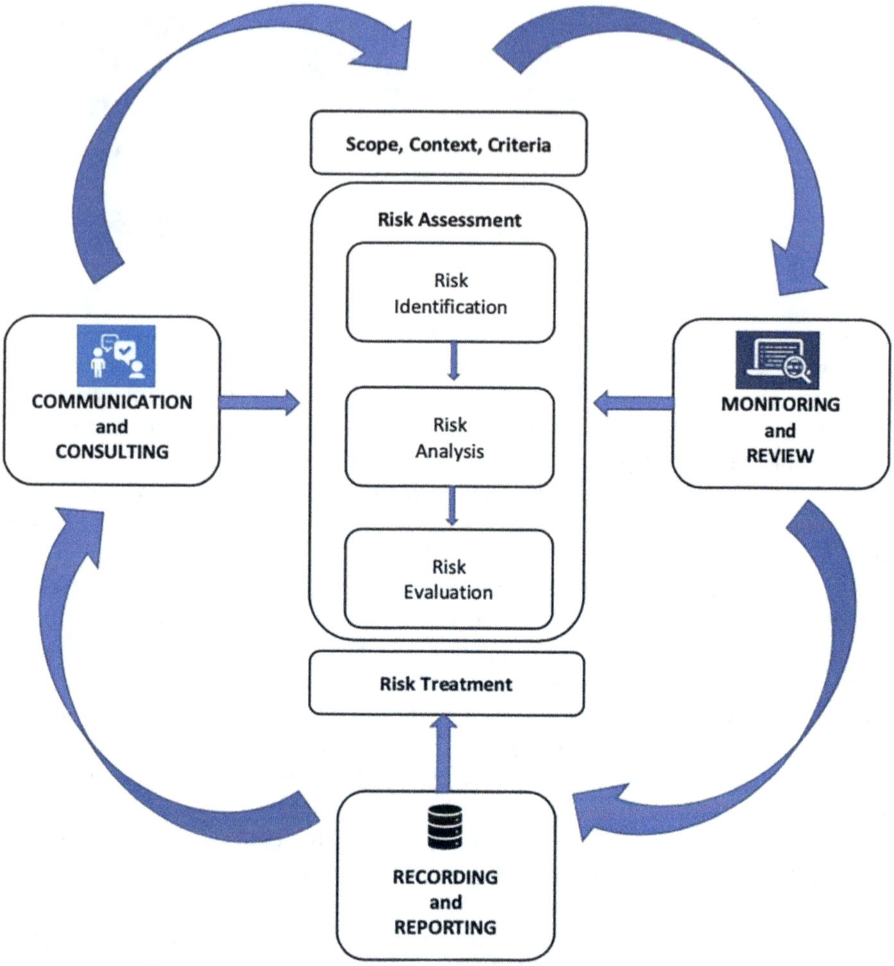

Fig. 3 Risk Management process, adapted from ISO/IEC (2018)

parameters (e.g. risk evaluation criteria, risk acceptance criteria or impact criteria) followed by another risk treatment. The risk acceptance assumes to achieve levels of acceptable risk explicitly accepted by the managers. Throughout the process, it is important that risks and their treatment are communicated to the appropriate managers and operational personnel. Information about identified risks collected before risk treatment can be valuable to managing incidents and can help reduce or mitigate potential harm. Moreover, managers and staff awareness of the risks and knowledge about the nature of controls used to mitigate the risks can assist the organisations to deal with incidents and unexpected events in the most effective manner. The choice of the controls specified in ISO 27002 should be based on a risk analysis process. However, and according to the standard itself, the organisation is not forced to use the described approach and should use the one that best suits their specific business application processes Pereira (2012).

In practise, assets have inherent security vulnerabilities, which need to be identified to support the definition plan including the implementation of the security mechanisms to mitigate impacts and guarantee the daily business activity. It is important to highlight the relevance to get a balance between the costs of applying security controls and the benefits realised from the operation of secured systems. Furthermore, the benefits should be viewed not only in the context of the activity itself, but also in relation to many and varied stakeholders who can be affected. Therefore, the risk management process should not be treated primarily as a technical function carried out by IT experts who operate and manage the IT system, but as an essential management function of the organisation. The investments in information systems protection are defined by the manager and from a business perspective, security is usually seen as an investment to be measured in euros/dollars, saved as a result of reduced losses from security breaches, or in profits from new commitments that would be too risky to undertake without investments in security.

Currently, one of the greatest problems in security is related to the difficulty of managers in defining the proper investments in information security, since it is difficult to quantify security. Beyond financial issues, measuring the efficiency and monitoring the protections of critical operations, whether to manage the Cybersecurity process, control the effects and even protect the construction of digital evidence, must be a primary concern of all agents involved. Not doing so is like purchasing an alarm and believing that it will continuously operate efficiently and without any maintenance, even if working conditions change or malicious actions target it. Measuring security controls efficiency has always been a research topic by itself, and security management success depends on how well this assessment is performed Bodnar and Hopwood (2001); Pendleton et al. (2016); Anu (2021).

3 Information Security Assessment and Metrics

The recent rise of Cybercrime resulted in the introduction of several national and international data protection laws in many countries, demanding organisations implement security and privacy policies to protect their stakeholders' data assets and personal information. Europe leads this trend Kalman (2019). Therefore, it became essential for organisations to develop efforts to ensure their ability to protect their information assets and IT infrastructures securely. Additionally, an increasing number of organisations seek security certification to guarantee compliance with enlarging demands from several business areas, like financial institutions, healthcare organisations, and insurance companies, to name just a few. Certification contributes to promoting trust in the organisations' capacity to implement security controls to manage and protect confidential client business information and contribute toward achieving the organisational operations commitments to reduce risk exposure. In all those strategic paths, security metrics and assessment play an important role.

The assessment of security performance is complex and challenging. Besides the absence of practical systematic approaches, there is a lack of organisational security culture and investment in skilled human resources in the field. Some of the most common approaches to accomplish the task usually involves performing some of the following tasks, with the indicated examples of the goals (and which, unavoidably, involve metrics) Scarfone et al. (2008):

Review Techniques (including internal and external audits)—measure the non-compliance finds; assess detected non-compliance situations; measure the number of security incidents and their frequency; assess the number of assets compromised and their criticality; assess the capability and timely response to incidents; assess the failed controls; measure the number of developed organisational initiatives to rising security culture; measure the number of failed logins; measure the number of tentative root logins; measure the number and type of errors reported by applications (e.g., web servers or databases).

Target Identification and Analysis Techniques—count the number of assets and ports; identify services and count the number of vulnerabilities found; assess the criticality of vulnerabilities in terms of their relevance and the impact of breaches on vital assets; and

Target Vulnerability Validation Techniques (including penetration testing)—assess the capacity to explore vulnerabilities, including human resources; count the number of passwords cracked (by password cracking tools); measure and assess the prediction or estimation of security incident scenarios; assess response to information security incidents;

None of the above assessment techniques can provide, *per se*, a complete picture of the Cybersecurity state of the organisation. We need to use a mixture of them, in practise, depending on security objectives and, indirectly, on the maturity level (as explained in Sect. 3.1). Furthermore, some of those techniques are performed by automatic tools, while others require manual intervention. Automatic tools can often give more rapid responses, almost real-time, while manual ones can only provide the state at a later point of time (static). Some environments, like the industrial sector, due to the rapid technological innovation (Industry 4.0) and the consequent priority to manage security within industrial processes, usually prioritise technical assessment, aiming to provide a type of continuous certification da Silva Oliveira and Santos (2022). Other activities, like forensic analysis, rely a lot more on manual processes to dig into the events and incidents, looking for solid digital pieces of evidence and supporting metrics. Response time is not a priority in this case, but even so, technical and operational metrics captured by real-time tools can provide valuable data Hou et al. (2020).

3.1 Security Metrics

Metrics, in general, can be described as quantifiable measurements of any specific characteristic of a system or a product. When applying the concept to Cybersecurity, we expect those characteristics to emerge framed by well-defined security objectives Payne (2006). As it was stated before, metrics are essential to assist the decision-making process related to privacy and security management issues. Some security experts believe that metrics are a key aspect in monitoring, controlling, and managing security aspects of information systems, which today are the principal support of a large range of organisational processes Chew et al. (2008). The terms metrics and measurements are frequently used interchangeably within the Cybersecurity community. The measurement can be seen as an elementary data item that translates a given observation within the information security objectives. In its turn, metrics are often derived from one or more correlated measurements, taking some reference value and aiming to support the decision-making process. The tools and requirements that support these security metrics and reference values can and should be audited and certified by some international standards Barabanov et al. (2011).

In practise, that difference usually has no impact when implementing a security assessment program, and that is why standards do not devote much attention to that detail. With higher impact, we should expect metrics/measurements to exhibit some fundamental properties Barabanov et al. (2011):

- **Being meaningful** in a given context. It should capture and transmit the target system's relevant attributes.
- **Objective and quantifiable**. Even so, there are situations where qualitative metrics (more subjective) is the only real alternative.
- **Repeatability**. Meaning different actors will get the same results when doing the same measurements.
- **Sample frequency**, which should be adapted to the expected target modifications.
- **Cost of the metric/measurement** should never exceed the benefit value it produces.

Several works focus on metrics' attributes. The list is extensive and reflects different perspectives, application areas and goals. Even so, it is not difficult to find common aspects among those lists, resulting in the above attributes, frequently referred to by the acronym SMART—Specific, Measurable, Attainable, Repeatable, and Time-dependent EDUCAUSE (2017).

Many research institutions, agencies and governments have been working on developing and cataloguing security metrics. Agencies like the Centre for Internet Security and The National Institute of Standards and Technology are currently dealing with these issues and even proposed a taxonomy based on three high-level dimensions: management, technical and operational metrics. They also highlight the role of maturity in the capacity to handle metrics properly Yusuf et al. (2017). Organisational or management metrics are linked to attributes of organisational

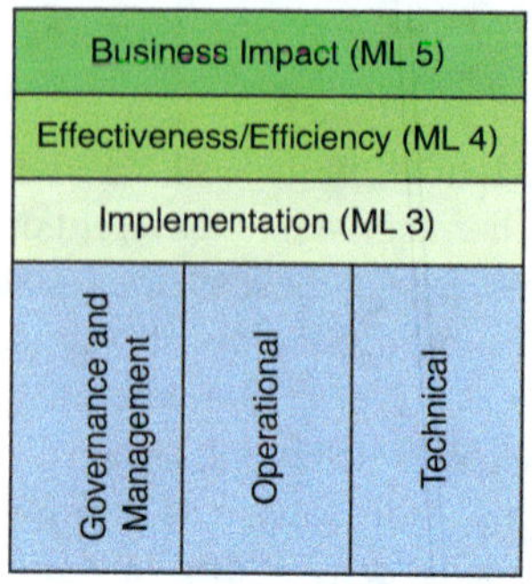

Fig. 4 Metrics taxonomy oriented by function and maturity level

programs and processes, technical metrics are related to computing and networking devices, and operational metrics pertain running systems in their environments Morrison et al. (2018). Putting it all together, as depicted in Fig. 4, we get the base of a taxonomy, which we will follow as the rationale of metrics categorisation. Given the impact on industrial sector, we will focus on the operational and technical metrics, which have a higher impact on continuous certification, as referred above.

Similar metrics can be perceived with different levels of detail. The maturity level has a significant influence on this fact. As suggested by Fig. 4, at level 3 of maturity (as defined in Chew et al. (2008)), organisations are usually capable of defining and handling implementation-related security metrics in any of the dimensions. Efficiency-oriented and business-oriented security metrics demand higher maturity levels, since they demand a broader and integrated knowledge of incident effects in all dimensions. Maturity assumes acquiring more profound education and training in Cybersecurity and a nonfunctional view over the production and supporting information systems. It is important to retain that many of the (really useful) metrics defined require a high maturity level—in a five levels maturity model, as defined in Chew et al. (2008)), meaningful security metrics are captured starting with a maturity level 3. For an illustrative purpose we next describe some possible entries in a security metrics program, in the technical and operational dimensions.

Examples of security objectives, metrics, and related measurements

- Operational
  - Objective 1: Ensure business continuity
  - Metric 1: Average maintenance time allowed <30 min
  - Measure 1: Maintenance time

  - Objective 2: Ensure that all devices/systems are supported by the supplier (bugs fixed)
  - Metric 2: Frequency of verification of device systems updates < 15 days
  - Measure 2: List of approved updates

- Technical
  - Objective 3: Ensure network integrity and healthy
  - Metric 3: The number of TCP ports used equals the number of TCP ports registered
  - Measure 3: Number of open TCP ports

  - Objective 4: Control the data traffic by a period of time
  - Metric 4: Volume of data transferred by device and by a period of time bellow a given limit
  - Measure 4: Volume of data transferred by device

Developing a proper security metrics program can be very hard and frustrating, especially if the team's maturity level is low and there are no clear guides. There are some frameworks developed to help with that task, and, oncerning metrics, the NIST SP 800-55 Chew et al. (2008) is an important asset. All security frameworks referred to so far aid organisations to achieve a higher security maturity level. The capacity to assess the maturity level itself can be used to quantify and qualify the implementation status of a security control in an organisation allowing to certify the relative Cybersecurity posture Wang et al. (2017).

Metrics help in the certification process, as they are conceived to support informed statements towards alleged security states. These states must be defined in a dedicated standard. It turns out that related to the industrial sector there are not many certification processes, and even less concerning Cybersecurity. Based on our previous research Santos et al. (2021); da Silva Oliveira and Santos (2022), we will follow the ISA/IEC 62443 standard to approach a definition of a certification process, which will be described in the next section.

4 Continuous Certification Schema

The most common definition of *certification* points to a formal validation or confirmation that someone is qualified to do some work or that an object or an organisation has a predetermined quality level. This confirmation is usually obtained by an external evaluation, assessment, or audit. Within the scope of this research work focused on the industrial sector, the most suitable certification benchmark is the ISA/IEC 62443 Leander et al. (2019).

4.1 ISA/IEC 62443 Standard

To address the Cybersecurity needs in Industrial Automation and Control Systems (IACS), the International Society of Automation (ISA) and the International

Table 1 Security Levels (SL)

Security Level (SL)	Definition
1	Protection against casual or coincidental violation
2	Protection against intentional violation using simple means with low resources, generic skills, and low motivation
3	Protection against intentional violation using sophisticated means with moderate resources, IACS-special skills, and moderate motivation
4	Protection against intentional violation using sophisticated means with extended resources, IACS-specific skills, and high motivation

Electrotechnical Commission (IEC) joined to create and publish the ISA/IEC 62443 multi-part standard, defining models, techniques and processes to address the Cybersecurity issues in the sector. Despite the initial focus, it has since been applied to other sectors such as building automation, medical, and transportation. Central to ISA/IEC 62443, there is a definition of *security level* as a "*measure of confidence that the system under consideration, security zone, or conduit is free from vulnerabilities and functions in an intended manner*" (ISA 2022, p. 7).

The standard defines three types of Security Level, focused on different phases of security project development, and four general Security Levels (SL) linked to the effective capacity of an organisation to handle security issues which are described in Table 1. The Security Level types are ISA (2022):

Capability Security Levels (SL-C) the security levels that systems or components can achieve when properly integrated and configured.

Target Security Levels (SL-T) the security levels desired by a particular automation solution.

Achieved Security Levels (SL-A) The actual security levels for an automation solution measured after it is approved, commissioned, and running.

The ISA Security Compliance Institute (ISCI) developed also a set of certification programs (ISA Secure®) for different aspects of IACS. In the context of continuous certification, the System Security Assurance (SSA) program emerges as an attractive alternative. SSA is composed of four fundamental elements ISA (2022):

- Security Development Lifecycle Process Assessment (SDLPA-S).
- Security Development Artifacts for Systems (SDA-S).
- Functional Security Assessment for Systems (FSA-S).
- Vulnerability Identification Testing for Systems (VIT-S).

The details of each element are beyond the scope, but it is important to note that the SSA certification requirements include all control systems and all process requirements. The control system requirements are described in IEC 62443-3-3 (Industrial communication networks—Network and system security—Part 3-3: System security requirements and security levels), and process requirements are specified in IEC 62443-4-1 (Security for Industrial Automation and Control Systems—Secure Product Development Requirements) ISASecure (2019).

Table 2 Requirements in the Identification and Authentication Control (IAC)

ID: FSA-S-IAC-	Requirement Name	SL1	SL2	SL3	SL4
1	Human user identification and authentication	X	X	X	X
1.1	Unique identification and authentication		X	X	X
1.2	Multifactor authentication for untrusted networks			X	X
1.3	Multifactor authentication for all networks				X
	...				
6	Wireless access management	X	X	X	X
6.1	Unique identification and authentication		X	X	X
	...				

Concerning our work's focus, the SSA's most relevant elements are FSA-S and VIT-S. FSA-S evaluation is applied to each security zone and the required security capabilities could differ based on the characteristics of the zone and the security level. To obtain a certain level of quality, an organisation needs to have implemented some technical requirements, labelled as Fundamental Requirements (FR), related to ISA (2022); Santos et al. (2021):

- FR1: Identification and Authentication Control (IAC)
- FR2: Use Control (UC)
- FR3: System Integrity (SI)
- FR4: Data Confidentiality (DC)
- FR5: Restricted Data Flow (RDF)
- FR6: Timely Response to Events (TRE)
- FR7: Resource Availability (RA)

For illustrative purposes, Table 2 shows an example of some requirements and how they match each security level under the FSA-S program and concerning the Identification & Authentication Control group of requirements—the first column contains the ID of each specific requirement considered in the example. These examples were chosen randomly and do not have a specific security objective. However, they illustrate the rationale behind the decision to endorse a given SL and the clear link between the requirements within the FSA-S program and the possible metrics. An identical relation is easily highlighted in the VIT-S program, which is why we choose them in the research undertaken here.

Example

Authentication is a security function within the Access Control, which is a fundamental security control implemented to prevent unauthorised access to systems and services ISO/IEC (2016). There are several authentication techniques, all based on three modalities: a secret, a token, and a biometric. By itself, none of these modalities provides a very high level of security. For that purpose, multifactor authentication is currently recommended (or mandatory). The users' identification and authentication is a security requirement, which can be measured mainly through system logs (number of failed logins, data and time of logins, frequency of password updates, origin of logins, among others). By policy, we may state that (1) after three failed

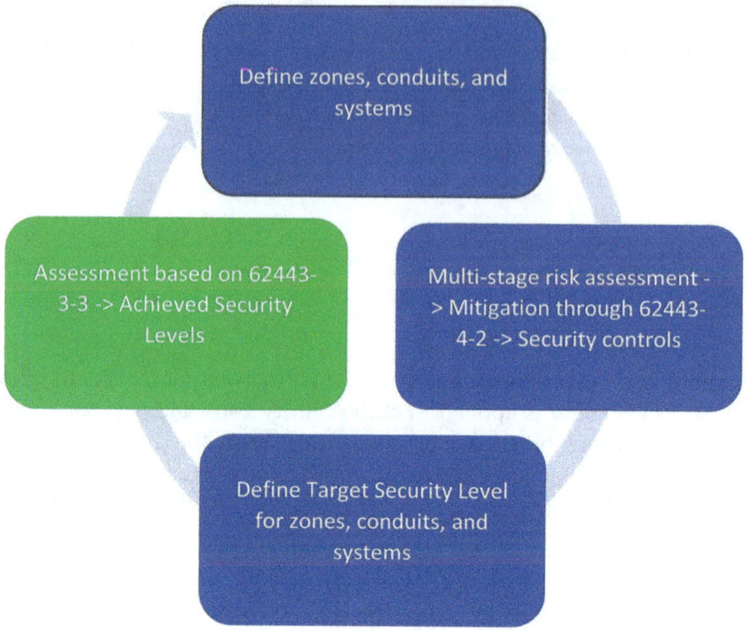

Fig. 5 Proposed model for a partial SSA certification cycle da Silva Oliveira and Santos (2022)

logins, the user will lose access, and (2) users in a given role should never access a particular resource during work times. In the first case, we can get the failed logins measurement and define the limit of three in the access control rule to accomplish the objective. The second example is much more complex. None of the measurements, per se, capture all the information necessary for the rule. We can aggregate the login attempt time and origin, but we still miss the role, which we need to get from other sources (e.g., user profile). These simple examples illustrate possible metrics defined by policies linked to the first security requirements presented in Table 2 and how the same requirement can affect several security levels presented in Table 1.

4.2 Proposed Certification Schema

For certification purposes the ISA/IEC 62443 standard demands an entire cycle through the system development process, possibly including software and hardware development—addressed by SDLPA-S, as referred to in Sect. 4.1. Although it is a complex scenario, in some industrial contexts, a much simpler scenario can be considered because it is possible to apply the proposed model represented in Fig. 5 and focused on FSA-S and VIT-S.

The vision behind the model is to develop a framework of constant analysis and monitoring, in real-time, that continuously assesses Information Systems. The advantage is twofold: it allows continuously improving the security level and provides a continuous certification of the security requirements (and related objectives), including the respective SLs.

The cycle adopts a Plan-Do-Check-Act model following the best practises in Risk management. It begins with the definition of the scopes, which can include a definition of systems (components tightly closed by architectural reasons), security zones (components with identical security requirements), and conduits (a particular case of zones where components have a communication channel). Next, using a multi-stage risk assessment mechanism, a set of security controls and requirements are identified, aiming to mitigate the identified risks. Once the security objectives and requirements are identified, it became possible to define the Target Security Levels, which should be within the Capability Security Levels of the desired security controls. At the same time, there is a selection of assessment metrics taking into account the 62443-3-3 framework.

Once in operation, the assessment module (green box in Fig. 5) continuously gathers the necessary metrics to achieve a pre-determined Security Level, which in the ultimate case, verifies the conformity with the selected components of the certification standard (mostly operational and technical elements). As stated before, this continuous assessment contributes to the unique and special feature that characterises the proposed model.

Considering the demand for new security solutions and approaches in the industrial sector and supply chains, in particular, the proposed model can be seen as an innovation. Once several inter-related organisations adopt this approach, they can empower trust and confidence in their relationship, besides establishing a shared knowledge platform that can help to better respond to Cyberincidents.

5 Metrics and Certification Challenges

Standards and certification help organisations align security practises and create trust relationships more easily. But to get there a long and difficult journey is required. In first place, it is very hard to define security objectives which are highly dependent on the organisational maturity level. Persistent analysis and monitoring of information systems, on a regular basis, contribute to increase security maturity and to improve security solutions. As a result, all stakeholders will be much more aware of the necessary metrics, their relevance, and how to handle them.

The security certification model based on the international standard ISA/IEC 62443 provides important guidance for defining security requirements for compliance purposes. The experience of the authors and the work already carried out to implement the model in the European project FISHY Masip-Bruin et al. (2021)—aimed at increasing resilience in supply chains—has been useful in evaluating the model and implementing a security assessment program in practise using a set of appropriate metrics. However, selecting adequate measurements and metrics is still a very challenging task. Usually, organisations have a myriad of security tools providing measurements mainly based on the performance, according each tool interpretation of the events. In fact, all the tools provide metrics, but the major challenge is on the organisational capacity to adjust those metrics and adding more tools, when necessary. These challenges are reinforced by the ability to balance the cost of a good metrics program and the benefit regarding security. Lastly, the lack of skilled human resources increases the difficulties of the process, and without specific tools to support decision-making it gets even worst.

Example

For the sake of illustration, let us assume that we want to achieve the target security level 4 (see Table 1), regarding the Identification and Authentication Control (IAC) of a specific production line component. For that purpose, we need to ensure requirement 1.3 (see also Table 2), which demands "multifactor authentication for all networks". We go for it and decide to modify all the software systems involved to accommodate it. But we also need to monitor its function and check if there are no breaches. Just assuming the multifactor authentication will work perfectly always is too risky since we know operational and environmental conditions can change—that is why a one-time static certification in this context is not the better solution. We can use logs from all involved components to measure the authentication types (in addition to success and failures). Still, we have no idea how to monitor the metric once there are many event sources (for instance, all network access controllers). After studying the possibilities, we found a new platform that can aggregate all the log information, but it is too expensive and is not worth the risk, since most of the access points are harmless. So, we decided to reduce the target security level to 3, which requires "multifactor authentication only for untrusted networks". Now, we only need to monitor one access controller, which is (more or less) a trivial operation. We know what metrics to use in this simple example, but we do not have enough expertise to measure them. As a consequence, we lower the expected security level. But we could also redefine the scope and exclude those harmless network segments. Anyway, we are now in a position to carry out continuous certification.

Fostering and continuously conducting the analysis and monitoring the organisational' systems and services' performance will certainly improve security levels and increase maturity, enabling a better response to security incidents, and thus achieve their security requirements and becoming closer to business goals. Furthermore, within the scope of a certification process, in addition to the documentary and procedural elements (of static nature and with longer temporal validity), the continuous monitoring of the controls most exposed to variations for technical or contextual reasons will represent an added value in the observability of these dimensions of certification. This capability will obviously increase the trust gained from a certification process in inter-organisational relationships. Suppose the dimensions in question involve a requirement of obtaining digital proof in the execution of transactions—not usual, but not unthinkable, too. In that case, we will have a valuable complement to resolve doubts in these relationships in a much more agile way.

6 Conclusions and Future Work

The world we live in is increasingly dependent on ICT in all sectors of activity. In particular, within the industry, ICT-based production and distribution chains have become a critical resource for the smooth functioning of all business processes. As a result, Cybersecurity has become a fundamental part of the management strategy of all organisations, which need to assimilate agile and adequate models for managing their Information Systems Security. However, to fully explore the potential of the interaction level, trust plays a critical role in allowing parties to recognise the extent to which all effectively implement Cybersecurity. Standards and certification are among the most effective responses to ensure an adequate level of trust.

This paper demonstrates that metrics and measurements play a crucial role in both cases. In Cybersecurity, metrics are the only way to measure the efficiency of security controls. Without a good metrics program, it is impossible to manage security properties. In certification, because of its dynamic component, namely the monitoring of security controls linked to the most sensitive to rapid changes dimensions, which demands a continuous assessment of the objectives achieved, requiring appropriate metrics. Otherwise, a static certification that is 'valid' over a long time can be meaningless due to frequent and unexpected context changes. The continuous certification model presented in this document seeks to respond to this challenge. Furthermore, metrics, by definition, are still a valuable source of information in the creation of digital evidence in cases of malicious exploitation of interconnections or vulnerabilities. However, identifying appropriate metrics proves to be an extremely challenging task. To begin with, metrics must be linked to well-defined security objectives, which depend a lot on the organisation's maturity level. Maturity requires a gradual transformation and it is not easy to change without a well-defined strategy from top management. But even defining the metrics well, getting them, and subjecting them to the necessary analysis demand expertise that organisations still do not have in abundance. The paper identifies some standards (in particular SP 800-55 and ISA/IEC 62443) that have proved to be beneficial throughout the experience of their application in a European project (FISHY).

In future work and to address the identified challenges, we will advance the construction of a metrics taxonomy based on the international standards ISA/IEC 62443 and SP 800-55, enabling us to create a solid foundation in the metrics definition and the certification goals. For practical reasons, we will highlight experimental research accompanying the development of the FISHY project. Within this context, we envisage significant improvements to information security metrics, information security management maturity, and the certification process, exploring the continuous dimension. Furthermore, and for efficiency reasons, a platform will be developed to support the technological live-cycle of the certification process, as described.

Acknowledgements This project has received funding from the European Union's Horizon 2020 research and innovation programme under grant agreement No 952644. Additionally, this work has been supported by FCT – Fundação para a Ciência e Tecnologia within the R&D Units Project Scope: UIDB/00319/2020.

References

Ahmed Y, Naqvi S, Josephs M (2019) Cybersecurity metrics for enhanced protection of healthcare it systems. In: 2019 13th International Symposium on Medical Information and Communication Technology (ISMICT), Oslo, Norway, IEEE, pp 1–9

Aldya AP, Sutikno S, Rosmansyah Y (2019) Measuring effectiveness of control of information security management system based on sni iso/iec 27004: 2013 standard. IOP Conference Series

Amran AR, Phan RCW, Parish DJ (2009) Metrics for network forensics conviction evidence. In: 2009 International Conference for Internet Technology and Secured Transactions, (ICITST), London, UK, IEEE, pp 1–8. Materials Science and Engineering 550:012020, https://doi.org/10.1088/1757-899X/550/1/012020.

Anu V (2021) Information security governance metrics: a survey and taxonomy. Inform Secur J Glob Persp:1–13. https://doi.org/10.1080/19393555.2021.1922786

Barabanov R, Kowalski S, Yngström L, Yngstrom L (2011) Information security metrics state of the art. Tech. Rep., Stockholm University, DSV Report series No 11-007, https://www.diva-portal.org/smash/record.jsf?pid=diva2:469570, cit. 2 Scholar 4/2021

Bodnar GH, Hopwood WS (2001) Accounting information systems, vol 8. Prentice Hall, London

Casola V, De Benedictis A, Rak M, Villano U (2018) A security metric catalogue for cloud applications. In: Complex, Intelligent, and Software Intensive Systems: Proceedings of the 11th International Conference on Complex, Intelligent, and Software Intensive Systems (CISIS- 2017), Springer, pp 854–863

Chew E, Swanson M, Stine K, Bartol N, Brown A, Robinson W (2008) Nist sp 800-55 revision 1 - performance measurement guide for information security. Tech. rep., NIST National Institute of Standards and Technology, https://csrc.nist.rip/CSRC/media/Events/ISPAB-SEPTEMBER-2007-MEETING/documents/Barker_ISPAB_Sept2007-SP800-55R1.pdf

da Silva Oliveira A, Santos H (2022) Continuous industrial sector cybersecurity assessment paradigm: Proposed model of cybersecurity certification. In: 2022 18th International Conference on the Design of Reliable Communication Networks (DRCN), Vilanova i la Geltrú, Spain, IEEE, pp 1–6, https://doi.org/10.1109/DRCN53993.2022.9758022

EDUCAUSE (2017) Effective security metrics. https://www.educause.edu/focus-areas-and-initiatives/policy-and-security/cybersecurity-program/resources/information-security-guide/toolkits/effective-security-metrics. Accessed 22 Apr 2022

Fielding J (2020) The people problem: how cyber security's weakest link can become a formidable asset. Comput Fraud Secur 2020(1):6–9. https://doi.org/10.1016/S1361-3723

Hou J, Li Y, Yu J, Shi W (2020) A survey on digital forensics in internet of things. IEEE Internet Things J 7:1–15. https://doi.org/10.1109/JIOT.2019.2940713

Houngbo PJ, Hounsou JT, Houngbo PJ, Hounsou JT (2015) Measuring information security: understanding and selecting appropriate metrics. Int J Comput Sci Secur (IJCSS) 9(108–120):q4

ISA (2022) Quick start guide: An overview of isasecure certification. https://www.isasecure.org/en-US/Documents/0920-ISASecure-QuickStart-Guide-FINAL. Accessed 15 Mar 2022

ISASecure (2019) System security assurance (ssa) certification. https://isasecure.org/certification/iec-62443-ssa-certification. Accessed 10 Mar 2022

ISO/IEC (2013) Iso/iec 27001:2013, information technology – security techniques – information security management systems – requirements. Tech. rep., ISO/IEC, https://www.iso.org/standard/54534.html https://www.iso.org/obp/ui/#iso:std:iso-iec:27001:ed-2:v1:en

ISO/IEC (2016) Information technology-security techniques–information security management systems–overview and vocabulary (international standard iso/iec 27000). Tech. rep., ISO/IEC, URL www.iso.org

ISO/IEC (2018) Iso 31000:2018 risk management – guidelines. https://www.iso.org/obp/ui/#iso:std:iso:31000:ed-2:v1:en. Accessed 20 Apr 2022

Kalman L (2019) New european data privacy and cyber security laws. Commun ACM 62:38–38. https://doi.org/10.1145/3310326

Leander B, Čaušević A, Hansson H (2019) Applicability of the iec 62443 standard in industry 4.0 / iiot. In: Proceedings of the 14th International Conference on Availability, Reliability and Security (ARES'19). ACM, Canterbury CA, UK, pp 1–8. https://doi.org/10.1145/3339252.3341481

Leszczyna R (2018) Standards on cyber security assessment of smart grid. Int J Crit Infrastruct Protect 22:70–89. https://doi.org/10.1016/j.ijcip.2018.05.006

Lu Y (2017) Industry 4.0: a survey on technologies, applications and open research issues. J Ind Inf Integr 6:1–10. https://doi.org/10.1016/j.jii.2017.04.005. 1468 cit (5/2022)

Masip-Bruin X, Marín-Tordera E, Ruiz J, Jukan A, Trakadas P, Cernivec A, Lioy A, López D, Santos H, Gonos A, Silva A, Soriano J, Kalogiannis G (2021) Cybersecurity in ict supply chains: key challenges and a relevant architecture. Sensors 21:6057. https://doi.org/10.3390/s21186057

Morrison P, Moye D, Pandita R, Williams L (2018) Mapping the field of software life cycle security metrics. Inf Softw Technol 102:146–159. https://doi.org/10.1016/j.infsof.2018.05.011

NA (2020) Nist sp 800-53 rev. 5 security and privacy controls for information systems and organizations. https://csrc.nist.gov/publications/detail/sp/800-53/rev-5/final, accessed 20 April 2022 (nd) CC (2018) Cis – center for internet security. https://www.cisecurity.org/controls. Accessed 20 Apr 2022

Olsen D (2022) Three-quarters of security pros believe current cybersecurity strategies will shortly be obsolete. https://www.infosecurity-magazine.com/news/security-pros-cybersecurity/. Accessed 26 May 2022

Payne SC (2006) A guide to security metrics. Tech. rep., SANS Institute, https://www.sans.org/reading-room/whitepapers/auditing/guide-security-metrics-55

Pendleton M, Garcia-Lebron R, Cho JH, Xu S (2016) A survey on systems security metrics. ACM Comput Surv 49:1–35. https://doi.org/10.1145/3005714

Pereira T (2012) A conceptual framework to support information security risk management. PhD thesis, University of Minho, Portugal., https://hdl.handle.net/1822/20869

Roy PP (2020) A high-level comparison between the nist cyber security framework and the iso 27001 information security standard. In: 2020 National Conference on Emerging Trends on Sustainable Technology and Engineering Applications (NCETSTEA), Durgapur, India, IEEE, pp 1–3, https://doi.org/10.1109/NCETSTEA48365.2020.9119914

Santos H (2022) Cybersecurity: a practical engineering approach. CRC Press

Santos H, Oliveira A, Soares L, Satis A, Santos A (2021) Information security assessment and certification within supply chains. In: The 16th International Conference on Availability, Reliability and Security (ARES 21), Vienna, Austria, August 17–20, 2021, ACM, pp 1–6. https://doi.org/10.1145/3465481.3470078

Savola RM (2013) Quality of security metrics and measurements. Comput Secur 37:78–90. https://doi.org/10.1016/j.cose.2013.05.002

Scarfone KA, Souppaya MP, Cody A, Orebaugh AD (2008) Technical guide to information security testing and assessment. Tech. rep., National Institute of Standards and Technology, https://doi.org/10.6028/NIST.SP.800-115., https://nvlpubs.nist.gov/nistpubs/Legacy/SP/nistspecialpublication800-115.pdf

Setzler T, Mountrouidou X (2021) Iot metrics and automation for security evaluation. In: 2021 IEEE 18th Annual Consumer Communications & Networking Conference (CCNC), IEEE, pp 1–4, https://doi.org/10.1109/CCNC49032.2021.9369533

Wang L, Jajodia S, Singhal A (2017) Network security metrics. Springer International Publishing. https://doi.org/10.1007/978-3-319-66505-4

Yusuf SE, Hong JB, Ge M, Kim DS (2017) Composite metrics for network security analysis. Softw Netw 2017:137–160. https://doi.org/10.13052/jsn2445-9739.2017.007

Zaber M, Nair S (2020) A framework for automated evaluation of security metrics. In: Proceedings of the 15th International Conference on Availability, Reliability and Security, ACM, vol 2020, pp 1–11, https://doi.org/10.1145/3407023.3409197

Henrique Santos received his first degree in Electric and Electronic Engineering, from the University of Coimbra, Portugal, in 1984. In 1996 he received the Ph.D. degree in Computer Engineering, from the University of the Minho, Portugal and the habilitation degree in 2013, by the same institution. Currently, he is an Associate Professor at the Information Systems Department, University of Minho, being responsible for several graduate and postgraduate courses. The research work has been framed within ALGORITMI Research Centre, at the same university, where he is responsible by the supervision of several postgraduate students and the coordination of several R&D projects, mainly in the Information Security area—emphasis on Intrusion Detection, biometrical technologies and Information Security Management—and Computer Architecture area—emphasis on Computer Vision and Cloud Computing. He authored and co-authored several scientific publications in journals, conferences and books within his field of interests and co-authored a patent with an industrial partner, in 2012, in the biometric area. He is also the President of a national Technical Committee (CT 136) for information system security standardization, Vice President for Conferences and Workshops of IEEE Education Society, between 2017 and 2021, President of the Portuguese Association for Data Protection (APPD) and integrates frequently advice and scientific committees supporting civil, governmental and military organizations, concerning Information Security subjects. During the second semester of 1990, under an ERASMUS program, he was teaching at the University of Bristol, United Kingdom, where he was recognized as University Academic staff.

Teresa Pereira holds a Ph.D (2012). in the area of Technologies and Information Systems at the University of Minho, Portugal. She has been a research member at ALGORITMI Research Centre, University of Minho. The main area of research is in Information Security Management, Cybersecurity and Digital Skills in the area of digital literacy, and microcredentials. Between 2017 and 2020, she was part of the Task Group Force of the Association for Computing Machinery (ACM) and the IEEE Computer Society (IEEE-CS), in the development of the report with the recommendations of curriculum competences in the area of computing (Computing Curricula 2020). Since 2016, I have been a member of the Technical Committee for Standardization CT 163—Information Systems Security.

Since 1.Feb.2022 Teresa Pereira has been full Professor at Department of Information Systems at Engineering School of Minho University. In addition, from Set.2004 to Jan.2022, was a lecturer on the Business Sciences School of Polytechnic Institute of Viana do Castelo (IPVC), Portugal; since 2012 to 31th January 2022 was an adjunct professor and from 31 of July of 2019 was deputy to director of the Business Sciences School of IPVC; was member of the Pedagogic Council of the Business Sciences school of IPVC; and Erasmus+ and Socrates/Erasmus coordinator.

André Oliveira holds an M.Sc. in the area of Technologies and Information Systems at the University of Minho, Portugal. After some professional experiences in the industry Portuguese sector, he's been a research member at ALGORITMI Research Centre and a member of the European Project FISHY which aims to develop a framework to increase cybersecurity resilience in the supply chains. Since September 2020, he is attending the Doctoral Program in Technologies and Information Systems and pursuing his Ph.D. in the field of cybersecurity certification and standardization in the industrial sector. In addition, he had some experience on national research projects focused on information systems management and security in the Portuguese health sector.

Cyberterrorism and the Portuguese Counter-Terrorism Act

Pedro Miguel Fernandes Freitas

Abstract Starting with an analysis of the international doctrine on the conceptualization of cyberterrorism, the aim of this article is to assess whether Law no. 52/2003 also foresees and punishes this form of terrorism. The countless meanings of cyberterrorism may be reconducted to cyberterrorism in a strict sense or cyberterrorism in a broad sense. The Portuguese law, although not taking a clear position on this distinction, foresees and punishes both modalities.

1 Introduction

The phenomenon of terrorism is complex, multifaceted and permeable to time and space. Part of the explanation for the absence of an agreed definition of terrorism lies in its historical background—from the *régime de la terreur* to contemporary terrorism. In the context of a signifiable longevity, terrorism has appeared with different characteristics, as it is sensitive to the specific socio-political, legal and cultural conditions of a certain period and place. These dissonances have generated doubts and uncertainties, still present today, about its exact contours.

It should also be added that the existence and features of terrorism depend to a large extent on its observer, as the "very word [terrorism] becomes a litmus test for dearly held beliefs, so that a brief conversation on terrorist matter with almost anyone reveals a special world view, an interpretation of the nature of man, and a glimpse into a desired future".[1] Idea that is crystal clear in the consecrated expression: "one man's terrorist is another man's freedom fighter".[2]

[1] Bell (1978).

[2] Laqueur (1987).

P. M. Fernandes Freitas (✉)
Faculty of Law Oporto, Catholic University of Portugal, Porto, Portugal
e-mail: pfreitas@ucp.pt

F. A. Carneiro Pacheco de Andrade et al. (eds.), *Legal Developments on Cybersecurity and Related Fields*, Law, Governance and Technology Series 60,
https://doi.org/10.1007/978-3-031-41820-4_7

2 The Features of Cyber-Terrorism

A consensus about the definition of terrorism brings with it an alignment, however minimal, in domains that are inherently polarising such as religion, ideology or politics. It is therefore not at all surprising that, faced with this conceptual difficulty,[3] coined by Brian Jenkins as a "Bermuda triangle" where "[e]ntire conferences sank in it without a trace",[4] we witness a certain fatalism and resignation on the part of scholars.[5]

One of their most audible voices is Walter Laqueur. In his words, "[n]o all-embracing definition will ever be found for the simple reason that there is not one terrorism, but there have been many terrorisms, greatly differing in time and space, in motivation, and in manifestations and aims".[6]

In summary, six arguments explain this conceptual difficulty of terrorism: complexity of the phenomenon; confusion about the relationship between terror and terrorism; diversity of targets; diversity of audiences for whom terrorist acts are carried out; confusion between terrorism and other forms of political violence; and the multiplication of types of terrorism.[7]

To some extent, the recognition of the difficulty (or even impossibility) of defining terrorism appears counterintuitive. "Most people", tell us Gus Martin, "likely hold an instinctive understanding that terrorism is politically motivated violence, usually directed against soft targets (i.e., civilian and administrative government targets), and with an intention to affect (terrorize) a target audience".[8] In other words, it seemingly isn't particularly difficult for the average citizen to say what constitutes terrorism. However, this apparent ease comes up against the reality of its operationalisation, or rather, the task of defining it. One of the most relevant studies in the field is the one carried out by Alex Schmid and Albert Jongman where 109 definitions of terrorism were gathered and 22 definitional elements were identified that were repeated in these definitions, e.g. violence (in 83.5% of the definitions), political (65%), terror/fear (51%), threat (47%), among others.[9] Years later, the same Alex Schmid (2011) presents a new list of definitions, which this time exceeds 250.

The lack of an agreed definition of terrorism entails negative consequences. Ben Saul (2021) essentially points to two: a decline in the efficiency of the investigation and prosecution of terrorism; inconsistency with international humanitarian law and international human rights law. With the first of the references, what the Author intends to underline is that a consensual definition of terrorism contributes,

[3]Marsili (2018).

[4]Brian Jenkins (2004).

[5]Schmid (2004).

[6]Laqueur (2007).

[7]Alex Schmid (2020).

[8]Gus Martin (2016).

[9]Schmid and Jongman (2005).

upstream, to a normative-substantive harmonization between the different national legal systems and, downstream, it allows the use of international judicial cooperation mechanisms in criminal matters. The absence of such a consensus, *a contrario*, "impairs inter-state cooperation to «bring to justice» terrorists" (Ben Saul 2021), which may lead to situations of impunity. It also calls into question strict compliance with international human rights law and international humanitarian law. Both because the principle of criminal legality is called into question at state level when the national legislator chooses a definition that is not sufficiently precise or clear, and, on other occasions, the incrimination of terrorism is so broad that results in discrimination or limitation of political freedoms. In the field of international humanitarian law, consequences arise from the uncertain delimitation of the boundary between terrorism and hostilities carried out by non-State armed groups.

Equally interesting is the contribution of James Dorsey regarding the 2017 Gulf crisis.[10] The Author emphasizes what, in his view, constitutes a fundamental point in international relations: "the absence of an agreed definition of terrorism that allows autocrats to abuse efforts to counter extremism by repressing non-violent critics and the ability of small states to chart their own course and punch above their weight". This absence has allowed authoritarian leaders to "suppress basic human rights, including freedoms of expression and the media, and to put tens of thousands of non-violent critics behind bars".[11]

Another author, Boaz Ganor, sees the definition of terrorism as a counterterrorist weapon. By this he means that "[w]ithout a definition of terrorism, it is impossible to formulate or enforce international agreements against terrorism", and "no responsibility can be imposed on countries supporting terrorism, nor can steps be taken to combat terrorist organizations and their allies".[12]

The same difficulty is found in the task of delimiting and clarifying the concept of cyberterrorism. "If you ask 10 people what 'cyberterrorism' is, you will get at least nine different answers!" (Gordon and Ford 2002).

In a seminal study led by Lee Jarvis and Stuart Macdonald, 118 academic researchers were asked about the "areas of consensus, disagreement, and ambiguity on core definitional questions around the term cyberterrorism".[13] The Authors concluded that, although most of the academic researchers agreed on the usefulness of a specific definition of cyberterrorism for policymakers and researchers, it was not possible to establish one. Only an approximation to such a definition. A number of elements of cyberterrorism were identified by most respondents: political or ideological motives, digital means or targets, and the production of fear. But without any agreement on an exact formulation of what cyberterrorism is.

In this domain, it is relevant to invoke the proposals of three authors: Dorothy Denning, Mark Pollitt and Barry Collin.

---

[10] James Dorsey (2017).

[11] James Dorsey (2017).

[12] Boaz Ganor (2002).

[13] Jarvis and Macdonald (2014).

According to Dorothy Denning:

> Cyberterrorism is the convergence of terrorism and cyberspace. It is generally understood to mean unlawful attacks and threats of attack against computers, networks, and the information stored therein when done to intimidate or coerce a government or its people in furtherance of political or social objectives. Further, to qualify as cyberterrorism, an attack should result in violence against persons or property, or at least cause enough harm to generate fear. Attacks that lead to death or bodily injury, explosions, plane crashes, water contamination, or severe economic loss would be examples. Serious attacks against critical infrastructures could be acts of cyberterrorism, depending on their impact. Attacks that disrupt nonessential services or that are mainly a costly nuisance would not.[14]

More recently, in 2007, the same Author revisits the concept of cyberterrorism as follows:

> Cyberterrorism is generally understood to refer to highly damaging computer-based attacks or threats of attack by non-state actors against information systems when conducted to intimidate or coerce governments or societies in pursuit of goals that are political or social. It is the convergence of terrorism with cyberspace, where cyberspace becomes the means of conducting the terrorist act. Rather than committing acts of violence against persons or physical property, the cyberterrorist commits acts of destruction and disruption against digital property (...).
>
> To fall in the domain of cyberterror, a cyber attack should be sufficiently destructive or disruptive to generate fear comparable to that from physical acts of terrorism, and it must be conducted for political and social reasons. Critical infrastructures, which include telecommunications, electrical power, oil and gas, water supply, transportation, banking and finance, emergency services, and essential government services, are likely targets. Attacks against these infrastructures that lead to death or bodily injury, extended power outages, plane crashes, water contamination, or billion dollar banking losses would be examples.[15]

In turn, Mark Pollitt defines cybterrorism as "the premeditated, politically motivated attack against information, computer systems, computer programs, and data which result in violence against noncombatant targets by sub-national groups or clandestine agents".[16] At the antipodes of the complexity of these definitions lies another one by Barry Collin (author of the word cyberterrorism): "the convergence of cybernetics and terrorism".[17]

In an attempt to systematise the countless meanings of cyberterrorism, we can narrow them down to one of two: cyberterrorism in the strict sense or cyberterrorism in the broad sense.[18]

Generally, the first class of cyberterrorism includes definitions according to which cyberterrorism corresponds to politically motivated attacks against information systems resulting in injuries to civilian targets. The abovementioned definition given by Mark Pollitt is a paradigmatic example of cyberterrorism in the strict

[14] Dorothy Denning (2000).

[15] Denning (2007).

[16] Mark Pollitt (1998).

[17] Plotnek and Slay (2021).

[18] Jarvis and Macdonald (2014); Brunst (2010); O'Brien (2021).

sense.[19] Exactly the same kind of cyber-terrorism exists even when, although under a not totally coincident nomenclature, we slightly widen its scope of meaning. Anna-Maria Talihärm, for example, refers to target-oriented cyberterrorism, as opposed to tool-oriented cyberterrorism, as "all politically or socially motivated attacks against computers, networks and information, whether conducted through other computers or physically, when causing bloodshed or serious damage, or fear".[20]

Cyberterrorism in a broad sense concerns the use of technological means by terrorists or terrorist organisations or, more specifically, the "use of the Internet for terrorist purposes".[21] This includes activities as diverse as fundraising for use in committing terrorist acts, recruitment, propaganda, communication, among others.[22]

The option for one or another meaning of terrorism brings with it profound differences in regard to the recognition of the current terrorist threat, the choice of prevention strategies and, naturally, the repression of the phenomenon.

Those who tend to advocate a narrower view of cyberterrorism will say that to date no acts of cyberterrorism have been recorded.[23] As an example, Maura Conway contests the reality of cyberterrorism—"cyberterrorism has never taken place"[24]–, because for an act to be coined cyberterrorist it must be proven the presence of political motives and the use of violence, or at least the threat of it. For the Author, four reasons stand out to explain why cyberterrorism does not exist: cost, complexity, destruction and media impact. In her opinion, the task of planning and executing cyber-terrorist acts is very expensive (cost) (in disagreement, Weimann[25]) and demands in-depth technical knowledge that members of terrorist organisations do not possess (complexity); the potential for producing damage by cyberterrorist acts is lower than traditional ones (destruction) and they are not as appealing to the media, since they do not have the same "theatricality" as conventional terrorist acts (media impact).

On the contrary, if a more expansive view of cyberterrorism is taken, there will be no doubt about its reality, although the borderline with mere cybercrime will be blurred, thus leading to terminological and conceptual confusion. This is the reason why Maura Conway rejects such an elasticity of the concept of cyberterrorism.[26] In her view, for a cyber-attack to acquire the epithet of terrorist, it must have an underlying political motivation and, at the same time, cause fear/terror as a consequence of deaths and/or large-scale destruction. She concludes that "[a]s regards the distinction between terrorist use of information technology and terrorism involving computer technology as a weapon/target, only the latter may be defined as

[19] Mark Pollitt (1998).

[20] Anna-Maria Talihärm (2020).

[21] Brunst (2010).

[22] Jarvis and Macdonald (2014).

[23] Clough (2010); Sieber (2022).

[24] Maura Conway (2014).

[25] Weimann (2005).

[26] Conway (2002).

cyberterrorism. Terrorist 'use' of computers as a facilitator of their activities, whether for propaganda, communication, or other purposes, is simply that: 'use'".[27]

James Holt agrees that, with reference to the narrowest definitions of cyberterrorism, particularly those that integrate elements such as the production of fear or physical damage, it cannot be said that we have seen cyberterrorist acts to date.[28] But he also adds that "while there is no single agreed upon definition for cyberterror, it is clear that this term must encapsulate a greater range of behavior than physical terror due to the dichotomous nature of cyberspace as a vehicle for communications as well as a medium for attacks. More expansive definitions, such as those provided by Britz[[29]] and Foltz[[30]], provide a much more comprehensive framework for exploring the ways that extremist groups utilize technology in support of their various agendas".[31]

Assuming a more comprehensive definition of cyberterrorism then the conclusion can only be one: "cyberterrorism is real and does pose a threat".[32] A phenomenon that can be embodied in the most diverse forms, such as the interference or disruption of the normal functioning of critical infrastructures, the unauthorised access, interception or modification of computer data, disinformation, among others.[33]

3 Why Cyberspace?

Cyberspace as an expression was popularised in the 1980s by William Gibson. In his novel "Neuromancer", he described cyberspace as a "hallucination experienced daily by billions of legitimate operators, in every nation, by children being taught mathematical concepts... A graphic representation of data abstracted from the banks of every computer in the human system. Unthinkable complexity. Lines of light

[27] Maura Conway (2002).

[28] James Holt (2012).

[29] "[Cyberterrorism is] the premeditated, methodological, and ideologically motivated dissemination of information, facilitation of communication, or attack against digital information, computer systems, and/or computer programs which requires advance planning and is intended to result in social, financial, physical or psychological harm to non-combatant targets and audiences; or any dissemination of information which is designed to facilitate such actions" (Britz 2009).

[30] "[A]n attack or threat of an attack (...), politically motivated (...), intended to interfere with the political, social (...), or economic (...) functioning of a group, organization, or country; or induce either physical violence (...) or the unjust use of power; or in conjunction with a more traditional terrorist action (...)." (Bryan Foltz 2004).

[31] James Holt (2012).

[32] Bryan Foltz (2004).

[33] Bryan Foltz (2004) argues, however, that the use of the internet as a means of planning or preparing terrorist acts (e.g. buying airline tickets or locating targets) cannot be regarded as cyberterrorist act.

ranged in the nonspace of the mind, clusters and constellations of data. Like city lights, receding…".[34]

Using a more recent definition of cyberspace, one could say that it is "the complex environment resulting from the interaction of people, software and services on the Internet by means of technology devices and networks connected to it, which does not exist in any physical form" (ISO/IEC 27032:2012).

Some factors explain the special suitability of cyberspace for the commission of criminal conducts. These are the scale, accessibility, anonymity, portability and transferability, global reach and absence of capable gatekeepers.[35] In cyberspace there is a confluence of billions of users and devices, distributed on a global scale, which expands criminal opportunities and raises them to an unprecedented level if we take as a reference the analogue context (scale). This has become possible with the democratisation of access to new technologies (accessibility). The simplification of the use of computing devices (e.g. computers, smartphones and tablets), the decrease in production, distribution and access costs, as well as the progressive increase in digital literacy, have significantly contributed to this. The spatial-temporal distance between the perpetrator and the victim and the use of technology to hide the perpetrator's identity are unavoidable aspects of this digital reality. It is relatively easy to find tools such as temporary mailboxes, proxies, virtual private networks, encrypted messaging applications or cryptocurrencies which, to a greater or lesser extent, guarantee privacy and anonymity to their users (anonymity).[36] Portability and transferability refer, in turn, to the miniaturisation of computing devices and the overwhelming evolution of their capacity to process, transmit and store computer data. Undoubtedly, the planning and execution of criminal conducts becomes simpler with the advent of truly mobile information systems, such as smartphones (portability and transferability). The exploitation of cyberspace with a criminal purpose takes advantage of its geographic fluidity. We observe a deconstruction of the traditional understanding of the notions of space and time. From a technological-communicational point of view, it is practically indifferent where the agent and the victim are.[37] An Internet connection (global reach) is enough. This translates into an enormous practical difficulty in carrying out effective criminal investigations and in the articulation between judicial and police authorities of the various countries involved, whose legal systems are governed by classic paradigms of territoriality and national sovereignty regarding the exercise of criminal action. Jonathan Clough is extremely clear when stating that "it is neither practical nor desirable that police be everywhere. The role of 'guardian' must be shared with others across the community, whether it be parents monitoring their children's use of the Internet, financial institutions looking for suspicious transactions or system administrators detecting network intrusions. All play an important guardianship

---

[34] Gibson (1984).

[35] Clough (2010). The author is followed closely in the explanation of these factors.

[36] Weimann (2005).

[37] Weimann (2005).

role, as do industry groups and government regulators. ISPs are particularly significant, being effectively the gatekeepers of data on the Internet".[38]

4 Cyber-Terrorism in the Context of the Counter-Terrorism Act

In compliance with the Council Framework Decision of 13 June 2002 on the fight against terrorism, Portugal approved Law No. 52/2003. Despite the successive amendments it has undergone—the most recent being the one resulting from Law No. 2/2023-, its object has remained the same since its beginning: the prevention and punishment of terrorist acts and organizations.

More precisely, the Portuguese legislator foresees the incrimination of terrorist organisations (articles 2 and 3), terrorist acts in a proper sense (article 4(1)(2)), public incitement to the commission of terrorist acts (article 4 (3)(4)), recruitment for terrorism (Article 4(6)), training for terrorism (Article 4(7)), public condoning of terrorist acts (Article 4(8)(9)), travelling for the purpose of training for the commission of terrorist acts (Article 4(10)), travelling to commit terrorist acts or to join terrorist organisations (Article 4(11)), travelling to Portugal to join terrorist organisations or for the purpose of training or to commit terrorist acts (Article 4-(12)) assistance for travelling to commit terrorist acts or to join terrorist organisations or for the purpose of training (Article 4(13)), and financing of terrorism (Article 5-A).

On a closer reading of Articles 2 and 3, it is immediately apparent that there is no reference to religious, political or ideological motivations.[39] Combining the abovementioned norms, the following definition of terrorism can be drawn: the commission of an act against the life, physical integrity or liberty of persons; or mass destruction of government or public buildings, transport systems, infrastructures, fixed platforms located on a continental platform, public places or private properties, susceptible to endanger human lives or provoke considerable economic loss; or capture of aircrafts, ships or other means of collective transport or merchandise; or manufacture, possession, acquisition, transport, supply or use of explosives, weapons or ammunitions; or the release of dangerous substances or the provocation of fires, floods or explosions that endanger human lives; or disturbance or interruption of electricity supply, water supply or any other fundamental natural resource; or illegal interference of information systems that can result in interference to a significant number of information systems, serious damage or hinderance of critical infrastructures; that may seriously affect the Portuguese State, a foreign State or an

[38] Clough (2010).

[39] Ganor (2001).

international organization; and are carried out with the aim of seriously intimidating certain people, groups of people or the population in general, unduly compel public authorities or an international organization to carry out or refrain from carrying out an act or from seriously disrupting or destroying the fundamental political, constitutional, economic or social structures of the Portuguese State, a foreign State or an international organization.

Rigorously speaking, the Portuguese legislator is following the European Union's lead.[40] Recital 3 of the Council Framework Decision of 13 June 2002 on combating terrorism reads: "[a]ll or some Member States are party to a number of conventions relating to terrorism. The Council of Europe Convention of 27 January 1977 on the Suppression of Terrorism does not regard terrorist offences as political offences or as offences connected with political offences or as offences inspired by political motives". And further on, in Article 1, when defining the offence of terrorism, there is no mention whatsoever to political, ideological or religious motivations. Under the terms of the first paragraph of this article, the aim of committing the acts referred to therein must fall within one of the following three categories in order to constitute an act of terrorism: serious intimidation of a population; undue coercion of public authorities or an international organisation to perform or abstain from performing an act; serious destabilisation or destruction of the fundamental political, constitutional, economic or social structures of a country or an international organisation.[41]

Therefore, it cannot be said that Article 1 of the Framework Decision and Articles 2 and 3 of Law 52/2003 require, for the incrimination of an act as terrorist, the presence of the subjective elements usually pointed out to the agents of terrorist acts. As Thomas Weigend reminds us:

> [T]errorists typically pursue a triple goal: they have 'normal' intent to commit the base crime of murder, bombing, assault, etc.; they intend, further, to intimidate a group or the population as a whole and/or to compel others to take action (e.g. to release political prisoners); and they have ulterior political or ideological motives, e.g. to destabilize the present government or to defeat a rival religion or ideology. Legal instruments differ as to the extent to which they require all or only some of these ideal-typical subjective elements for a terrorism conviction.[42]

[40] Within the scope of the Council of Europe, the 1977 European Convention on the Suppression of Terrorism is relevant. Article 1 of the Convention enshrines the rule that, for the purposes of extradition, the crimes referred to therein shall not be considered a political offence or an offence connected with a political offence or an offence inspired by political motives. The reason for this choice is simple: categorizing a terrorist act as a political or politically motivated crime would make it impossible to extradite its perpetrator (Council of Europe, 1977). See also article 3 of the European Convention on Extradition.

[41] The same definition is found in the Directive (EU) 2017/541 of the European Parliament and of the Council of 15 March 2017 on combating terrorism and replacing Council Framework Decision 2002/475/JHA and amending Council Decision 2005/671/JHA.

[42] Weigend (2006).

It may be argued that the rejection as a normative element of any political (or other) motivation follows the reasoning that it would constitute a factor of greater complexity and/or confusion. Kalliopi K. Koufa, United Nations Special Rapporteur on terrorism and human rights, in a report prepared in the context of the United Nations (E/CN.4/Sub.2/2003/WP.1), expresses this reasoning:

> [I]n any event, while broad or general categorizations can hardly reach precision and do full justice to the variety and complexity of the terrorist phenomena, attemp ts to devise analytical and more sophisticated subdivisions and distinctions providing more precise delimitations of, or information on, subgroups of terrorism - such as their organizational structure, size, potential relationships with States and degrees of such relationships, their identity, characteristics, social, political, cultural and psychological motivations, and so forth - are too complicated and diverse and, above all, they only serve the needs of the particular user. As useful as they are for illuminating particular aspects of the phenomena of terrorism and of terrorists, and for contributing to our understanding of the wide-ranging nature of the *problematique* surrounding them, they are of little utility in identifying exactly what constitutes terrorism and who the terrorists are.[43]

There are also those who argue that, in addition to this layer of complexity that would seriously hinder criminal investigations and punishment, especially when the motivations behind a terrorist act are not clear, evident or manifest, the non-inclusion of political, ideological or religious motives explaining the meaning and scope of these words (politics, ideology and religion) allows for greater compatibility with legal systems where motives are not a relevant normative element.[44]

The result of this option is clear: the interpretation of the concept of terrorism in the light of those legal instruments waives the presence of a political, ideological or religious motive as an additional subjective element, despite the fact that these are considered by academic researchers as fundamental characteristics of terrorism.[45] This leads to an expansion of the incrimination and to the classification as terrorism of acts that, following the indications of the generality of international scholars, are not strictly terrorism.[46]

Putting aside this debate on the nature of terrorism and focusing our attention on the question whether cyberterrorism is in fact supported by Portuguese law, the answer is affirmative.

On the one hand, if we take into account the common crimes referred to in the various subparagraphs of Article 2(1), it would not be unreasonable to envisage the punishment of cyberterrorism, even in its narrowest sense. Barry Collin puts forward some hypotheses that may be useful to us: "[a] CyberTerrorist will remotely access the processing control systems of a cereal manufacturer, change the levels of iron

---

[43] Koufa (2003).

[44] Borgers (2012).

[45] Borgers (2012); Dumitriu (2004); Weigend (2006).

[46] Borgers (2012). Take the case of the attack on the Alcochete Academy in Portugal. Relevant, Nuno Brandão, "O caso do ataque à Academia de Alcochete sob a perspectiva do crime de terrorismo. Anotação ao acórdão do Juízo Central Criminal de Almada (Juiz 3) de 28 de Maio de 2020", Revista Portuguesa de Ciência Criminal, ano 30 (2020), pp. 403–430.

supplement, and sicken and kill the children of a nation enjoying their food"; "[a] CyberTerrorist will attack the next generation of air traffic control systems, and collide two large civilian aircraft"; "[a] CyberTerrorist will remotely alter the formulas of medication at pharmaceutical manufacturers"; [t]he CyberTerrorist may then decide to remotely change the pressure in the gas lines, causing a valve failure, and a block of a sleepy suburb detonates and burns".[47]

Generically, any of the common crimes whose *iter criminis* is not normatively described in full may constitute a situation of cyberterrorism in a strict sense.

If our theoretical framework is, rather, of cyberterrorism in a broad sense, i.e., of classification as a terrorist act the "use of the Internet for terrorist purposes",[48] there are many hypotheses foreseen in Law No. 52/2003. For example, public incitement to the commission of terrorist acts, by means of electronic communication, with dissemination of messages accessible through the internet (article 4, paragraph 3 and 4), apologia by means of electronic communication, accessible through the internet, of the commission of terrorist acts (article 4, paragraph 8 and 9).

5 Conclusion

The concept of terrorism and, inherently, of cyberterrorism has been widely discussed in the international sphere for decades, without achieving a result worthy of consensus. Although it has not prevented the standardisation of strategies for the prevention and repression of terrorism (and its financing), both at a national and international level, the normative description of what is terrorism, foreseen in those legal instruments, is subject to profound doubts regarding its sense and scope, precisely due to its polyhedral and controversial character.

The use of cyberspace as a new stage for the phenomenon of terrorism—in its multiple dimensions: financing, propaganda and apology, recruitment, planning and execution—is, to some extent, expected and explainable by its scale, accessibility, anonymity, portability and transferability, global reach and absence of capable guardians.[49] Supporters of a stricter notion of cyberterrorism place this phenomenon in a merely theoretical or academic dimension, to the extent that, in their view, there has not been, to date, a politically motivated attack against information systems resulting in civilian victims. At the other end of the spectrum, there are proposals, with different tones, which recognise in cyberterrorism a more comprehensive phenomenon where the use of digital tools assumes a more prominent role in the materialisation of its constitutive elements.

Turning our attention to the Portuguese Law on the fight against terrorism—Law No. 52/2003—we do not find any reference to this dispute of a markedly theoretical

[47] Collin (1996).

[48] Brunst (2010).

[49] Clough (2010).

nature. However, a careful reading of the norms therein provided allows us to conclude that not only the phenomenon of terrorism in its traditional sense is punished, but also cyberterrorism, in both of its dimensions.

References

Bell J (1978) A time of terror: how democratic societies respond to violence. Basic Books, New York

Borgers M (2012) Framework decision on combating terrorism: two questions on the definition of terrorist offences. New J Eur Crim Law 3(1):68–82

Brandão N (2020) O caso do ataque à Academia de Alcochete sob a perspectiva do crime de terrorismo. Anotação ao acórdão do Juízo Central Criminal de Almada (Juiz 3) de 28 de Maio de 2020. Revista Portuguesa de Ciência Criminal 30:403–430

Britz M (2009) Computer forensics and cyber crime, 2nd edn. Prentice-Hall, Upper Saddle River

Brunst P (2010) Terrorism and the internet: new threats posed by cyberterrorism and terrorist use of the internet. In: Wade M, Maljevic A (eds) A war on terror?: The European stance on a new threat, changing laws and human rights implications. Springer, New York, pp 51–78

Bryan Foltz C (2004) Cyberterrorism, computer crime, and reality. Inf Manag Comput Secur 12(2): 154–166

Clough J (2010) Principles of cybercrime, 1st edn. Cambridge University Press, Cambridge

Collin B (1996) The future of cyberterrorism: where the physical and virtual worlds converge

Conway M (2002) Reality bytes: cyberterrorism and terrorist 'use' of the internet. First Monday 7(11)

Conway M (2014) Reality check: assessing the (un)likelihood of cyberterrorism. In: Chen T, Jarvis L, Macdonald S (eds) Cyberterrorism. Springer, New York, pp 103–121

Denning D (2000) Cyberterrorism: testimony before the special oversight panel on terrorism

Denning D (2007) A view of cyberterrorism five years later. In: Himma K (ed) Internet security: hacking, counterhacking, and society. Jones and Bartlett Publishers, London, pp 123–140

Dorsey J (2017) The Gulf Crisis: Grappling for a face saving solution. [Blog] South Asia Journal. Available at: <http://southasiajournal.net/the-gulf-crisis-grappling-for-a-face-saving-solution/ >. Accessed 5 Mar 2022

Dumitriu E (2004) The E.U.'s definition of terrorism: the council framework decision on combating terrorism. German Law J 5(5):585–602

Ganor B (2001) Terrorism: no prohibition without definition. ICT

Ganor B (2002) Defining terrorism: is one Man's terrorist another Man's freedom fighter? Police Pract Res 3(4):287–304

Gibson W (1984) Neuromancer. Penguin Group, New York

Gordon S, Ford R (2002) Cyberterrorism? Comput Secur 21(7):636–647

Holt T (2012) Exploring the intersections of technology, crime, and terror. Terrorism Polit Viol 24(2):337–354

ISO (2012) ISO/IEC 27032:2012 Information technology — Security techniques — Guidelines for cybersecurity, 1st edn. [Pdf], in https://www.iso.org/standard/44375.html

Jarvis L, Macdonald S (2014) What is cyberterrorism? Findings from a survey of researchers. Terrorism Polit Viol 27(4):657–678

Jenkins B (2004) Semantics are Strategic in the War on Terror. [Blog] The RAND Blog. https://www.rand.org/blog/2004/09/semantics-are-strategic-in-the-war-on-terror.html

Koufa K (2003) Specific human rights issues: new priorities, in particular terrorism: additional progress report. Nações Unidas, Geneva

Laqueur W (1987) The age of terrorism. Weidenfeld and Nicolson, London

Laqueur W (2007) Terrorism: A Brief History. US Department of State EJournal. https://www.hsdl.org/?view&did=474007/
Marsili M (2018) The war on cyberterrorism. Democr Secur 15(2):172–199
Martin G (2016) Essentials of terrorism: concepts and controversies, 5th edn. Sage Publishing, Thousand Oaks
O'Brien C (2021) What is cyber-terrorism, and is it a threat to U.S. national security?. Small Wars J. n.p
Plotnek J, Slay J (2021) Cyber terrorism: a homogenized taxonomy and definition. Comput Secur 102:102–145
Pollitt M (1998) Cyberterrorism — fact or fancy? Comput Fraud Secur 1998(2):8–10
Saul B (2021) The Legal Black Hole in United Nations Counterterrorism. [Blog] International Peace Institute. https://theglobalobservatory.org/2021/06/the-legal-black-hole-in-united-nations-counterterrorism/
Schmid A (2004) Terrorism - the definitional problem. Case Western Reserv J Int Law 36(2): 375–419
Schmid A (2011) The Routledge handbook of terrorism research. Routledge, London
Schmid A (2020) Revisiting the wicked problem of defining terrorism. In: Brunton G, Wilson T (eds) Terrorism: its past, present & future study - a special issue to commemorate CSTPV. Contemp Voices: St Andrews J Int Relat 1(4):3–11
Schmid A, Jongman A (2005) Political terrorism. Transaction Publishers, New Brunswick
Sieber U (2022) The threat of cybercrime. In: da Europa C (ed) Organized crime in Europe: the threat of cybercrime. Council of Europe, Strasbourg, pp 81–217
Talihärm A (2020) Cyberterrorism: in theory or in practice? Defence Against Terrorism Rev 3(2): 59–74
Weigend T (2006) The universal terrorist: the international community grappling with a definition. J Int Crim Just 4(5):912–932
Weimann G (2005) Cyberterrorism: the sum of all fears? Stud Confl Terrorism 28(2):129–149

Pedro Miguel Fernandes Freitas holds a PhD in Public Legal Sciences (Criminal Sciences branch) from the Law School of the University of Minho, Portugal. Lecturer and researcher in the areas of Criminal Law and Procedure, Cybercrime and Law and Technology at the Universidade Católica Portuguesa (Portugal). He is a founding member of the Lusophone Institute of Criminal Justice and a member of the Secure Platform for Accredited Cybercrime Experts. Participated in teaching courses organized by the University of Massachusetts Lowell (USA), the University of Turin (Italy), the Polytechnic University of Valencia (Spain), and the Jean Piaget University (Angola), among others. Currently coordinates the Postgraduate Course on Law and Technology at the Universidade Católica Portuguesa, Portugal.

Part II
Cybersecurity and Law: Specific Topics

Towards Cyber Security Regulation of Software in the European Union

Arno R. Lodder and Joeri J. Toet

Abstract Under European Union law, software, the defining asset class of the twenty-first century, carries broad rights. It is subject to only a limited and fragmented set of responsibilities or obligations in relation to quality generally and security in particular. Other than in respect of select situations where software may pose a danger to consumers, there is no generally recognised expectaton of security when procuring software. In most cases this means that security must be pursued deliberately and relies on custom contractually arrangements for enforcement. In this chapter we discuss a selection of existing and leading EU regulatory initiatives that deal with software and its security. The core of the paper is a discussion and analysis of norms in the GDPR relevant for software and security. We highlight how these different initiatives leave significant gaps in the governance of security for the information society, and how this may be problematic.

1 Introduction

Companies and governments have their mouth full about digitization, digitalization and the process of digital transformation. In many cases the (use of) electronic data takes centerstage. Electronic data creates an obvious need for information security. However, electronic data itself is inert. Software is the actuator and the proxy for human operation on data. It is information technology—and mostly software—that powers the digital society. Also, it is through software that data must be kept secured and applied for its intended purposes.

In a famous article in the *Wall Street Journal* from 2011, Mark Andreessen posited that "Software is eating the world", and more recently in 2020 Parker indicated this is still the case. Andreessen had three claims. First, he claimed that every product would become a software product. Secondly, as a consequence, every

A. R. Lodder (✉) · J. J. Toet
Vrije Universiteit Amsterdam, ALTI - Amsterdam Law and Technology Institute, Amsterdam, Netherlands
e-mail: a.r.lodder@vu.nl; j.j.toet@vu.nl

F. A. Carneiro Pacheco de Andrade et al. (eds.), *Legal Developments on Cybersecurity and Related Fields*, Law, Governance and Technology Series 60,
https://doi.org/10.1007/978-3-031-41820-4_8

company would become a software company. And, lastly, that the best software *company* would win each market. The tendency towards market dominance expressed in the third point is something that occupies many nowadays. There are indeed signs that it may hold some merit given what we see happening in many sectors, with single big players like Amazon, Uber, Airbnb, Netflix, Spotify and others emerging. One may question whether these are the best software companies and how inevitable market dominance is. For this paper, we will not further discuss competition law aspects, an issue already high on the legislative agenda of the European Union.[1] We are however inspired by Andreessen's third claim to question whether the best software *companies* also produce the best software, in particular when one considers security as a key aspect of software quality. Although this might have seemed like hyperbole at the time, there is little to argue against the fact society nowadays practically runs on software. There is a significant amount of trust placed in software and, by extension, in its manufacturers.

Daley links the omnipresence of software to cybersecurity,[2] and calls for regulative initiatives: "As physical objects increasingly rely on software-embedded systems, regulation must keep pace." We witness the increasingly visible disruption due to both high-profile attacks as much as unintentional consequences of deficient software quality (development) and operational failures.[3] Societies around the world are coming to grips with this, and this translates into a wave of new legislation. Where policy initiatives have long addressed—and seemingly continue to focus on—various types of data, comparatively limited attention seems to go out to coherently addressing the modern asset needed to process this, hence, software.

Given the prominent role of software, it is surprising if not concerning that there does not appear to be any general understanding or definition of "software" under the laws of the European Union. It is not like there are no (statutory) legal requirements applicable to software. There are many present in said laws about data use. Software developers are mostly just not the subject or addressee of these legal requirements. This may appear appealing from an individual firm's perspective as it places the onus to identify and account for compliance with requirements on its customers. Historically, it was also argued that this would benefit innovation.[4] The risk it also poses, however, is that developers and their solutions increasingly fail to identify and govern requirements, or become subject to a patchwork of overlapping and conflicting legal requirements that are increasingly hard to reconcile with other legitimate software requirements. This can only increase the complexity and fragility of software, increase the direct cost as well as opportunity costs associated with software manufacturing and overall result in lower quality and more vulnerable

[1] Proposal for a Regulation of the European Parliament and of the Council on contestable and fair markets in the digital sector (Digital Markets Act), Brussels, 15.12.2020, COM(2020) 842 final, 2020/0374(COD).

[2] Daley (2016), p. 533.

[3] CISQ, "*The Cost Of Poor Software Quality In The US: A 2020 Report*", 1 January 2021.

[4] [Regulation for software development impedes innovation].

software. The consequences thereof are externalized and by default land on customers and society more widely. This in turn obscures visibility of the true cost of software.

Quality in general and more specifically security of software appears to have become the elephant in the room of the information society (Degli-Esposti and Mocholí Ferrándiz 2021). It is questionable that there is no legislation with direct and general applicability to software or software developers. It only stands to reason then that we think hard about the role this important asset class plays in our society, and what normative imperatives arise out of this. The observation that software must meet overlapping and conflicting quality and legal requirements raises the question to what extent the current legal framework can efficiently and effectively address the concerns of modern society, and can reconcile the different interests at stake.

In this chapter we approach cybersecurity against the background of the European Union. Immediately ENISA (European Agency[5] springs to mind. We will, however, focus on regulation, and so will not discuss the activities of this Agency. We do not focus on the security of networks, but ordinary software used in the daily practice, so do not address the NIS Directive.[6] In the absence of a legislative framework that governs software or the acts of its creation and distribution, in the European Union the relation between developers and their customers is subject to contractual freedom. We are thus interested in what categories of statutory requirements do exist and, directly or indirectly, impose generic quality requirements or specific security requirements. The information technology market as we know it essentially functions as a global market. As such, we focus on European Union law and ignore legislation of individual Member States. We assume that software quality requirements will generally be common to the European market, and that a pan-European perspective helps keep requirements in the European market to a minimum while being necessary for effective enforcement of requirements in a global market whether that be by private action or regulatory supervision.

This chapter is structured as follows. We start with exploring some old and some of the most recent EU initiatives regarding or related to the regulation of software. The core of this chapter covers the General Data Protection Regulation as an example of data centered norms that indirectly address the security of software (Marotta and Madnick 2021). We will discuss privacy by design (Horák et al. 2019), data protection impact assessments and specific security norms. Our analysis focusses on what these Articles regulate, and suggests areas for further consideration when attempting to improve the quality and in particular security of software through regulation.

---

[5]Regulation (EU) 2019/881 of the European Parliament and of the Council of 17 April 2019 on ENISA (the European Union Agency for Cybersecurity) and on information and communications technology cybersecurity certification and repealing Regulation (EU) No 526/2013 (Cybersecurity Act).

[6]The Directive on Network and Information Security (NIS Directive). For an interesting analysis see Cole and Schmitz (2019).

2 Software in EU Regulative Initiatives

We do not pretend to give a comprehensive or fully representative overview of initiatives, but rather to touch upon the in our view most prominent EU regulatory initiatives relevant for software. Probably one of the oldest EU legislative initiatives related to software is the 1991 Software Directive. This directive deals with intellectual property, like the 1996 the Database Directive that we discuss as well. Next we cover product liability. We finish with the over the last couple of years most discussed 'software application', viz. Artificial Intelligence and the related Act proposed in 2021.

2.1 Software and Database Directive

The development of software has long been recognized as comprising an intellectual effort. As a result the creator of a software product is afforded copyrights in relation to the creation. The Software Directive from 1991 introduced copyright protection on software, or, in terms of the Directive: computer programs.[7] The rationale for the introduction of this legislation was that computer programs were not clearly protected in the European Union, while "the development of computer programs requires the investment of considerable human, technical and financial resources while computer programs can be copied at a fraction of the cost needed to develop them independently."

Five years later, in 1996, the European Union adopted the Database directive.[8] The rationale for protection was similar, databases were not sufficiently protected. The efforts being invested in the development of databases needed protection, in those cases where "there has been qualitatively and/or quantitatively a substantial investment in either the obtaining, verification or presentation of the contents".

These legislative acts, together with other acts governing aspects of software in the field of intellectual property, primarily afford entitlements to the rights' holder.[9] An intellectual property holders' rights may be conditional or subject to limitation, even in ways that affect the delivery of software from a technical perspective. [10] Intellectual property rights under EU law are not afforded or denied on conditions relating to the quality of software, however. Where afforded, intellectual property rights also do not

---

[7]Directive 91/250/EEC of 14 May 1991 on the legal protection of computer programs, *Official Journal* L 122, 17/05/1991, pp. 42–46. In 2009 replaced by Directive 2009/24/EC of the European Parliament and of the Council of 23 April 2009 on the legal protection of computer programs.

[8]Directive 96/9/EC of the European Parliament and of the Council of 11 March 1996 on the legal protection of databases, OJ L 77, 27.3.1996, pp 20–28.

[9]See also DIRECTIVE of 16 December 1986 on the legal protection of topographies of semiconductor products, 27.1.1987, *Official Journal of the European Communities*, L 24/36.

[10]CJEU, C-13/20 (Top System SA v. Belgian State), 6 October 2021.

create liabilities or warranties for the object of protection. There are arguably limits a software developer's ability to oversee all situations for which a general purpose piece of software may be used, and thus for the requirements that this software would need to satisfy. However, software is nevertheless often advertised and procured for its distinct functionality. In that light it is somewhat peculiar that a practice has emerged where most software licenses seem to disclaim all warranties including in particular fitness-for-purpose. A party obtaining a software license will thus have to ensure that this can (be used to) meet its own needs and obligations. It cannot by law rely on legal protection for qualitative requirements of software per se.

2.2 *Product Liability*

If we move on from the view of software as an intellectual property asset, one of the first areas where one would expect accountability for software quality and manufacturing to be addressed would be in product centered legislation (Howells et al. 2017). Recall that we referred in the introduction to the claim "every product is a software product".

The European Union has adopted a harmonized liability regime for defective products and product safety within the general market by means of two directives as far back as 1985 and 2001 respectively.[11] These directives and the national legislation that implemented these originate from an era before mainstream adoption of information technology, and a key limitation of this legislation is that it does not recognize software as a product per se.

On 30 June 2021 the European Commission published both the Impact Assessment *Adapting liability rules to the digital age and circular economy*[12] and a proposal for a general product safety regulation[13] that aims to build on and further integrate the two aforementioned directives. Software as such is not covered, namely product is defined in Article 3(1) as:

> any item, interconnected or not to other items, supplied or made available, whether for consideration or not, in the course of a commercial activity including in the context of providing a service – which is intended for consumers or can, under reasonably foreseeable conditions, be used by consumers even if not intended for them;

---

[11] Directive 2001/95/EC of the European Parliament and of the Council of 3 December 2001 on general product safety and Directive 85/374/EEC of 25 July 1985 on the approximation of the laws, regulations and administrative provisions of the Member States concerning liability for defective products.

[12] See https://ec.europa.eu/info/law/better-regulation/have-your-say/initiatives/12979-Civil-liability-adapting-liability-rules-to-the-digital-age-and-artificial-intelligence_en.

[13] Proposal for a Regulation of the European Parliament and of the Council on general product safety, amending Regulation (EU) No 1025/2012 of the European Parliament and of the Council, and repealing Council Directive 87/357/EEC and Directive 2001/95/EC of the European Parliament and of the Council, COM/2021/346 final.

The objective of the proposed regulation is to better protect consumers against health and safety risks of products, including where this includes software, so-called embedded software. This sets a high threshold for intervention since software failures at the current state of affairs are probably not highly likely to affect the health and safety of consumers and extremely hard to attribute and evidence.

In judging the admissibility of a product to the common market, the proposal presumes that a product is safe—and does not intervene—if the product meets relevant EU standards or Member State legislation to protect against relevant risks (Article 6). In the absence of both, or where a product fails to meet these requirements, a product's safety is to be judged by means of a non-exhaustive list of safety relevant aspects (Article 7(1)). This includes characteristics of the product's design (e.g. quality criteria), and where relevant, the product's effect on other products as well as other products' effect on the product under assessment (e.g. interoperability).

The presence of "appropriate cybersecurity *features* necessary to protect against *external influences*" as a safety aspect to be considered deserves separate mention. This dimension is arguably already covered by the aforementioned general aspects if we consider that software development best practices and software quality management standards already call for this.[14] The separate mention thereof suggests that from a legal perspective this should not be assumed. The overall list of aspects is non-exhaustive however, and it is not clear whether the criteria constitute a minimum or an indicative set of aspects to consider. We question what the net effect of including this requirement is.

We find the mention of protection against *external influences* interesting for another reason. All of the criteria under Article 7 will increase the need for documentation to evidence these criteria have been satisfied. Unlike the general interoperability aspects under sub b and c, this aspect appears to assume, and can be read as calling for, a form of threat assessment as it places the existence of protection against external influences squarely in a cybersecurity context.

To this point the proposed regulation does not use the term software. Undeniably, many products are at least partly software products, so more explicit mention of software would appear to have been practical. The proposal does not avoid the term in its entirety, but only uses this in circumspect ways. It uses it when describing online market places and online interfaces (Articles 8(14) and 8(15)):

> 'online marketplace' means a provider of an intermediary service using software (...)
>
> 'online interface' means any software (...) that is operated by or on behalf of an economic operator.

Then it mentions software where it addresses necessary updates (Article 35(2)). And, surprisingly, Article 37(1)(c) mentions in the context of a Safety Gate portal and

[14]For example: ISO, "ISO/IEC 25010:2011 Systems and software engineering – Systems and software Quality Requirements and Evaluation (SQuaRE) – System and software quality models," 2011.

Safety Business Gateway for financing activities "a public, non-restricted software interface", where one would expect the use of the term online interface.

The proposed regulation introduces a general statutory recognition for software quality—and most notably security—for software this is part of a consumer product. It reserves legal consequences however only to those situations where a lack of this quality amounts to a risk to a health or safety risk.

The proposal was open for consultation until January 2022, so maybe this will change. Late 2022 a next version of the proposal is expected.

2.3 *Proposal for AI Act*

The kind of software dominating the news, and academics for over 5 years now are applications based on Artificial Intelligence. On 21 April 2021 the European Commission proposed the so-called AI Act.[15] Artificial Intelligence is defined in Article 3(1) as special software:

> developed with one or more of the techniques and approaches listed in Annex I[16] and can, for a given set of human-defined objectives, generate outputs such as content, predictions, recommendations, or decisions influencing the environments they interact with.

As we know from other upcoming technologies, the EU always wants to be leading and at the time preserve (human) rights:

> It is in the Union interest to preserve the EU's technological leadership and to ensure that Europeans can benefit from modern technologies developed and functioning according to Union values, fundamental rights and principles.

Cybersecurity is mentioned at several places, most notably in recital 51:

> Cybersecurity plays a crucial role in ensuring that AI systems are resilient against attempts to alter their use, behavior, performance or compromise their security properties by malicious third parties exploiting the system's vulnerabilities. Cyberattacks against AI systems can leverage AI specific assets, such as training data sets (e.g. data poisoning) or trained models (e.g. adversarial attacks), or exploit vulnerabilities in the AI system's digital assets or the underlying ICT infrastructure. To ensure a level of cybersecurity appropriate to the risks, suitable measures should therefore be taken by the providers of high-risk AI systems, also taking into account as appropriate the underlying ICT infrastructure.

Cybersecurity concerns are addressed in the proposed act in several articles. That is in itself is consistent with the intentions of the act. However, in light of the stated concerns, it is surprising to see such a fundamental topic restricted to only high-risk AI systems.

[15] Proposal for a Regulation of the European Parliament and of the Council Laying Down Harmonised Rules on Artificial Intelligence (Artificial Intelligence Act) and Amending Certain Union Legislative Acts, COM/2021/206 final.

[16] Annex I refers to (a) Machine learning approaches; (b) Logic- and knowledge-based approaches (c) Statistical approaches.

3 Building on notions from the GDPR

The European Union has maintained a harmonized omnibus personal data protection legislation since Directive 95/46/EC was enacted in 1995. A key consideration driving the introduction of Europe's personal data protection legislation was the advent of automated data processing and the recognition that the processing of personal data at scale would entail risks for individuals. The most recent major development was the adoption of the General Data Protection Regulation in 2016, applicable since May 2018. The EU personal data protection framework regulates the processing of personal data, and its requirements essentially lay down a data management framework in which security features prominently. European data protection legislation does not directly address software manufacturers. However, in today's world, the GDPR's requirements essentially can only be met if software manufacturers integrate them into the design of data processing software.

The primary addressee of legal obligations under the GDPR is the 'controller', which is the party that cf. Article 4(7) "determines the means and the purposes of the processing of personal data". We consider that the processing of personal data is a practical necessity for any type of modern organization, even if that is solely for purposes of running a financial administration and managing human resources. Not all organizations will develop software themselves, but where software is not developed within the company it will be procured.

The requirements to which the controller is subject under the GDPR will have to be facilitated by means of the software used for the processing of personal data. Where the controller develops—or procures the development of—this software, it will be legally held to identify and embed the relevant characteristics in that capacity. Where the data controller relies on a third party for the development and supply of the relevant software, whether that be in a capacity as a "processor" under the GDPR or as a licensee of a software product, it will need to ensure that the product or service enables it to meet the security requirements of the GDPR. Every controller will thus have to deal with the quality and security of software.

It follows that the developer of a software solution is only an addressee of legal requirements under the GDPR where it also operates the software it develops for the processing personal data. This may be either in a capacity as a controller—in which case it will be the direct addressee of the majority of legal obligations—or in a capacity of processor—in which case it works on behalf of the controller but is also the direct addressee of a select number of obligations that relate to security. In the latter case the developer or processor will need to facilitate the controller with its compliance in respect of certain functionality in its solution.

However, there are many other companies that develop software and that do so for others. The norms of the GDPR do not apply to them when no personal data processing is involved and, where it is, they do not apply to them directly if they are not involved in the operation of the software. This creates a mismatch between the ability to control risks and accountability for the manifestation thereof, which risks leading to ineffective and economically inefficient risk management (Anderson et al.

2008). We discuss three examples from the GDPR, viz. data protection by design, data protection impact assessment, and security of processing. We will indicate how it is regulated now, and propose an alternative focused on the software.

3.1 *Cybersecurity by design for all software development*

A classic scenario of software development within a company is the following. The developers work for days, months and sometimes even more than a year on the software. Then, in the week the software is to be put on the market, the lawyers are asked to check the compliance. Not only is one or two days to check compliance quite short, but in case the lawyers discover legal hurdles there might be no time left to repair them. This particular is the case if a legal flaw is caused by some design decision made at the beginning of the development process. To remedy this, the GDPR introduced the notion of data protection by design, better known as privacy by design. In an earlier version of the GDPR this common term was used, but at a certain stage the drafters decided to delete all occurrences of the word privacy. Probably because they wanted to respect the distinction made in the Charter of the EU between the fundamental right of privacy (Article 7) and data protection (Article 8). The GDPR obviously deals with the latter. So now the word privacy does not appear a single time in the text of the GDPR, except for one footnote referring to the E-privacy Directive.

Article 25(1) indicates what the controller should do in terms of data protection by design. The starting point is that "the state of the art, the cost of implementation and the nature, scope, context and purposes of processing" are taken into account. The 'state of the art' is a term that already appeared in the Directive 95/46 but then solely referred to security in recital 46 "(. . .) must ensure an appropriate level of security, taking into account the state of the art (. . .)". Similarly, Article 17 on the security of processing indicated "(. . .) Having regard to the state of the art and the cost of their implementation, such measures shall ensure a level of security appropriate to the risks (. . .)". The scope of data protection by design does cover security but is broader.

Also, a controller must take into account "the risks of varying likelihood and severity for rights and freedoms of natural persons posed by the processing". So data protection by design is related to a risk assessment, as is the data protection impact assessment to be discussed next but we will see that only high risks are covered by a DPIA. As for the timing, the controller should pay attention to risks, state of the art etc. "at the time of the determination of the means for processing", which is the early stage of design. Also, since design of software never stops, not even when it is already used the controller "at the time of the processing itself". What is it that the controller must do to cover any risks detected? He should "implement appropriate technical and organizational measures (. . .) in an effective manner". So the design is not only related to the software per se, but also guidelines for the people who are going to use it (e.g. authorisations) should be dealt with. The aim of all this is "to integrate the necessary safeguards into the processing in order to meet the requirements of this Regulation and protect the rights of data subjects." This is, as with many data protection norms, something that should be considered normal business for a company. The years before the GDPR demonstrated that this was not the case, reason to introduce data protection by design.

In case the software is developed by the company using the software for data processing the controller has to comply to the principle of data protection by design. But off the shelf software is developed by a company that is not going to use it. In that case the just discussed norms do not apply. One would hope that software developers think about norms applicable to their customers, the companies who are going to use the software. Legally they are not required to do so however. The obligation to comply with the requirement of privacy-by-design rests on the shoulder of the controller, which will need to actively engage with its supplier to ensure that it satisfies the conditions for it to meet its obligations. It is not surprising that in practice many suppliers do not adequately address this requirement, or where they do that this comes at significant cost either directly in terms of the price paid for professional experience or indirectly in the form of compliance overhead and economic friction. We believe this to be an error in the GDPR's design. We suggest that data protection by design becomes a principle within the European Union for all developers designing software to be used to process personal data. Even, more generally, we propose a so-called cybersecurity by design norm applicable for all software developers, so also if no personal data are going to be processed.

3.2 New obligation: Software developer and DPIAs

Also new in the GDPR is the data protection impact assessment. For the same reason just discussed, this assessment is not referred to by the common term privacy impact assessment. In case of data protection by design you could argue that you need to think about data protection principles from the beginning of software development. As for an assessment, the impact that needs to be assessed for sure is the impact on people's privacy, not data protection. So the term is wrong. That being said, here the controller has to take into account "the nature, scope, context and purposes of the processing". For sure, the impact of processing data about special categories of data have more impact than the data about people ordering from a supermarket. This is something to consider here. These considerations are not necessary for all processing activities, but only for those that are "likely to result in a high risk to the rights and freedoms of natural persons." One example explicitly mentioned is the use of new technologies, that by default ("in particular") should be assessed. Under the described circumstances the controller should "prior to the processing, carry out an assessment of the impact of the envisaged processing operations on the protection of personal data." Although the assessment is only necessary in case of high risks, we do advise controllers to assess the impact in all situations, referred to us as a DPIA light. Then, only if this DPIA light is leading to the conclusion that the risks are high the full DPIA has to be carried out.

Article 35(3) does describe three cases where, next to the already mentioned new technologies, a DPIA is required:

(1) systematic evaluation based on automated processing and leading to legal decision (makes sense since this is in principle prohibited cf. Article 22(1);
(2) processing on a large scale;
(3) systematic monitoring of the public area.

The aim of the assessment is to mitigate any risks identified. Just like with data protection by design, the controller has the obligation to do the assessment. For the specific situations described (new technologies, and Article 35(3)) as well as in general, we suggest that EU law introduces a norm that requires companies that develop software meant to process personal data should also carry out an impact assessment. In case software is developed that does not process personal data, the law should require software companies to assess the security risks and either mitigate them and in case mitigation is not possible inform the party that buys the software about the existence of the risk.

3.3 *Proposing a Unified EU Legal Framework for Software Security Principles*

Article 32 GDPR addresses security in respect of a personal data processing activity. The requirement succeeds an almost identical article on obligations in respect of security in Directive 95/46. The GDPR expands on this in more general terms however in that security is also added to the existing five principles of data protection in Article 5(1)(f) as a sixth principle relating to the processing of personal data:

> Personal data shall be (. . .) processed in a manner that ensures appropriate security of the personal data, including protection against unauthorised or unlawful processing and against accidental loss, destruction or damage, using appropriate technical or organisational measures ('integrity and confidentiality').

The GDPR does not merely introduce a substantive security requirement by means of this paragraph. It also adds an explicit obligation for the controller to demonstrate compliance with these principles by means of Article 5(2). This so-called accountability requirement means that a controller must consider these foundational principles of personal data protection, determine what they mean for the data processing within the organization, and additionally account for how these principles are being satisfied (Troisi 2021). The explicit requirement to demonstrate compliance makes this stricter than merely having "to ensure that the principles are complied with" as was the phrasing in Directive 95/46.

Article 5 is the normative core of the GDPR, and it stands to reason that security was included as a key part of this. It is questionable then how much Article 32 really adds to the security regime embedded in Article 5. The measures listed in Article 32 may serve as indicative measures to comply with Article 5(1)(f), but do not describe a comprehensive security regime and appear somewhat selective:

(a) the pseudonymisation and encryption of personal data;
(b) the ability to ensure the ongoing confidentiality, integrity, availability and resilience of processing systems and services;
(c) the ability to restore the availability and access to personal data in a timely manner in the event of a physical or technical incident;
(d) a process for regularly testing, assessing and evaluating the effectiveness of technical and organisational measures for ensuring the security of the processing.

That said, these and other security measures are all important measures for controllers to take in respect of the processing of personal data. The need to already embed (some of) these measures during the design and development of software is arguably even more pressing than for the principle of privacy-by-design and the performance of data protection impact assessments. The same issues apply here, which suggests again that security related principles should generally not have to be negotiated with suppliers of software or supervised at a transactional level. It would appear preferable for EU legislation addressing developers of software to apply a cohesive set of principles they have to account for. A Regulation or Directive on the Security of Software, could apply a principle similar to Article 5(1)(f) and be supported by an Article similar to Article 32.

General security obligations similar to the above requirement in the GDPR are present in a myriad of other European Union laws.[17]

4 Conclusion

Under European Union law, software, the defining asset class of the twenty-first century, carries broad rights. It is subject to only a limited and fragmented set of responsibilities or obligations in relation to quality generally and security in particular. Other than in respect of select situations where software may pose a danger to consumers, there is no generally recognised expectaton of security when procuring software. In most cases this means that security must be pursued deliberately and relies on custom contractually arrangements for enforcement.

The current approach to software security heavily depends on the functioning of markets to achieve desirable levels of security. This, combined with key characteristics of software, suggests that the present form of governance might be unlikely to deliver an adequate level of cybersecurity. Our concerns are not only limited to the

[17] For example: article 14-1 of Directive 2016/1148 ("NIS Directive"), article 95 of Directive 2015/2366 ("Payment Services Directive II").

inability of achieving significantly improved security (Liu and Wong 2017). The cost at which security must be pursued under the present circumstances is already significant (Moore 2010). In light of society's vast and increasing dependence on software, the markets' struggle to correctly allocate responsibilities and risks[18] increases significantly.

We are generally considered to be in a digital transformation. This means that companies that would not traditionally identify or be seen as information technology companies nowadays develop and deploy software as a key competitive enabler. The software they develop may be deployed for internal purposes only, but also increasingly underpins or forms part of products and services they deliver to their customers. Unless the responsibility for security of software is naturally recognized and treated as an integral part of any products and services supplied, consequences of security failures are in practice likely—and generally probably unknowingly—to be passed on to customers. We are concerned this may create a form of systemic risk to the information society.

We believe accountability for software security—and quality more generally—calls for an integrated and holistic approach in which software manufacturers are recognised as much as rewarded in that capacity for their crucial role in today's society. The introduction of a general software accountability framework is likely to be disruptive in that it will require affected companies to introduce new forms of governance and thereby organizational change. This will likely introduce additional costs. Quality improvements resulting from a more efficient allocation of accountability should eventually reduce overall cost on society in the form of a decreasing number of security incidents.

In this chapter we discussed a selection of existing and leading EU regulatory initiatives that deal with software and its security. We then focused on norms in the GDPR relevant for software and security. We highlighted how these different initiatives leave significant gaps in the governance of security for the information society (Tagarev 2020), and how this may be problematic. We hope this provides inspiration for a more holistic and integrative look at the role of software manufacturers, and an appreciation for software quality, within the European legal environment.

References

Anderson R et al (2008) Security economics and the internal market. Report to the European Network and Information Security Agency

Cole MD, Schmitz S (2019) The Interplay Between the NIS Directive and the GDPR in a Cybersecurity Threat Landscape, (December 31, 2019). University of Luxembourg Law Working Paper No. 2019-017, in https://ssrn.com/abstract=3512093

[18] For example: the information a-symmetry that exists between buyers and licensors in respect of software quality; and the inability of buyers/licensors to control risks at their origin in the software value chain.

Daley J (2016) Insecure software is eating the world: promoting cybersecurity in an age of ubiquitous software-embedded systems. Stanford Technol Law Rev 19:533

Degli-Esposti S, Mocholí Ferrándiz E (2021) After the GDPR: cybersecurity is the elephant in the artificial intelligence room. Eur Bus Law Rev 32(1):1–24

Horák M, Stupka V, Martin Husák M (2019) GDPR compliance in cybersecurity software: a case study of DPIA in information sharing platform. In: ARES '19: Proceedings of the 14th International Conference on Availability, Reliability and Security, August 2019 Article No.: 36, pp 1–8

Howells G, Twigg-Flesner C, Willett C (2017) Product liability and digital products. In: Synodinou TE, Jougleux P, Markou C, Prastitou T (eds) EU internet law. Springer, Cham

Liu F, Wong M (2017) Challenges of cyber security and a fundamental way to address cyber security. In: Khajuria S, Sørensen L, Skouby KE (eds) Cybersecurity and privacy - bridging the gap. River Publishers, pp 189–212

Marotta A, Madnick S (2021) A framework for investigating GDPR compliance through the lens of security. In: Bentahar J, Awan I, Younas M, Grønli TM (eds) Mobile Web and Intelligent Information Systems. MobiWIS 2021. Lecture Notes in Computer Science, vol 12814. Springer, Cham

Moore T (2010) The economics of cybersecurity: principles and policy options. Int J Crit Infrastruct Protect 3:103–117

Tagarev T (2020) Towards the design of a collaborative cybersecurity networked organisation: identification and prioritisation of governance needs and objectives. Future Inter 12(4):62

Troisi E (2021) GDPR accountability principle and EU political strategy on cybersecurity: the cybersecurity act. Eur J Priv Law Technol

Arno R. Lodder is a professor of Internet Governance and Regulation at Vrije Universiteit Amsterdam, ALTI—Amsterdam Law & Technology Institute. In his research and lecturing he focuses on topics related to law and internet, such as liability, contracting, security, privacy, freedom of speech, cybercrime; and phenomena related to algorithms, big data, social media, cyberwar, internet of things, smart devices and apps.

Joeri J. Toet is lecturer/researcher at Vrije Universiteit Amsterdam, ALTI—Amsterdam Law & Technology Institute. He is specialized in privacy and cyber security, and is a practicing lawyer in this field for over 10 years.

The Importance of the Computer Undercover Agent as an Investigative Measure Against Cybercrime: A Special Reference to Child Pornography Crimes

Almudena Valiño Ces

Abstract The Internet is a scenario in which a wide range of criminal activities can be carried out and, in addition, it is a medium in which it is very difficult to identify the people who commit crimes using the Internet and new technologies: cybercriminals. Many of them take refuge in the network to carry out practices that harm minors. We are referring to a typical online crime: the production, possession, and exchange of child pornography. In this context, the undercover computer agent becomes important, as it represents a specific measure of technological investigation in the criminal process aimed at identifying these people. This figure is presented as appropriate for the investigation of these crimes related to the sexual exploitation of minors, being able to act as a kind of spy on the network that, using false identities, can impersonate pedophiles to exchange illegal files with child pornography. The aim is therefore to determine whether this exchange during Internet-related investigations will be sufficient to identify suspected pedophiles and thus put an end to this type of practice, which represents a major social scourge.

1 Introduction

The Information and Communication Technology (ICT) revolution has contributed to the emergence of new forms of crime and, fortunately, also of crime prevention and response. For this reason, police forces, through the means of investigation and detection, as well as legislators and legal operators, have had to evolve in parallel to offer effective solutions to a whole series of new criminal behaviours or new manifestations of the commission of traditional conducts linked to technological development. However, we must not forget that these solutions must in no way limit

A. Valiño Ces (✉)
Department of Special Public and Business Law, University of Santiago de Compostela, Santiago de Compostela, Spain
e-mail: almudena.valino@usc.es

F. A. Carneiro Pacheco de Andrade et al. (eds.), *Legal Developments on Cybersecurity and Related Fields*, Law, Governance and Technology Series 60,
https://doi.org/10.1007/978-3-031-41820-4_9

or restrict the fundamental rights and freedoms of citizens—especially when it comes to minors—and the principles and values inherent in the rule of law.[1]

In response to this challenge, the Spanish legislator addressed in the second half of 2015 important legislative reforms, such as those operated in the Criminal Code by Organic Laws 1/2015 and 2/2015, both of 30 March,[2] and the one carried out in the Criminal Procedure Law by Organic Law 13/2015, of 5 October, for the strengthening of procedural guarantees and the regulation of technological investigation measures and by Law 41/2015, of 5 October, for the streamlining of criminal justice and the strengthening of procedural guarantees.

Specifically, with Organic Law 13/2015, new technological investigation procedures have been approved that take on enormous relevance with respect to crimes perpetrated by computer means, that is, those crimes linked to computer data.[3] Thus, these proceedings are a reality and represent a very necessary step in the adaptation of the old Criminal Procedure Law to the new circumstances that affect both the way crimes are committed and the crimes themselves. These include: the undercover computer agent; the interception of telephone and telematic communications; the capture and recording of oral communications by electronic devices; tracking, tracing, and image capture devices; the search of mass storage devices; and the remote search of computer equipment.

Except for the first of these -the undercover computer agent- these measures are subject to common provisions provided for in Article 588 *bis* a) of the Criminal Procedure Law, which can be summarised as requiring judicial authorisation based on the principles of speciality, suitability, exceptionality, and necessity of the measures, as well as proportionality when deciding to adopt them. Without prejudice to the importance of each of them, we must highlight the consolidation of the figure of the undercover agent in the Spanish legal system and the demonstration of its effectiveness in the investigation of certain crimes, such as drug trafficking.

However, beyond other types of criminal acts, we are aware that child pornography[4] is one of the social phenomena that concerns all countries, especially when,

---

[1]Prosecutor's Office Annual Report 2017, pp. 642 and 643. Available at https://www.fiscal.es/memorias/memoria2017/FISCALIA_SITE/index.html. Accessed 15 October 2021.

[2]These reforms were aimed, among other things, at criminalising new offences and/or adapting existing offences to the forms of criminal execution that have arisen as a result of technological developments.

[3]In the opinion of Miró Llinares, the category of computer crimes included typologies of conducts and not criminal types (Miró Llinares 2012, p. 37). For this reason, computer-related crime does not exist as such in our legal system, there is no such heading in the Criminal Code and there is no specific dogmatic of these crimes (Choclán Montalvo 2006, p. 698). Because of these interpretative problems, the doctrine has adopted the term cybercrime, which encompasses crime related to the use of ICTs. However, it should be noted that there is a common denominator between the definition of cybercrime and that of computer-related crime. Thus, the former comprises all crimes related to computer data and cybercrime encompasses those computer crimes that are committed on computer networks, that is, crimes related to global cyberspace (Sieber 2009, p. 162).

[4]According to Article 189 of the Criminal Code "*child pornography or pornography involving persons with disabilities in need of special protection shall be considered to be child pornography:*

due to the confinement caused by the state of alarm decreed in March 2020, it has spread even further using the Internet and virtual social networks. The Internet is a network that allows millions of users to communicate with each other and to access a huge amount of information from all over the world. Its main characteristics are interactivity, free choice of content and the absence of a controlling authority to limit its content. Unlike television, radio or cable, the Internet presents very few barriers to access for those who want to provide or distribute information, allowing any individual to communicate with a worldwide audience.

In view of this, there is no doubt that the influence of new technologies in changing education, interpersonal relationships and the way knowledge is disseminated and generated in society has been reflected in an increase in child pornography offences. Precisely, the digital era has brought with it a qualitative and quantitative leap in the trafficking of pornographic material, both in terms of the material available and the production by means of increasingly smaller image and video devices with discreet and inexhaustible virtual supply routes that allow for the easy production of this type of pornography, which makes it even more difficult for law enforcement agencies to detect it.

Given this scenario, the figure of the undercover computer agent plays a fundamental role in the Spanish legal system, which is why it is necessary to focus on its analysis—taking the figure of the conventional undercover agent as a starting point—especially when the need for its regulation has become clear in recent years.[5]

(a) *Any material that visually depicts a minor or a person with disabilities in need of special protection engaging in real or simulated sexually explicit conduct.*
(b) *Any depiction of the sexual organs of a child or a person with a disability in need of special protection for primarily sexual purposes.*
(c) *Any material that visually depicts a person appearing to be a minor engaged in real or simulated sexually explicit conduct, or any depiction of the sexual organs of a person appearing to be a minor, for primarily sexual purposes, unless the person appearing to be a minor is found to be in fact eighteen years of age or older at the time the images were obtained.*
(d) *Realistic images of a minor engaged in sexually explicit conduct or realistic images of the sexual organs of a minor, primarily for sexual purposes*".

[5]By way of example, on 23 March 2001, the Plenary Session of the Senate approved a motion urging the Government to submit to the Cortes Generales a Bill regulating the figure of the undercover agent on the Internet, especially with regard to child pornography. Thus, it was understood that this regime had important shortcomings. Firstly, because of the singularities of the virtual organisation resulting from the interaction of criminals on the Internet, which is usually more diffuse than a non-virtual criminal organisation, with unaccustomed methods of coercive imposition of discipline, scarce or unnecessary means and effects at the service of the organisation and aims, in principle, alien to any economic benefit; and, secondly, because Article 282 bis of the Criminal Procedure Code raised doubts as to this type of group because of the powers that the undercover agent may have and, in particular, the possibility of exchanging or providing child pornography to the community. Issues such as these were particularly foreseen by the Supreme Court in Ruling 767/2007, of 3 October, in a case in which the Civil Guard detected a chat room in which the subject of sexual relations with minors was discussed. In this case, the agents, without revealing their status, contacted one of its users, who sent them files with child pornography, telling them about the existence of a group of paedophiles on the internet called "the big family" who met

2 From the Concept to the Characteristic Notes of the Undercover Agent Figure

Today we are aware of the serious social problem of organised crime, which requires the adoption of special investigative techniques by the police to effectively combat this type of criminal activity.[6] Indeed, most countries are heavily involved in the fight against this type of crime, as it is a phenomenon that concerns them, especially if we take into account that the investigative techniques that had been used—house searches or interceptions of communications—were not sufficient.[7] Therefore, it was understood that an effective response to organised crime implied the adoption of means of investigation that would make it possible to confront "*the opacity and clandestinity with which the major criminal organisations operate*".[8]

One of these is the undercover agent, who is one of the most appropriate agents for combating the alleged acts of criminal organisations. It is the members of the Security Forces and Corps themselves, with a specific professional and personal profile, who develop this technique. Its importance is such that, without their work, it would have been difficult to dismantle some criminal groups in Spain.

Undercover agents, whose origin is in German law, are governed by Article 282 *bis* of the Criminal Procedure Law.[9] This precept was introduced ex novo into

---

with their underage children to have sexual relations with them. From this point on, by decree of the Public Prosecutor, the undercover agent was authorised to act.

[6]Expósito López (2015), p. 251.

[7]The Explanatory Memorandum to Organic Law 5/1999, of 13 January, recognises the inadequacy of traditional investigation techniques in the fight against organised crime.

[8]Gimeno Sendra (2015), p. 575.

[9]Article 282 *bis*: "*1. For the purposes set out in the previous article and in the case of investigations involving organised criminal activities, the competent investigating judge or the Public Prosecutor's Office, immediately informing the judge, may authorise officers of the Judicial Police, by means of a substantiated decision and taking into account their need for the purposes of the investigation, to act under assumed identity and to acquire and transport the objects, effects and instruments of the offence and defer the seizure of the same. The assumed identity shall be granted by the Ministry of the Interior for a period of six months, extendable for periods of the same duration, and they shall be legitimately authorised to act in all matters related to the specific investigation and to participate in legal and social traffic under such an identity. The decision granting the authorisation shall state the real name of the agent and the assumed identity under which he will act in the specific case. The decision shall be confidential and shall be kept outside the proceedings with appropriate security. The information obtained by the undercover agent shall be brought to the attention of the person who authorised the investigation as soon as possible. This information must also be brought to the proceedings in its entirety and shall be assessed in all conscience by the competent judicial body.*

2. Judicial Police officers who have acted in an investigation under a false identity in accordance with the provisions of section 1 may maintain this identity when testifying in the proceedings that may arise from the facts in which they have intervened, provided that this is agreed by means of a reasoned judicial decision, and provided that the provisions of Organic Law 19/1994, of 23rd December, shall also apply to them. No officer of the Judicial Police may be obliged to act as an undercover agent.

our legal system by Organic Law 5/1999, of 13 January, amending the Criminal Procedure Law to improve the investigative action related to illegal drug trafficking and other serious illegal activities. Its provision was motivated by the desire to improve this investigative action with regard to the circulation and controlled delivery of prohibited substances, in addition to drugs, as until then there was no reference to this figure. In this way, the undercover agent is being provided with a legal empowerment in the framework of investigations related to organised crime, being able to use an assumed identity, under strict judicial and prosecutorial control.[10]

Due to the importance of this figure, the active position of the undercover agent cannot be occupied by just any police officer, but, by legal provision, it is necessary that a member of the Judicial Police is the one who carries out the infiltration. Although it is not very clear who will form part of this corps, it can be understood that it will be those members of the State Security Forces and Corps who have the necessary specialisation in crime investigation techniques. In the opinion of Zafra Espinosa de los Monteros, it would be appropriate to "*create a specific body of Judicial Police with jurisdiction throughout the national territory and with organic and functional dependence on the Public Prosecutor's Office, from which they will be commissioned*".[11]

An undercover agent can therefore be defined as a specialised officer of the Judicial Police who, with the authorisation of the competent jurisdictional body, is appointed to enter criminal organisations, concealing his identity or assuming a fictitious identity on a temporary basis, pretending to be part of it or to be interested in carrying out the punishable acts perpetrated by that organisation.[12] It is therefore a tool for police infiltration[13] aimed at identifying the perpetrators and participants, the

---

3. When the investigative actions may affect fundamental rights, the undercover agent shall request from the competent judicial body the authorisations established in this respect by the Constitution and the law, as well as complying with the other applicable legal provisions.

4. For the purposes indicated in paragraph 1 of this article, organised crime shall be considered to be the association of three or more persons to carry out, on a permanent or repeated basis, conduct aimed at committing one or more of the following offences: [...].

5. The undercover agent shall be exempt from criminal liability for those actions that are a necessary consequence of the development of the investigation, provided that they are duly proportionate to the purpose of the investigation and do not constitute a provocation to commit a crime. In order to be able to proceed criminally against him/her for the actions carried out for the purposes of the investigation, the judge competent to hear the case shall, as soon as he/she becomes aware of the actions of any undercover agent in the same, request a report on such circumstances from the person who authorised the supposed identity, in view of which he/she shall decide what he/she deems appropriate".

[10] Paz Rubio et al. (1999), p. 395.

[11] Zafra Espinosa de los Monteros (2015), p. 559.

[12] For other definitions of undercover agents, see the sixth legal basis of Supreme Court Judgement 1140/2010 of 29 December and the third legal basis of Supreme Court Judgement 395/2014 of 13 May: Valiño Ces (2016).

[13] Gascón Inchausti (2001), p. 34.

actions or *modus operandi* of the criminal structure, its plans of action, contacts, means and results of the criminal activity, etc.

In view of the above, the undercover agent is sometimes confused with other related concepts. One of these is that of the agent provocateur,[14] insofar as he is a member of the security forces who, with the aim of uncovering a criminal act, instigates or encourages the commission of the crime with the requests made to those under investigation. For this reason, his participation in the activities of a criminal gang goes beyond those of an undercover agent.[15] The jurisprudence rejects the means of evidence obtained with the intervention of these agents,[16] since the Supreme Court ruling of 8 November 1993 states that "*the provocation of the criminal offence by an agent of the Authority is a means of evidence incompatible with the general principles that guarantee the legality of the process, with the interdiction of arbitrariness and with the dignity of the person*".[17]

On the other hand, there is the figure of the informant who is another of the traditional means of investigating crimes, whose intervention is limited to police investigations. This is generally a person belonging to the criminal milieu who provides the police with information, not always for altruistic purposes, but generally in exchange for money or certain favourable treatment by the police officers.

And finally, the figure of the repentant, which can be defined as the individual who, while originally belonging to the criminal organisation, from a certain moment onwards collaborates with the justice system, providing information about those crimes in which he or she has or has not participated, in exchange for procedural benefits. This is done for various purposes: to clarify a criminal act or to identify its

---

[14] On the distinction between undercover agent and agent provocateur in general, see, among others: García San Martín (2014), p. 11 and Muñoz Marín (2014), pp. 189–194.

[15] Moreno Catena y Cortés Domínguez (2019), p. 266.

[16] See the judgments of the Supreme Court of 16 July 1999 and those of 14 July and 29 June 2000.

[17] Even so, this ruling justifies police intervention and "*it is understood that provocation is excluded when the action of the undercover agent in instigating the criminal act really pursues and uncovers a previous criminal conduct, the channel through which a pre-existing criminal activity is taking place, which is nothing more than an investigative action that is part of the task of the judicial pólice*". This statement departs from an interpretation which guarantees fundamental rights and freedoms and omits the rule of Article 11.1 of Organic Law 6/1985, of 1 July, of the Judiciary, which excludes evidence obtained, directly or indirectly, by violating these rights or freedoms from the process.

In accordance with the ruling of the European Court of Human Rights of 9 June 1998 (Teixeira case), the situation of agent provocateurs would exist in several cases, such as when the police operation was not part of an open investigation; when the person under investigation had no previous record; if he was not directly known by the agents; when, in the case of drug trafficking, the drugs were not found in his home, but were obtained from a third party; or also when the person under investigation only had the quantity requested by the police. In spite of all this, this court considers that there was a violation of the Convention and states: "*it must be deduced that the two policemen did not limit themselves to examining in a purely passive manner the criminal activity of Mr. Teixeira de Castro, but that they exercised an influence to incite him to commit the crime*", so that the police intervention "*goes beyond that of an undercover agent since they provoked the crime and that nothing indicates that, without their intervention, it would have been perpetrated*".

perpetrators or participants; to prevent its consummation; or to detect related acts. However, it should be noted that the term "repentant" is, to a certain extent, inadequate, as the willingness to cooperate does not necessarily have to be motivated by repentance. For this reason, it would be more appropriate to identify him as a collaborator, given that he is a person under investigation who provides information to achieve an improvement in his personal situation.[18]

On another level, and in accordance with the aforementioned precept, this figure presents a series of characteristic features. Thus, its action is limited to activities typical of organised crime, this being understood as the association of three or more persons to carry out, permanently or repeatedly, conduct aimed at one of the offences provided for in Article 282 bis (4).[19] However, some of these offences raise doubts as to the proportionality stricto sensu of the means of investigation. Indeed, it can be understood that the legislator was consistent with the idea that the criminal phenomenon cannot go hand in hand exclusively with the quantitative nature of the offence, since, as Gimeno Sendra states, "*precisely the greatest unjustness of the offence is produced by the commission of the punishable act within a criminal organisation*".[20]

In addition, the authorisation of the examining magistrate or of the Public Prosecutor's Office is necessary, with immediate notification to the judge, to "*fulfil the requirement of the measure's jurisdictionality, which is an integral part of the principle of proportionality and of obligatory validity in any measure limiting fundamental rights*".[21] This will be done by means of a well-founded decision and provided that it is necessary for the purposes of the investigation. Therefore, this authorisation will be granted so that the undercover agent, under an assumed identity provided by the Ministry of the Interior,[22] can forge personal relationships, gain the trust of the group, and gain access to knowledge of crimes perpetrated or being prepared, as well as to a whole set of private elements about the subjects under investigation. It will also enable them to act and to acquire and transport the objects, effects, and instruments of the crime and to postpone their seizure.

---

[18] For further discussion see: Díaz-Maroto y Villarejo (1996); Jordán Díaz-Roncero and Comes Raga (2010), pp. 67–90; Lamarca Pérez (2011).

[19] Article 282 *bis* (4) includes a list of the following offences: Offences of obtaining, illicit trafficking in and transplantation of human organs; offence of kidnapping of persons; offence of trafficking in human beings; offences relating to prostitution; offences against property and against the socio-economic order; offences relating to intellectual and industrial property; offences against workers' rights; offences against the rights of foreign citizens; crimes of trafficking in endangered species of flora or fauna; crimes of trafficking in nuclear and radioactive material; crimes against public health; crimes of counterfeiting currency, provided for in Article 386 of the Criminal Code, and of counterfeiting credit or debit cards or travellers' cheques; crimes of trafficking and deposit of weapons, ammunition or explosives; crimes of terrorism; and crimes against historical heritage.

[20] Gimeno Sendra (2015), p. 576.

[21] Gimeno Sendra (2015), p. 575. See Constitutional Court judgments 56/2003, of 24 March; 123/2002, of 20 May; 70/2002, of 3 April.

[22] This assumed identity includes, as a general rule, a false name, address, telephone line, criminal record, bank account, as well as all kinds of accreditations: ID card, passports, residence cards, credit cards, degree or graduate degree, etc. (Zafra Espinosa de los Monteros 2010, p. 345).

As for the duration of this false identity, as provided for in the provision, it will be "*six months, extendable for periods of the same duration*".[23] As this is an exceptional measure restricting fundamental rights, it cannot be allowed to remain indefinitely and without controls, as an excessive length of time could be disproportionate to the aims it seeks to achieve. Moreover, respect for the principle of proportionality requires that the duration of the measure be reduced to the minimum necessary for the success of the criminal prosecution. However, determining a priori the duration of the covert operation is considered extremely complex, due to the need to assess the situation based on the specific case and its various circumstances.

It is also characterised by its voluntary nature, in other words, no judicial police officer may be obliged to act as an undercover agent. The reason for this optional nature lies, on the one hand, in the legislator's awareness of the risks that this type of operation entails and, on the other hand, in the fact that some agents may be reluctant to adopt false names, due to the professional and personal consequences that this activity may entail for them. In view of this, it will be essential to have the consent of the acting agent, which, if possible, should be in writing.[24]

Finally, there is an exemption from criminal liability for his actions, provided that they are a necessary consequence of the investigation and, furthermore, they are proportionate to the conduct of the investigation and do not constitute an inducement to commit a crime.[25] The reason for this provision is the knowledge that the officer

[23] At the international level, we can refer to Article 14 of the European Convention on Mutual Assistance in Criminal Matters of 14 November 2000, which states in the context of covert investigations that "*Member States shall agree on the duration of the covert investigation, the specific conditions and the legal status of the officers concerned, in accordance with their respective national laws and procedures*".

[24] Marchal Escalona (2011), p. 758.

[25] As far as the nature of the exemption from liability is concerned, on the one hand, it can reside in a cause of justification, exempting from liability the person who breaks the law in the fulfilment of a duty or in the legitimate exercise of an office, or, as the case may be, for acting in a state of necessity. On the other hand, it can be considered as an excuse for acquittal, by virtue of reasons of criminal policy. In this case, it affects the punishability of the act which, therefore, is unjust, giving rise to the appropriate civil liability for the damage caused and which applies to those in whom it occurs, but not to the rest of the participants. Thus, Supreme Court Judgment 395/2014, of 13 May, in its third legal basis, seems to opt for the latter option, stating that "*It must be a member of the judicial police who, by reasoned decision, receives a kind of authorisation to transgress the rule with respect to one of the crimes listed in art. 282 bis, a kind of exemption from acquittal improperly included in a procedural rule. The exemption from criminal liability for the crimes that the undercover agent may have committed refers to those offences committed and which are a direct consequence of the authorisation for which the status of undercover agent is conferred*". In opposite direction, the majority doctrine understands it to be a cause of justification, which, together with unlawfulness, excludes both criminal and civil liability. Specifically, it is included in article 20.7 of the Criminal Code, which means that the exemption from liability, if applicable, reaches the participants, and operates in the sphere of civil liability, including the subsidiary civil liability of the State, which, if applicable, will be liable in administrative proceedings for normal or abnormal functioning. This is the line taken by the 2012 draft, Article 409 of which refers to the scope of exemption from liability, stating that "*1. The undercover agent shall be exempt from liability for those actions that are a necessary consequence of the development of the investigation, provided*

may commit criminal acts during the operation. Accordingly, it could be argued that, although case law allows for the sacrifice of the right to privacy, the action will be lawful if it does not become an inducement to crime and does not infringe fundamental rights.

Beyond the characteristics of the undercover agent described above, one aspect that should be emphasised is that, through this measure, the state infiltrates the lives of the persons under investigation in a secret manner to obtain information about the iter criminis. What happens is that this practice results in greater interference in the sphere of privacy of the persons under investigation, as the infiltrated police officer not only maintains a relationship of trust with the so-called cybercriminals, but also carries out actions that, if his true identity were known, he would not have been able to carry out. In these circumstances, the possible problem raised by the action of this figure lies in the possibility of implying an additional harm to the exercise of the fundamental rights of the persons under investigation.[26] Therefore, the question arises as to how this measure will affect the safeguarding of the rights to privacy and secrecy of communications of the persons under investigation, which protect the exchange of files online. The answer is not complex. This measure complies with all the parameters of legality and proportionality,[27] that is, the limitation of a fundamental right is legitimised by the rule of law as long as it is carried out within the criteria established by law.

In short, these rights will be guaranteed by the need for prior judicial authorisation to carry out these actions, which will ensure that they are fully respected. In this way, it will be the judge who will control, beforehand and in any case, based on certain criteria: the existence of sufficient evidence, the suitability of the measure and its necessity or the seriousness of the conduct under investigation and its motivation. In short, even when the infiltration of an agent restricts fundamental rights, the situation does not entail any inconvenience, given the need to obtain authorisation from the competent investigating judge and to assess, with special attention, the necessity and proportionality of the means of investigation used.

that the interest sacrificed is of a proportionally lower value than that which the investigation seeks to safeguard. 2. In no case shall provocation to crime be authorised".

[26] As Zafra Espinosa de los Monteros understands when he points out that it is a "*special investigative measure because it implies an additional interference in the system of guarantees of the persons under investigation*" (Zafra Espinosa de los Monteros (2010), p. 563).

[27] In this respect, Cardoso Pereira understands that the figure of the undercover agent entails "*the implementation of an essential instrument in the fight against organised crime as long as it is used in accordance with the constitution, respecting especially the requirements of legality and proportionality*" (Cardoso Pereira (2012)).

3 The Undercover Computer Agent

A broad analysis of the legal regime of undercover agents shows the fundamental role that they play as an extraordinary means of investigation in the prosecution of certain types of crime. However, as there were legal loopholes in its actions, this led to an urgent need for reform and updating to provide it with the necessary legal coverage.[28] This reality motivated Organic Law 13/2015, of 5 October, on the modification of the Trial Law for the strengthening of procedural guarantees and the regulation of technological investigation measures,[29] to perfect this precept 282 bis through the incorporation of sections 6 and 7:

> 6. *The investigating judge may authorise officers of the Judicial Police to act under assumed identity in communications maintained on closed communication channels in order to clarify any of the offences referred to in section 4 of this article or any of the offences provided for in article 588 ter a.*
>
> *The undercover computer agent, with specific authorisation to do so, may himself exchange or send illegal files by reason of their content and analyse the results of the algorithms applied for the identification of such illegal files.*
>
> 7. *In the course of an investigation carried out by an undercover agent, the competent judge may authorise the taking of images and the recording of conversations that may take place during the planned meetings between the agent and the person under investigation, even if they take place inside a home.*

In view of this, it can be seen that the legislator, influenced by technological developments, is taking sides and intends to reinforce the figure of the undercover agent that existed until then in our legal system. Consequently, based on the existing regulation and, about technological research, we can define the undercover computer agent as a member of the State Security Forces and Corps who, voluntarily, and having received the relevant judicial authorisation, temporarily infiltrates the network under an assumed identity in a closed communication channel, with the aim of obtaining information on criminal practices produced through it and identifying their perpetrators and participants.[30] The aforementioned infiltration would take place through the mechanism of concealment of the true identity, in order to gain the trust of a group of criminals, thereby obtaining sufficient evidence of the illegal acts perpetrated by them.

In this way, the regulation of this figure is extended with the aim of bringing criminal justice closer to the repression not only of organised crime, but also of crimes committed via the Internet. Its creation is associated with the prosecution of specific crimes committed with the help of new technologies, which the legislator

---

[28] See Valiño Ces (2017), pp. 377–388.

[29] In Barona Vilar's opinion, this 2015 reform comes to fill a perceptible gap in the digital society: the need to grant substantivity to other forms of telematic communication existing in reality and without the corresponding legal coverage that would protect them, causing a gap between the norm and reality (Barona Vilar 2021, p. 525).

[30] Rizo Gómez (2017), p. 102.

cannot ignore. Even so, it will be necessary to strike a balance between investigating and prosecuting crime and safeguarding the fundamental rights and freedoms of individuals.

3.1 Target Scope of Police Infiltration

The basis of the figure of the undercover computer agent is to be found in the possibility of providing cover for the agent's actions, by means of an assumed identity, in closed communication channels, implying that this refers to social networks or other means of Internet connection. This idea is clear from the precept, insofar as it indicates that the figure is aimed not only at clarifying some of the crimes perpetrated in the framework of organised crime, those provided for in paragraph 4, but also those that can be committed through computer tools or any other information or communication technology, as contemplated in the new Article 588 *ter* a,[31] which, in turn, explicitly refers to some of the crimes referred to in Article 579.1.[32] It can be seen how the legislator, in a glimmer of light, extends the scope of action of the undercover agent to online investigations, precisely because of its usefulness in clarifying illegal acts perpetrated through the network and for determining their authorship in the framework of investigations related to cybercrime,[33] or at least in those in which the victims are minors.

The main reason for this inclusion may lie in the fact that until 2015 the possibilities of using the figure were limited to the types of offences listed in section 4 of the precept itself, constituting a "*closed number*". This circumstance limited the

[31] This precept was provided for by Organic Law 13/2015, by creating a new Chapter V in Title VIII of Book II, which regulates the interception of telephone and telematic communications. Specifically, it states that "*Authorisation for the interception of telephone and telematic communications may only be granted when the purpose of the investigation is one of the offences referred to in Article 579.1 of this law or offences committed by means of computer tools or any other information or communication technology or communication service*".

[32] Article 579.1 provides that "*The judge may order the detention of private, postal and telegraphic correspondence, including faxes, bureaufaxes and money orders, which the person under investigation sends or receives, as well as their opening or examination, if there are indications of obtaining through these means the discovery or verification of any fact or circumstance relevant to the case, provided that the investigation is for any of the following offences: 1. Crimes punishable by a maximum sentence of at least three years' imprisonment; 2. Crimes committed within a criminal group or organisation; 3. Terrorist offences*".

[33] Cybercrime can be understood as: "*any unlawful or abusive activity related to computers and communications networks, either because the computer is used as a tool of the crime, or because the target of the crime is the computer system or its data*" (Mitchison and Urry (2001), pp. 19–24). In this respect, it can be understood that the handicap of this type of crime is the singularity of the circulation through which the criminal object passes, because while in the conventional world, being physical, its control is simple, in the virtual world there is the added disadvantage for police agents of guaranteeing adequate control of everything that circulates through the telecommunications that are carried out through the network (Velasco Nuñez (2011)).

options for use in online investigations, especially if we take into account that most of the frequent illegal activities -such as the harassment of minors or everything related to child pornography or even attacks on computer systems[34]- did not fall within the framework of organised crime groups and, therefore, were not included in this list of offences.[35]

This list of offences places us in a situation of legal vacuum and, furthermore, is not very operative. Given the progress made in technology, it would be a mistake to draw up this closed list, and it would be more appropriate to establish a system of numerus apertus based on classes of offences rather than on specific offences. In this way, it would be possible to avoid other classifications that would quickly become outdated.[36]

Beyond the possibility of specifying the types of computer crime a little more, the fact is that this provision, which undoubtedly extends the scope of action of the undercover agent to investigations carried out on the Internet, should be considered positive. Rizo Gómez takes this line, considering this extension to be praiseworthy, bearing in mind that limiting this figure to cases in which organised crime activities are investigated and, more specifically, to the criminal offences envisaged in the aforementioned section 4, would mean a failure of the measure.[37] Nevertheless, the need to extend the operability of the undercover computer agent to other types of crime is considered unavoidable.

3.2 The Undercover Computer Agent's Acquisition of Images and Recording of Conversations

In the event that in the development of a specific investigation it is necessary to carry out any of the activities provided for in paragraph 7 of Article 282 bis—obtaining images and recording conversations that may take place in the meetings planned between the agent and the person under investigation—the agent must request the appropriate authorisation, with the competent judicial body assessing the viability of the measure in accordance with its suitability, proportionality and necessity.

About image and sound recordings, taking into account that there is no specific regulation on undercover agents, these will be carried out in accordance with the specific rules set out in Chapter VI of Title VIII of Law 13/2015—Article

[34] There are a series of circumstances that contribute to the increase in cybercrime, such as, among others: its impersonal nature, providing anonymity to those who do not want to be discovered in their illegal actions; its wide dissemination; the ease of obtaining and disseminating multimedia content favours criminal behaviour; or the global nature of the system and the lack of limits which, together with the immediacy of the transmission of information, encourages the perpetration of crimes.

[35] See the analysis of this list of offences in Valiño Ces (2016).

[36] Bueno de Mata (2012), p. 297.

[37] Rizo Gómez (2017).

588 *quater*- as it regulates the capture and recording of oral communications through the use of electronic devices. Without prejudice to these rules, ad maiorem, the general rules of Chapter IV, which are contained in Article 588 *bis*, must be applied. This is because they should complement each other, even if the resulting text is in many cases repetitive, in others incomplete, or even almost incompatible on some points.[38]

3.3 Sharing or Sending of Illegal Files and Analysis of the Results of the Algorithms Applied for the Identification of Such Files

A key area for the conduct of undercover investigations, and where the relevance of this agent is undeniable, is that of child pornography.[39] Indeed, it is precisely in this context that a problem of concern to all countries emerges: the production, possession, and exchange of child pornography on the Internet. It is a practice that has been reinvented in the light of technology, which has adapted perfectly to the multiple possibilities of communication and exchange of information today and which has taken advantage of the factors of transnationality and anonymity that characterise the use of the network.

The reality is that, in the history of humanity, few issues have as much demagogic power as the fight against this social scourge, even to the point of restricting reason and uniting people of different ideologies. The threat of this type of behaviour in a country like Spain places it in second place in the world in terms of child pornography consumption and paedophile file sharing, after the United States and ahead of Mexico, as reflected in data from the Alia2 Foundation.

The difficulty in these circumstances is that consumers of child pornography are in restricted forums, where gaining their trust is, more often than not, the only way to locate and arrest those who produce and distribute pornographic material.[40] In addition, the severe blows suffered by child pornography networks in recent years have made paedophiles increasingly cautious about exchanging material online, be it videos or photographs of children, making it more difficult to detect them. Technological developments have even allowed for an increase in the production of child pornography, whereas previously only the distribution and possession of such material was a crime. This context was the reason why the heads of the technological investigation brigades of both the National Police and the Guardia Civil agreed that child pornography represents a problem that is difficult to eliminate and that, due to

[38] Conde-Pumpido, pp. 3 and 4.

[39] De La Rosa Cortina (2012).

[40] In order to get to the sources of production of pornography, it will be necessary to make personal and direct contact with those who could provide access to a particular crime group. While this is an activity that does not ensure the success of the investigation, it is an essential precondition for it.

the multiplying effect of the Internet, it has become one of the most common crimes today.

For this reason, it was necessary for the legislator to react by introducing this undercover computer agent, especially when the figure of the conventional undercover agent was hardly used in child pornography investigations due to the lack of legal coverage.[41] This figure was regulated to improve the effectiveness of agents, allowing police officers to pose as paedophiles or pretend to be children in Internet forums to catch the depraved in flagrante delicto, as well as being able to access closed groups where it is necessary to offer certain captious material in order to become a member and thus combat child pornography from the inside. To achieve this, a specific regulation was undoubtedly needed to determine, with full legal certainty, the scope of action of these agents in the prosecution of child pornography, given that its design was based on the example of drug trafficking offences.

In accordance with the provision analysed, in the actions of the undercover computer agent, it is worth highlighting, on the one hand, the possibility of analysing the results of the algorithms applied to identify illegal files. In this respect, the Report of the Public Prosecutor's Council to the Preliminary Draft is very clear,[42] for whom the secure identification of computer files is usually carried out by means of hashing. It states that "*The hash is the alphanumeric key resulting from the analysis of the contents of any computer file and its specificity is such that the slightest alteration in the content of the file would determine the modification of the hash result. In turn, the term algorithm is used to define the steps and tools necessary to obtain a result such as the hash*". Consequently, for the Prosecutor's Office, what is relevant in this regard is not the analysis of the algorithms, but "*the analysis of the results of the algorithms applied to identify the illicit files*". On the other hand, the exchange or sending of files with illicit content by the undercover agent is provided for, which is, in view of the above, an absolutely necessary measure for combating crimes committed on the Internet.

Thus, paragraph 6 of 282 *bis* provides for possible covert police intervention in file-sharing networks (p2p), which will consist of the possibility of using files with illicit content in a justified manner to obtain the identity of the recipient, who would request them in this type of network. In this case, the judicial decision will again have to be reasoned and specific to this kind of police intervention. This activity on p2p networks will make it possible to analyse the algorithms, that is, the mathematical-electronic operations that can identify the routes taken by cybercriminals on the networks, their protocols or rules of action and the nature of the material being exchanged. In other words, the role of the undercover agent, who becomes a kind of spy on the network, includes the possibility of sending or

[41] In contrast to the main countries around us, such as France, Germany, Italy and the United States, where this figure exists and is used to dismantle this type of criminal networks from within.

[42] See the Report of the Public Prosecutor's Council on the Draft Bill of the Organic Law amending the Criminal Procedure Act for the streamlining of criminal justice, the strengthening of procedural guarantees and the regulation of technological investigation measures, presented in Madrid on 23 January 2015, pp. 26 and 27.

exchanging illicit files and then being able to examine the algorithms associated with these files, while guaranteeing the privacy and secrecy of the communications of those potentially affected.

For this reason, prior judicial authorisation is necessary to carry out interventions of this type, and all the more so in cases where illicit files are shared, given that this is an action that is contrary to the law. The truth is that, on this point, a problem arises, as the text of the law itself does not contain any provision about the concept of "illicit file", which can sometimes lead to a legal vacuum and, therefore, to insecurity in the actions of the agent in these spaces which are no longer private, but intimate to the person under investigation.

In this respect, for the undercover agent to infiltrate effectively, it was initially envisaged that criminal material from previous raids would be exchanged. However, this practice did not prove to be appropriate, as it was understood that, in addition to involving minors in the whole procedure, the punishable act would continue to be committed by the agents as this material was circulating on the internet. Therefore, the use of real images would undermine the rights of the victims, without considering the fact that the protection of children is considered to be above any criminal investigation.

Precisely because of the harm caused using real images in the investigation of these crimes, graphic designers have created a digitised image of a minor to simulate pornographic videos that can be used in the investigation of this crime without resorting to real images. An example of this is the Dutch NGO Terre des Hommes which computer generated the image of a virtual girl -a ten-year-old Filipino girl they called "Sweetie"—which has been used by the police to identify sex offenders.[43]

Another option was to allow the exchange of camouflaged material created ad hoc, that is, to exchange pornographic material in which pornographic actors and actresses of legal age appear posing as minors or in tweets or threats created against fictitious persons to generate confidence in the investigated person.[44] In this way, the actions of the agent and the material itself would be deceptive, but without violating the image of any minor, or of children as a whole, since we would be dealing with material specifically created to fight against this purpose, and in which minors would not be implicated at any time.

However, this whole question deserves some reflection, since giving the agent the power to exchange illicit material with the person under investigation could lead the defence to accuse the agent himself of inducing the crime.[45] This could lead to

[43] Terre des Hommes is an NGO active in Asia, Africa and Latin America that aims to prevent child exploitation and promote the development of children in a safe environment. Thanks to the creation of this child sex offender recruitment site, in ten weeks, 20,000 adults from all over the world were attracted to the Internet to abuse her, demonstrating the unstoppable growth of child sexual abuse on the Internet. See news at https://elpais.com/sociedad/2013/11/04/actualidad/1383586504_108141.html and https://www.bbc.com/mundo/ultimas_noticias/2013/11/131104_ultnot_paidofilia_virtual_wbm.

[44] Bueno de Mata (2013), p. 322.

[45] Bueno de Mata (2015).

the nullity of the investigation on the grounds that the undercover agent has become an agent provocateur, as it would make it possible for the person under investigation to develop a criminal intent and use the commission of crimes as an investigative tool.[46]

In view of the above, it will be difficult for the court to determine when the offenders have acted spontaneously and naturally, or whether the agent has used trickery or deception for the mere fact of uploading illegal content onto the network, due to the way file-sharing networks work. If the actors make illegal files available to third parties, the next thing to be expected is that they will download them, so one could speak of "provocation" in the strict and unlawful sense. However, even if they can say that the agents uploaded the files only to contact suspects in their distribution, it is considered very difficult to fit this justification.

Ultimately, to overcome this drawback, the legislator envisaged the need for a specific authorisation to exchange or send illegal files by reason of their content during an investigation.[47] Thus, the undercover agent will have to act clandestinely under an assumed identity, in accordance with the law and with judicial authorisation to repress or prevent the crime.

3.4 The Probative Value of Their Performance

To analyse the special features derived from the environment in which the undercover computer agent intervenes, it is convenient to address the evidential value of his or her actions. This is because there is no doubt as to the importance of his statement at the oral trial, in that it constitutes evidence against him capable of rebutting the presumption of innocence, and it is for the court of first instance to assess its importance.[48]

---

[46] See the third legal basis of the judgement of the Criminal Division of the Supreme Court 601/2000, of 14 July 2000.

[47] This authorisation was not provided for in the Draft Organic Law amending the Criminal Procedure Law for the strengthening of procedural guarantees and the regulation of technological investigative measures. By stating that "*The undercover computer agent may exchange or send illegal files by himself/herself because of their content and analyse the algorithms associated with these illegal files*", it was inferred that it was not necessary to have the authorisation of the judge to carry out these actions. However, given the illicit content of the files, it seems advisable that the judge should expressly authorise the exchange (Lafont Nicuesa (2015)).

[48] See the judgement of the Criminal Chamber of the Supreme Court 104/2011, of 1 March, in which it reasons on the validity of the testimony of the undercover agent as sufficient prosecution evidence to break the presumption of innocence: "*The Court of first instance grants credibility to this testimony and we have already said - for all Supreme Court Judgment 545/2010 of 15. 6- that the witness statements in the plenary session of police officers on facts of their own knowledge, as they are provided with the procedural guarantees of the act itself, constitute sufficient evidence for the prosecution to overturn the presumption of innocence (Supreme Court Judgment 284/96 of 2.4). In this sense, art. 717 of the Criminal Procedure Law provides that the declarations of the*

Strictly speaking, police infiltration takes place at the pre-trial stage of the proceedings and will have its effects at the trial stage, where the specific means of evidence, which will serve as a vehicle for introducing the information at trial, will depend on its nature. It is common for the testimony of the undercover agent to be proposed, whose statement will refer not only to what he has directly perceived himself during the infiltration, but also to those known facts that have been related to him by others, in this case as a reference witness. Similarly, their testimony will serve to confirm the testimony of other third parties who, without their intervention, might be reluctant to testify or even to tell the truth.

In view of the above, if the undercover agent does not ratify his statement in the oral trial, the statements made by that subject in the investigation as a result of the investigative activity carried out will have no evidential value, and will only have the value of a mere denunciation and will therefore be subject to evidential activity.[49]

An exceptional case is the action of an officer who intervenes without judicial authorisation. In this case, the evidence obtained, as it violates fundamental rights because of the lack of a judicial decision authorising its adoption, will be null and void in accordance with the provisions of Article 11.1 of Organic Law 6/1985 of 1 July 1985 on the Judiciary.

One of the special features regarding the statement of the undercover agent in the oral trial is paragraph 2 of Article 282 *bis* of the Criminal Procedure Law,[50] since it allows the false identity to be maintained if this is agreed by means of a reasoned judicial decision, in which case the provisions of Organic Law 19/1994, of 23 December, on the protection of witnesses and experts in criminal cases, will also be applicable. To this end, it should be recalled that Article 4.3 provides that "*Without prejudice to the foregoing, if any of the parties should make a reasoned request in their brief of provisional qualification, prosecution or defence, to know the identity of the proposed witnesses or experts, whose testimony or report is considered relevant, the judge or court hearing the case, in the same order in which it declares the relevance of the proposed evidence, must provide the names and surnames of the witnesses and experts, respecting the other guarantees recognised for them in this Law*".

In this way, the maintenance of the false identity in the trial phase may not violate the right of defence, nor prevent the fullness of the principle of contradiction, having to disclose the status of judicial police and identify the official through his Personal

---

authorities and judicial police officers will have the value of witness statements, which can be assessed as such, according to the rules of rational criterio" (second legal basis).

[49] Rizo Gómez (2017), pp. 119 and 120.

[50] Article 282(2) *bis* provides: "*Judicial police officers who have acted in an investigation under a false identity in accordance with the provisions of paragraph 1, may maintain this identity when testifying in the proceedings that may arise from the facts in which they have intervened and provided that this is agreed by means of a reasoned judicial decision, provided that the provisions of Organic Law 19/1994, of 23 December, also apply to them*".

Identification Number or his Professional Identity Card in case his testimony is admitted.[51]

Lastly, the photographs, image and/or sound recordings obtained by the undercover agent will be brought to the trial for judicial assessment and may, where appropriate, be the subject of expert opinions.[52] In line with this, it is worth citing Supreme Court judgment 652/2016, of 15 July, in which the validity of evidence consisting of a recording of the content of a meeting held inside a company between the accused and four of the company's employees is questioned. The recording that had been played during the hearing was one of the fundamental elements for a conviction by the Provincial Court of Guipúzcoa.[53]

[51] Rodríguez Caro (2015).

[52] Rodríguez Caro (2015).

[53] Faced with the appeal in cassation lodged by the defence, the Supreme Court ended up stating in the twelfth legal basis: "*1. The use in criminal proceedings of recordings of private conversations recorded by one of the interlocutors does not in any case violate the constitutional right to secrecy of communications.*

2. Nor does it infringe the constitutional right to privacy, except in exceptional cases in which the content of the conversation affects the intimate core of the personal or family privacy of one of the interlocutors.

3. They violate the fundamental right not to testify against oneself and not to confess guilt, and consequently incur in evidential nullity, when the recordings have been made from a position of institutional superiority (agents of the authority or hierarchical superiors) to obtain an extra-procedural confession obtained by deception, except in cases of recordings authorised by the judicial authority in accordance with art. 588 and following of the Criminal Procedure Law (Criminal Code).

4. They do not violate the fundamental right not to testify against oneself and not to confess guilt, when they have been made in the private sphere.

5. They may violate the right to a trial with all guarantees, when the person recorded has been brought to the meeting using trickery with the premeditated intention of making them state facts that could be used against them, in which case the set of concurrent circumstances must be weighed up.

6. Case law does not classify the statements made by the accused in these recordings as a confession, using the recordings as ratification of the statements of the other participants in the conversation, which have the value of reference testimony on the statements of the accused.

In the present case, as has been pointed out, the evidence is unnecessary, as there is more than sufficient evidence to rebut the constitutional presumption of innocence. Furthermore, the participants in the conversation have testified and confirmed its content, apart from the recording. Lastly, there is no evidence of any trickery, since it is clear that the meeting was intended to seek an agreement, and was held days after the fact was discovered, before the proceedings were initiated, and without seeking to obtain a confession, which, moreover, did not take place. Consequently, there is no grounds for the nullity sought".

4 Conclusions

Reality shows us how today the Internet is a scenario of human activity, where the factor of anonymity and technology contribute to the possibility of harbouring unlawful conduct. There are people who act through this channel for criminal purposes, which undoubtedly constitutes a great threat to our society, especially when the targets of these actions are particularly vulnerable people, such as minors.

For this reason, the fight against criminality in the context of pornography-related offences is an arduous and complex matter. Hence, the need to articulate new investigative measures that would make it possible to effectively combat this type of criminal conduct, one of which is the provision for undercover computer agents. With this figure, and its possibility of exchanging or sending illegal files, the infiltration of a judicial police officer in a virtual environment is facilitated, with the aim of dealing with criminal conduct perpetrated on the Internet and thus ascertaining the identity of cybercriminals.

In short, although the figure of the undercover computer agent is considered a good solution in the fight against this type of action, it should be pointed out that it cannot be considered a panacea for all the shortcomings in the investigation of crimes in this digital environment. This is because its regulation, far from being a daring text, should be more solid and coherent with the very nature of the measure, avoiding legal loopholes that could generate legal uncertainty in its use.

References

Barona Vilar S (2021) Algoritmización del Derecho y de la Justicia. De la inteligencia artificial a la Smart Justice. Tirant lo Blanch

Bueno de Mata F (2012) El agente encubierto en internet: mentiras virtuales para alcanzar la justicia. In: Pérez-Cruz Martín AJ, Ferreiro Baamonde X (Dirs) Los retos del Poder Judicial ante la sociedad globalizada. Actas del IV Congreso Gallego de Derecho Procesal (I Internacional). A Coruña, 2 y 3 de junio de 2011. Universidade da Coruña

Bueno de Mata F (2013) Un centinela virtual para investigar delitos cometidos a través de las redes sociales: ¿deberían ampliarse las actuales funciones del agente encubierto en Internet? In: Pérez Gil J (Coord.) El proceso penal en la sociedad de la información: Las nuevas tecnologías para investigar probar el delito. La Ley

Bueno de Mata F (2015) Comentarios y reflexiones sobre la Ley Orgánica 13/2015 de modificación de la Ley de Enjuiciamiento Criminal para el fortalecimiento de las garantías procesales y la regulación de las medidas de investigación tecnológica. *Diario La Ley*, Núm. 8627, Sección Doctrina

Cardoso Pereira F (2012) Agente encubierto y proceso penal garantista: límites y desafíos (Tesis doctoral). Department of Administrative, Financial and Procedural Law, University of Salamanca

Choclán Montalvo JA (2006) Infracciones patrimoniales en los procesos de transferencia de datos. In: Romeo Casabona CM (Coord.) El Cibercrimen. Nuevos retos jurídico-penales, nuevas respuestas político-criminales. Comares

Conde-Pumpido P. Captación y grabación de comunicaciones orales mediante la utilización de dispositivos electrónicos, in https://docplayer.es/30240711-Captacion-y-grabacion-de-comunicaciones-orales-mediante-la-utilizacion-de-dispositivoselectronicos-paloma-conde-pumpido-fiscalia-especial-antidroga.html

De La Rosa Cortina JM (2012) Delitos de pornografía infantil: otra vuelta de tuerca. Diario La Ley, Núm. 7817

Díaz-Maroto y Villarejo J (1996) Algunos aspectos jurídico-penales y procesales de la figura del "arrepentido". Diario La Ley, Sección Doctrina, Ref. D-293, tomo 5

Expósito López L (2015) El agente encubierto. Revista de Derecho UNED, Núm. 17

García San Martín J (2014) Los límites entre el agente encubierto y el agente provocador en la persecución de los delitos de tráfico ilícito de drogas. La ley penal: revista de derecho penal, procesal y penitenciario, Núm. 107

Gascón Inchausti F (2001) Infiltración Policial y "agente encubierto". Comares

Gimeno Sendra V (2015) Derecho Procesal Penal. Aranzadi

Jordán Díaz-Roncero MJ, Comes Raga I (2010) El arrepentimiento postdelictual en España: un ensayo acerca de su viabilidad como instrumento combativo del crimen organizado. La Ley Penal, Núm. 77, Sección Legislación aplicada a la práctica, pp 67–90

Lafont Nicuesa L (2015) El agente encubierto en el Proyecto de reforma de la Ley de Enjuiciamiento Criminal. Diario La Ley, Núm. 8580, Sección Doctrina

Lamarca Pérez C (2011) Atenuación por arrepentimiento en el delito de tráfico de drogas. La Ley Penal: revista de derecho penal, procesal y penitenciario, Núm. 86, Sección Legislación aplicada a la práctica

Marchal Escalona AN (2011) Manual de lucha contra la droga. Aranzadi

Miró Llinares F (2012) El cibercrimen. Fenomenología y criminología de la delincuencia en el ciberespacio. Marcial Pons

Mitchison N, Urry R (2001) Delitos y abusos en el comercio electrónico. The IPTS Report 57:19–24

Moreno Catena V, Cortés Domínguez V (2019) Derecho Procesal Penal. Tirant lo Blanch

Muñoz Marín Á (2014) El agente encubierto y su diferenciación con la provocación para delinquir. CEF Legal: revista práctica de derecho. Comentarios y casos prácticos, Núm. 158:189–194

Paz Rubio JM, Mendoza Muñoz J, Ollé Sesé M, Rodríguez Moriche R (1999) La prueba en el proceso penal. Su práctica ante los Tribunales. Colex

Rizo Gómez B (2017) La infiltración policial en Internet. A propósito de la regulación del agente encubierto informático en la Ley Orgánica 13/2015, de 5 de octubre, de modificación de la Ley de Enjuiciamiento Criminal para el fortalecimiento de las garantías procesales y la regulación de las medidas de investigación tecnológica. In: Asencio Mellado JM (Dir.) Fernández López M (Coord.), Justicia penal y nuevas formas de delincuencia. Tirant lo Blanch, pp 98–123

Rodríguez Caro MV (2015) La infiltración policial: en el límite del Estado de Derecho. El inminente agente encubierto informático. Noticias Jurídicas. in http://noticias.juridicas.com/conocimiento/articulos-doctrinales/10222-la-infiltracion-policial:-en-el-limite-del-estado-de-derecho-el-inminente-agente-encubierto-informatico/

Sieber U (2009) El control de la complejidad en el ciberespacio global: la armonización de los delitos informáticos. In: Delmas-Marty M, Pieth M, Sieber U (eds) Los caminos de la armonización penal. Tirant lo Blanch

Valiño Ces A (2016) Una lectura crítica en relación al agente encubierto informático tras la Ley Orgánica 13/2015. Diario La Ley, Núm. 8731

Valiño Ces A (2017) La actuación del agente encubierto en los delitos informáticos tras la Ley Orgánica 13/2015. In: Fuentes Soriano O (Coord.) El proceso penal. Cuestiones fundamentales. Tirant lo Blanch

Velasco Nuñez E (2011) Novedades técnicas de investigación penal vinculadas a las nuevas tecnologías. Revista de Jurisprudencia, Núm. 4

Zafra Espinosa de los Monteros R (2010) El policía infiltrado. Los presupuestos jurídicos en el proceso penal español. Tirant lo Blanch

Zafra Espinosa de los Monteros R (2015) La lucha contra el crimen organizado en el borrador del Código Procesal Penal: el agente encubierto. In: Moreno Catena V, Ruiz López C, López Jiménez R (Coords), Reflexiones sobre el nuevo proceso penal. Tirant lo Blanch

Almudena Valliño Ces is Professor of the Procedural Law Area of the University of Santiago de Compostela. Participation in various research projects. Member of the Research Group "The conflict and the solution mechanisms with a gender perspective". Member of the Teaching Innovation Groups: "Group of innovation in conflict resolution techniques" and "Arte, lingua e Dereito (ARLIDE)". Author of more than 80 publications. She has participated as a speaker and communicator in more than 70 national and international congresses, conferences and courses in Spain, Chile, Mexico and Portugal, in addition to having directed a collective work and coordinated 5. She has participated in the organization of numerous activities. And she has carried out a research stay for 3 months at the Faculty of Law of the University of Porto.

Post-Mortem Data Protection and Succession in Digital Assets Under Spanish Law

Marta Otero Crespo

Abstract This contribution analyses a hot topic across Europe: the issue of *post-mortem* data protection and succession in digital assets focusing on Spanish Law. Their protection through the instruments provided by the Spanish Organic Law 3/2018, of 5 December, on the Protection of Personal Data and Guarantee of Digital Rights, and the Catalonian Law 10/2017, of 27 June, on digital wills and amending the Second and Fourth Books of the Catalonian Civil Code, provide good examples of the interaction amongst data protection, contract law and inheritance law in this field, which will be the subject matter of our study.

1 Introduction

Over the last few years, the issue of *post-mortem* data protection and succession in digital assets has become topical under Spanish law from a general perspective.[1] In this regard, the concrete purpose of this chapter is to contribute to this recent debate focusing on the *post-mortem* protection of the deceased's data and the inheritance of digital content or digital assets,[2] protected as personality or as property elements

[1]There are a series of previous contributions in which I have dealt with the topic. See Otero Crespo (2019), pp. 89–133; Otero Crespo (2020), pp. 1–10; Otero Crespo (2021), pp. 367–378.

[2]In this context, 'digital content' does not always have the meaning established in Directive (EU) 2019/770 of the European Parliament and of the Council of 20 May 2019 on certain aspects concerning contracts for the supply of digital content and digital services. Article 2 of Directive (EU) 2019/770 states that 'For the purposes of this Directive, the following definitions apply: (1) 'digital content' means data which are produced and supplied in digital form'. On the other hand, the concept of 'digital assets' has been embraced by the American Revised Uniform Fiduciary Access to Digital Assets Act (RUFADAA, 2015). According to this instrument, Section 2. Definitions '(10) 'Digital asset' means an electronic record in which an individual has a right or interest. The term does not include an underlying asset or liability unless the asset or liability is itself an

M. Otero Crespo (✉)
University of Santiago de Compostela, Santiago de Compostela, Spain
e-mail: marta.otero.crespo@usc.es

F. A. Carneiro Pacheco de Andrade et al. (eds.), *Legal Developments on Cybersecurity and Related Fields*, Law, Governance and Technology Series 60,
https://doi.org/10.1007/978-3-031-41820-4_10

respectively. On this matter, it is required, as a preliminary question, to differentiate between the personal and the patrimonial aspects of succession, even though the two are sometimes intertwined and difficult to dissect in the digital environment. For the former, the idea of the digital trace or fingerprint, connected to the protection of the digital identity, means that the personal data of the deceased must be protected *post-mortem*; for the latter, the legal notion of inheritance determines the succession *mortis causa* in the digital assets.[3]

To achieve the abovementioned aim, a series of general issues will be outlined, so as to take into greater prominence in a *sui generis* field in which there is a clear intersection amongst inheritance law, data protection law and contract law.

The starting point is the indisputable intensive use of the Internet, both for professional and personal purposes. Focusing on the second one—the personal sphere—it seems obvious to point out that any average digital citizen of the twenty-first century uses e-mail accounts and instant messaging applications for communication; social networks to publish ideas, photographs or share other content; stores documents, videos or snapshots in the cloud; acquires goods and contracts services in digital media; and even opens a bank account or stores an online balance to make certain payments. The activities described have in common the fact that they are options facilitated by the development of the Internet; at the same time, they provide a good example of the heterogeneity of actions that could be adopted as Internet users, the repercussions of which could go, and often do go, beyond the end of the physical existence of their 'owner'.[4] And this statement is based on the fact that, on the one hand, the digital fingerprint, typically made up of non-patrimonial contents, transcends the physical existence of the individuals, and on the other hand, the activity of the individuals may have created a 'digital' or 'virtual estate', so called in contrast to the traditional 'analogue estate'.[5] Thus arises the category of what the American doctrine has baptized as 'digital assets' (or also, 'digital estate'), that is, elements, goods, or digital assets,[6] which in our Spanish literature have been denominated as 'herencia digital' or 'herencia virtual'.[7]

---

electronic record'. This Act governs access to a person's online accounts when the account owner dies or loses the ability to manage the accounts. Furthermore, it extends the power of the fiduciary to manage not only the tangible property but also digital assets (See https://www.uniformlaws.org/viewdocument/final-act-with-comments-40?CommunityKey=f7237fc4-74c2-4728-81c6-b39a91ecdf22&tab=librarydocuments. Accessed 1 April 2023).

[3] Cámara Lapuente (2020a), pp. 57–58.

[4] In many cases there is not an issue related to ownership as licenses of use are applicable.

[5] Navas Navarro (2020), pp. 60–61.

[6] From a general perspective, it comprises any information or file of digital nature stored locally or online. See Santos Morón (2018), p. 416.

[7] Authors have distinguished between 'herencia analógica' (analogue estate) and 'herencia digital' (digital estate). However, it should be noted that this division is artificial when dealing with inheritance law as the so-called 'digital estate' must follow the general succession law rules. In this regard, Article 659 of the Spanish Civil Code states that 'An estate comprises all properties, rights and obligations pertaining to a person, unless they are extinguished as a result of his death'. See Fernández-Bravo Francés (2016), p. 54; Navas Navarro (2020), p. 60; Ginebra Molins (2020),

As can be inferred from the foregoing, in a broad sense, the category of 'digital assets' or 'digital content' is a complex one and, consequently, difficult to conceptualize and systematize.[8] It would include, first, email accounts, web pages, blogs, social network accounts, documents, videos, or photos stored in the cloud, etc.: in essence what we have just referred to as digital contents of a typically non-patrimonial nature, which value is normally sentimental and lacks clear economic significance for the deceased and for those who survive him. Secondly, also included in this non-exhaustive catalogue are other items with a clear economic value, such as music, movies, books or, in a more obvious way, the balance available in certain payment applications or cryptocurrencies, as well as redeemable points obtained in loyalty programs.[9]

In the face of this heterogeneity, a common point emerges: the *mortis causa* transferability of these 'digital assets' (and even at an earlier point in time, their accessibility) is conditioned in most cases by the existence of a binding contractual relationship between the company providing the product or service (e.g., Google, Facebook, Apple, Amazon, etc.), and the person making use of these services or acquiring these products (who has adhered to the terms and conditions that they are usually unaware of). As it could not be otherwise, on many occasions these contracts or agreements of use (typically 'free of charge'[10]) prevent or limit access to the information stored in the service provider's systems, making it impossible or, at least, very difficult to obtain effective knowledge of potential patrimonial contents that may integrate the estate of the deceased person (and even non-patrimonial contents).[11] Closely connected with the problem of accessibility and the need to combine it with the protection of personality rights (typically the right to privacy or

p. 916; Solé Resina (2018), pp. 421–422; Otero Crespo (2019), p. 103; Otero Crespo (2021), p. 375. However, it has been suggested that there might be nuances in the light of the peculiarities of certain digital goods and services, in order to protect other interests in addition to those of the deceased (secrecy of one's own and third parties' communications, the contours of the defence of the deceased's memory, intellectual property of third parties, etc.). See Cámara Lapuente (2019), p. 411.

[8] Otero Crespo (2019), pp. 92 ff.

[9] According to Navas Navarro, up to nine different legal relationships related to the digital behaviour of the deceased could be considered as part of his or her estate: social networks ('redes sociales'), email accounts ('cuentas e-mail'), online game accounts ('cuentas para juegos online'), accounts to use contents online ('cuentas para usar contenido online'), cloud computing services ('servicios de almacenamiento de datos en la nube'), sharing economy platforms ('plataformas de la economía colaborativa'), forums, blogs and chats ('foros, blogs y chats'), online stores ('tiendas online'), and, online banking services or online payment systems ('banca online' and 'sistemas de pago virtuales'). For further details, Navas Navarro (2020) pp. 63–65.

[10] In some cases, the service is apparently provided free of charge. However, there is always a consideration on the part of the user, which consists of the transfer of certain data to the internet service provider. See, e.g., Santos Morón (2018), p. 416.

[11] Under Spanish law these aspects may be studied in connection with the laws on the protection of consumers and users and the unfair terms regulations. In this regard, some of these contractual terms might be examined from the General Law for the Protection of Consumers and Users ('Real Decreto Legislativo 1/2007, de 16 de noviembre, por el que se aprueba el Texto Refundido de la Ley

secrecy of communications) is, once these are known, their transferability. Its limitation or prohibition contractually established by service providers may clash with the traditional foundations of inheritance law, insofar as it would call into question the universality of the inheritance phenomenon or the very principles on which each system is based.[12]

In short, what happens after the death of the person with these contents or digital patrimonial and non-patrimonial assets will be the subject of our study over the next pages. For this purpose, it should be born in mind that these digital assets comprise both personal or non-patrimonial and patrimonial elements which, from the perspective of personal data protection legislation, could be considered 'personal data'.[13] However, as we shall see, their processing is excluded from the scope of application of the 2018 Spanish *ad hoc* data protection rule (Organic Law 3/2018, of 5 December, on the Protection of Personal Data and Guarantee of Digital Rights), without prejudice to the fact that persons linked to the deceased for family or *de facto* reasons, or their heirs, are allowed to request access to the data, their rectification or deletion, where appropriate, in accordance with the directions provided by the deceased (article 3). Furthermore, and connected to the inheritance law aspects, the Organic Law 3/2018 refers also to the 'Right to a digital will' (article 96). Additionally, the regional Catalonian legislator, prior to the Spanish, had passed a Law on digital wills in 2017 (Law 10/2017, of 27 June, on digital wills and amending the Second and Fourth Books of the Catalonian Civil Code).

2 The General Data Protection Regulation of 2016 and the Spanish Organic Law 3/2018, of 5 December, on the Protection of Personal Data and Guarantee of Digital Rights

As is well known, Regulation (EU) 2016/679 of the European Parliament and of the Council of 27 April 2016 on the protection of individuals with regard to the processing of personal data and on the free movement of such data and repealing Directive 95/46/EC (General Data Protection Regulation, hereinafter GDPR) assumed among its objectives to lay down rules on the protection of individuals

---

General para la Defensa de los Consumidores y Usuarios y otras leyes complementarias') perspective and considered as unfair terms. For further details, Navas Navarro (2020), pp. 68 ff.

[12] One outstanding European example of this is the German Supreme Court's decision of 2018 (BGH 12.7.2018, Case III ZR 183/17) where the Court held that social network accounts, like most contractual positions, pass to the heirs (in the case, the parents of a 15-year-old girl who has died as a result of a subway accident in Berlin, probably committing suicide). The BGH considered that the principle of universal succession must prevail. See Resta (2018), pp. 201–204; Cámara Lapuente (2019), pp. 379–381; Patti and Bartolini (2019), p. 1183.

[13] Navas Navarro (2020), pp. 66–67.

with regard to the processing of personal data and rules on the free movement of such data. However, it excludes from its scope the protection of personal data of deceased persons, without prejudice to the possibility for Member States to adopt their own rules.[14] In the light of this wording, some Member States have established rules encouraging the protection of the data of deceased persons. For example, legitimising the heirs or other subjects to exercise the data subject's rights upon death (Italy), or empowering the heirs to request the data controller to update the data in order to reflect the death of the data subject (France).[15]

In the case of Spain, the entry into force of the GDPR imposed the need to review and adapt Organic Law 15/1999, of 13 December, on the Protection of Personal Data. And the result of this work of revision and adaptation to the European regulation is Organic Law 3/2018, of 5 December, on the Protection of Personal Data and Guarantee of Digital Rights (hereinafter OLPPDGDR).

According to its first article, the OLPPDGDR is intended to adapt the Spanish legal system to the GDPR, to complete its provisions and to guarantee the digital rights of citizens, all in accordance with the provisions of article 18.4 of the Spanish Constitution.[16] As is the case with the European instrument, it does not generally focus on the data of deceased persons, excluding them—albeit with a nuance—from its scope (article 2.2c) OLPPDGDR) and with the exception of two theoretically coordinated provisions, articles 3 and 96, whose content and scope is analysed in the next sections.[17]

2.1 *Article 3 OLPPDGDR: The Processing of the Data of Deceased Persons*

Firstly, article 3 OLPPDGDR provides a right of access and, where appropriate, of rectification or erasure of data in favour of 'persons related to the deceased for family

[14] 'This Regulation does not apply to the personal data of deceased persons. Member States may provide for rules regarding the processing of personal data of deceased persons' (Recital n. 27 GDPR). See also Recitals n. 158 and n. 160. It has been argued that the margin of freedom inferred from Recital n. 27 GDPR is high, since national legislators may or not may apply data protection to deceased persons. And in the affirmative case, they could decide whether to establish their own specific legal regime or, on the contrary, to extend all or part of the rules of the general legal regime applicable to the data protection of living persons. See Minero Alejandre (2018), pp. 159–160.

[15] See Resta (2019), p. 97.

[16] Article 18 of the Spanish Constitution regulates a fundamental right on the right to intimacy and the inviolability of the home. Its paragraph 4 states that 'The law shall limit the use of data processing in order to guarantee the honour and personal and family privacy of citizens and the full exercise of their rights'.

[17] A (previous) version of Sects. 2 and 3 is published in Otero Crespo (2019), pp. 112 ff.

or *de facto* reasons as well as their heirs'.[18] Paragraph 1 states that these persons (or groups of persons) may contact the controller or processor, unless the deceased has expressly prohibited it, or a law so provides. However, 'such prohibition shall not affect the right of the heirs to access the data related to the deceased's estate'. The wording of the first paragraph raises several controversial issues.

(1) The Spanish legislator makes no mention to the extent or degree of the relationship (kinship or factual), so that the list of persons potentially entitled to proceed accordingly could be dangerously high. This wide scope seems to respond to the fact that such intervention is not based on the hereditary succession—legatees are not explicitly mentioned, as we will resume in our reflections on article 96 OLPPDGDR[19]—so that it is not personalised in those called to the inheritance, but on the need to protect the (virtual) *memoria defuncti.*[20] Additionally, the provision does not address the potential conflicts in the event of the concurrence of several legitimated parties. The issue is not trivial, because these entitled parties may raise identical claims (e.g., rectification) or incompatible requests (e.g., two entitled parties request in a contradictory manner one the rectification and the other the erasure of data). In this point, the Spanish legislator has omitted or distanced itself from the order established in the early eighties by the Organic Law 1/1982 on Civil Protection of the right to honour, personal and family privacy and one's own image,[21] so it seems that in the absence of such priority and agreement between those who claim to have standing, it would be for a third party (e.g., Courts, arbitrators, etc.) to settle the dispute. In the absence of a clear criterion (and always bearing in

[18]The regulation of data protection of deceased persons is considered to be one of the major novelties introduced by the new OLPPDGDR. See Plaza Penadés (2018), p. 1.

[19]In this regard, there is a clear lack of coherence or coordination between the two branches of law which are at stake: succession law and data protection law.

[20]Otero Crespo (2020), pp. 1–2.

[21]Article 4 of the Organic Law 1/1982 (amended in 2010) states that: 'One. The exercise of civil actions for the civil protection of the honour, privacy or image of a deceased person shall be the responsibility of the person designated for this purpose in the will. The designation may fall on a legal entity.

Two. If there is no designation or if the designated person has died, the spouse, descendants, ascendants, and siblings of the person concerned who were alive at the time of his or her death shall be entitled to seek protection.

Three. In the absence of all of them, the exercise of the actions for protection shall be the responsibility of the Public Prosecutor's Office, which may act *ex officio* at the request of the interested party, provided that no more than 80 years have elapsed since the death of the person concerned. The same time limit shall be observed when the exercise of the aforementioned actions corresponds to a legal person designated in a will.

Four. In cases of unlawful interference with the rights of the victims of a crime as referred to in Article 7(8), the injured party or person harmed by the crime committed, whether or not they have brought a criminal or civil action in the preceding criminal proceedings, shall be entitled to exercise the actions for protection. The Public Prosecutor's Office shall also have standing in all cases. In the event of death, the provisions of the previous sections shall apply'. On the legal standing foreseen in this article 4, see Minero Alejandre (2018), pp. 91 ff; Gutiérrez Santiago (2016), pp. 216 ff.; Ammerman Yebra (2021), pp. 174–176.

mind that these are cases where no express designation has been made by the deceased), we would advocate for the analogical application of the rule established in paragraph 2 of article 4 Organic Law 1/1982, which contains a 'cascading list' of subjects entitled to file civil actions for the civil protection of the honour, privacy or image of a deceased person against offences committed after his or her death.[22] The underlying reason is that the philosophy of article 3 OLPPDGDR is to protect the digital fingerprint of the deceased, which might be understood as the transposition to the digital sphere of the protection of the *memoria defuncti* foreseen in the Organic Law 1/1982.[23] Should our proposal be accepted, the spouse (or person linked by an analogous relationship of affectivity, applying article 3 of the Spanish Civil Code), descendants, ascendants and siblings of the deceased would be entitled to seek protection.[24] In this group of subjects, both family reasons (or *de facto*) and the condition of heirs may concur.

(2) Similarly, no light is shed on the exception concerning the express prohibition on the part of the deceased. In the absence of formal requirements, the question arises as to the validity of oral statements, which are certainly not advisable given the difficulty of proving them; also disputable is the case of express statements recorded in documents that are contradictory in their content.[25] It seems necessary to wait for the implementation of the register provided for in the OLPPDGDR,[26] although it is not expressly mentioned in this first paragraph, to find out whether the opposition on the part of the deceased must be formulated in accordance with some kind of *ad solemnitatem* requirement (not necessary by law).

(3) But undoubtedly, the part of the provision that most attracts our attention is the last clause of the first paragraph: 'Such prohibition shall not affect the right of the heirs to access the data related to the deceased's estate'.[27] This wording has several drawbacks. Thus, in the first place, although the legislator's intention is laudable in that it seems to recognise the dichotomy between content—or data—of an extra-patrimonial nature and of patrimonial significance, it is no less so that it would be

[22] However, the protection granted in the area of *post-mortem* data protection does not concern defence actions against unlawful intrusions by third parties, but the availability of the deceased's personal data to the persons entitled to do so, including the right of access. See Cámara Lapuente (2020a), p. 60.

[23] On legal standing, Cámara Lapuente seems to disagree with the similarities between the Organic Law 1/1982 and the OLPPDGDR (and even article 18 of the Law 41/2002, of 14 November, regulating patient autonomy and rights and obligations regarding clinical information and documentation). For instance, the legal interests protected are very different in the three laws: in the Organic Law 1/1982, the broad legal standing is justified in the defence against violations of the right to privacy, honour or image of the deceased; in the access to the clinical history, contents that could be accessed are very restricted and there must be some justification related to health risks; and finally, accessing the social network accounts of the deceased has nothing to do with the previous laws. See Cámara Lapuente (2019), pp. 424–425.

[24] In the absence of all of them, see Article 4 paragraph 3 of the Organic Law 1/1982 above.

[25] The express prohibition could be included in a will.

[26] In early 2023, this Register has not been set up yet.

[27] Again, legatees are out of the picture.

very difficult to know *a priori* whether there is patrimonial content behind the deceased person's data. It would be easier if there is a will, or a manifestation externalised in another way by the deceased in which this information is revealed. If this does not exist, it seems unlikely that it would be known by those entitled under the OLPPDGDR. As a logical derivation, it could not be ruled out either that these patrimonial contents end up disappearing or becoming very difficult to trace or identify, especially if one of the entitled parties requests the erasure of the digital fingerprint and the provider proceeds to complete the request. We could even be faced with a case of liability of the provider *vis-à-vis* the heirs—and even legatees when the asset or right that is bequeathed is linked to the deceased's digital assets. This would happen if, for example, they comply with the demand of one of the entitled parties (not the specific heirs—nor legatees) by cancelling the data, and it subsequently becomes known that among those data there were some revealing information on patrimonial content, access to which would no longer be possible.[28]

Secondly, but no less relevant, the will of the deceased prohibiting access could lack *post-mortem* effectiveness. Once again, the wording of the provision would allow access to the heirs simply by arguing the existence of potential contents (or data) with patrimonial relevance. The rule does not require even the slightest indication of proof to render inoperative any provision of the deceased vetoing access to his or her data.

Moreover, the wording of the remaining paragraphs of article 3 OLPPDGDR is not exempt from criticism either. In this regard, paragraph 2 provides that 'the persons or institutions that the deceased had expressly designated for this purpose may also request, in accordance with the instructions received, access to the deceased's personal data and, where appropriate, their rectification or erasure'. The provisions contained in the previous paragraph are replicated with respect to the rights of access, rectification, or erasure, always following the mandate of the *de cuius*. However, no reference is made to the right of the heirs to access the data of the deceased's estate. Even so, we understand that this right remains untouched, as it would make no sense to allow it in the cases of the first paragraph and not in those of the second.

The last clause of the paragraph adds that 'a Royal Decree shall establish the requirements and conditions for accrediting the validity and effectiveness of these mandates and instructions and, where appropriate, their registration'. As noted above, in this case there is a reference to a future regulation in charge of establishing these 'mandates and instructions'.

Finally, the provision closes with two references to the death of minors or persons with disabilities. Thus, 'In the event of the death of minors, these powers may also be exercised by their legal representatives or, within the framework of their

[28] A different case may occur if the heir does not exercise the action of petition for inheritance, which is subject to the limitation period of 30 years *ex* art. 1963 of the Spanish Civil Code, within a reasonable time after the death of the deceased and the assets are lost (the doctrine of unfair delay might be applicable).

competences, by the Public Prosecutor's Office, which may act *ex officio* or at the request of any interested natural or legal person'. It seems that in the case of minors, we could not ignore the fact that in most cases they would be minors of a certain age, since the terms of access to goods and services require minimum ages. Theoretically, such minors, depending on their degree of maturity, could have expressed their will *post-mortem,*[29] but it seems that it would be common for the powers before the service providers to be exercised by their legal representatives or by the Public Prosecutor's Office, acting *ex officio* or at the request of any interested party.[30]

In the case of the death of persons with disabilities, these powers may also be exercised, 'in addition to those mentioned in the previous paragraph, by those who have been designated for the exercise of support functions, if such powers are understood to be included in the support measures provided by the designated person'. At the time of passing out the OLPPDGDR, the Spanish legislator was updated on this point, following the path set by the Draft Bill for the reform of the Spanish Civil Code on disability, aimed at adapting Spanish law to the requirements of the UN Convention on the matter. This Draft Bill has led to the Law 8/2021, of 2 June, which reforms civil and procedural legislation to support people with disabilities in the exercise of their legal capacity.[31]

Lastly, the systematic organisation of the provision is not free from criticism. From our point of view, it would have been more appropriate to provide, firstly, for the autonomy of will and, secondly, to insert the rule applicable in the alternative (in the absence of instructions, the list of persons entitled to act *vis-à-vis* service providers).

2.2 *Article 96 OLPPDGDR: The Normative Enshrinement of the 'Right to a Digital Will'*

Apart from the regulation on the personal data of deceased persons, article 96 OLPPDGDR—entitled 'Right to a digital will'—is found in another section,

[29] Under the application of the rules contained in the Spanish Civil Code, minors, from the age of fourteen, may make a will, except for a holographic will (See articles 663 and 688 of the Spanish Civil Code).

[30] See Bastante Granell (2022), pp. 118 ff.

[31] On 3 September 2021, Law 8/2021 reforming civil and procedural legislation to support people with disabilities entered into force. See García Rubio (2021), *passim*.

referring to the Guarantee of Digital Rights (Title X).[32] This is not a right in the technical sense, and its virtuality is reduced to a merely pedagogical function,[33] insofar as a legal instrument acknowledges the possibility for subjects to decide on the destiny of digital content. Not only does the legislator err in considering it as a 'right' but is also mistaken in the use of the term 'digital will', which is totally non-technical.[34]

What the provision enshrines is a right of access, not to the personal data for which its counterpart, article 3 OLPPDGDR, is responsible, but to the content managed by the providers of information society services. This right could be exercised because it has been provided for by the deceased, by means of a positive choice or, failing that, by the rules established in a supplementary capacity. Furthermore, it establishes which actions could be carried out by the entitled parties on the social networks or equivalent services, how the possible mandates and instructions would be materially and formally implemented, and what the coexistence regime would be between this rule and possible provisions passed by Spanish Autonomous Communities.[35]

(I) The right of access to contents

The first paragraph of article 96 OLPPDGDR establishes that all access to content managed by information society service providers about deceased persons shall be governed by the following rules.

Firstly, 'persons related to the deceased by family or *de facto* reasons, as well as their heirs, may contact the information society service providers in order to access said content and give them the instructions they deem appropriate regarding its use, destination or deletion'. However, 'As an exception, the aforementioned persons may not access the content of the deceased, nor request its modification or deletion, when the deceased person has expressly prohibited it or when so established by law. This prohibition shall not affect the right of the heirs to access the contents that may form part of the estate'.

[32]The Spanish literature has been critical on the regulation of the guarantees of digital rights in Organic Law 3/2018, considering that a more intense and calm reflection would have been necessary. See Piñar Mañas (2019), pp. 1 and 8–11. The author also states that a specific regulation of fundamental rights in the digital society would be more appropriate than a Title of a Law. It should be remembered that this regulation on the digital will was incorporated into the text of the Organic Law by way of an amendment presented in Congress during the processing of its Draft.

[33]E.g., Otero Crespo (2021), pp. 373–374; Cerrillo i Martínez (2021) p. 4331.

[34]Otero Crespo (2021), pp. 369 ff. However, other authors are less critical and value positively the regulation of the right to a digital will, considering that it establishes a series of 'clear and precise rules of conduct for cases that until now lacked them, despite the defects observed in the parliamentary processing of the Law'—author's own translation—(González García 2018, p. 5).

[35]The Spanish Constitution establishes a division of regulatory powers between the State and the Autonomous Communities ('Comunidades Autónomas'). In general terms, this means that, depending on the legal sphere, we could find Autonomous Community and State regulations. This distribution of competences is contained in articles 148 and 149 of the Spanish Constitution. In addition, we must pay attention to the assumption of competences according to the different Statutes of Autonomy ('Estatutos de Autonomía').

Without prejudice to the criticisms made of certain paragraphs of article 3, which are identical in article 96 OLPPDGDR, the general rule would be that of access to digital content by 'third parties'—legatees are not expressly mentioned again, and some of them might have a direct interest if the legacy left in the will is related to the 'digital inheritance'[36]-, unless there is explicit opposition from the deceased. To a certain extent, the expected rule is reversed, with the right of access by relatives, related persons and heirs prevailing over the right to protection of the privacy of the person and those with whom he or she has communicated digitally. The explanation could be found, albeit with nuances, in the doctrine of the Spanish Data Protection Agency ('Agencia Española de Protección de Datos', hereinafter AEPD) referring to Organic Law 15/1999, of 13 of December, on the Protection of Personal Data. In this sense, regarding the right of access to data (not content) of deceased persons, the AEPD has—on many occasions—recognised the right of access by relatives in order to protect the memory of the deceased. In this sense, 'it would be possible for the heirs to have access to the data of the deceased provided that they are directly related to their own status as heirs (for example, access to the data necessary to know the estate or the state of certain assets of the inheritance). However, the access to information to which we refer could not be understood as related to the right of access enshrined in the legislation on the protection of personal data, but would be derived from the right of all heirs to know the estate and the state of the same, as well as to carry out the necessary actions for its determination and defence, given that the heir succeeds the deceased in all his rights and obligations as a consequence of his death, as determined in articles 651, 659 and 661 of the Civil Code'.[37] It would therefore be a right of access linked to the field of succession, but not to that established by the legislation on personal data, showing (once more) the clear disconnection between the recent regulations on the protection of personal data and the fundamentals of succession law.

In any case, we consider—and have defended elsewhere[38]—that an unlimited right of access could never be granted, as it may collide with other fundamental rights such as the right to privacy, not only of the deceased person—extinguished with the end of the personality—but also of other subjects, potentially together with the right to secrecy of communications.[39] As a result of the concurrence of these

[36] It has been sustained that the legatees should be considered included as well. See Navas Navarro (2020), p. 77. However, the exclusion might be related to the position of the heir, who is the person replacing the deceased on a universal basis.

[37] See Report 63/2016 ('Informe 63/2016') and Report 010601/2019 ('Informe 010601/2019') of the AEPD, p. 25.

[38] Otero Crespo (2019), p. 121.

[39] The secrecy of communications is a fundamental right also foreseen in Article 18 of the Spanish Constitution. According to its paragraph 3, 'Secrecy of communications is guaranteed, particularly of postal, telegraphic and telephonic communications, except in the event of a court order to the contrary'. However, this right to secrecy of communications applies while the process of communication is taking place (See Spanish Supreme Court judgements, Criminal Chamber, 342/2013, of 17 April and 786/2015, of 4 December). Once the message has reached the receiver, we leave the

rights, it is very difficult to know to what extent it is proportionate to provide a generalised right of access. The correct option would be the costliest one: a case-by-case assessment in which a tailor-made solution would be found. Respect for these fundamental rights would be weighed against safeguarding the heirs' (and even legatees) right to know whether there are assets that could be included in the estate, a fact that is also of interest to potential creditors or to the tax authorities. However, if we examine again this power legally granted to the heirs, i.e., their right to know the contents that may be included in the estate, it seems that the letter of the law sweeps aside any respect for other rights of a fundamental nature.

Moving forward in our criticisms of the provision, nothing is laid down about how the opposition/ prohibition of access is to be instrumented, and even less about who is responsible for proving its existence, leaving it to a future regulatory development to establish 'the requirements and conditions for accrediting the validity and effectiveness of the mandates and instructions and, where appropriate, their registration' (art. 96.3 OLPPDGDR). In practice, over the last few years, most internet service providers have started to allow users to declare their preferences and to decide about the *post-mortem* destiny of their digital assets during their lifetime. However, the awareness of these options offered by the service providers, as well as their effective use, could still be qualified as quite residual.

Secondly, art. 96 OLPPDGDR legitimises 'the executor of the will and any person or institution that the deceased has expressly designated for this purpose may also request, in accordance with the instructions received, access to the contents in order to comply with such instructions'. For this to be the case, there must have already been an express action by the deceased during his or her lifetime, in the sense of establishing guidelines for the executor or of the natural or legal person selected by himself or herself. The only disadvantage that could arise would be that of the previous disappearance of those expressly called upon to execute these digital wills, because the natural person has died or has lost the autonomy to do so, or the legal person has been extinguished. It would then be possible to consider the subrogation of the heirs in the absence of the previous ones. Furthermore, when a designated natural or legal person acts, it should be noted that this third party must refrain from executing wills that, although established by the deceased, may be harmful to the interests of the heir(s) or legatee(s). In this regard, it would be possible that a

scope of article 18.3 of the Spanish Constitution, without prejudice, where appropriate, to the right to privacy proclaimed in paragraph 1 of the same provision (See Supreme Court judgement, Criminal Chamber, 864/2015, of 10 December). Considering these restrictions, the right to secrecy of communications would be remotely put into question.

mandate to suppress the content affects the inherited estate. Therefore, this third party could not execute wills that are contrary to the legal system.[40]

Thirdly, and like article 3 OLPPDGDR, the provision refers to cases of death of minors or disabled persons. For the first of these cases, the powers described in the previous paragraphs may also be exercised 'by their legal representatives or, within the framework of its powers, by the Public Prosecutor's Office, which may act *ex officio* or at the request of any interested natural or legal person'.[41] For the second, 'in the event of the death of persons with disabilities, these powers may also be exercised, in addition to those mentioned in the previous paragraph, by those who have been designated to exercise support functions if such powers are understood to be included in the support measures provided by the designated person'.

(II) The actions that the entitled persons may carry out on the social networks or equivalent services and the formal and material requirements that the instructions or directions of the deceased must comply with.

Paragraph 2 of article 96 OLPPDGDR insists on the need to heed the instructions or directions of the deceased, and only in the absence of such instructions, 'the persons entitled in the previous paragraph may decide on the maintenance or deletion of the personal profiles of deceased persons on social networks or equivalent services'. In these circumstances, 'the person responsible for the service who is notified, in accordance with the previous paragraph, of the request to delete the profile, must proceed without delay to do so', without establishing a maximum period for action or the need for reliable notification of such a fact. The question also arises as to what would happen should the deceased have left contradictory instructions. Although paragraph 3 states that a Royal decree shall establish the requirements and conditions for recognizing the validity and effectiveness of the mandates and instructions, as well as, where appropriate, their registration, the fact is that we are still left with this regulatory lacuna. This Royal decree should shed light on some controversial questions, easily imaginable in the event of disagreement: Should the will expressed and recorded in this possible register or the dispositions of the will prevail? Or the option selected by the service provider? Or should the clauses established by the service provider be ineffective if the deceased has opted to express his will through this register or in the will?

(III) The coexistence between state and (potential) autonomous regulations

Article 96 OLPPDGDR ends with a rather ill-advisedly worded paragraph 4 specifying that 'the provisions of this article in relation to persons deceased in the Autonomous Communities with their own civil, foral or special law shall be governed by the provisions of the latter within their scope of application'. The legislator is wrong in connecting the application of autonomous civil law with passing away in such territories. As far as personal status is concerned, regional

[40] See, with reference to the executor, Article 901 of the Spanish Civil Code ('The executors shall have all the powers expressly conferred on them by the testator and which are not contrary to the law').

[41] Again, Bastante Granell (2022), pp. 118 ff.

status ('vecindad civil') is the determining factor for the application of ordinary law or regional ('special or foral') civil law. This is governed by article 14 of the Spanish Civil Code, the place of death of the deceased being irrelevant. Therefore, it seems that the legislator should have referred to 'deceased persons with regional status in an Autonomous Community with its own civil law'. On the other hand, the regulatory capacity of the Autonomous Communities with their own law is indirectly recognised, although in the Catalonian case their competence to regulate certain aspects has been attacked, as discussed in the following section.[42]

3 Law 10/2017, of 27 June, on Digital Wills and Amending the Second and Fourth Books of the Catalonian Civil Code

More than a year before the approval of Organic Law 3/2018, the Catalonian legislator undertook the first specific regulation in the Spanish legal sphere, with Law 10/2017, of 27 June, on digital wills and amending the Catalonian Civil Code (hereinafter CCCat).[43] The Catalonian lawmaker was thus at the forefront of the Spanish State insofar as it crystallised an *ad hoc* regulation, admitting, even indirectly, that existing positive law was not in a position to provide a response to these new realities.[44]

This Law, issued under the civil law competence of article 129 of the Catalonian Statute of Autonomy, amends Book II, relating to the person and the family, and Book IV, relating to inheritance. The Law also regulated digital wills in the event of death and 'supervening loss of capacity' and included a reference to minors/persons under guardianship.

Certain articles were the subject to an action of unconstitutionality ('recurso de inconstitucionalidad'), decided by Judgement of the Plenary of the Constitutional Court 7/2019 of 17 January of 2019.[45] This ruling declared the unconstitutionality and nullity of a series of provisions, affecting articles 6, 8, 10, 11 and the first final provision of the Law 10/2017. In this regard, the Constitutional Court endorsed the

42 Otero Crespo (2019), pp. 124–125; Otero Crespo (2020), p. 8.

43 Ginebra Molins (2020), pp. 919 ff.

44 The Preliminary Draft of the Law in its Preamble stated that 'the current legislation on inheritance does not provide an answer to these questions'—author's own translation—(Ruda González 2017, pp. 227–230), in which the author reflects on the need or otherwise for the Catalonian regulation when it was still at the preliminary draft stage). However, it has also been considered a 'marketing law' or one that fulfils a pedagogical function (Ginebra Molins 2020, p. 916).

45 Decision available at https://www.boe.es/buscar/doc.php?id=BOE-A-2019-2033. Accessed 1 April 2023.

theory of the invasion of powers already 'suggested' by the Opinion of the Council of State of 21 September 2017.[46]

In accordance with the regulation in force after the ruling of the Highest Constitutional interpreter, it is possible to manage the digital footprint for cases of death through clauses that are inserted in a will, in a codicil or in testamentary memoirs (with the option of using a document that could be registered in the electronic register of digital wills having been erased from the Catalonian legal system). Through the expression of these digital wills, the heir,[47] the universal executor or the designated person would act before the digital service providers with whom the deceased had active accounts (article 411-10, paragraph 1 CCCat).

The content and scope of the assignment to be undertaken by any of these three 'executors' is limited to a series of options, the exercise of which may be all-encompassing or limited to a specific action. Namely: '(a) To notify digital service providers of his/her death; (b) To request digital service providers to cancel his/her active accounts; (c) To request digital service providers to execute the contractual clauses or to activate the policies established for cases of death of active account holders and, if applicable, to provide them with a copy of the digital files on their servers'.

Following the declaration of unconstitutionality of paragraph 3(b), which provided for the possibility of recording these digital wills in an *ad hoc* document to be entered in the Register created for this purpose, it seems that paragraph 4 of the provision has been left orphaned in terms of systematic interpretation. It provides that 'the document of digital wills may be amended and revoked at any time and has no effect if there are last will provisions'. It is evident that a document containing a digital will could be amended and revoked at any time. What does not make sense is the addition of 'and has no effect if there are last will provisions', because after the ruling of the Constitutional Court and the declaration of nullity of paragraph 3 (b), such wills must necessarily be expressed in wills, memoirs, or codicils, in other words, in last will instruments.

In the absence of the expression of such digital wills, 'the heir or the universal executor, if applicable, may execute the actions of letters a, b and c of paragraph 2 in accordance with the contracts that the deceased has entered into with the digital service providers or in accordance with the policies that these providers have in force'. In this sense, the Catalonian legislator does not incur in the vagueness of the State lawmaker in establishing who the potential applicants against the service providers are; at the same time, it shows respect for the terms of the contracts concluded between such service providers and the deceased.

The regional legislator also expresses its views on access to the contents of digital accounts and files. In this case, the default rule is that of non-access unless the deceased has established otherwise in his or her digital wills. In any event, it

[46] 'Dictamen del Consejo de Estado de 21 de septiembre de 2017', available at https://www.boe.es/buscar/doc.php?id=CE-D-2017-725. Accessed 1 April 2023.

[47] The Catalonian regulation also omits the reference to the legatee.

provides for recourse to the courts for the corresponding judicial authorisation to be granted. We assume that such authorisations would be granted in cases where, among others, there is a suspicion of the existence of digital assets with patrimonial content or even, as has happened in the comparative sphere, where there are indications that behind this digital fingerprint there may be information potentially shedding light on the causes of death (for example, because there are suspicions of suicide or help those closest to the deceased to find out the last letters written by the person who dies in combat).[48]

The article closes with a paragraph 7 establishing that, unless the deceased has provided otherwise, the expenses arising from the execution of the digital wills shall be borne by the estate ('activo hereditario'). Consequently, and again in the absence of an express statement to the contrary, they form part of the liabilities as inheritance expenses, as they arise due to the death of the deceased and as an automatic reaction to the opening of succession.

Finally, the Catalonian legislator also allows the determination of digital wills in anticipation of a supervening loss of capacity. It does so in the area of 'preventive powers' in Book II of the CCCat relating to the person and the family. In line with the provisions on succession, the principal, when he or she has full capacity, may organise his or her digital wills in the event of a 'supervening loss of capacity'.

4 The Spanish Digital Rights Charter

Together with the OLPPDGDR and the CCCat, a final reference should be made to the Digital Rights Charter, made public in July 2021.[49] The drafting of the Digital Rights Charter followed a participatory process, including contributions from experts in the digital rights field and advocacy associations, as well as from private citizens, together with input from the private sector, service providers, and the public

[48] One of the most media-acclaimed was that of Marine Justin Ellsworth, who died at the age of 20 in a bombing in Fallujah, Iraq, in November 2004. His father, John Ellsworth, launched a legal battle against Yahoo to gain access to his son's emails. Finally, despite the company's opposition on privacy grounds, the Oakland County Probate Court in Michigan in 2005 upheld his father's claims, forcing Yahoo to turn over the contents of Justin's email account to him. Yahoo complied with the decision by delivering the emails on CD (more than 10,000 pages) and indicating that it would also provide them in paper format. See https://www.nbcnews.com/id/wbna7581686. Accessed 1 April 2023.

[49] Available at https://www.lamoncloa.gob.es/presidente/actividades/Documents/2021/140721-Carta_Derechos_Digitales_RedEs.pdf. See also the Portuguese Charter of Human Rights in the Digital Era, approved by Law 27/2021, of 17 May, available at https://dre.pt/dre/legislacao-consolidada/lei/2021-164870244. More recently, the European Declaration on Digital Rights and Principles for the Digital Decade has been adopted (2023/C 23/01), available at https://eur-lex.europa.eu/legal-content/EN/TXT/?uri=OJ:JOC_2023_023_R_0001. Accessed 1 April 2023.

sector with relevant competences in the matter.[50] In its Introductory remarks ('Consideraciones previas'), it is stated that 'The objective of the Charter is descriptive, prospective, and assertive. Descriptive of the digital contexts and scenarios that determine conflicts, sometimes unexpected, between the rights, values, and goods, but which require rethinking; this mere description helps to visualise and become aware of the impact and consequences of digital environments and spaces. Prospective by anticipating future scenarios that can already be predicted. Assertive in the sense of re-validating and legitimising the principles, techniques, and policies that, from the very culture of fundamental rights, should be applied in present and future digital environments and spaces.

The Charter is not normative in nature, but aims to recognise the very new challenges of application and interpretation that the adaptation of rights to the digital environment poses, and to suggest principles and policies relating to them in this context (. . .)'.

In spite of its lack of normative character, the Digital Rights Charter is of utmost importance because it recognizes the so-called 'Right to digital inheritance'[51] under Spanish law ('Derechos de libertad' point VII).

According to its wording, '1. In accordance with the law governing the succession, the right to digital inheritance is recognised in respect of all assets and rights which, in the digital environment, were held by the deceased person.

2. It shall be for the legislature to determine the digital assets and rights of a digital nature that may be the subject of protection, preservation, and memory, as well as the persons called upon, where appropriate, to perform such a function, in the absence of the deceased designation.

3. Legislation shall be encouraged to provide for those cases in which, in view of the rights of the deceased person or of third parties, and in particular the protection of their privacy and the secrecy of their communications, it is appropriate to extinguish the digital assets or to make it inaccessible outside the persons to whom it was distributed or to whom access was allowed, in cases where the deceased has not left an express destination'.

In an admittedly superficial analysis of the provision, the following remarks could be made. Firstly, paragraph 1 is just superfluous insofar as it adds nothing to the inheritance setup, be it analogue or digital; secondly, paragraph 2 contains flawed wording and content as it states that it would be left to the legislator to decide which assets of a digital nature would form part of the inheritance. This could not be the case, precisely because of existing article 659 of the Spanish Civil Code, where the legislature already specifies that the inheritance is made up of all assets, rights and obligations, even if it does not refer to those of a digital nature; thirdly and finally, paragraph 3 shows once again how the *pseudo*-legislator in matters of digital rights is

[50] Additionally, an Expert Group on Digital Rights was established, and two public consultations were carried out, receiving more than 250 contributions. See https://www.lamoncloa.gob.es/lang/en/gobierno/news/Paginas/2021/20210713_rights-charter.aspx. Accessed 1 April 2023.

[51] See Cámara Lapuente (2020b), pp. 5–6; Otero Crespo (2021), pp. 375–376.

unaware of basic issues of inheritance law. Thus, it is established that legislation should be encouraged providing for cases in which, taking into account the rights of the deceased or third parties, and in particular the protection of their privacy and the secrecy of their communications, it is appropriate to extinguish the digital assets or to prevent its accessibility outside the persons to whom it was distributed or to whom it was made accessible. It seems peculiar that any prospective law could advocate for the destruction of digital assets which are part of the inheritance, irrespectively of the protection of fundamental rights such as privacy and, to a lesser extent, the secrecy of communications.[52]

5 Conclusion

Over the last few years there has been a growing concern in the Spanish academia on the issue of *post-mortem* protection of personal data and the so-called digital inheritance. As shown, the topic has been subject of attention by the Spanish legislators, both at national and regional levels, passing the Organic Law 3/2018, of 5 December, on the Protection of Personal Data and Guarantee of Digital Rights (specific provisions) and the Law 10/2017, of 27 June, on digital wills and amending the Second and Fourth Books of the Catalonian Civil Code, and even of the 'pre-legislator', with the adoption of the Digital Rights Charter.

However, as detailed above, articles 3 and 96 of the OLPPDGDR are far from providing adequate solutions to the critical issues related to *post-mortem* data protection and succession in digital assets. In this sense, criticisms also apply to the Catalonian regulation.

To sum up, there is sometimes a lack of adequate coordination between succession law and data protection law as the legislators, bearing in mind the digital nature of the assets or goods at stake, seem to forget about basic elements pertaining to inheritance law. From our perspective, a reform on the topic is necessary, in order to offer a coherent solution which takes duly into account the intersection between inheritance law and the protection of personal data (and even contract law—a third element which has been mostly excluded from our picture[53]).

---

[52]See above footnote 39 and the relevant case law of the Spanish Supreme Court (Criminal Chamber) on the secrecy of communications.

[53]It has been argued that the Spanish OLPPDGDR takes an important step forward as it recognises that the will of the individual in the preservation of his or her identity and digital assets prevails over any contractual impositions. See Cámara Lapuente (2019), pp. 384–385.

References

Ammerman Yebra J (2021) El derecho a la propia voz como derecho de la personalidad. Colex, A Coruña

Bastante Granell V (2022) Menor de edad y últimas voluntades digitales. Revista de Derecho Civil IX(4):51–135

Cámara Lapuente S (2019) La sucesión *mortis causa* en el patrimonio digital. Anales de la Academia Matritense del Notariado 59:375–432

Cámara Lapuente S (2020a) ¿Vida (digital) eterna o muerte digna en la nube? La protección de los datos y contenidos digitales de las personas fallecidas. El Cronista del Estado Social y Democrático de Derecho 88-89:56–69

Cámara Lapuente S (2020b) Informe/contribución (20.12.2020), Consulta pública para la elaboración de una "Carta de Derechos Digitales" por parte del Ministerio de Asuntos Económicos y Transformación Digital: 1–13. Available at https://portal.mineco.gob.es/es-es/ministerio/participacionpublica/audienciapublica/Paginas/SEDIA_Carta_Derechos_Digitales.aspx

Cerrillo i Martínez A (2021) Derecho al testamento digital (Comentario al artículo 96 LOPDGDD). In: Troncoso Reigada A (ed) Comentario al Reglamento General de Protección de Datos y a la Ley Orgánica de Protección de Datos Personales y Garantía de los Derechos Digitales, Tomo II. Civitas, Thomson-Reuters, Cizur Menor, pp 4317–4335

Fernández-Bravo Francés L (2016) Testamento, legado, herencia. . . ¿digital? In: Oliva León R et al (eds) Testamento ¿Digital?, Desafíos Legales, Juristas con Futuro, pp 53–55

García Rubio MP (2021) Contenido y significado general de la reforma civil y procesal en materia de discapacidad. Editorial Jurídica SEPIN, Junio, SP/DOCT/114070

Ginebra Molins ME (2020) Voluntades digitales en caso de muerte. Cuadernos de Derecho Transnacional 12(1):908–929. https://doi.org/10.20318/cdt.2020.5229

González García A (2018) El derecho al testamento digital. Tribunal Empresa Familiar, Uría Menéndez: 2–5

Gutiérrez Santiago P (2016) La llamada 'personalidad pretérita': datos personales de las personas fallecidas y protección post mortem de los derechos al honor, intimidad y propia imagen. Actualidad Jurídica Iberoamericana, IDIBE 5:201–238

Minero Alejandre G (2018) La protección post mortem de los derechos al honor, intimidad y propia imagen y la tutela frente al uso de datos de carácter personal tras el fallecimiento. Aranzadi Thomson Reuters, Cizur Menor

Navas Navarro S (2020) Herencia y protección de datos de personas fallecidas. A propósito del mal llamado 'testamento digital'. Revista de Derecho Privado 1:59–88

Otero Crespo M (2019) La sucesión en los 'bienes digitales'. La respuesta plurilegislativa española. Revista de Derecho Civil 6(4):89–133

Otero Crespo M (2020) Las disposiciones *post mortem* sobre el llamado 'patrimonio digital': una primera aproximación desde el sistema plurilegislativo español. Encontro de Investigadores EDUM 2019, Escola de Direito da Universidade do Minho, pp 1–10

Otero Crespo M (2021) El Derecho de sucesiones en clave digital. Algunas consideraciones a propósito del "testamento digital" y de la "herencia digital" en el ámbito del Derecho común. In: Blandino Garrido MA, Cervilla Garzón MD (eds) Declaración de voluntad en un entorno virtual, Aranzadi, pp 367–378

Patti FP, Bartolini F (2019) Digital inheritance and post mortem data protection: the Italian reform. Eur Rev Priv Law 5:1181–1194

Piñar Mañas JL (2019) ¿Qué regulación de los derechos en la sociedad digital? Derecho digital e innovación 1:2

Plaza Penadés J (2018) El Proyecto de la nueva Ley Orgánica de Protección de Datos. Revista Aranzadi de Derecho y Nuevas Tecnologías, núm. 46/2018, BIB 2018\7463

Resta G (2018) Personal data and digital assets after death: a comparative law perspective on the BGH facebook ruling. Journal of European Consumer and Market Law 7(5):201–204

Resta G (2019) La successione nei rapporti digitali e la tutela post-mortale dei dati personali. Contratto e Impresa 1:85–105

Ruda González A (2017) Vida más allá de la muerte (digital). La protección de las voluntades digitales en la reforma del Derecho civil catalán. In: Managing risk in the digital society, 13th international conference on internet, law & politics. UOC, Huygens Editorial, Barcelona, pp 226–239

Santos Morón MJ (2018) La denominada "herencia digital": ¿necesidad de regulación? Estudio de Derecho español y comparado. Cuadernos de Derecho Transnacional 10(1):413–438. https://doi.org/10.20318/cdt.2018.4128

Solé Resina J (2018) Las voluntades digitales: marco normativo actual. Anuario de Derecho Civil LXXI(II):417–440

Marta Otero Crespo is a Senior lecturer in Civil Law at the Universidade de Santiago de Compostela (Spain).

Her main fields of interest involve Civil Law, Tort Law, Contract Law and Comparative Law, taking part in several European and national projects.

Dr. Otero Crespo publications include, amongst others, a monograph, several book chapters and contributions to law journals (especially on topics related to precontractual, contractual and tort liability, consumer protection and collective redress).

The Suitability of the Regime of Technological Measures for Copyright Protection in the Face of Modern Cybersecurity Risks

Pedro Dias Venâncio

Abstract Technological protection measures (TPM) are Information and Communication Technologies (ICT) applications, devices or other technologies used to block, limit or perform any sort of control to the access to certain protected works or performances made available digitally. They represent a way for holders of copyright and related rights to control the economic exploitation of their works in the digital environment. Given the risks posed by the Information Society to unauthorised access, sharing and use of protected works and performances, TPM's play a central role in protecting the interests of the holders of these rights. The international protection of TPM's was initially recognised in the 1996 WIPO International Treaties on Copyright and on Performances and Phonograms. Later in Section 1201 of the Digital Millennium Act of 1998 in the US. And finally, in Article 6 of Directive 2001/29/EC of the European Parliament and of the Council of 22 May 2001, it has been made compulsory for the member states of the European Union to implement it. This directive was transposed by Portugal through Law No. 50/2004 of 24 August 2004. In this chapter we analyse the provision made in EU law on TPM's (in Sect. 2) and their transposition into Portuguese law (in Sect. 3). In Sect. 4 we analyse the risks that the digitalisation of works and performances pose to their protection, and in Sect. 5 we present our conclusions on the adequacy of the legal regime established for the protection of TPM's as a legal mechanism that seeks to reconcile the exclusive ownership of copyright owners and related rights with citizens' rights of access to education, culture and information.

P. D. Venâncio (✉)
Escola de Direito da Universidade do Minho, JusGOV, Braga, Portugal
e-mail: pdv@pdv.pt

F. A. Carneiro Pacheco de Andrade et al. (eds.), *Legal Developments on Cybersecurity and Related Fields*, Law, Governance and Technology Series 60,
https://doi.org/10.1007/978-3-031-41820-4_11

1 Introduction

According to a common definition, "Technological protection measures (TPM) encompass software, devices or other technologies used to block or limit access to a work, or certain actions with respect to the work (e.g., copying). TPMs include such things as encryption, passwords, and access controls".[1]

In 2008, Oliveira Ascensão already envisaged that these measures could serve four distinct purposes:

> (a) measures to control access to works or performances, aimed, for example, at providing it only in return for a payment;
> (b) measures which prevent or restrict certain uses of such works or subject-matter, for example, the printing of text or reproduction in digital form;
> (c) measures aimed at preserving the integrity of such works or subject-matter by preventing their modification; and
> (d) measures which enable the number or duration of uses made to be controlled, thereby facilitating the economic exploitation of such works or performances.[2]

With the development of Information and Communication Technologies (ICT), as well as of digital exploitation models of works and services, it is easy to foresee a multiplicity of new "functions" that these technological protection measures may cover. Imagine, for example, limiting access (or price) according to the user's geo-referencing.

The legal protection against the circumvention of technological protection measures, "so-called third layer of protection of digital works",[3] was introduced at the international level through the WCT and the WIPO Performances and Phonograms Treaty, both adopted on December 20, 1996.

In the United States the DMCA was signed into law on October 28, 1998. In Title I, it implemented the WIPO Treaties of 1996—the WCT and the WIPO Performances and Phonograms Treaty—and created the new Chapter 12 of Title 17 of the U.S.C. § 1201 that implements the international treaties by protecting technological measures against circumvention.

And finally, Article 6 of Directive 2001/29/EC of the European Parliament and of the Council of 22 May 2001, on the harmonisation of certain aspects of copyright and related rights in the information society, makes compulsory for the member states of the European Union to implement legal protection against the circumvention of technological protection measures.

It is in the sequence of the latter that Portugal introduced this protection into national law, through Law No. 50/2004 of 24 August 2004, which added to the Copyright and Neighbouring Rights Code a Title VI under the epigraph "Protection

[1] https://itlaw.wikia.org/wiki/Technological_protection_measures, accessed on 17 October 2021.

[2] Ascensão (2008), p. 500.

[3] Gasser (2006), p. 43.

of technological measures and of information for the electronic management of rights".[4]

On the following sections we will start analysing the provision made by EU law on TPM's (Sect. 2) and their transposition into Portuguese law (Sect. 3). We will pay attention both to the purposes that these diplomas aim to satisfy and to the provisions adopted and their different solutions (between the European directive and Portuguese law).

In Sect. 4 we analyse the risks that the digitalisation of works and performances pose to their protection, and we conclude in Sect. 5 by presenting our findings on the adequacy of the legal regime established for the protection of TPM's as a legal mechanism that seeks to reconcile the exclusive ownership of copyright owners and related rights with citizens' rights of access to education, culture and information.

2 The European Union Directive on Technological Protection Measures

For the correct interpretation of the treatment of technological protection measures under Portuguese national law, it is essential to understand the purposes and obligations resulting from Directive 2001/29/EC for Member States.

Directive 2001/29/EC aims the harmonisation of certain aspects of copyright and related rights in the information society. It is a dense legal text with sixty-one recitals, setting out the aims of the European legislator. And, despite containing only fifteen articles, it deals with central issues of copyright protection in the European Union. We will not address all the matters dealt with in this Directive, focusing on its article 6, which deals with TPM's issues.

In relation to technological protection measures, the Directive foresees in its recital 47 that "Technological development will allow right holders to make use of technological measures designed to prevent or restrict acts not authorised by the right holders of any copyright, rights related to copyright or the sui generis right in databases. The danger, however, exists those illegal activities might be carried out to enable or facilitate the circumvention of the technical protection provided by these measures. In order to avoid fragmented legal approaches that could potentially hinder the functioning of the internal market, there is a need to provide for harmonised legal protection against circumvention of effective technological measures and against provision of devices and products or services to this effect".

This recital summarises the possibilities and risks that the legal guardianship of TPM's should consider. On the one hand, the growing evolution of technology and of models for making works available to the public by digital means provides the holders of copyright and related rights with a set of mechanisms capable of

[4] All translations of Portuguese legal texts and doctrine are of our sole responsibility. To help with these translations we used the free version of the software DeepL (www.DeepL.com/Translator).

controlling the uses that the public can make of the work made available. On the other hand, the same technological knowledge expands the risk of these measures being illegally circumvented.

The directive also safeguards the protection of other measures provided for in Community legislation. In this regard, recital 50 says that TPM's should not undermine "the specific provisions on protection provided for by Directive 91/250/EEC. In particular, it should not apply to the protection of technological measures used in connection with computer programs, which is exclusively addressed in that Directive. It should neither inhibit nor prevent the development or use of any means of circumventing a technological measure that is necessary to enable acts to be undertaken in accordance with the terms of Article 5(3) or Article 6 of Directive 91/250/EEC".

The legislator's concern to ensure that TPM's do not affect the functioning and free interoperability of computer systems is also felt, as well as that they do not represent an obstacle to scientific research and development. Namely in the recital 48 where it states that "such legal protection should respect proportionality and should not prohibit those devices or activities which have a commercially significant purpose or use other than to circumvent the technical protection. In particular, this protection should not hinder research into cryptography".

Finally, the European legislator also warns that legal recognition of TPM's may also restrict the rights of free use which the various States recognise for "consumers" of cultural works, by virtue of compliance with the fundamental rights of access to culture and information. The legal regime must therefore strike a balance between protection of the exclusive rights of rightsholders and the free access rights of users.

These concerns of the European legislator can be found in recital 51 when it states that "The legal protection of technological measures applies without prejudice to public policy, as reflected in Article 5, or public security. Member States should promote voluntary measures taken by rightsholders, including the conclusion and implementation of agreements between rightsholders and other parties concerned, to accommodate achieving the objectives of certain exceptions or limitations provided for in national law in accordance with this Directive. In the absence of such voluntary measures or agreements within a reasonable period of time, Member States should take appropriate measures to ensure that rightsholders provide beneficiaries of such exceptions or limitations with appropriate means of benefiting from them, by modifying an implemented technological measure or by other means. However, in order to prevent abuse of such measures taken by rightsholders, including within the framework of agreements, or taken by a Member State, any technological measures applied in implementation of such measures should enjoy legal protection".

Moving on to the enacting part of the Directive, it is mainly in articles 6 that we find the provision for the protection of TPM's.

Article 6(3) of the Directive defines "the expression 'technological measures' means any technology, device or component that, in the normal course of its operation, is designed to prevent or restrict acts, in respect of works or other subjectmatter, which are not authorised by the right holder of any copyright or any right related to copyright as provided for by law or the sui generis right provided for in Chapter III of Directive 96/9/EC. Technological measures shall be deemed 'effective' where the use of a protected work or other subject matter is controlled by the right holders through application of an access control or protection process, such as encryption, scrambling or other transformation of the work or other subject-matter or a copy control mechanism, which achieves the protection objective."

Whereas paragraph 1 of the same article requires that "Member States shall provide adequate legal protection against the circumvention of any effective technological measures, which the person concerned carries out in the knowledge, or with reasonable grounds to know, that he or she is pursuing that objective".

This protection is reinforced by paragraph 2 which states that "Member States shall provide adequate legal protection against the manufacture, import, distribution, sale, rental, advertisement for sale or rental, or possession for commercial purposes of devices, products or components or the provision of services which: (a) are promoted, advertised or marketed for the purpose of circumvention of, or; (b) have only a limited commercially significant purpose or use other than to circumvent, or; (c) are primarily designed, produced, adapted or performed for the purpose of enabling or facilitating the circumvention of; any effective technological measures."

The same article imposes on member states the obligation to take legal measures to ensure both the exercise of free uses and private copying rights and that such TPM's respect the terms on which the works have been made public.

In all these provisions, the European legislator does not specify what these "appropriate measures" are, thus leaving a large margin of discretion in the transposition into member states domestic law.

3 Technological Protection Measures in Portuguese Law

As we mentioned in the introduction, the protection of technological protection measures was introduced in Portugal, by transposition of the European directive, by Law 50/2004, which added this matter to the Portuguese Copyright and Neighbouring Rights Code. Despite its provision in this diploma, the protection covers not only all holders of copyright and related rights, but also the holders of the sui generis right on databases, enshrined in Directive 96/9/EC of 11 March 1996 (implemented by Decree-Law 122/2000 of 4 July).

Article 217, number 2, (all articles quoted hereafter refer to Portuguese Copyright and Neighbouring Rights Code) defines technological measure as "any technique, device or component that, in the normal course of its operation, is intended to prevent or restrict acts relating to protected performance works and productions, which are not authorised by the owner of the intellectual property rights". This part of the definition complies with international standards, as well as with the aforementioned definition in Article 6(3) of the European Directive.

In a second part, the Portuguese standard strangely excludes from the concept "a protocol, a format, an algorithm or a method of encryption, conditioning or transformation". An addition not included in the European definition and that some Portuguese authors[5] even consider contradictory to it. We believe that this part of the rule should be interpreted restrictively as referring to such technologies when they do not fulfil any of the typical functions of copyright or related rights protection that may exist over the work or performance.

The introduction of a technological protection measure in a digital copy of the work constitutes, under Portuguese law (article 217/4), an exclusive right of the intellectual creator and cannot therefore be used by a third party without his express consent.[6] This is an imposition whereby the Portuguese legislator goes beyond Community law, which does not provide for such a requirement. In the opinion of Oliveira Ascensão, this is not exactly a new requirement in Portuguese law as article 68/3 "already reserves to the holder of the copyright the faculty of freely choosing the processes and conditions for the use of the work".[7] The requirement enshrined herein is thus merely a reflection of this right.

The protection conferred is the prohibition to circumvent any technological protection measures, by any means or procedure, to make an unauthorised use of the work (article 217, paragraph 1). This prohibition also includes preparatory acts to the infringement, such as any form of production or making available devices or techniques intended for the unlawful circumvention of these technological measures (Article 219). Which, in short, meets the requirements of paragraphs 1 and 2 of the Directive, as quoted above.

Violation of these technological protection measures will make the offender liable for both civil liabilities, for the damage caused, and criminal liability.

The neutralization of technological protection measures is foreseen as a legal type of crime in article 218, with a penalty of 1 year of imprisonment or 100 days of fine. Attempts are also punishable, but only with a fine of up to 25 days. In addition to the material act of neutralisation of the protection measure, the legal type provides as a subjective requirement that the offender acts "knowing this or having reasonable grounds to know this". It means that "not knowing" the imperative nature of the technological measure is foreseen as an "excusable" factor of the criminally punishable conduct.[8] Article 219 also criminalises the preparatory acts referred to above with a penalty of imprisonment of up to 6 months or a fine of up to 20 days.

As is evident from the penalties provided for in the articles cited, the sanctions predicted in criminal law are far from the potential damage that the neutralisation of technological protection measures in the digital environment may cause. Oliveira Ascensão justifies the reduced scope of the criminal sanction by the fact that "at least some of the technological measures in question (...) are not strictly speaking aimed at

[5] For all, Ascensão (2008), p. 507.

[6] Leitão (2011), pp. 370–371.

[7] Ascensão (2008), p. 509.

[8] This negative requirement is contested by some Portuguese doctrine. Menezes Leitão states that "we have difficulty in conceiving cases in which this element is not fulfilled and therefore its provision may be a source of jurisprudence doubts" Leitão (2011), p. 372.

protecting copyright or related rights, but rather at ensuring payment of the remuneration due for the use of the work or performance made available to the public".[9] Which would justify why this crime has a lower sanction that other crimes against protected works.

Civil liability protection, under general legal terms, is therefore essential. Civil liability is independent from criminal protection, as expressly stated in Article 226. Law also provides for the right of the injured party to resort to the precautionary procedures provided for in the general law (Article 227).

Copyright is caught in a constant conflict between the exclusive rights of the intellectual creator and the general community's right of access to culture. The protection of technological protection measures does not escape this dichotomy.

Since these technologies aim to limit the ways in which the work, performance or production made available can be used, it is clear that they pose "serious problems in relation to the public's right of access to the work, in the context of the free uses that are permitted".[10] As mentioned in the previous section, this concern was also reflected in Article 6 of the European directive.

In fact, the new modalities of making works or performances available in digital format, which can only be accessed online, give the right holder control over the private use of the work or service, which until now was in the private (and therefore free) sphere of the user. The protection now conferred on TPM's provides legal coverage for this control of the private use of works and performances, reinforcing the need to safeguard users' rights.

In the Portuguese Copyright and Neighbouring Rights Code this conflict is dealt with in Article 221, which seeks to combine this mechanism for protecting the exclusive rights of the intellectual creator with the free uses provided for in Article 75. In summary, the article provides that the TPM's must include means for the user to benefit from the free uses to which he is entitled, and the right holder must deposit with the public entity competent for the regulation and supervision of cultural activities the means allowing the user to benefit from free uses in relation to the works and performances made available with the associated TPM's. In case of non-compliance, any person interested in a free use may request the competent public authority to lift the TPM's that are blocking such access (article 222/3).

The mechanisms foreseen are essentially based on the promotion of the adoption by the rights holders of practices in conformity with the guarantee of access for the purposes of free use, and the recourse to mechanisms for the resolution of urgent extra-judicial disputes. Which are legitimised to impose compulsory financial penalties with a view to the prompt restoration of the violated free access. As referred by Victoria Banti-Markouti "The Directive in article 6(4) recognises the importance of private agreements and non-institutional mechanisms of settling disputes between the right holders and the users such as mediation. The lack of sufficient legal

[9] Ascensão (2008), p. 511.

[10] Leitão (2011), p. 374.

framework in the digital environment permits mostly voluntary arrangements among users rather than state intervention".[11]

A central criticism to the options of the Portuguese legislator on this point is the fact that this rule does not include all foreseen free uses (in fact, the rule expressly states that it only applies to the uses set forth in paragraphs (a), (e), (f), (i), (n), (p), (r), (s), and (t) of Article 75(2), in paragraph (b) of Article 81 and in Article 152(4); all others are left out!). On the other hand, it is also criticised that the law allows the limitation of the number of reproductions that can be made, even in the exercise of the private copying right (Article 221/8).[12] In both cases, restrictions on access to information and culture seem to go further in cyberspace than they ever did in the analogue world. As already pointed out by Oliveira Ascenção in 2008, "it now seems to be a general trend in copyright law in the European Union and the United States of America".[13] This issue is not at all pacific in the Portuguese doctrine.[14]

In fact, the same criticism has been made to the directive itself by European doctrine. Victoria Banti-Markouti points out that "Furthermore, article 6 (4) (2) allows the extension of the rights of the rightholders for the disadvantage of the users. Then, inevitably, the question that arises is whether the 'fair use/fair dealing' exemption has any future in the digital arena. Member states may take measures for private copying but are not obliged to do so. Accordingly, if a TV station prevents by technological protection measures the private recording of a programme then the users are deprived of their right to private copy".[15]

4 The Risks of Digitalization for Copyright Protection

Cybersecurity is presented as a central issue of the new organization of modern society, as a cyber-connected society. As stated in the recent Report Cybersecurity in Portugal—Ethics & Law: "The increase of connections (and dependence) between States' critical infrastructures and networks and information systems and services has brought new risks and vulnerabilities to the security of States, motivating the adoption of measures to ensure the protection of networks and infrastructures".[16]

---

[11] Banti-Markouti (2007), p. 581.

[12] Oliveira Ascensão states that "due to its potentially restrictive nature on the free use of protected works and performances, especially those available online, it is actually likely to negatively affect the access to information, scientific research and teaching; which, in a country that is highly deprived and dependent on foreigners in this area, such as the new one, can only be seen with concern". Ascensão (2008), pp. 517–518.

[13] Ibid., p. 523.

[14] Criticizing these choices of the legislator, in addition to the work already cited: Ascensão (2009); Rocha (2017), pp. 27–28.

[15] Banti-Markouti (2007), p. 582.

[16] Andrade (2020), p. 10.

The (in)security of cyber infrastructures is, however, not only a risk for the state, but for all activity in this increasingly digitised society.

The issue is particularly relevant for copyright and related rights, given the global and exponential growth that the digital exploitation of these works has experienced in recent years.

According to a news article in *Revista Exame* from 2019, "While CD sales have continued to fall, revenues from streaming services have exploded in recent years and reached $9 billion in 2018, almost half of the total. According to a recent study by German market consultancy Statista, later in 2019, for the first time the music streaming market is expected to reach 1 billion listeners, between subscribers and people who access the services for free. It is a milestone for an industry that sold a measly 52 million CDs in 2018 in the United States, 94% less than the 943 million sold in 2000, according to the American association that represents the industry, the Riaa".[17]

Also in the book sector, a news item from the "Inter Saberes" Blog of 26 April 2021 states that: "The digitalisation of the contemporary world is a trend that shows no signs of receding. Characters and algorithms dictate the pace of companies from all sectors, following the new consumption habits that settle among audiences of varied profiles. To measure the recent breaking of the taboo regarding digital solutions and the reduction of resistance to new media, books are a good example. With printed books in full circulation in the market, digital book revenues grew 115% within 3 years".[18]

Furthermore, according to the study Digital Economy in Portugal (2020 Edition), published by ACEPI, the continuous growth of the digital economy suffered a significant increase with the restrictive measures of analogue commerce during the period of combat against the Covid-19 Pandemic. In fact, according to the study "Post COVID-19 forecasts predicted an increase in 2020 to 46%, accelerating convergence with the European Union in 2025, where it is estimated that 69% a of the Portuguese will buy online.".[19] The same study points out that in the European Union the percentage of the population that shops online could grow to 85% in 2025 (whereas before the pandemic the forecast for the same period for the European Union was only 78%).

On the other hand, in addition to the increase in the variety and volume of works exploited in the digital environment, the technologies and business models associated with the multiple and innovative forms of use and communication that digital allows are also multiplying. In a news item dated 23 April 2021, the "MoreThanDigital" Blog[20] points out eleven digital business models differentiated

[17] In https://exame.com/revista-exame/musica-o-digital-da-lucro/, accessed on 28-10-2021.

[18] In https://www.intersaberes.com/blog/tendencia-de-consumo-faturamento-com-livros-digitais-cresce-115-em-3-anos/, accessed on 28-10-2021.

[19] IDC (2020), p. 19.

[20] In https://morethandigital.info/pt-pt/11-modelos-de-negocios-digitais-que-deve-conhecer-incluindo-exemplos/, accessed on 28-10-2021.

both by the technologies used and by the contractual relations established between economic agents and consumers.

This movement of consumers to the digital market will not fail to be reflected in the consumption habits of copyrighted works, exacerbating the challenge that such a transition poses to the risks associated with unauthorised access, reproduction and use of protected works.

Furthermore, as Maria Victória Rocha states, "the dissemination raises complex issues, which we can only point out here, regarding applicable law and competent jurisdiction, given the diversity of protection periods and exceptions or limits of national Copyrights. The Internet is global, copyright is, by essence, territorial".[21] We will not elaborate on these territoriality issues in this text, as we focus on the Portuguese legal regime.

The multiple forms of data transmission allowed by computerised networks raise an equal number of problems for copyright protection. From the already traditional methods of communication by email or file uploading and downloading protocols (File Transfer Protocol) via a server accessible online; to temporary storage technologies for viewing (caching, browsing or streaming); to file sharing technologies (peer-to-peer); or web chat technologies (sometimes with encrypted content); and even the latest blockchain technologies.[22]

All these technologies present different access control opportunities for rightholders of protected works and performances, and risks of infringement by unauthorised users. However, it is certain that the control over all forms of digital communication is more and more utopian.

First and foremost, because when comparing the protection of property rights of protected works and performances with the fundamental right to privacy and confidentiality of electronic communications, it seems virtually impossible for copyright holders to have absolute control over the countless possible uses of works in the digital environment. The difficulty that the traditional press has encountered in preventing unauthorised sharing of digital publications on encrypted networks is a clear example of this.[23]

---

[21] Rocha (2017), pp. 27–28.

[22] On the different ways of sharing protected works: Vieira (2020), pp. 628–698.

[23] According to a report in *Jornal de Notícias* of 29-10-2021: "The illegal sharing of newspapers and magazines (in pdf format) on social networks increased with the pandemic, with monthly losses estimated at around 3.5 million euros for the national press. On average, 88 publications are shared per day. The analysis was made by Visapress and the results shared by its executive director, this Friday, during the conference "(I)literacy and Piracy: the same fight", promoted by the Portuguese Press Association." In https://www.jn.pt/nacional/partilhados-88-jornais-e-revistas-de-forma-ilegal-todos-os-dias-14270839.html, accessed on 29-10-2021.

5 Conclusions

In view of the inevitability of the transfer of the economic exploitation of protected works and performances to the digital environment, which was fully demonstrated above, a new challenge in the protection of Copyright and Related Rights is presented to the legislator.

The issue is not limited to the guarantee of the author's or artist's exclusivity over the work or performance. Copyright lives in a permanent conflict between the right to cultural creation and the right of access to culture, between the cultural creator's exclusivity and the citizen's rights of access to education, culture and information.

This conflict has not been solved with the promised democratisation of access to information provided by the advent of the Information Society. On the one hand, the free use of works in digital environment is being strangled (as demonstrated by the criticism we pointed out above to the solutions of the Portuguese law regarding restrictions to TPM's), on the other hand, unauthorised use is being multiplied, boosted by multiple anonymised, encrypted and massified channels, which are virtually impossible to trace by the rights holders.

The solution does not seem easy, and the vertiginous speed of ICT evolution does not allow the legislator to keep up with the pace, finding itself hopelessly one step behind technology.

It is not by chance that Portuguese law, following the path of the EU Directive, opts for a legal system that seeks to promote the proactivity of the holder of copyright or related rights in the design of the technological protection measures, as well as in the facilitation mechanisms of the free uses allowed to the user, which are more adequate to the type and mode of exploitation of the work or performance adopted.

In fact, the most appropriate TPM's for the protection of the work or performance will depend not only on the nature of that work or performance, but also on the medium, model or technology adopted to make it available to the public.

We recall that TPM's may be designed not only to control access to the work or performance, but also to prevent its transformation; to control the day, time, place or duration of access; to restrict some types of possible uses; or whatever else the technology used allows. Since it is the exclusive right of the copyright or related right holder to authorise or prohibit any form of use.

It is therefore not an easy task for the legislator to anticipate the exact terms under which TPM's should operate, and it is only up to the legislator to safeguard the resulting balance between the preservation of the rightholder's exclusive rights and users' free access rights.

In this system, it is the holder of the rights over the works or performances who has the burden of following the evolution of the Information Society, opting for the TPM's that best guarantee a satisfactory control of the economic exploitation he/she intends to make of the works or services made available to the public. It cannot be anyone other than those interested in the economic exploitation of works or performances in the digital environment, to foresee the risks and to configure the TPM's that best satisfy the security they desire.

The path mapped out internationally, since the nineties of the last century, towards the universal recognition of the legal protection of TPM's, both through criminal penalties for their contravention and through the provision of mechanisms for conflict resolution and rapid enforcement of their civil protection, remains relevant today (perhaps even more so). The option for a regime focusing not on the regulation of technologies, but rather on guaranteeing the balance of interests in conflict (although not always with solutions applauded by the doctrine) seems equally correct.

As a final comment, I quote Jane C. Ginsburg, when she states that "The word "copyright owner" more often than not evokes a large, unloveable, multinational (or American), corporate entrepreneur, in short, an Evil Troll. It is easy to deplore technological protections if one thinks of them only in those apocalyptic terms. But one might instead focus on the opportunities technological protections extend to individual authors to disseminate their works, and to condition further copying or exploitation on remunerating the creators. Digital media, by making the means of production and dissemination available to any computer-equipped author, give authors a realistic opportunity to bring their works to the public without having to put themselves in thrall to traditional intermediaries".[24]

References

Andrade FPD et al (2020) Relatório Cibersegurança em Portugal - Ética & Direito, p 10

Ascensão J d O (2008) Direito de Autor e Medidas Tecnológicas de Protecção. Direito da Soc da Informação VII:499–523

Ascensão J d O (2009) Dispositivos Tecnológicos de protecção, direitos de acesso e uso dos bens. Direito da Soc da Informação VIII:101–122

Banti-Markouti V (2007) The Interface between Technological Protection Measures and the Exemptions to Copyright under Article 6 Paragraph 4 of the Infosoc Directive and Section 1201 of the Digital Millennium Copyright Act. Sci Inf Technol 4:573–600. https://doi.org/10.28945/973

Gasser U (2006) Legal frameworks and technological protection of digital content: moving forward towards a best practice model. Fordham Intellect Prop Media Entertain Law J 17:40–113. https://doi.org/10.2139/ssrn.908998

Ginsburg JC (2005) Legal protection of technological measures protecting works of authorship: international obligations and the US experience. Colum J Law Arts 29:05–93. https://doi.org/10.2307/1321345

IDC (2020) Economia Digital em Portugal. Associação da Economia Digital (ACEPI), Lisboa

Leitão LMT d M (2011) Direito de Autor. Almedina, Coimbra

Rocha MV (2017) Impressão 3D e Direito de Autor. Rev Bras Estud Jurídicos 12:13–48

Vieira JA (2020) Direito de Autor - Dogmática Básica. Almedina, Coimbra

[24]Ginsburg (2005), p. 26.

Pedro Dias Venâncio holds a PhD. in Legal Private Sciences from the Law School of the University of Minho, Portugal. Teacher in higher education since 2004, currently is Auxiliary Professor at School of Law, University of Minho, Portugal, and guest lecturer at School of Technology and Management of Polytechnic Istitute of Oporto, Portugal. Researcher at JUSGOV—Research Center for Justice and Governance, School of Law, University of Minho, Portugal, and guest researcher at CIICESI—Center for Innovation and Research in Business Sciences and Systems, School of Technology and Management, Polytechnic Institute of Porto, Portugal. From 2016 to 2018 was international legal advisor to the VI and VII Constitutional Governments of the Democratic Republic of Timor-Leste. Lawyer, registered in the Portuguese Bar Association, with professional license no. 7332p, and effectively practicing law from February 1999 to September 2015.

Digital Signatures and Quantum Computing

Francisco António Carneiro Pacheco de Andrade and José Carlos Bacelar Almeida

Abstract The legal framework of electronic signatures in the European Union is mainly based on the use of Public Key cryptography systems or asymmetric cryptography. This system, currently regulated by Regulation 910/2014 (eIDAS Regulation) appears to be quite safe under current technology but may be at huge risk with the developments of Quantum Computing. To better understand this we must start by considering digital signatures (and the characteristics of symmetric and asymmetric encryption) and further analyzing the threats of quantum computation for this system, the need of a post quantum cryptography and of long term validation preservation.

1 Digital Signatures

The concept of signature is not defined in Portuguese Law. In general terms, signature is a way of identifying someone and showing one's agreement with a certain fact, object or content. The signature appears as a symbol that someone uses or executes with the real intention of authenticating a writing.[1] And the classical

[1] "A traditional signature must be (1) a symbol; (2) executed or adopted; (3) by a party; (4) with present intention; (5) to authenticate; (6) a writing", Fischer (1997), pp. 545–570. This statement can be adapted in view of the use of an electronic "signature" by a software agent? As for the use of token(s) and authentication there doesn't seem to be any problem. Even if encryption mechanisms are used, there is a use of symbols that ensure a real authentication (even if this authentication concerns the electronic agent). As for execution by a party, there are no major issues either, as long as one understands the electronic agent as a real party (which is not problematic, even if one sees the software agent as a mere tool. As for writing, it is necessary to see what is understood by writing in

F. A. Carneiro Pacheco de Andrade (✉)
School of Law, University of Minho, Braga, Portugal
e-mail: fandrade@direito.uminho.pt

J. C. B. Almeida
School of Engineering, Computer Science Department, University of Minho, Braga, Portugal
e-mail: jba@di.uminho.pt

F. A. Carneiro Pacheco de Andrade et al. (eds.), *Legal Developments on Cybersecurity and Related Fields*, Law, Governance and Technology Series 60,
https://doi.org/10.1007/978-3-031-41820-4_12

doctrine defines a signature as a distinctive sign, proper of the author of the signature, by which the person himself becomes known before others. Therefore, the admissibility of a non-manuscript signature must be considered taking into account a functional analysis of the signature.[2] That is, the signature must be "a strictly personal and undoubtedly distinctive mark, such that it certifies beyond doubt the will of the person who signs with it".[3] Vincent Gautrais,[4] referring to the signature, tells us that it essentially has two main functions: the identification of the signer and the manifestation of his will.

But the idea of electronic signature, because it is usually applied to forms of long-distance contact and contracting, necessarily appeals to a broader functional content than that of the traditional handwritten signature. Thus, as mentioned by Carlos Vattier Fuenzalida,[5] the electronic signature allows the receiver of data transmitted by electronic means not only to check the origin of the message (authentication of the origin of the data and identification of the sender, as a guarantee of the authenticity of the document[6]) but also to verify that the message transmitted is the one actually originated by the Author and that it has not been altered in any way (guarantee of the integrity of the document[7]), and, depending on the electronic signature method adopted, eventually even guarantee what the doctrine calls "non-repudiation" of messages, that is, guarantee that the party sending a message cannot later claim that it did not send it. Furthermore, in the electronic exchange of messages it can be also important to ensure the "confidentiality of messages", that

digital environments, understood in the broad sense, as anything that can be represented in writing. A more debatable question is whether there is a real intention to authenticate (see below about the intentional states of software agents). In any case, Fischer (1997), op. cit., p. 567, goes beyond this issue by stating that if the agent "has exercised the principal's present intention to perform the task", then the intention, even if referred to the principal, will be present as the intention that the agent perform the authentication process. Cf. Fischer (1997), op. cit. But of course the issue is complicated when the electronic agent authenticates messages without the knowledge of the principal. In this case, two hypotheses arise: either we understand the agent as a mere "nuncio", and the principal "really wanted" the electronic agent to process the message and, consequently, to authenticate it—which can be understood as part of the user's instructions—or we should consider the agent as having a will of his own and, ultimately, as capable of acting autonomously on behalf of the principal. (See below on the issue of representation). In any case, John P. Fischer ends up considering that if a software agent authenticates ("signs") a document, it must be presumed that it is acting the principal's real intention. Cf. Fischer (1997), op. cited above, p. 569.

[2] "Важно обеспечить так называемый"функционально-эквивалентный" подход к бумажной и безбумажной документации", Вершинин А П, "Электронный документ: правовая форма и доказательство в суде" Городец, Москва, 2000, стр. 31—("It is thus important to ensure the so-called functional equivalence of paper and paperless documentation", cf. Vershinin (2000), p. 31.

[3] Bensoussan (1992), p. 183.

[4] And also the integrity of the message. Vincent Gautrais « La formation des contrats en ligne », https://www.jurisint.org/pub/05/fr/guide_chap4.pdf (consulted on 2nd June 2022).

[5] Fuenzalida (1999), p. 81.

[6] Correia (2006), pp. 277–317.

[7] Correia (2006), idem.

is, the guarantee that they will not be accessed by "unauthorized persons".[8] Let's not forget that, in electronic communication, messages exchanged between two parties will usually travel a long way, through different servers and communication ports, which is why it is very important to ensure a high level of security of the message exchange.

Having said this, we must distinguish the concept of electronic signature from that of digital signature. The latter is a more restricted concept, referring to the use of cryptographic techniques[9] for data transmission,[10] allowing not only the identification of the author of the message sent, but also to prove its integrity,[11] whereas the concept of electronic signature is a broad concept, which refers to any method of signing an electronic document that is able to identify its author. In addition, the concept of electronic signature also includes other types of requirements, such as the need to ensure the integrity, authenticity, non-repudiation and even confidentiality of messages.[12]

The Council of the European Union, in its Common Position 28/99, approved on June 28th, 1999,[13] distinguishes between the terms "electronic signature" and "digital signature".[14] In fact, the first term is broader than the second (which is only a specific subtype of electronic signature). On the other hand, and no less

---

[8] Correia (2006), idem.

[9] These techniques have the advantage that they can be used both in the case of inter-personal electronic contracting (digital signature used by natural persons—humans) and in the case of inter-systemic electronic contracting, namely in the case of contracting between software intelligent agents; in this case, "the identification of agents in VMs" (Virtual Worlds) "through the use of cryptographic tools, giving rise to identification schemes that are of extreme relevance for EC systems" (Electronic Commerce). "The identification of agents is made from the predicates Name, Code and Key, that is, "the agent's name, the agent's code that identifies it univocally in the community where it belongs, and a cryptographic key that serves as a reference for general identification schemes", see Brito and Neves (2003). However, the use of digital signatures by software "agents", which is technically possible, is not foreseen in our legal system. And the eIDAS Regulation (Reg. 910/2014) even expressly provides, in art. 3 no. 9, that only a natural person can be a signatory.

[10] The use of authenticated messages depends on the ability to determine, with absolute certainty, their origin; i.e., in closed network environments (typically with specific point-to-point connections) it is possible to determine the origin; on the other hand, in open environments, such as the Internet, the use of cryptographic tools is essential. Brito and Neves (2003), op. cit.

[11] On the difference between electronic signature and digital signature, see Barbagalo (2001).

[12] Sorge (2006), p. 13.

[13] Barbagalo (2001), referred, p. 42.

[14] Sorge (2006), referred, p. 13, footnote 7, says that: ""Beide Begriffe werden synonym verwendet; in der juristischen Literatur findet sich teilweise jedoch eine Unterscheidung, wonach der Begriff "elektronische Signatur" technologieneutral ist, der Begriff'digitale Signatur" hingegen ausschließlich im Kontext asymmetrischer Kryptographie verwendet wird" (Both concepts are used as synonyms; however, in legal literature there is sometimes a differentiation, according to which the concept "electronic signature" is technology-neutral and the concept "digital signature", on the contrary, is only used in the context of asymmetric cryptography).

importantly, by talking about "electronic signature" we are addressing the issue of signature in virtual environments in a more technologically neutral way.[15]

The digital electronic signature—so called because it allows identifying the party that issues the message, using the electronic mode[16] and the so-called binary language, in which all data are encoded by a combination of only two possible states or situations, 0s and 1s,[17] is a mathematical function of the message content which allows identifying the issuer and authenticating the content. To be considered a true signature it must fulfill two essential requirements: identify the author of the document and reasonably "guarantee" its acceptance and agreement with the content. Regarding the digital electronic signature, two primary issues should now be analyzed: the security problem (is it easy, or at least reasonably possible, to forge a digital signature, which would allow a person to try to impersonate another person and consequently contract using his name or electronic identification?); the legal problem (when the law requires a document to be dated and signed, is it possible, in a legally valid way, to use electronic document and digital signature?) The answer to the first question requires a closer look at the main systems or methods used in digital signatures; the answer to the second question should be achieved by analyzing and interpreting the law.

Digital signatures are achieved by using cryptographic methods. There are well established digital signature algorithms that are widely used, with an established legal framework.[18] However, this paradigm may soon be at risk of being compromised due to developments in the field of quantum computation.[19] Despite

[15]Jos Dumortier and Sofie Van den Eynde, "De juridische erkenning van de elektronische handtekening" https://www.law.kuleuven.be/citip/en/archive/copy_of_publications/72eh-computerrecht-juli20012f90.pdf (consulted 2nd June 2022): "Het begrip elektronische handtekening" in juridische zin is technologieneutral (The notion of "electronic signature" in a legal sense is technologically neutral); also Vicente (2005), refers that "in the legal discipline . . . a principle of technological neutrality of Law must certainly be observed, which is essential to the opening of the legal system to technological innovation".

[16]Reed (1990), p. 268: "as a stream of digital information".

[17]Sloane (1994), p. 17.

[18]See https://ec.europa.eu/digital-building-blocks/wikis/display/DIGITAL/What+is+the+legislation+-+esignature (consulted 2nd June 2022).

[19]It is however important to distinguish between Quantum Cryptography and Post Quantum Cryptography: « "It is important to make a distinction between Post-Quantum Cryptography (PQC)and Quantum Cryptography. PQC is about designing cryptographic solutions that can be used by today's [non-quantum] computers and that we believe are resistant to both conventional and quantum cryptanalysis. On the other hand, Quantum Cryptography is about cryptographic solutions that take advantage of quantum physics to provide certain security services. Quantum Key Distribution (QKD) is a good example of the latter.", Post-Quantum Cryptography: current state and quantum mitigation", ENISA—European Union Agency for Cybersecurity, May 2021, v. 2. It is predicted that ". . .the quantum computers of the future will be able (probably in the next decade) to break today's most sophisticated encryption algorithms, entailing serious security problems", i.e. "data that is securely encrypted today will be easy to decrypt with the quantum computing of the future". https://www.digicert.com/resources/industry-report/2019-Post-Quantum-Crypto-Survey.pdf. Blockchain itself may be subject to obvious vulnerabilities. Cf. Haney (2020), p. 117.

the difficulties encountered for a widespread use of quantum computers[20] and considering that it is unlikely that this technology will be available for widespread use soon,[21] some large companies,[22] in addition to powerful states,[23] have been developing ambitious projects in this field. This situation may in fact create evident inequalities between individuals, between individuals and companies, and even between states.[24] The security of electronic identification systems, the protection of personal data and the security of communication infrastructures may be at stake.[25] Therefore, it is pertinent to question the need for regulation in the use of these technologies.[26]

2 Symmetric and Asymmetric Encryption

To contextualize the threat of quantum computation to digital signatures, let us briefly review some notions of cryptography and how it accomplishes the requisites of signatures. Broadly speaking, cryptographic methods are classified among symmetric or asymmetric schemes, depending on whether the secret protecting the communication is known to all legitimate players or not. Example of symmetric cryptography are symmetric encryption,[27] such as the Advanced Encryption

---

[20] "The construction and operation of quantum computers involves high costs and expertise". "They require ultrahigh vacuum and ultra low temperatures (at times as low as −273.15 °C)". Jeutner (2021), pp. 52–59.

[21] Jeutner (2021), pp. 52–59.

[22] "Google has claimed that its quantum computer can resolve a mathematical problem which would take conventional computers around 10,000 years to complete in less than 4 minutes", idem.

[23] "The USA and China are also fighting for dominance in the field with the help of ambitious funding programmes and in close cooperation with private companies such as Google, IBM, Alibaba and Baidu.", idem.

[24] "This inequality can play out among individuals, between individuals and companies, among companies, between companies/individuals and states, and, on a geopolitical level, among states.", idem.

[25] "Regulators must ensure that the potential of quantum communication is not used by states and/or non-state actors to undermine existing security infrastructures or data protection.", idem.

[26] "The establishment of an authority licencing and supervising those entrusted with the development of quantum computers… regulate not (only) the developers but (also) their products by imposing registration requirements on hardware or software", idem. In addition to the need to establish regulations regarding the export of quantum cryptographic products ("""…lawmakers must reassess regulations for the exportation of cryptographic products for the quantum regime", Rand and Rand (2021).. On the other hand, regulating the use of these technologies also has preventive features: The regulation of quantum computing software will become important in preventing bad actors from taking advantage of quantum computing's capacity for decryption", Vermeer and Peet (2020), pp. 36–37.

[27] "Encryption is, at its essence, the process of transforming readable information so that it is not immediately recognizable", Kuhn et al. (2001).

Standard (AES).[28] It can be used to protect the confidentiality of messages—there, and depending on the intended security level, a key with 128/192/256 bits is used by the sender and receiver to scramble/descramble the message content. An attacker, without knowing the key, won't be able to extract any information from the transmitted data. Similarly, a Message Authentication Code (MAC) is a symmetric primitive designed to protect the integrity and authenticity of messages. It acts as a kind of secure fingerprint, used to ensure the contents of the message are not manipulated while in transit. Both the sender and the receiver need a secret key to generate/verify the fingerprint, which makes it unfeasible to perform undetected changes on the message by outsider attackers.[29] Notice that a MAC also provides authenticity—upon successful validation of the fingerprint, the receiver "knows" the message has been originated from the emitter since he is the only, besides himself, knowing the secret key. But it falls short of achieving what is expected from a digital signature, where the message should be bound "uniquely" to the sender (non-repudiation)—the receiver could itself be the source of the message, since he holds the very same key.[30] To provide non-repudiation, the capabilities of the signer and verifier need to be asymmetric.

The critical observation towards a cryptographic mechanism able to reproduce the guaranties of hand-written signatures was made in a seminal paper by W. Diffie & M. Hellman,[31] where they put forward the concept of public-key cryptography. The key ingredient is that the secret underlying the cryptographic scheme could be split in two—a key-pair—one component that is kept secret by the owner while the other can be made public. Those two components are inter-related, but the knowledge of the public part shall not give any information on the corresponding secret part (hence the names of public and secret keys). For digital signatures, the signer generates a key-pair, keeps for himself the secret-key, and publishes the corresponding public-key. When signing, he uses his secret key to generate the signature from a message-digest (a fixed-sized sequence of bits resulting from applying a so-called cryptographic hash algorithm[32] to the message). Anyone knowing the corresponding public-key would be able to verify the signature,

[28] *Advanced Encryption Standard (AES)*, NIST FIPS-197. https://doi.org/10.6028/NIST.FIPS.197.

[29] If the message is changed, it won't be validated by the original fingerprint, and without knowing the key, the attacker won't be able to generate a new fingerprint.

[30] "Strong evidence that it could have emanated only from one or other of the keyholders". Cfr. Reed (1990), op. cit. p. 268.

[31] Diffie and Hellman (1996), pp. 644–654.

[32] Sorge (2006), op. citada, p. 15: "An eine kryptographische Hash-Funktion werden zusätzlich drei Anforderungen gestellt: Es muss sich um eine Einweg-Funktion handeln, d.h. es darf nicht effizient möglich sein, zu einem gegebenen Funktionswert (Hash-Wert) ein Urbild zu bestimmen. Es darf nicht effizient möglich sein, zu einer gegebenen Nachricht eine zweite zu finden, der der gleiche Hash-Wert zugeordnet wird (schwache Kollisionsresistenz). Es darf nicht effizient möglich sein, zwei Nachrichten zu konstruieren, die auf den gleichen Hash-Wert abgebildet werden (starke Kollisionsresitenz)". [It must be a one-way function, i.e. it must not be possible to determine efficiently the original image of a given function value (Hash value). It must not be possible, in an efficient way, to find, for a given message, a second message that has the same Hash value (weak

establishing message's authenticity. Notice that the verifier is no longer able to generate the signature, making it possible to bind the signed message to the sender (non-repudiation). Similarly, a public-key encryption scheme can be devisable to protect message's confidentiality—in that case, the public-key is used for the encryption operation, and the secret-key for decryption. Other uses of public-key cryptography, also known as asymmetric cryptography, include the so-called key-agreement protocols where a (symmetric) key is securely agreed between the communication parties, hence avoiding the difficult problem of secure pre-distribution of secrets needed by symmetric cryptography.[33]

There are two important observations to be made at this point. The first one is of a more theoretical nature and concerns the feasibility of the whole concept of asymmetric cryptography: given that part of the key is made public (the public-key), isn't it always the case that an attacker could "in principle" be able to find a "matching" private-key (e.g., through scanning all possible private-keys). In fact, asymmetric cryptography is intrinsically bound to the notion of computational security, where the computational power of adversaries is reasonably bound. This way, those "brute-force" attacks are excluded since, under reasonable computational assumptions and properly chosen key sizes, they would result into huge execution times (e.g., the age of the universe). So, we could say that a suitable asymmetric primitive depends on a "hard-problem" that makes the task of relating the public-key to the matching private-key unfeasible.

A second observation is of a more practical nature and concerns the premisses of its use. The security guaranties of digital signatures (and asymmetric cryptography in general) are inexorably tied with a correct association between public-keys and entities/identities. In the case of digital signatures, a successful verification with a given public-key would assert that the signer made use of the corresponding private-key—to lift the guaranty to a concrete entity such as a physical person, one must be confident that is using the "correct" public-key. This is the source of the well-known "man-in-the-middle" attack, where an adversary replaces a legitimate user public-key by its own public-key, allowing it to forge any signature on behalf of the legitimate user. In practice, to circumvent these attacks, asymmetric cryptography must be complemented with a public-key certification mechanism, enabling a secure bind between public-key and entities/identities. Incidentally, this mechanism is itself a use-case of asymmetric cryptography, and specifically of digital signatures, as those public-key certificates are in essence a digital document comprising both the representation of the identity and its public-key, being itself signed by some trusted third-party—the Certification Authority (CA), sometimes also called "electronic notary".[34] Everyone trusting a CA and knowing its public-key, would be able to

---

collision resistance). It may not be possible to efficiently construct two messages that are represented by the same Hash value (high collision resistance)].

[33] Incidentally, this was the application detailed in op. cit. Diffie and Hellman (1996).

[34] Rotger and Garau (1995), pp. 131–136. Which does not mean that with the expression "electronic notary" we are referring to a true notary public, but rather to the intervention of the so-called

verify (the signature of) a public-key certificate, and access its data to obtain the public-key/identity association.

One of the firsts and most successful instantiation of the public-key paradigm for public-key encryption and digital signatures was the RSA algorithm.[35] Its security is based on the difficulty of finding prime factorisation of numbers. A prime number is an integer that cannot be written as the product of simpler integers. As an example, 15 can be written as 3*5, but both 3 and 5 cannot be further simplified—they are primes. Any number can be prime factorised in an essentially unique way, but when the number fulfils certain criteria (e.g., with at least a sufficiently big prime factor) no known algorithm is able to compute its factorisation effectively (that is, in reasonable time). The RSA algorithm uses a key pair where both keys are related in a way such that, deriving the private-key from the corresponding public-key essentially amounts to factoring a product of two large prime numbers. That means that RSA is secure as long as we aren't able to factor a number embedded in its public-key, which is believed to be the case for numbers of order of magnitude of a few thousands of bits (e.g. 2048 bit, which corresponds to around 600 decimal digits).

The RSA algorithm, although being one of the first proposals for asymmetric primitives, is still widely used as a digital signature scheme, normally in its probabilistic variant RSA-PSS[36] for increased security guaranties. Other widely used algorithm is the NIST standardised Digital Signature Algorithm (DSA),[37] whose security is based on the difficulty of the so-called "discrete logarithm problem"—a mathematical problem somewhat related to the factorisation problem. An interesting property of discrete logarithms is that they can be framed in other mathematical domains such as in Elliptic Curves over finite fields Curve—what is called Elliptic Curve Cryptography (ECC). By doing so, one is able to obtain equivalent security levels with shorter keys/signatures. As an example, ECDSA amounts to the DSA algorithm defined over an elliptic curve, and a 256-bit key size corresponds roughly to the security level of a 3072-bit key with DSA or RSA. The downside of the ECC is that it depends on additional curve parameters (often standardised), which increases the implicit/assumed trust base.

"certifying entities". Regarding the issues related to the relations between notaries and telematic services, see the interesting work, Colegios Notariales de España (2000). Regulation 910/2014 (eIDAS Regulation) article 3 nr. 16: "trust service' means an electronic service normally provided for remuneration which consists of:

(a) the creation, verification, and validation of electronic signatures, electronic seals or electronic time stamps, electronic registered delivery services and certificates related to those services, or
(b) the creation, verification and validation of certificates for website authentication; or
(c) the preservation of electronic signatures, seals or certificates related to those services;"

[35] So named after the initials of its inventors: Rivest et al. (1978), pp. 120–126.

[36] PKCS #1: RSA Cryptography Specifications Version 2.2. IETF RFC-8017.

[37] Digital Signature Standard (DSS). NIST FIPS-186-4. https://csrc.nist.gov/publications/detail/fips/186/4/final (consulted 2nd June 2022).

3 The Threat of Quantum Computation

Quantum Computation (QC) exploit the laws of quantum mechanics to solve computational problems. The way quantum computer represent information is fundamentally different from classic (current) computers. Instead of bits (0 or 1), a quantum state is formed by their quantum analogue—qubits—which exhibit very weird capabilities when compared with their classical counterparts. Instead of further detailing the quantum computation world, we are interested in understanding how such a different computational model might impact the hardness of problems that are currently used to support security in asymmetric cryptography. To that respect, in 1994 Peter Shor presented a quantum algorithm that would allow a quantum computer to factorise a number efficiently.[38] Of course, it has a dramatic impact on cryptography as, as already mentioned, factorisation is the hard problem used to establish the security of RSA.[39] Even worse, a small adaption on the algorithm allows it to solve other widely used hard problems: the discrete logarithm used in DSA, including its elliptic curve variants, such as ECDSA. In short, the very existence of Shor's algorithm compromises the security of the generality of signature schemes currently in use. It must be emphasised however that they should not be considered outright insecure—to run Shor's algorithm on currently used key sizes one would need a quantum computer whose capability is (still) out of reach. It can even be the case that it won't be possible to construct a quantum computer with the needed capabilities, but the current pace of research and investment in developing quantum computer technology strongly suggests that we need to be prepared for that eventuality.

As a side note, we can also add that the impact of QC is not restricted to asymmetric crypto. QC can also be deployed to speed up attacks to symmetric cryptography, benefiting from the Grover's quantum search algorithm.[40] However, the impact of such uses is not as devastating as for the asymmetric case—there's strong evidence that QC would only enable a quadratic speedup on symmetric crypto attacks,[41] which roughly means that one should double the security parameters (e.g. key sizes) to obtain equivalent pre-quantum security levels (e.g. AES-256 in a QC setting provides the security of AES-128 in a pre-quantum setting).

The crucial question is: when should we expect QC to reach the capability of breaking realistic instances of RSA, such as RSA-2048. Theoretically, such an instance could be break in around 10 sec. in a quantum computer with 4099 perfectly stable qubits (also known as logical qubits). As we have already hinted, currently

[38] Shor (1994), pp. 124–134.

[39] However, with quantum computing there is a risk of such a reversal: "The first vulnerability stems from exposure of public keys after transactions occur. Once a public key is exposed, the private key counterpart is at risk of being stolen with quantum algorithms", Haney (2020), p. 130.This is confirmed by a Royal Society Open Science Report (2018).

[40] Grover (1996), pp. 212–219.

[41] Bennett et al. (1997), pp. 1510–1523.

available quantum computers are very far from that threshold—IBM as recently announced a 127-qubit quantum computer.[42] But, to some extent, this is a fallacious comparison as those qubits are noisy in the sense that one must deal with errors that might scramble calculations. Current attempts to overcome these errors require quantum-error correction codes in which a logical qubit could be formed with up to a thousand physical qubits.[43] In a recent study, a realistic bound on breaking the RSA-2048 has been established 20 million noisy qubits[44]—such a huge number might not seem much impressive, but it must be understood in context: in 2012, an estimate along the same lines was around one billion gates, and since then we have assisted an impressive decrease in a 7-year span. Moreover, there is also the prospect of other contributions from the field of quantum computation might become a much bigger risk in breaking realistic RSA key sizes, such as the use of quantum annealing—quantum annealing devices[45] cannot run Shor's algorithm, as they are not universal quantum computers. But they can nevertheless be used to speed up the factorisation problem and have been recently used to factor a 20-bit number—the biggest number factored with quantum computers.[46] Current estimates from the research community place the horizon of QC-enabled breaking of RSA-2048 at around 10 years.

It is important to realise that a failure in cryptographic components in a near future do pose a real threat today. This is particularly the case for confidentiality—an attacker, knowing of the possibility of breaking a cipher in a near future, might simply collect and store encrypted data to decrypt it later. That means that currently used public-key encryption schemes should already be deemed unable to provide long-term secrecy protection. For digital signatures, the nature of the threat is somewhat more benign—someone might sign a document today to attest its authenticity for the coming years—if, meanwhile, the signature scheme happens to be broken, the security guaranties of the signature will become void. However, the act of signing does not entail a risk on itself (as was the case for encryption). Indeed, it is conceivable that the same user re-signs the document when threat of breaking the original signature becomes eminent, or even that a trusted third-party independently "promotes" the signature into a safer one, as will be discussed below.

[42] Ball (2021), p. 542.

[43] Fowler et al. (2012), p. 032324.

[44] Gidney and Ekerå (2021).

[45] E.g., https://www.dwavesys.com (consulted 2nd June 2022).

[46] Wang et al. (2020), p. 7106.

4 Post-Quantum Cryptography (PQC)

The previous discussion leads us to the inevitable question of how the cryptographic community might adjust to a world where quantum computing is disseminated. As previously noted, the main concern respects the uses of asymmetric cryptography, and the culprit is to devise alternative asymmetric schemes whose security is based on hard-problems that preserve the hardness status even in the presence of QC. Notice that, in theory, it could be even the case that QC might jeopardise the whole possibility of asymmetric crypto (and digital signatures in particular), if it proves effective in solving any possible hard-problem usable in crypto. A variety of lower bound results on the speedup allowed by QC in specific problems[47] provide strong evidence that it "is not the case"—there appears to exist hard-problems that retain their status in a QC setting. Hence, the question is to find the most suitable and which provides better guaranties—these are the aims of what had been known as post-quantum cryptography (PQC).

The US National Institute of Standards and Technology (NIST) initiated a standardisation effort for PQC in 2016.[48] A total of 69 submissions have met the acceptance criteria, from which 26 have been selected for moving to the second round (Jan. 2019), and further refined to 6 third-round finalists, as well as 8 alternate candidates that will be subjected to further evaluation. In July 2022 NIST announced the selection of four candidates to be standardized. Regarding digital signature schemes, the selected algorithms are Cristals-Dilithium,[49] Falcon,[50] and Sphincs +.[51] The first two are based on so called structured lattices, which are acknowledge as providing the most compact combined public-key and signature sizes (between 1.5 KByte and 7 Kbyte). The latter is a hash-based signature, which allow for short public-keys (~ 50 Byte), at the expense of fairly bigger signatures (> 15 KByte). Besides the NIST reports describing the evaluation process, several Security

[47] Such as the op. cit. *The strengths and weaknesses of quantum computation.*

[48] See https://csrc.nist.gov/projects/post-quantum-cryptography/post-quantum-cryptography-standardization (consulted 2nd June 2022).

[49] See https://pq-crystals.org/dilithium/ (consulted 2nd June 2022).

[50] See https://falcon-sign.info (consulted 2nd June 2022).

[51] See https://sphincs.org/ (consulted 2nd June 2022).

Agencies have provided detailed comments on the finalists and prospects for the transition to PQC.[52,53,54,55,56]

Some general remarks on compromises and drawbacks that appear emerge on the transition to PQC:

1. Bigger sizes and/or efficiency issues for related security levels—in general, PQC demands bigger keys and/or bigger signature sizes. If we restrict attention to the lattice-based finalists, which offer the best compromise in this respect, the ratio on the combined sizes compared to ECC signatures is between are between 12 and 30. Efficiency wise, the differences of speed are marginal.
2. Drop-in replacement unlikely—the differences between pre- and post-quantum schemes makes it unlikely that it would allow simple drop-in replacements in protocols, standards, etc. It is believed that after PQC selection phase, a throughout revision of protocols and standards would be needed.
3. Theoretical immaturity—the novelty of the mathematical foundations for the proposed schemes raises concerns on the confidence on the hardness assumptions, parameter selection, etc., which poses a considerable risk in a rushed transition.[57]

[52] European Telecommunications Standards Institute—ETSI (EU). ETSI TR 103616 V1.1.1 *Quantum-Safe Signatures*. https://www.etsi.org/deliver/etsi_tr/103600_103699/103616/01.01.01_60/tr_103616v010101p.pdf (consulted 2nd June 2022).

[53] European Euro Agency for Cybersecurity—ENISA (EU). *Post-Quantum Cryptography: Current state and quantum mitigation.* https://www.enisa.europa.eu/publications/post-quantum-cryptography-current-state-and-quantum-mitigation/ (consulted 2nd June 2022).

[54] Agence Nationale de la Sécurité des Systèmes d'Information—ANSSI (FR). *ANSSI Views on the Post-Quantum Cryptography Transition.* https://www.ssi.gouv.fr/en/publication/anssi-views-on-the-post-quantum-cryptography-transition/ (consulted 2nd June 2022).

[55] Bundesamt für Sicherheit in der Informationstechnik—BSI (DE). "*Quantum-safe cryptography – fundamentals, current developments and recommendations*". https://www.bsi.bund.de/SharedDocs/Downloads/EN/BSI/Publications/Brochure/quantum-safe-cryptography.html (consulted 2nd June 2022).

[56] National Cyber-Security Center—NCSC (UK). "*Preparing for Quantum-Safe Cryptography*". https://www.ncsc.gov.uk/whitepaper/preparing-for-quantum-safe-cryptography (consulted 2nd June 2022).

[57] . . . the maturity level of the post-quantum algorithms presented to the NIST process should not be overestimated. Many aspects lack cryptanalytical hindsight or are still research topics, e.g. analysis of the difficulty of the underlying problem in the classical and quantum computation models, dimensioning, integration of schemes in protocols and more importantly the design of secure implementations. This situation will probably last some time after the publication of NIST standards.". In op. cit. "ANSSI Views on the Post-Quantum Cryptography Transition.

5 Transition to PQC

The standardization effort for PQC is only the first step towards a transition to a quantum-safe security environment. A whole set of challenges need to be addressed by a variety of players, ranging from each business/organization; software and service providers; hardware manufactures; etc. Due to the pressing timeline imposed by the prospects of QC enabled attacks in a near future, businesses and organizations should plan and deploy transition plans alongside ongoing developments in standardization efforts. Recommendations and guidance for the planning and execution of the PQC transition are being articulated by Security Agencies across the world.[58] Such a pressure on the transition to PQC poses its own risks. In the words of the ANSSI:[59]

> Acknowledging the immaturity of PQC is important: ANSSI will not endorse any direct drop-in replacement of currently used algorithms in the short/medium term. However, this immaturity should not serve as an argument for postponing the deployments. ANSSI encourages all industries to initiate in the next months a gradual overlap transition in order to progressively increase trust on the post-quantum algorithms and their implementations while ensuring no security regression as far as classical (pre-quantum) security is concerned.

The apparent contradiction stated above can be solved by what has been known as hybridization. In the context of the PQC transition, a hybrid scheme is the combination of an established pre-quantum scheme with a post-quantum analogue. The rational is that the security of the combination shall be at least the security granted by any of its components, hence guaranteeing that under no circumstance a regression on security might occur. We note that the increase of sizes of public-keys, etc. caused by hybridization is not significant, as sizes in PQC are always much bigger than those of pre-quantum schemes. For digital signatures, a simple way of building a hybrid digital signature scheme is to combine the results of a pre- and post-quantum signatures. Such a dual signature can also provide a simple path for compatibility with legacy systems during the transition period, by allowing them to focus on the pre-quantum portion.

Hybridization is a well-established method from the research community perspective but, as of the time of writing, it is not clear if it is going to be enforced, recommended, or even supported by the main standardization bodies.[60] Consensual however is that we are entering a period where security systems should be able to

---

[58] E.g., European Telecommunications Standards Institute. ETSI—TR 103619—CYBER. *Migration strategies and recommendations to Quantum Safe schemes.* Jul. 2020. https://www.etsi.org/deliver/etsi_tr/103600_103699/103619/01.01.01_60/tr_103619v010101p.pdf (consulted 2nd June 2022).

[59] ANSSI, op. cit.

[60] ANSSI emphasizes that the role of hybridization and makes it mandatory in the early phases of the transition—c.f. "*...ANSSI emphasizes that the role of hybridization in the cryptographic security is crucial and will be mandatory for phases 1 and 2 presented in the sequel.*", ANSII, op. cit. On the other hand, ETSI opens the prospect of using hybrid solutions, but without any explicit recommendation—c.f. "*Are hybrid solutions quantum safe?—Hybrid solutions are a*

rapidly replace cryptographic algorithms and/or parameters—a property termed as crypto-agility.

What have been said regarding digital signatures applies also to the Public Key Infrastructure (PKI), which is itself a critical ingredient supporting digital signatures. A hybrid certificate includes both the pre- and post-quantum public-keys and is itself signed by both schemes.[61] Besides being a natural support for hybrid signatures, they can also be used just to promote a smooth transition to PQC, by letting the legacy systems rely on the pre-quantum key/signature while adding support to PQC.

6 Long-Term Validation and Signature Preservation

It has been hinted that, in the event of breakthrough development in QC, documents signed with currently used signature schemes would lose its cryptographic guaranties. But this is not a specificity of the signing algorithm losing its cryptographic strength, but rather the mismatch between the signing and verification times that might change the premises concerning the validity status of the signature. To better understand the issue, let us recall the verification procedure of a digitally signed document:

1. Obtain the signer public-key—the verifier should access to the signer's certificate,[62] and check its validity. Checking certificate's validity is itself a task that comprises several steps, such as checking the data on the certificate (e.g. identities of the owner and issuer, validity periods, etc.); checking the certificate's signature;[63] check if the certificate was not; and, if the issuer is not on the verifier's trusted list, repeat the whole process for the next certificate on the certificate chain (that is, the issuer's public-key certificate).
2. Use the signer's public-key obtained by the previous step to verify the signature.

The goal of (1) is to establish that the public-key used in (2) is tied to the signer's identity. Consider now that, after the signing of a document, some event changes the validity status of the corresponding certificate(s) (e.g., it expires, or get revoked)? One can argue that the signature should be deemed valid, since it was valid at signing time. The problem is that the verifier cannot independently verify that information.

Long-Term Validation (LTV) signatures precisely address this problem, by complementing the data provided in the signature to include all the necessary information for its validation, namely:

waypoint on the path to QSC and do not represent the end state (thus a system with hybrid solutions has not achieved FQSCS"). ETSI, op. cit. Annex B (FAQ).

[61]International Telecommunication Union (ITU). Recommendation ITU-T X509 (ISO/IEC 9594–8). "*Public-key and attribute certificate frameworks*".

[62]The signer's certificate is always sent alongside the signed document.

[63]Recall that a certificate is, itself, signed by the certification authority.

- a trusted timestamp[64] that bounds the time of signing to the signed document.
- validation data attesting that the signer's certificate was valid at the time of signing.

Both items rely on trusted third parties, respectively, a Time-Stamp Authority (TSA) that issue timestamps, and a Validation Authority (VA) that issues evidence of the signer's certificate validation status.[65]

LTV signatures add a layer with validation information to basic digital signatures. Moreover, it is not strictly required that this layer is included in the original signed document, not even by the original signer. Moreover, additional LTV signature layers can be added to refresh/extend/upgrade the cryptographic security of signed documents. LTV signatures are normally offered as a Preservation Service, where the end-user promotes the security of signed document. The EU Regulation 910/2014 (eIDAS)[66] contemplates trust-services for (qualified) time stamps, validation, and preservation of signatures, providing a legal framework for their use.[67]

Returning now to the subject of QC, signature preservation can be used to effectively promote a document signed with a pre-quantum signature into a quantum resilient signed document, as long as the added LTV layer is quantum resilient. It is thus predicable that reliance on preservation services of digital signatures will increase substantially during PQC transition.

7 Conclusions

This article aims to highlight some threats posed by quantum computation in the setting of digital signatures of documents. It was explained why signature algorithms currently in use are at risk of being compromised, and what are the quantum-safe alternatives that are being developed to overcome it. Businesses and organizations are being urged to initiate the planning for the transition to the post-quantum setting, even if much of the required technological support is being finalised in parallel. It was also highlighted the role that signature preservation services might provide in ensuring that the security guaranties of pre-PQC signed documents are transferred to a PQC setting.

[64] A timestamp is a digital token, signed by a trusted third-party, that includes a fingerprint (cryptographic hash) of the signed document and the time collected from a reliable source. Regulation 910/2014 (eIDAS Regulation) article 3 nr. 33: "'electronic time stamp' means data in electronic form which binds other data in electronic form to a particular time establishing evidence that the latter data existed at that time".

[65] Or "trust service", Regulation 910/2014 (eIDAS Regulation) article 3 nr. 16.

[66] See https://www.eid.as (consulted 2nd June 2022).

[67] Detailed technical specifications are published by the Electronic Signatures and Infrastructures (ESI) technical committee of the ETSI—https://www.etsi.org/technologies/digital-signature (consulted 2nd June 2022).

References

Ball P (2021) First 100-qubit quantum computer enters crowded race. Nat News 599:542. https://doi.org/10.1038/d41586-021-03476-5

Barbagalo EB (2001) Contratos Eletrônicos. Editora Saraiva, São Paulo

Bennett CH, Bernstein E, Brassard G, Vazirani U (1997) The strengths and weaknesses of quantum computation. SIAM J Comput 26(5):1510–1523. https://doi.org/10.1137/s0097539796300933

Bensoussan A (1992) Les Telecommunications et le droit. Memento-Guide Alain Bensoussan. Hermés, Paris

Brito L, Neves J (2003) Uma abordagem multiagente à problemática do comércio electrónico. Grupo de Inteligência Artificial, Departamento de Informática, Universidade do Minho

Colegios Notariales de España (2000) Notariado y Contratación Electrónica. Consejo General del Notariado

Correia MP (2006) Assinatura electrónica e certificação digital. In: Direito da Sociedade da Informação, vol VI. Coimbra Editora, pp 277–317

Diffie W, Hellman M (1996) New directions in cryptography. IEEE Trans Inf Theory 22(6): 644–654. https://doi.org/10.1109/TIT.1976.1055638

Dumortier J, Van den Eynde S. De juridische erkenning van de elektronische handtekening. https://www.law.kuleuven.be/citip/en/archive/copy_of_publications/72eh-computerrecht-juli20012f90.pdf

Fischer JP (1997) Computers as agents: a proposed approach to revised U.C.C. article 2. Indiana Law J 72(2):545–570

Fowler AG, Mariantoni M, Martinis JM, Cleland AN (2012) Surface codes: Towards practical large-scale quantum computation. Phys Rev A 86:032324. https://doi.org/10.1103/PhysRevA.86.032324

Fuenzalida CV (1999) En torno a los contratos electrónicos. In: Revista General de Legislación y Jurisprudência, vol 1. Enero-Febrero

Gautrais V. La formation des contrats en ligne. https://www.jurisint.org/pub/05/fr/guide_chap4.pdf

Gidney C, Ekerå M (2021) How to factor 2048 bit RSA integers in 8 hours using 20 million noisy qubits. Quantum 5:433. https://doi.org/10.22331/q-2021-04-15-433

Grover LK (1996) A fast quantum mechanical algorithm for database search. In: Proceedings of the twenty-eighth annual ACM symposium on theory of computing. STOC '96. Association for Computing Machinery, pp 212–219. https://doi.org/10.1145/237814.237866

Haney BS (2020) Blockchain: post-quantum security & legal economics. NC Bank Inst 24:117

Jeutner V (2021) The quantum imperative: addressing the legal dimension of quantum computers. Morals Mach 1(1):52–59

Kuhn DR et al (2001) Nat'l Inst. of Standards & Tech. Introduction to public key technology and the federal PKI infrastructure 9. Available at https://apps.dtic.mil/sti/pdfs/ADA394230.pdf

Rand L, Rand T (2021) The 'prime factors' of quantum cryptography regulation. In SSRN: https://papers.ssrn.com/sol3/papers.cfm?abstract_id=3904342

Reed C (1990) Computer law. Blackstone Press Limited

Rivest R, Shamir A, Adleman L (1978) A method for obtaining digital signatures and public-key cryptosystems. Commun ACM 21(2):120–126. https://doi.org/10.1145/359340.359342

Rotger LH, Garau GA (1995) Seguridad en la transmisión electrónica (EDI): validez jurídica. In: Encuentros sobre Informática y Derecho 1994–1995. Aranzadi Editorial

Royal Society Open Science Report (2018) According to a Royal Society Open Science Report: quantum computers are capable of deducing the private key from a formerly revealed public key with little effort. R Soc Open Sci. no. 6, at 3. https://doi.org/10.1098/rsos.180410 [https://perma.cc/U47R-5KZB]

Shor PW (1994) Algorithms for quantum computation: discrete logarithms and factoring. In: Proceedings 35th annual symposium on foundations of computer science. IEEE Computer Society Press, pp 124–134. https://doi.org/10.1109/sfcs.1994.365700

Sloane A (1994) Computer communications – principles and business applications. McGraw Hill Book Company

Sorge C (2006) Softwareagenten – Vertragsschluss, Vertragsstraffe, Reugeld. Universitätsverlag Karlsruhe

Vermeer MJD, Peet ED (2020) Securing communications in the quantum computing age: managing the risks to encryption. RAND CORP, pp 36–37. https://www.rand.org/pubs/research_reports/RR3102.html

Vershinin AP (2000) Electronic document: legal form and evidential force in court. Gorodiets, Moscow

Vicente DM (2005) Direito Internacional Privado - Problemática Internacional da Sociedade da Informação. Almedina, p 19

Wang B, Hu F, Yao H et al (2020) Prime factorization algorithm based on parameter optimization of Ising model. Sci Rep 10:7106. https://doi.org/10.1038/s41598-020-62802-5

Francisco António Carneiro Pacheco de Andrade holds a PhD in Law (Legal Privatistic Sciences) from University of Minho and a MSc in Electronic Information Management from the University of Sheffield (United Kingdom). He is auxiliary professor at Universidade do Minho Law School and he has been, for 11 years, the Director of the Master Course in Law and Informatics. He is also lecturer in the same Master in the Units of "Cryptography, Electronic Identification and Documents", "Privacy and Data Protection", "Electronic Commerce and Electronic Contracting". He is an integrated member of JUSGOV – Research Center on Justice and Governation at University of Minho Law School.

José Carlos Bacelar Almeida holds a Ph.D. in Informatics Engineering and an M.Sc. from the University of Minho, and a degree in Electrical and Computer Engineering from the University of Porto. He is an auxiliary professor at the University of Minho, and a lead researcher at IHASLAB/NESCTEC. His research interests include cryptography, provable security, program verification and theorem proving. He has been involved in several international research projects with multiple contributions on the areas of formalisation of security proofs and tool development for certified cryptographic implementations.

No Words Needed? Emojis as Evidence in Judicial Proceedings

Ana Rodríguez Álvarez

Abstract Emojis have become an integral part of our daily communications. Through them, we express our emotions, complete the content of messages, qualify our words and, sometimes, we completely replace the text. It has not taken long for these pictograms to move from the keyboards of our devices to the courts. And the fact is that, not so long ago, the court rulings have been taking emojis into account to resolve both civil and criminal proceedings. Thus, the aim of this paper is to analyse what role emojis are playing as evidence, what problems and doubts are arising in practice and what challenges we will have to face in the future.

1 About Emoticons, Emojis and the Rest of the Family

Before addressing the role that emojis are playing as evidence in legal proceedings, it is necessary to clarify the meaning of this term, as it is not always used properly. To do so, we will begin by talking about the emoticon, the predecessor of the current emoji.

The emoticon is generally a representation of a facial expression made up of orthographic signs: full stops, commas, brackets, etc.[1] Its origin dates back to 1982, the year in which the researcher Robert E. Fahlman and his colleagues at Carnegie

A Spanish version of this work was published in *Revista de la Facultad de Derecho de México*, num. 275, 2019, pp. 675–698. DOI: https://doi.org/10.22201/fder.24488933e.2019.275-2.71117; https://revistas.unam.mx/index.php/rfdm/article/view/71117.

[1]The *Real Academia Española*'s Dictionary defines emoticon as "a representation of a facial expression used in electronic messages to allude to the sender's mood".

A. R. Álvarez (✉)
Department of Special Public Law and Company Law of the University of Santiago de Compostela, Santiago, Spain
e-mail: ana.rodriguez.alvarez@usc.es

F. A. Carneiro Pacheco de Andrade et al. (eds.), *Legal Developments on Cybersecurity and Related Fields*, Law, Governance and Technology Series 60, https://doi.org/10.1007/978-3-031-41820-4_13

Mellon University were victims of a misunderstanding following an exchange of messages: what was a statement made in jest was interpreted by some people as something serious. As a result, and in order to avoid further misunderstandings, Fahlman proposed including the emoticon :-) to distinguish more informal or joking messages from formal ones.[2]

For its part, the kaomoji is the Eastern equivalent of the emoticon. The differences between the two are mainly two: firstly, the kaomoji, unlike the emoticon, is not read "sideways"; secondly, kaomojis tend to focus much more on the expression of the "eyes" than emoticons, apparently for cultural reasons. An example of a kaomoji would be the following: (^_^). In this case, it would represent a smiling expression.

Finally, emojis are pictograms, drawings that represent a wide variety of moods, people and objects.[3] They were created in 1995 by Japanese engineer Shigetaka Kurita, who created the first one hundred and seventy-six emojis as a result of designing a platform for the telephone company where he worked.[4]

Although the familiarity with which we use them today[5] leads us to think that emojis have been with us for a long time, in reality, they did not reach the western world until 2011. They did so through Apple devices, although they quickly spread to other companies.

Its immense diffusion and popularity is well known. Proof of this is, for example, that the Oxford Dictionary, in a decision not without controversy, chose the emoji "face with tears of joy" as word of the year in 2015.[6] Or that the catalogue of the Unicode[7] consortium—responsible for creating and regulating them—increases year after year. Or that their use—if not abuse—is increasingly widespread among people of all ages and walks of life. Or that with them we not only make up for the lack of non-verbal communication in written electronic communications, but also, on occasions, we directly replace words (the applications themselves suggest them to us when we write).[8] In short, if one thing is clear, it is that emojis are here to stay.

---

[2]However, it is not uncommon to cite other precedents. For example, Cuadrado Gordillo et al. (2015), p. 184, point out that the origin seems to go back to a 1967 article in *Reader's Digest* magazine, although they recognize that Fahlman is credited with being the first to use it in an interactive context. Martín-Mora Parra (2017), pp. 199 *et seq.*, also points to other precedents.

[3]The *Real Academia Española*'s Dictionary defines emoji as "small digital image or icon used in electronic communications to represent an emotion, an object, an idea, etc."

[4]*Vid.* Sampietro (2016), pp. 58–59.

[5]On all types of devices and particularly on instant messaging services such as WhatsApp.

[6]We even have a "novel" in emoji version: *Emoji Dick*, an adaptation of Herman Melville's famous work by artist Fred Benenson. However, he is not the only one, as artist Ken Hale has also done the same with Lewis Carroll's *Alice in Wonderland.*

[7]*Cfr.* http://unicode.org/.

[8]There is even an emoji grammar that explains how to construct verb tenses using these pictograms. *Vid.* Vv. Aa. (2018).

2 The Emoji Landing: From the Keyboards to the Courts

2.1 Some Examples from Comparative Law

Not even a decade has passed since emojis arrived in the West. However, it has been more than enough time for them to reach the courts from our terminals.

One of the first cases to hit the media spotlight took place in the United States in 2015. At that time, a minor in New York was prosecuted for making a terrorist threat after posting on his Facebook profile—which was open to the public—among other messages, one in which the emoji of a policeman could be seen followed by three guns pointed at him.

In another court case, held in France in 2016, a young French man was sentenced to 3 months in prison for threats after sending his ex-partner a message with the gun emoji.

Emojis matter. They matter a lot. A good example of this is the 2015 United States case Silk Road, in which the criminal liability of Ross Ulbricht, creator of a black market on the deep web, was sought. At one point in the trial, the prosecution read out an email but failed to mention that there was a smiley emoji accompanying the words. The defence highlighted this omission and the judge instructed the jurors to be mindful of the emojis included in the electronic communications, judiciously considering that these were also an integral part of the text and therefore of the evidence.

The issues are, of course, not limited to criminal cases. For example, the case of Ghanam versus Does, decided by the Michigan Court of Appeals in 2014, involved the possible infringement of the right to honour of a municipal official due to a series of comments posted on an internet forum. One such comment was: "They are only getting more garbage trucks because Gus needs more tires to sell to get more money for his pockets :P".

In this case, the use of the emoticon was decisive. In its judgment, the court reasoned that the discordant statement could not be taken seriously, as the use of the emoticon made it clear that it was a joke. Consequently, no reasonable reader would regard the comment as infringing on the right to honour.[9]

Another civil case was decided by an Israeli court in 2017. In this case, the owner of a house claimed compensation from potential tenants. The potential tenants, in the course of a conversation about renting a house, sent him a message stating that they wanted the house, but needed to go over the details. This was accompanied by various emojis: a smiley face, dancers, a bottle of champagne.

Convinced that the negotiations had come to a successful conclusion, the owner withdrew the rental advert. But those who were going to be his new tenants

[9]Literally, the court states: "This statement on its face cannot be taken seriously as asserting a fact. The use of the :P emoticon makes it patently clear that the commenter was making a joke. As noted earlier, a :P emoticon is used to represent a face with its tongue sticking out to denote a joke or sarcasm. Thus, a reasonable reader could not view the statement as defamatory".

disappeared. As we pointed out, the man claimed compensation and the court upheld his claim, understanding that, although the message did not constitute a binding contract between the parties, it did give the landlord a reasonable expectation that the contract would be completed.[10]

2.2 *Emojis Before Spanish Courts*

2.2.1 Determinant or Not for the Ruling? There Are No More Emojis, Your Honour

As in other countries, emojis have also reached the Spanish courts. An analysis of the case law allows us to conclude that the results can be divided into two large groups: firstly, there are those cases in which, although emojis are referred to in court rulings, they are not decisive. In other words, although they are elements that are valued in the judgment, the court's decision would not have changed if they had not been present.

An example of this first block can be found in Provincial Court of Sevilla's decision 437/2017, September 22nd, concerning a continuous offence of threats. Despite the fact that the messages include the emoji representing a gun, the words uttered were more than enough to justify, on their own, the conviction.

Something similar happened with Provincial Court of Valencia's decision 115/2018, February 27th, in which a man who sent a series of messages to his ex-partner was convicted of a minor offence of insult. The messages contained various insults, together with six emojis representing a hand with a raised middle finger. Once again, the words were sufficient to support a conviction, regardless of the pictograms that accompanied them.

Similar approach is adopted in the decision 117/2018, July 23th of the Provincial Court of Ciudad Real, which dealt with a violation of the prohibition of communication through the sending of emojis, but also text messages and telephone calls.

The case of the Provincial Court of Islas Baleares's decision (second Section) 186/2016, September 1st, is different: in this case, a man was convicted in the first instance for threats against his ex-wife. The accused had posted the following message on Facebook: "my revenge begins, get ready, you remember what you did to me, now I'm going to kill you to death, I will not stop, like you did when I had my partner", to which he added six emojis of laughter.

Far from understanding that these emojis indicate that the content of the message is not serious, that it is a joke—even if it is in bad taste—the court, with good judgement, reasoned: "The fact that these expressions are accompanied by emoticons smiling with laughter does not lower the tone and the threatening sense of the

[10]These and other cases can be found referenced in: Berels (2017), pp. 21–26; Delaney (2016) pp. 2–3; El Khouri (2017); Janssen (2018) pp. 708 *et seq.*; Kauffman (2018), pp. 26–29; Kirley and McMahon (2018), pp. 517–570; Kramer (2018), pp. 407–409; Mashile (2017), pp. 16–17.

sentences, but rather emphasises the cynicism of the author and the fact that the sender enjoys the evil he is announcing to the appellee and the uneasiness and disquiet that he knows such expressions may cause her, in which he warns her that he is going to take revenge on her, that he will not stop and that he is going to make her die, all of this, moreover, communicated on a social network, in such a way that the threat is reinforced by its public communication so that it reaches the recipient's ears, using this publicity to show her intentions to other people who may access her social profile".

On the other hand, in a case of sexual abuse by a teacher of his underage pupil, the Provincial Court of Barcelona's decision 407/2018, July 9th, explains that the aggressor and victim established a coded language, using different emojis.

Also in a case of multiple robberies in bank branches resolved by the Provincial Court of Burgos's decision (1st Section) 157/2017, May 12th, reference is made, among other much more decisive evidence—such as DNA—to emojis. Specifically, to those representing wads of banknotes, sent by one of the accused on the same dates as some of the robberies took place. The sentence states: "On the same day, November 20th at 10.36 a.m., the accused [. . .] sent a person called Juliana emoticons with wads of money telling her that he had succeeded, followed by a congratulatory message received from Juliana. [. . .] on 17 December, the day of the robbery in Bakio, [. . .] sends emoticons with bundles of banknotes telling Fermín: 'you already have a car'".

Along with this first block, there is another block made up of legal proceedings in which emojis are at the centre of the discussion. That is, those where their presence is decisive in the judge's decision. These are the most interesting cases, for obvious reasons. Although there are not many yet, we can predict that their number will increase sooner rather than later.

A first example can be found in Provincial Court of Alicante's decision 203/2018, April sixth, concerning an offence of breach of sentence for failing to comply with the prohibition of communication: a man convicted of harassing a woman infringes this prohibition by sending her two messages via Messenger: according to the sentence, one is "an emoticon of a face"—it is not made clear which one–; the other, "an emoticon of thumbs up".[11] The sending of these emojis, even if they are not accompanied by any words, is sufficient to satisfy the requirements of the criminal offence, which is why he was convicted at first instance.

The convicted person appeals on the grounds of "error in the assessment of the evidence". Strictly speaking, the appellant does not dispute the reality of the messages, but his authorship. In his defence, he maintains that he did not send them, but a third party whose identity he does not know. The Court, on its part, upheld the appellant's assessment, as there was not the slightest indication of manipulation in the sending of the messages: "there is no evidence of manipulation or alteration, [. . .] the mere allegation that there has been manipulation without any proof that a third party had accessed the Facebook account is not sufficient [. . .]".

[11] As we can see, the Spanish courts use the words emoji and emoticon interchangeably.

On the other hand, the case resolved by Provincial Court of Barcelona's decision 345/2015, June 30th, refers to a crime of threats in which the defendant avoided his conviction, precisely, thanks to the thumbs-up emoji.

It is a proven fact that the defendant sent the following text to a young woman: "you'll see when we get out of here", accompanied by the aforementioned emoji. A certain intimidating tone could be inferred from the words, but the pictogram that accompanies them does not have—in the sense commonly used—any kind of negative connotation.

Faced with doubts about the interpretation of the message, the Barcelona Provincial Court emphasises that the emoji "appears in previous moments of the conversation [. . .] as a symbol of agreement, which is its usual meaning, so that the doubts that may arise about its meaning cannot be resolved to the detriment of the accused and therefore his right to the presumption of innocence must prevail".

In short, the classic *in dubio pro reo* applies, which determines the acquittal of the appellant, who had been convicted at first instance.

In relation to threats, we also find Provincial Court of Cantabria's court order 475/2014, October 13th, which confirms the provisional dismissal ordered in favour of a man denounced by his ex-partner after publishing a message in his whatsapp status in which he inserted emojis of a target, a woman, a man and a gun with the barrel pointing towards the man, accompanied by the phrase "this does not end here".

The Court upheld the dismissal on the basis of various arguments.[12] Among them, that the interpretation of such a whatsapp status was subjective, insofar as it could be understood "as a suggestion of a possible suicide of the person who is in that 'state of mind' due to the separation. In any case, any interpretations that may be made are mere conjecture".

The Provincial Court of Álava's court order 566/2018, November 22th, which shares certain similarities with the previous one, also resolves an appeal against a provisional dismissal. In this case, the defendant had a prohibition of communication with the complainant as a precautionary measure. The latter informed the authorities that the man had written a phrase—it is not indicated which one—on his whatsapp profile, accompanied by "emoticons of 'peinetas'"—due to the meaning that is sometimes given to the Spanish word "peineta", we assume the "middle finger" emoji.

The Court upheld the dismissal, in view of two concurrent circumstances: the first, the place where the message is located—a whatsapp status. In this regard, the court points out: "A sentence on a whatsapp profile is like putting it on a sign on the door of a house: it constitutes a message and, therefore, a one-way communication for anyone who looks at the profile or passes by the door of the author of the sentence. In any case, it must be approached to be read, and the addressee is anyone who does so. This does not show that the defendant intended the message to reach

[12] Another was, for example, that the woman did not ask for a protection order because she stated that she did not feel threatened.

the complainant one way or the other. There is no evidence that there was any certainty that she read it or that anyone informed her of the existence of the message".

The second circumstance taken into account by the Provincial Court has to do with the content of the message itself, which is described as ambiguous and open to interpretation, since it does not contain any explicit reference to the complainant. In our opinion, this is the real key which, in the present case, can justify the dismissal of the case.

Let us start from the following premise: for the purposes of breaching the prohibition on communication, it is completely different to send a "direct" message to the victim—in which case the prohibition imposed will always be breached regardless of the content of the message—than to post a message in the whatsapp status. In the latter circumstance, as a general rule, the prohibition will not be infringed. However, in contrast to the Álava Provincial Court, we consider that, on occasions and with due caution, it could be breached, provided that it is accredited that the whatsapp status is used as a subterfuge to establish communication with the victim.[13]

Be that as it may, the court itself specifies that its decision "is based on a matter of nuance" and, by way of prevention, warns the defendant: "in the future [...] you could get some criminal displeasure if you read this decision as an authorisation to put anything on your whatsapp profile. Prudence".

Ambiguity is also one of the criteria used by Provincial Court of Madrid's decision 809/2016, December 14th, to resolve a case. In this case, the accused had sent his wife, among other messages, three emojis representing a gun—a case practically identical to that of the young Frenchman mentioned above.

The defendant argued in his defence that he had sent the gun icons by mistake, as he actually wanted to send kisses. According to his version, they are next to each other on his terminal—which is probably due, in our opinion, to the fact that they are

[13] In the same sense that we defend, see Provincial Court of Valladolid's decision 119/2015, April 13th: "The appellant states in his appeal that the 'WhatsApp statuses' are not a form of communication, given that all forms of communication require a sender, a message and a receiver, and, in this case, there was no message addressed to the complainant with the intention of breaching the court order. This Chamber does not share the appellant's assessment, but does share that of the Court of First Instance. The information that is placed in the 'WhatsApp status' by a user of the aforementioned application is information that is placed so that it can be viewed and known by all those who have that mobile phone number incorporated into their phone, but in this case the accused took advantage of the subterfuge of the 'WhatsApp status' to break the prohibition of communication that had been imposed on him, because instead of offering any information that could be used to identify him, what he did was to send communications that could be used to identify him, specifically addressed to the person with whom he had been told that he could not communicate, communications that also had a clearly offensive content, and in which, in addition, due to the method used, he caused his offensive expressions to enjoy a certain amount of publicity, precisely among all his 'WhatsApp' contacts, which is why it is agreed that the accused has indeed breached the communication prohibition order he had and that he has also committed the offences of insult for which he has been convicted".

among the most frequently used by this user. The accused explained that, after noticing the error, he spoke to his wife to clarify this point.

The Court itself recognises that this explanation is not very credible, although "the literal tenor of the messages sent by the accused to his wife is not conclusive, being, in the same words used in the plenary session by the representative of the Public Prosecutor's Office, ambiguous phrases".

This ambiguity of the messages, together with the context of the conversation between the complainant and the accused—in which the couple referred on several occasions to the possibility of resuming their relationship—led the Court to consider that the mere reference to the emojis of guns "cannot be interpreted as necessarily threatening, and could simply be a joke". As a result, it reversed the lower court's ruling, acquitting the defendant.

Leaving aside the threats, in the case resolved by Provincial Court of Madrid's decision 302/2017, May 18th, the defendant was acquitted of the minor offence of insult for which his ex-partner had denounced him. The alleged insulting message consisted of the phrase "How little you have left", accompanied by six emojis representing the face of a pig.

With regard to the phrase, the Court ruled out its criminal relevance, understanding that it could refer to the "announcement of the end of the civil proceedings that both parties had pending, insinuating or anticipating the possible failure of the complainant's claims". Together with this, it merely states that the pig emojis, on their own, also lack criminal relevance, referring to the reasoning made in the judgment under appeal on this point.

Despite the fact that most of the decisions we have found and which we have presented so far are criminal, there are also some in the civil sphere. For example, in matters of machinery leasing, as shown in Provincial Court of Valladolid's decision 365/2018, November 8th.

In this case, the plaintiff and the defendant disagreed on the total number of hours of use of the leased machinery. These hours ultimately determined the total amount to be paid. One of the pieces of evidence submitted to the proceedings was a whatsapp conversation between the parties, a conversation about which there was no discussion—as is the case on other occasions—about its possible lack of validity or the existence of manipulations. Here, on the contrary, the debate was about the interpretation of an emoji. In the disputed fragment, the lessor wrote: "Total hours. Total 272 hours". The tenant replied by sending a thumbs-up emoji.

The lower court ignored the emoji, which it described as an informal act. However, contrary to its criterion, the Court considered that, taking into account the context of the conversation they had been having, it could be logically deduced that the defendant was accepting those 272 h. As a result, the respondent was ordered to pay an additional five thousand euros: "The emoticon that the judge describes as an informal act of acceptance of the number of hours claimed by the plaintiff cannot be disassociated from the context of the conversations held by both parties regarding the number of hours of the machine and from the data presented by the plaintiff it must be concluded that the emoticon is the consequence of other previous conversations in which they specify the number of hours worked with the machine to which the defendant does not object, so the logical inference is that he accepts them, which culminates in the emoticon with which he agrees to the plaintiff's message detailing the total number of hours worked at 272".

2.2.2 Defence Strategies?

A reading of the case law shows us how the defendants' lawyers sometimes interpret the emojis sent by the alleged victims of the crimes in order to articulate their defence strategy. Specifically, there are examples in cases involving minor offences of threats, which seek to demonstrate how the use of emojis makes it possible to prove that the recipients of the messages in question were not the least bit disturbed when they received them.

For example, in the case resolved by the Provincial Court of Vizcaya's decision 90047/2016, February 17th, the appellant argues that "an essential element is missing in order to appreciate the crime, which is that the complainant loses his peace of mind due to the threatening content of the threat, which does not occur in this case since in the messages it can be seen that he sends an emoticon of a wink or a greeting, which is not consistent with a state of unease".

The court, ratifying the assessment of the lower court, dismissed the appeal, in view of what was stated by the complainant in the trial and the nature of the threatening phrase itself.

Also in the Provincial Court of Ourense's decision 308/2016, October 14th, it is explained that, in the appellant's opinion, the expressions made lacked the requirements of seriousness, firmness and credibility. Among other reasons, because the complainant replied to the messages received in a mocking tone and even with emojis of smiley faces. His allegation, however, was unsuccessful. The judgment explains how at first the complainant thought that the sender was someone else and, after discovering the identity of the real sender, "he put the smiley face emoticon because it was funny that (sic) he was being accused of something he had not done". However, after receiving subsequent threatening messages, he no longer uses any emoji.

However, as the Court explains, "even if the defendant had not managed to frighten the complainant, this does not affect the consummation of the offence, which is one of danger, and it is sufficient that the expression uttered by itself is capable of disturbing the tranquillity of the passive subject".

More curious is the defence articulated in the case of Provincial Court of Santa Cruz de Tenerife's decision 70/2016, February 25th: a man breaks a ban on approaching the victim—he went to her home—and tries to provide as evidence a conversation in which he uses an emoji—it is not specified which one—which, according to him, would prove that when the events took place he was under the influence of drugs. As is easy to imagine, his argument was unsuccessful: "With regard to the allegations on the application of the mitigating circumstance of Article 21. 1, which the appellant links to the circumstance that the emoticon makes it certain that Celso was under the influence of cocaine, it must be pointed out that the proven facts, which the court has taken as valid, make no reference to the fact that the appellant was under the influence of drugs and that this had affected his abilities, since when it refers to the consumption of intoxicants by the appellant, it refers to an earlier date and takes this into account to conclude that when the events in question occurred, he was not with his friends, as he argued. Nor does the legal reasoning reflect such a conclusion and it certainly cannot be based on an emoticon from a mobile phone application".

3 The Emoji Challenge

The arrival of emojis in the courts leads us to consider some difficulties that may arise in practice. Regardless of the general problems derived from the provision and eventual challenge of electronic evidence, which we are not going to go into here.[14]

The first has to do with their interpretation.[15] It is true that, in many cases, emojis allow us to clarify the meaning or intention of a message.[16] Just think of a simple example: the phrase "get ready, you're going to pay for this" accompanied by a smiley emoji will be interpreted in a very different way—rather antagonistically—if we change that emoji for another with an angry expression or one that represents a gun followed by a hospital.

This being the case, emojis definitely condition the interpretation of the words that accompany them. In this regard, it is worth mentioning the so-called "Poe's Law", named not after the famous writer, but after the person who enunciated it in 2005: Nathan Poe.

In the context of a Christian internet forum in which creationism was being discussed, Poe posted: "Without a winking smiley or other blatant display of humor, it is utterly impossible to parody a Creationist in such a way that someone won't mistake for the genuine article". That is to say, if it is generally stated, without some emoji or other element that denotes its humorous or jocular nature, it is

[14]On this question, *cfr.* Arrabal Platero and Fuentes Soriano (2019), pp. 1–12; Arrabal Platero (2016), pp. 351–362; Rodríguez Álvarez (2019), pp. 321–346; Rodríguez Álvarez (2018), pp. 1–14; Rodríguez Álvarez (2016), pp. 339–349.

[15]Notes Janssen (2018), p. 714, that one of the reasons emojis are difficult to interpret lies in their close association with emotions. He adds that two or more emojis together can further change the meaning of a message. In this sense, Evans (2017), p. 13, points out that the repetition of emojis serves to emphasise.

[16]The fact that a different element of a word influences or conditions the meaning of a sentence is certainly not new. Conan Doyle himself gives us an example in his *Study in Scarlet*: "Upon rising next morning he found, to his surprise, a small square of paper pinned on to the coverlet of his bed just over his chest. On it was printed, in bold straggling letters:

'Twenty-nine days are given you for amendment, and then—'

The dash was more fear-inspiring than any threat could have been".

practically impossible to distinguish between a statement that expresses an extremist opinion and another that parodies, precisely, that opinion.

On this basis, we pose the following question: do emojis always help to clarify the meaning of a message? In our opinion, the answer is no. This is mainly due to the ambiguity inherent in some of these pictograms, whose true meaning is either not always known or is subject to different interpretations.

For example, the emoji called "folded hands", which represents two hands joined palm to palm, is used to mean apologising, thanking, praying or high-fiving.

For its part, the emoji "face with steam from nose" evokes for many of us feelings of anger, weariness. However, in its original conception, it intends to convey an attitude of triumph, pride or empowerment (in fact, its original name was "face with look of triumph").[17]

In short, despite attempts at "codification" such as Emojipedia,[18] the meaning of these pictograms is not always univocal and, therefore, the meaning attributed to them by one person may be different from that assigned to them by another.

In addition to this, there is another considerable drawback: the differences in format between the different operators. Apple's emojis differ from those of Samsung, which in turn differ from those of WhatsApp, Microsoft, Twitter, Facebook, Mozilla, Google, etc. It is true that, on most occasions, the differences between one system and another are nuanced. But not always. Let's take an example: in 2016, the Apple company modified the gun emoji. It went from representing a real gun to a water pistol. Some companies imitated Apple and also introduced this change in their emoji catalogue, while others kept the revolver.

At this point, let's go back to the case of the young Frenchman we were talking about at the beginning. If that young man had sent a message with a water pistol, would he then have been convicted? Most probably the answer is no.

The disparity in format between operators also means that the emoji we send may be received differently from how we see it on screen. For example, if we send the water gun emoji from an Apple device, the person who receives it may see it as a gun if their operator did not introduce the aforementioned change.

Given this different appearance, for legal purposes it would logically be the emoji sent that should be taken into account, not the one actually received.[19] Again taking the French case as a reference, if the young man had sent a water pistol, we understand that he could not be convicted of threats even if his ex-partner visualised it on his terminal as a weapon—unless, of course, the emoji was accompanied by words with sufficient substance to constitute such a criminal offence.

Be that as it may, the difficulties we have pointed out cannot lead us to ignore the presence of emojis: the courts will have to analyse and assess them like any other piece of evidence. They cannot ignore their presence in a text, just as they cannot

[17] Not to mention the interpretation that some have made of the aubergine emoji, banned on certain platforms as a phallic reference.

[18] Emojipedia is, so to speak, the emoji "dictionary". *Cfr*. http://emojipedia.org/.

[19] It is also understood by Berels (2017), p. 32, in the same way.

ignore the presence of any other sign or word that makes up a text: it is by considering all these elements as a whole that we will be able to better interpret the message. Without forgetting, of course, the importance of context.[20]

As we have seen throughout these pages, emojis have only just appeared in our courtrooms. In the coming years we will see how their presence as evidence increases quantitatively and qualitatively in court decisions; and we will surely also witness the appearance of new challenges and questions that this new form of global communication, this *newspeak*—hopefully not in an Orwellian sense—poses. Among them, some as classic as the question of whether a picture is worth a thousand words. The answer will most likely be the same as for other big questions: it depends.

References

Arrabal Platero P (2016) El whatsapp como fuente de prueba. In: Fuentes Soriano O (ed) El proceso penal. Cuestiones fundamentales. Tirant lo Blanch, Valencia, pp 351–362

Arrabal Platero P, Fuentes Soriano O (2019) Impugnación de la prueba tecnológica: práctica de prueba instrumental y exigencia de un "principio de prueba". Comentario a la STS 375/2018, de 19 de julio. Revista General de Derecho Procesal 47:1–12

Berels RA (2017) Take me seriously: emoji as evidence. Digital Commons at Michigan State University College of Law:1–38. http://digitalcommons.law.msu.edu/king/261

Cuadrado Gordillo I, Martín-Mora Parra G, Fernández Antelo I (2015) La expresión de las emociones en la comunicación virtual: el ciberhabla. Icono 14 13(1):180–207

Delaney JF (2016) Mixed messages: courts grapple with emoticons and emoji. Socially Aware Social Media Law Update 7(4):2–3

El Khouri C (2017) #PopLaw: how emojis are creeping into the courtroom. http://bucketorange.com.au/emojis-creeping-courtroom/

Evans V (2017) The emoji code. How smiley faces, love hearts and thumbs up are changing the way we communicate. Michael O'Mara Books Limited, London

Janssen E (2018) Hearsey in the smiley face: analyzing the use of emojis as evidence. St Mary's Law J 49(3):699–725

Kauffman RH (2018) If it looks like a duck: emojis, emoticons and ambiguity. Florida Bar Family Law Sect Comment xxxi(3):26–29

Kirley E, McMahon M (2018) The emoji factor: humanizing the emerging law of digital speech. Tennessee Law Rev 85:517–570

Kramer X (2018) Challenges of electronic taking of evidence: old problems in a new guise and new problems in disguise. In: Vv. Aa (ed) La prueba en el proceso. Atelier, Barcelona, pp 391–410

Martín-Mora Parra G (2017) Caracterización de los usos y funciones de los emojis en la comunicación mediada electrónicamente. http://dehesa.unex.es/handle/10662/6173

Mashile TC (2017) Think before you emoji. De rebus. SA Attorney's J 572:16–17

[20] On the importance of context, Evans explains an example given by Stephen C. Levison: let us imagine that we find a bottle floating in the sea containing the following message: "Meet me here in a week's time with a stick of this size". We do not know who wrote the message, or when, or where, or the size of the stick we should carry. We have no context and therefore cannot properly understand the message. *Vid.* Evans (2017), p. 42.

Rodríguez Álvarez A (2016) Proceso penal y redes sociales: aportación por las partes de la información contenida en ellas. In: Fuentes Soriano O (ed) El proceso penal. Cuestiones fundamentales. Tirant lo Blanch, Valencia, pp 339–349

Rodríguez Álvarez A (2018) Los contenidos de redes sociales como prueba en el proceso civil: un estudio jurisprudencial. Diario La Ley 9195:1–14

Rodríguez Álvarez A (2019) Redes sociales y proceso penal: una radiografía. In: Castillejo Manzanares R (ed) El nuevo proceso penal sin Código Procesal Penal. Atelier, Barcelona, pp 321–346

Sampietro A (2016) Emoticonos y emojis: análisis de su historia, difusión y uso en la comunicación digital actual. http://infoling.org/repository/PhDdiss-Infoling-83-5-2016.pdf

Vv. Aa (2018) Emojigraphy. The international emoji language, vol 1. Emojigraphy Team

Ana Rodríguez Álvarez is a Graduate in Law from the University of Santiago de Compostela with an Extraordinary Degree Award, Master's Degree in Private Law, Master's Degree in Mediation and Doctorate in Law with an international mention and Extraordinary Doctorate Award from the same University.

At present, she is an Assistant Professor of Procedural Law (certified as Associate Professor) at the University of Santiago de Compostela.

She is the author of more than ninety scientific publications including articles, book chapters and books; and has participated as a lecturer in more than a hundred national and international conferences, seminars and courses in Spain, Costa Rica, Chile, Mexico, Peru, Italy and Portugal.

She has carried out research stays at the Universities of Pavia, Bologna, Complutense de Madrid, Carlos III de Madrid and the Institute of Advanced Legal Studies in London.

She has also coordinated a dozen collective books and has participated in six research projects.

Part III
Cybersecurity, Ethics and Fundamental Rights

Bug Bounties: Ethical and Legal Aspects

João Paulo Magalhães

Abstract Bug bounty programs are a new approach to pen-testing. Through them, organisations are willing to test their products taking advantage of hackers spread all over the world. So, the number of vulnerabilities found increases and the cost of detecting them becomes lower. To maintain some control over what hackers can do, organisations specify a set of rules. Through these rules, organisations try to limit the actions to be performed and to give confidence to ethical hackers conduct activities that are typically illegal without being worried with the risk of legal violations. This article presents an analysis of the current state of bug bounty programs. The analysis focuses on economic, ethical, and legal aspects and highlights several problems related to these aspects. Given the current state of these programs, it is important that national bodies responsible for cybersecurity, address the challenges imposed by these programs. National and international rules are needed to both ethically and legally protect the parties and contribute to regulate an activity that many still consider illegal. Without that, a set of alternative solutions to "legalize" them in an ad-hoc and unclear way will continue to proliferate creating ethical and legal problems.

1 Introduction

Two absolute truths exist in the IT field. The first is that every software has bugs and the second is that no one can say that its system is 100% secure. Knowing these truths, organisations are left to continuously test computer systems in search of bugs to timely mitigate them. If this is not done, organisations run the risk of their systems being exploited by a third party, intentionally or not, causing serious harm to the company. The impact of a cyber-attack varies from organisation to organisation and

J. P. Magalhães (✉)
CIICESI, Escola Superior de Tecnologia e Gestão, Politécnico do Porto, Porto, Portugal
e-mail: jpm@estg.ipp.pt

F. A. Carneiro Pacheco de Andrade et al. (eds.), *Legal Developments on Cybersecurity and Related Fields*, Law, Governance and Technology Series 60,
https://doi.org/10.1007/978-3-031-41820-4_14

can affect the reputation, have strong economic impacts or, due to the integration of technology into our daily lives, put human lives at risk.

To reduce the likelihood of problems, organisations turn to auditing and pen-testing services. To perform such tests, organisations use dedicated security testing teams that perform black-box, grey-box, white-box penetration tests to discover and proof the existence of vulnerabilities in a firm product. Although these tests allow discovering and enhance the mitigation of vulnerabilities, it has been verified that they are not enough to address the problem. The fact that they are carried out only periodically, associated with the complexity of computer systems nowadays, means that many of the vulnerabilities are not identified in time and therefore potentially exploited by malicious actors. It is also known that the more eyes there are looking for vulnerabilities, the more vulnerabilities will be found and mitigated. These facts lead many organisations to resort to crowdsource to help them identify vulnerabilities that their internal teams may not catch. In this context, Vulnerability Disclosure Program (VDP) or Bug Bounty Programs (BBP) are launched by organisations to identify and fix vulnerabilities within their production applications. Both programs give ethical hackers, also known as white hats, permission to test if organisation applications contain certain types of vulnerabilities. While a VDP solely gives clear guidelines for how an organisation would like to be notified of potential security vulnerabilities found by external third parties, a BBP incentives external third parties to find security vulnerabilities in software and report them to the company so they can be mitigated. In a BBP, the finders of the vulnerabilities are rewarded with monetary prizes.

The primary benefit of a bug bounty program is that organisation identifies and fix a few vulnerabilities within their applications. If these vulnerabilities were discovered and exploited by a malicious actor before the organisation could fix them, then the impact to the organisation could be significant. This helps to protect the company reputation and decreases the likelihood of high-value hacks, but, if not planned right bug bounties can go terribly wrong.

From the perspective of an ethical hacker, bug bounty programs are seen with a lot of interest. Most of the participants recognise various motivation factors, such as monetary benefits, increasing reputation, or job opportunities. Others aim to acquire knowledge by identifying bugs in systems. Individuals who previously shared this information to build their reputations as experts in information security are now considering trading this knowledge on security vulnerability markets to increase their income. But it cannot be ruled out that these programs, even if authorised by organisations, entail legal and ethical risks that cannot be ignored. In this article, we focus on the current state of bug bounty programs with emphasis on the ethical and legal aspects associated with these programs. More specifically, we:

- analyse the growth of bug bounty programs;
- depict the terms and conditions of the main programs available;

- review the state of the art on bug bounty programs with an emphasis on ethical and legal aspects;
- make considerations about the current state of bug bounty programs, namely about:
  - the business model;
  - the ethical aspects for the parties involved (organisations, platform owners, hackers);
  - the legal aspects for the parties involved.

The analysis presented, as well as the discussion, is relevant at several levels. It promotes general knowledge about how these programs work. It highlights the current state, as well as its advantages and disadvantages. It points out questions for future research work. And, since this is a borderless problem that encompasses ethical and legal risks, it reinforces the need to create regulations on bug bounty programs that safeguard the parties and that could be applied as globally as possible.

This article is organised as follows: Sect. 2 describes the related work. Section 3 presents a characterisation of bug bounty programs. Section 4 focus on the results of the analysis. Section 5 concludes the paper.

2 Related Work

In this section we present a review of the literature on bug bounty programs (BBP). The literature review encompasses studies carried out within the scope of scientific works and considerations made by specialists around bug bounty programs. During the review, we realised that the most work focuses on two main topics:

- the topic related to the number of reports submitted to organisations operating BBP programs that are considered out of scope;
- The pros and cons of BBP programs with an emphasis on coverage of outcomes and related economic issues.

The ethical and legal issues end up being neglected in the state of the art analysed. In this context, we mainly resorted to comments from experts in the field, leaving in this section a summary of what was found.

2.1 Meaningless Reports

Mitigation of invalid reports is a serious concern of organisations running bug bounty programs as well as security researchers. In (Malladi and Subramanian 2020) authors refer that BBP attract large numbers of invalid reports, pointing 50–70% for HackerOne (the largest bug bounty platform). The number of invalid reports is serious and raises challenges to platforms. The nature of these platforms allows virtually anyone to participate and so organisations may be overwhelmed by low-value reports.

In (Shafigh et al. 2021) authors conducted an empirical study on disclosed invalid reports in HackerOne to examine the reasons these reports are invalid. They studied 1028 publicly available and fully disclosed invalid reports on HackerOne and analysed the policy pages of all programs on HackerOne and Bugcrowd. The reports showed at first place the main causes of rejection: reports evidencing vulnerabilities already fixed are the top cases of rejection, false positive vulnerabilities are the second, out-of-scope the third, duplicated reports the fourth and the inexistent of proof-of-concept the fifth reason. The analysis conducted by the authors, focused primarily on the out-of-scope reasons and they found that out-of-scope followed by false-positive are the two main reasons for a report to be deemed invalid and this happens mainly due to the attribute type of vulnerability (with more than 40%) of out-of-scope reports. Other attributes associated with the out-of-scope invalidation are the information disclosure type and attack surface. Understand the reasons behind the reports rejection is important since it may help ethical hackers to classify the reports properly to maximise it acceptance.

In (Zhao et al. 2017) authors refer that bounty amount is positively correlated with the number of valid reports received. However, at the same time, organisations that run bug bounty programs could be easily overwhelmed by invalid reports (also referred as noise). In fact, bug bounty platforms acknowledge that the key challenge companies face in running a public program at scale is "managing noise, or the proportion of low-value reports they receive". According to the study, the percentage of valid reports is lower than 25% for all programs and BBP in the platforms Facebook, Google, BugCrowd and HackerOne.

The high number of invalid reports is complex for organisations that operate bug bounty programs, but also for ethical hackers. On the ethical hackers' side, a report sent and for which they do not have timely answers or are considered invalid can lead to situations of frustration and inadequate exposure of what was found.

2.2 Economic Aspects

In (Walshe and Simpson 2020) authors derive a set of significant questions from a main global question "Is it beneficial for a company to make use of bug bounty programs, instead of hiring additional software engineers?". From this question four other were derived. The first question was "What is the expected cost per year of operating a bug bounty program, and what results can be expected?" and authors concluded that with an average annual cost of $83,815, the cost of running a full-time program is greater than the $65,133 required to hire an additional software engineer. Regarding the question "What is the expected benefit per year?" authors refer that newly released programs can expect an initial spike in the number of reports submitted as hackers use automated testing to find vulnerabilities. After this initial period, a stable level of 156 vulnerabilities per year can be expected. Another question addressed was "How does the program activity vary across its lifetime?" and the conclusion is that after an initial high rate of reported vulnerabilities after the program is launched, most programs continue with a constant rate of vulnerability discovery. The fourth question was "Does the promise of higher bounty pay-outs result in an increased number of vulnerabilities being reported?" and the analysis done concludes that there is a weak correlation between the success of a program and the average bounty pay-out. Hackers value the challenge or opportunity to learn almost as much as the bounty pay-outs when selecting programs in which to participate. The non-linear relationship between the number of reports and the average bounty makes it difficult to model the effect of increasing the average bounty of a program, however, the weak correlation suggests there is some benefit in increasing the average bounty. In line with the conclusions achieved by Walshe and Simpson (2020), in Hata et al. (2017) authors analysed datasets collected from Chromium and Mozilla, and reported that both bug bounty programs are economically efficient, compared to the cost of hiring full-time security researchers.

In (Sridhar and Ng 2021) authors affirm that security researchers have a price elasticity of supply between 0.1 and 0.2 at the median, indicating that they are largely motivated by non-pecuniary factors. Second, they found that a company size and profile do not have an economically significant impact on the number of reports it receives, reinforcing the value of bug bounties for smaller, less prestigious companies. Many firms are sceptical about receiving reports of cybersecurity vulnerabilities from third-party researchers. According to HackerOne, 93% of companies in the Forbes Global 2000 list do not have vulnerability disclosure policies, which stipulate how security researchers can submit the vulnerabilities they find to organisations without fear of being sued. This has a chilling effect, preventing companies from learning about the blind spots in their cybersecurity posture. In late 2019, the US Department of Homeland Security, the federal government agency tasked with cybersecurity, instructed all government agencies to create a VDP (Sridhar and Ng 2021).

In (Sivagnanam et al. 2021) authors analysed: if external bug hunters discover vulnerabilities that are significantly different from ones that are discovered by internal security teams; how often vulnerabilities are rediscovered, and which vulnerability characteristics determine the probability of rediscovery; if bug hunters discover vulnerabilities that are significantly different from ones that are exploited by threat actors. The key findings include that externally reported security issues significantly differ from internally reported ones, which suggests that external bug hunters provide benefits by complementing internal security teams; rediscovery probabilities are non-negligible, which means that finding and patching vulnerabilities is beneficial as many vulnerabilities are easy to discover; and vulnerabilities exploited by threat actors significantly differ from issues that are reported either internally or externally, which suggests that security could be improved by shifting the focus of vulnerability discovery efforts.

According to the various studies analysed, companies that embark on the execution of bug bounty programs end up having economic advantages, as the discovery of vulnerabilities increases and the price to discover them is substantially lower than hiring/having teams dedicated for this purpose.

2.3 *Ethical and Legal Aspects*

In Hata et al. (2017) authors conduct a survey with several questions. From the set of questions, question 5 is what fits our analysis. The question is “Do you have options to sell security bugs in black/grey markets?” and the answers achieved were “Yes, if someone will buy them with high value. No. I will sell them to the vendors (most voted). Others argued that receiving a bounty sum is a factor, but it is more important feel that the work is appreciated by the vendor.”. The answer to this question highlights much of the ethical aspects related to the bug bounty programs.

In (Böhme 2006) authors report a problem that can lead to less ethical behaviours. They say that delays in responding to a submitted report or wrongly classifying a valid report as invalid could lead to exposure of vulnerability and dissatisfaction of the ethical hacker reporting a vulnerability. As consequence, ethical hackers may resort to other means to disclose the findings, compromising the security of the organisation in which the vulnerability was discovered.

In Zhao et al. (2017) authors refer that bug bounty is often perceived as a risky approach to improve security, because an organisation is asking largely anonymous and independent hackers from all over the world to test its software systems. Organisations could worry that some hackers might damage the production system or steal user data when doing vulnerability research, or disclose vulnerabilities found to other parties. On the other hand, hackers would also worry that they might face legal charges for vulnerability research and disclosure. One might expect to have regulatory policies to control the risk, however, as of today, regulatory policies for bug bounty are a murky area. The most common form of engagement policy is the development of bug bounty rules. These rules specify which part of the system can be assessed and what kind of actions are permitted. These rules aim to regulate the behaviour of white hats/ethical hackers, but also bind these organisations to certain actions (Laszka et al. 2018). In the scope, out-of-scope, eligible vulnerabilities, non-eligible vulnerabilities, prohibited or unwanted actions (e.g., DoS), legal issues, participants origin (employees, country), submission guidelines, disclosure guidelines (e.g., time to fix before turning it public), reward criteria are some of the rules used in bug bounty programs.

Ethical issues are not just on the participants’ side. Organisations operating the programs must also have good faith in the practices they adopt. In (Salter 2021) is revealed a scenario where three iOS zero-day vulnerabilities were revealed by a researcher frustrated with the Apple bug bounty program. The researcher argues that he asked for an explanation and warned then that he would make the research public if he do not receive an explanation. The request was ignored, so he published the findings. Another scenario of frustration reported was due to the silent patching where organisations receive the reports and apply patches without recognising and award the work done by researchers (Culafi 2021).

This equation also includes other types of organisations that operate in the market. In more ethically grey territory, there are several "zero-day brokers" like Zerodium that will buy and sell exploits. A potential issue with zero-day brokers and marketplaces is that there is no guarantee on who the buyer will be or what are the buyer plans for the exploits. For example, the buyer could be a nation-state or a spyware vendor such as the NSO Group. On the flip side, zero-day brokers can pay significantly more than most vendors. This situation raises several ethical and legal issues.

3 Bug Bounty Programs: Characterization

In this section we present a characterization of the main bug bounty programs. The characterization includes: the types of existing bug bounty programs (BBP), the number of projects, participants, amounts paid in rewards and a review of the rules provided by bug bounty programs regarding the ethical and legal aspects.

3.1 Types of Bug Bounty Programs

Existing bug bounty programs to date, as shown in Table 1, can be organised into three types: Institutional, Platform and Brokers.

A common pattern observed is that bug bounty programs of the institutional type are limited to large organisations. To allow access to smaller organisations, bug bounty platforms were created. These act as an aggregating system between organisations looking for bug bounty services and ethical hackers who are willing to provide these services in favour of a reward. A study, carried out by the company HackerOne, the largest platform in the area, found that bug bounty platforms give greater confidence to ethical hackers. According to the study available in Bannister

Table 1 Types of bug bounty programs

Type	Examples	Characteristics
Institutional	Microsoft, Facebook, Google, Mozilla, European Union	Hosted directly by organisations who set policies and compensation.
Platform	Bugcrowd, HackerOne	Legitimate intermediary host of simultaneous BBP for multiple organisations. Reward amount is determined by the host.
Brokers	Zerodium	Purchase vulnerabilities from researchers to sell downstream. Rewards higher prices compared to the other program types.

(2020), the most common reason for withholding the discovery, cited by 38% of respondents, was threatening legal language used on the organisations website related with the reporting of vulnerabilities, followed by the lack of an obvious reporting channel (21%), and the organisation having been unresponsive to previous bug reports (15%). The bug bounty platforms contribute to mitigate some of these problems.

3.2 Projects, Participants, and Rewards: Stats

In Table 2 is presented a compilation of results achieved by different bug bounty programs over time. The analysis considers the number of projects, the number of ethical hackers involved, and the rewards paid considering valid vulnerability reports submitted.

The analysis provided in Table 2 allows to observe common features between the various programs, The growing number of programs and reports submitted, the growing number of prizes awarded by ethical hackers and the geographical dispersion of the participants is common to all, and still increasing every year. In the case of Zerodium, the analysis cannot be done in the same way as the bounty to be attributed varies according to the vulnerability reported and the company protects as much as possible the findings submitted by participants.

3.3 Bug Bounty Programs Rules: Terms and Conditions

As referred in (Laszka et al. 2018) the most common form of engagement policy is the development of bug bounty rules. These rules are important to define the permitted kind of actions and to create conditions that allow outside and unknown hackers to carry out intrusion tests (which are, by definition, illegal), under some form of protection against legal sanctions.

In this section we present an analysis regarding the existence of rules by organisations that operate bug bounty programs. More specifically, we went through the terms and conditions of the different programs to verify if they clearly consider the following rules:

- In-scope and Out-of-Scope: This analysis consists of checking whether the list of rules clearly defines the scope of the tests that ethical hackers can perform.
- Safe harbor: This analysis consists of verifying whether the programs owner clearly says that the ethical hacker will never be prosecuted by the company and under what conditions.
- Participants' origin: This analysis consists of verifying whether the program owner limits the participation of some types of ethical hackers, for example preventing them from being employees of the company, from collaborating

Table 2 BBP evolution

Bug bounty program	Stats
Microsoft[a]	Between July 2020 and June 2021, 17 programs existed, 1261 reports were eligible for rewards, 341 researchers awarded, $200 K was the biggest award and a total of $13.6 M in awards was registered.
Facebook[b]	Since 2011, 50 K researchers subscribed the program, 1500 researchers awarded a bounty from 150 different countries, more than 130 K reports were submitted and 6900 reports were awarded. In 2020, $1.98 M was distributed in awards, 17 K reports were submitted and 1000 were awarded. The top three countries with more contributions are India, Tunisia, and EUA.
Google[c]	In 2020 $6.7 million in bug bounty rewards to 662 security researchers across 62 countries were paid, 180 security researchers received grants in 2020, which submitted back 200 bug reports that yielded 100 confirmed vulnerabilities in Google products. Numbers updated in Jul 2021 reveal that $29 M were paid in rewards, 2022 bug hunters were paid and an impressive number of 11,055 individual rewards was achieved.
Mozilla[d]	Between 2017–2019 the average pay-out was $2.755. $965,750 for the disclosure of 348 bugs were paid. In 2019, Mozilla doubled web pay-outs for vulnerabilities impacting critical services and core sites, and triplicated pay-outs for remote code execution (RCE) bugs on critical sites.
Bugcrowd[e]	In 2020 Bugcrowd observed 50% more submissions than the year before. Throughout the period, there was a 65% increase in the most critical vulnerabilities.
HackerOne[f]	The community of hackers, pen testers, and security researchers has nearly doubled year-on-year. It has grown to over one million registered hackers, spanning 170 countries. Some 850 new recruits are joining the platform each day. In the past year, hackers reported over 50 K valid vulnerabilities to organisations, with a 63% increase in the number of hackers submitting valid reports in the past year alone. Bug hunters together earned around $40 million.
Zerodium[g]	Pay-outs range from $10 k to $2.5 M depending on the zero-day type and impact.

[a] https://msrc-blog.microsoft.com/2021/07/08/microsoft-bug-bounty-programs-year-in-review-13-6m-in-rewards/, Oct 2021
[b] https://about.fb.com/news/2020/11/bug-bounty-program-10th-anniversary/, Oct 2021
[c] https://bughunters.google.com/about/key-stats, Oct 2021
[d] https://portswigger.net/daily-swig/firefox-bug-bounty-mozilla-raises-payouts-and-abandons-first-reporter-wins-policy, Oct 2021
[e] https://www.bugcrowd.com/resources/reports/priority-one-report/, Oct 2021
[f] https://www.hackerone.com/resources/reporting/the-2020-hacker-report, Oct 2021
[g] https://zerodium.com/program.html, Oct 2021

with the company at a certain level or from belonging to a country in the sanctions list.

- Disclosure policy: This analysis consists of verifying whether the program owner clearly defines how the findings should be communicated.
- Defined times: In line with the disclosure policy, this analysis checks whether there are well-defined deadlines in which a vulnerability found should be kept

secretly (only shared with the affected organisation) and the deadline after which it can be made public.

The results of the analysis are shown in Table 3. The value "Y" is used when the terms and conditions are clear about the existence of the rule. "N" is used when the rule is not in the program list of rules. "U" is used when the rule exists but is considered ambiguous (e.g., the ethical hacker decides when to publish the vulnerability after communicating the intention to the program manager; platforms delegates restrictions on the programs it supports). "-" is used when the information is not provided in the program main page.

Even though most programs refer to the safe harbor as a way of protecting ethical hackers against legal sanctions, it should be noted that the terms and conditions contain exceptions that refer to the local law. Statements like "You understand that your participation in the program is at your own risk. To the extent permitted under your local law, we exclude any implied warranties in connection with the program. You may have certain rights under your local law". As the systems are complex and integrate various technologies, issues related to third parties are also mentioned, that is, organisations that may indirectly be affected by the discovered vulnerabilities. In this regard, there is only one principle of good faith, which indicates the non-disclosure of data that may affect third parties (unless required by court), and in case of legal sanctions against the ethical hacker, the company operating the program will only act as a witness in the process.

4 Bug Bounty Programs: Ethical and Legal Aspects

Considering the state of the art and an analysis of the economic, ethical, and legal aspects, in this section we make some considerations about the pros and cons found. These considerations aim to highlight aspects that, in the first instance, organisations and program participants should consider. In the second instance, we highlight aspects that in our opinion, as in the understanding of other research works, suggest the creation of regulatory policies for the area.

4.1 Ethics

As can be seen from the economic factors presented in this article, bug bounty programs are very interesting. They provide ethical hackers with an excellent source of income while allowing substantial economic savings for organisations due to the crowdsource model adopted. However, and with the lack of regulation on the functioning of the area, it is verified that there is fierce competition within it. For example, government agencies or their brokers often pay much higher rewards compared to bug bounty programs offered by organisations (e.g., Apple launched

Table 3 BBP Rules

	Microsoft	Facebook	Google	Mozilla	Bugcrowd	HackerOne	Zerodium
In-scope and Out-of-Scope defined?	Y	Y	Y	Y	Y	U	Y
Safe harbor adopted?	Y	Y	N	Y	Y	Y	–
Restricts participants origin?	Y	N	N	Y	U	Y	Y
Has disclosure policy?	Y	N	Y	Y	Y	Y	–
Has clearly defined times?	N	U	Y	U	U	U	–

a bug bounty program that is expected to pay up to $200,000, while Zerodium, a vulnerability broker company offers up to $1.5 M for top iOS vulnerabilities). This situation raises ethical issues for those involved. An ethical hacker has ways of selling his findings more profitably and with identical guarantees of confidentiality and criminal liability. Intermediary companies (aka brokers) and states compete with companies that have the vulnerability in their products, and that vulnerability can be used for other purposes (e.g., espionage) rather than being reported for mitigation. In this regard, there is a need to create regulatory mechanisms to balance supply and demand, as well to balance the practiced values and rules for operating in the market.

Another ethical issue that arises stems from the disclosure policies that bug bounty programs implement. Most of the programs define a form of disclosure for the findings made by the ethical hackers, however, they leave open the way the reports are handled, and particularly the response times. For an ethical hacker, submitting a report is an important thing. The finding can really affect the security of the affected organisation and from its analysis it comes the mitigation and the corresponding monetary and reputation reward. The absence of a response, whether for temporal reasons or for other reasons, creates frustration in the ethical hacker. Frustration, as admitted by some ethical hackers, makes them to consider disclosing their findings on an ad-hoc basis or selling the findings to other organisations to monetize the effort made. A company that launches a bug bounty program does not know in advance how many reports it will receive. As described in the state of the art, one of the problems in the area is related to the number of reports that are not significant but need to be analysed. This is not an easy problem to address, however, organisations will have more to gain from clearly defining analysis and response deadlines than to lose. The definition of these deadlines contributes to the ethical behaviour of the parts involved.

There are ethical issues that also arise for a company affected by a vulnerability. Faced with an identified and reported vulnerability, it is up to the affected organisation to act to mitigate it. Failure to do so could lead to the organisation and its users exposed to cyber-attacks. In this context, the company fails to protect the information of third parties and can be held responsible for such failure.

The ethical hacker community is very international. HackerOne, the leading bug bounty platform in the United States, reported that only 19% of the hackers are self-identified as US-based. Many of the organisations that operate bug bounty programs are clear in specifying the minimum age of participants, conflict of interest issues with the company and restrictions regarding their geographic location, mainly due to sanctioning reasons existing between countries. But there are others that do not specify anything and may, in this sense, create false expectations in the ethical hackers community. Faced with frustrated expectations, an ethical hacker can choose to share findings with others leaving the organisation exposed to cyber-attacks. In this sense, it is considered important that the program clearly defines the kind of participants allowed to participate.

4.2 Regulatory Policies

An analysis of the policies implemented by bug bounty programs allows us to conclude that they are mainly engagement policies and not so much regulatory policies. In practice the policies are just a list of topics that can be considered as contracts between organisations and ethical hackers that permit limited vulnerability research and always based on good faith principles. For example, Facebook bug bounty program explicitly states that "If you comply with the policies below when reporting a security issue to Facebook, we will not initiate a lawsuit or law enforcement investigation against you in response to your report". However, there will be times when ethical hackers and organisations disagree on the interpretation of those rules. This happens because of the challenges and complexity that the activity itself imposes.

The first challenge of creating regulatory policies is that it is hard to separate vulnerability research from malicious hacking. Both, typically include collecting information about the system, reverse-engineering a piece of software, sending exploit payload through different channels (input vectors) or attempting to escalate privilege to access critical data. So, security researchers engaging in vulnerability disclosure often move in grey areas, particularly when there are no established processes for vulnerability identification or disclosure. Unauthorised access to or control of software, hardware or services is often illegal, even in the presence of a valid, identified security vulnerability, sometimes even when there is a policy in place.

Bug bounty programs define rules that ethical hackers must comply with in a unilateral approach (without margin for agreements). Ethical hackers are not law experts making it difficult for them to evaluate the possible personal legal implication of participating in a BBP. In addition, it is also common that security researchers discover vulnerabilities in software products and systems without associated bug bounty programs by organisations. For out-of-scope findings organisations could consider them as illegal cyberattacks. In a recent case (Lin 2016), a Chinese online dating company reported an ethical hacker to the police, who was then arrested based on the charge of illegal intrusion and acquisition of user data. In addition to organisation-level legal actions, governments might also take actions against bug bounty organisers and white hats. For example, Wooyun, the oldest and largest bug bounty platform in China, was shut down in the summer of 2016, followed by the arrest of its key members (WSJ 2016).

Leading bug bounty organisations and platforms are found to embrace the safe harbor principles. These principles contribute to a clarification of the participants, but it should be noted that these principles are not always verified. For example, the DJI bug bounty program was a fiasco in the past, when security researcher walked away from a $30,000 bug bounty after drone maker DJI threatened him with legal action. Most organisations say they will never bring the ethical hacker to court, but here they impose conditions that raise other issues:

- The first has to do with the exception—ethical hackers are safeguarded by the safe harbor, but they should at the same time comply with all applicable laws, including local laws of the country or region in which you reside;
- An ethical hacker found something relevant, but it does not fit the scope. What to do? (This is the question that arises for him);
- An ethical hacker does not know about laws, he is a professional in his field. What does it mean to follow local laws, which specific laws? What are the consequences of not following?

It turns out that, for the questions that each ethical hacker raises for himself, there are no concrete answers. The grey areas remain. In our opinion, this lacks regulation, more specifically a local regulation allied with broad coalition (e.g., Wassenaar Arrangement), that clarify how each country supports and protects citizens who apply their skills and knowledge in favour of better security for organisations.

In this matter, we have identified space for cybersecurity and cyber defence bodies in each country, or member states, to create regulations that clarify the way in which the parties involved (companies, platforms, and ethical hackers) act. There is already work done but much more is yet to do.

5 Conclusion

The intrusion testing paradigm is changing. Traditionally, tests were carried out by specialised teams hired while nowadays there are more and more crowdsource initiatives that encourage unknown hackers to carry out such tests.

Bug bounty programs provide significant cost savings to an organisation in a couple of different ways. One of these is the fact that paying a bounty to learn about a vulnerability is much cheaper than remediating a cybersecurity incident caused by that same vulnerability. While bounty values can vary greatly, even the most expensive bounties are often an order of magnitude cheaper than a data breach. The other cost saving associated with bug bounty programs is the fact that an organisation only must pay bug bounty hunters if they find something. Bug bounty programs provide access to a huge pool of labour as hunters look for potential vulnerabilities, which may be difficult to obtain otherwise given the scarcity of human resources in the area.

The financial aspects are interesting and promote the programs, both in supply and in demand, but there are associated ethical and legal issues that still need to be clarified. In this article, the terms and conditions of the main bug bounty programs were analysed, and the associated ethical and legal challenges were surveyed. The analysis highlights the importance of clarifying some aspects in favour of safeguarding the parties involved. Among the aspects to be clarified, we highlight the issue of the conditions for the disclosure of discoveries, making them clearer and more binding. In this regard, we consider that deadlines must be well defined, as conditions must be created so that discoveries can be validated more quickly and responses to those who discovered faster. The consequences of disclosure that undermine these rules must be clear in the regulations, inhibiting the sale to third parties or the public disclosure before going down a certain path. As an example, a country can define that before a finding is made public, it must be reported to a national entity responsible for formal communication and sanctions, i.e., a national CERT (Computer Emergency Response Teams) can be used as central point, forwarding a finding to the corresponding CERT of the country to which the vulnerability is located. Sanctions may be imposed to organisations if they are contacted by the CERT after being alerted by the ethical hacker for the problem.

Regarding the existence of brokers, it is considered that the legislation should clarify the *modus operandi* of this type of companies in the market. The vulnerabilities found should be reported to product owners and not used for other purposes such as spying or massive surveillance.

If, instead of prohibiting or recriminating, each country, through its own channels, for example via country CERT, regulates the role of ethical hackers, they will be more safeguarded in their actions and, consequently, a greater number of vulnerabilities can be revealed and mitigated in useful time.

References

Bannister A (2020) Bug bounty earnings soar, but 63% with held security flaws study. Online, https://portswigger.net/daily-swig/bug-bounty-earnings-soar-but-63-of-ethical-hackers-have-withheld-security-flaws-study

Böhme R (2006) A comparison of market approaches to software vulnerability disclosure. In: Müller G (ed) Emerging trends in information and communication security, international conference, ETRICS 2006, Freiburg, Germany, June 6–9, 2006. Proceedings, Lecture Notes in Computer Science, vol 3995. Springer, pp 298–311. https://doi.org/10.1007/11766155_21

Culafi A (2021) Burned by apple, researchers mull selling zero days to brokers. Online, https://searchsecurity.techtarget.com/news/252508220/Burned-by-Apple-researchers-mull-selling-zero-days-to-brokers

Hata H, Guo M, Babar MA (2017) Understanding the heterogeneity of contributors in bug bounty programs. In: 2017 ACM/IEEE international symposium on empirical software engineering and measurement (ESEM). IEEE, pp 223–228

Laszka A, Zhao M, Malbari A, Grossklags J (2018) The rules of engagement for bug bounty programs. In: Meiklejohn S, Sako K (eds) Financial cryptography and data security. Springer, Berlin, pp 138–159

Lin MS (2016) Are China's 'ethical hackers' cyber heroes or criminals? Online, http://english.caixin.com/2016–10-17/100997728.html

Malladi SS, Subramanian HC (2020) Bug bounty programs for cybersecurity: practices, issues, and recommendations. IEEE Softw 37(01):31–39. https://doi.org/10.1109/MS.2018.2880508

Salter J (2021) Three iOS 0-days revealed by researcher frustrated with apple's bug bounty. Online, https://arstechnica.com/information-technology/2021/09/three-ios-0-days-revealed-by-researcher-frustrated-with-apples-bug-bounty/

Shafigh S, Benatallah B, Rodríguez C, Al-Banna M (2021) Why some bug-bounty vulnerability reports are invalid? study of bug-bounty reports and developing an out-of-scope taxonomy model. In: Proceedings of the 15th ACM/IEEE international symposium on empirical software engineering and measurement (ESEM), ESEM '21. Association for Computing Machinery, New York. https://doi.org/10.1145/3475716.3484193

Sivagnanam A, Atefi S, Ayman A, Grossklags J, Laszka A (2021) On the benefits of bug bounty programs: a study of chromium vulnerabilities. In: Workshop on the Economics of Information Security (WEIS)

Sridhar K, Ng M (2021) Hacking for good: Leveraging HackerOne data to develop an economic model of Bug Bounties. J Cybersecur 7(1):tyab007. https://doi.org/10.1093/cybsec/tyab007

Walshe T, Simpson A (2020) An empirical study of bug bounty programs. In: 2020 IEEE 2nd international workshop on intelligent bug fixing (IBF), pp 35–44. https://doi.org/10.1109/IBF50092.2020.9034828

WSJ (2016) China's 'white-hat' hackers fear dark times after community founde ris detained. Wall Street J. https://www.wsj.com/articles/BL-CJB-29440

Zhao M, Laszka A, Grossklags J (2017) Devising effective policies for bug-bounty platforms and security vulnerability discovery. J Inf Policy 7:372–418. http://www.jstor.org/stable/10.5325/jinfopoli.7.2017.0372

João Paulo Magalhães is Professor and researcher at ESTG - Porto Polytechnic, and director of the Graduation in Computer and Networks Security at ESTG. He holds a PhD in dependable systems from University of Coimbra and is author of several scientific publications in dependability and cybersecurity. He is a member of the Multinational Cyber Defense Education and Training Project (MNCD E&T) NATO Smart Defense Project and contributed to the development of academic curricula for postgraduate courses in cyber-security and cyber-defense and postgraduate education in cyber-law. He keeps a close relationship with the industry, having been the co-founder and CTO at Globinnova Cyber Intelligence (Malware Analysis, Digital Vigilance, Big Data Security, Cyber Awareness). Previously, João worked as team coordinator and sysadmin (UNIX) at SONAE.

Profiling and Cybersecurity: A Perspective from Fundamental Rights' Protection in the EU

Alessandra Silveira

Abstract In this text we will be assessing to what extent personal data protection is related to the development of AI systems, as well as testing to what extent the General Data Protection Regulation (GDPR) (Regulation 2016/679 of 27 April 2016 on the protection of natural persons with regard to the processing of personal data and on the free movement of such data, and repealing Directive 95/46/EC.) enables the defense of individuals in the face of some AI applications—especially with regard to profiling and automated decisions. Considering the GDPR regulates the processing of data of an identified or identifiable natural person, it would apply when AI systems are building on everyone's data, as well as when such systems are used to analyze data and produce inferences on individuals (Datatilsynet - The Norwegian Data Protection Authority, Artificial intelligence and privacy, Report: Oslo, 2018). Herein lies the problem of the opacity of inferences or predictions resulting from data analysis by AI systems—inferences whose application to everyday situations determines how each of us, as personal data subjects, are perceived and evaluated by others. It is important to assess the existence of legal remedies to challenge operations that result in automated inferences that are not reasonably justified. Thus, we intend to clarify whether the GDPR adequately protects inferred data, in the light of the fundamental right to the protection of personal data provided in Article 8 of the Charter of Fundamental Rights of the European Union (CFREU), under penalty of violating our insusceptibility to instrumentalization and objectification—in other words, human dignity itself.

This contribution was supported by the Portuguese Foundation for Science and Technology (FCT) with the reference UID/05749/2020.

A. Silveira (✉)
University of Minho, Braga, Portugal
e-mail: asilveira@direito.uminho.pt

F. A. Carneiro Pacheco de Andrade et al. (eds.), *Legal Developments on Cybersecurity and Related Fields*, Law, Governance and Technology Series 60,
https://doi.org/10.1007/978-3-031-41820-4_15

1 Introduction: Data Protection as a Fundamental Right

Profiling is often used to make predictions about individuals [Article 4(4) GDPR], and may, or may not, lead to automated decisions within the meaning of the GDPR. Profiling involves the collection of information about a person and the assessment of their characteristics or behavioral patterns in order to place them in a certain category or group and drawing upon that an inference or prediction—whether of their ability to perform a task, of their interest or presumed behavior.[1] To this extent, such automated inferences demand protection as inferred personal data,[2] since they also make it possible to identify someone by association of concepts, characteristics, or contents. The crux of the matter is that people are increasingly losing control over such automated inferences and over how they are seen and evaluated by others.[3]

Article 22 GDPR (apparently) provides a general prohibition of individual decisions based solely on automated processing, including profiling. However, as set out below, its provisions raise doubts to the doctrine, not yet clarified by the Court of Justice of the European Union (CJEU).[4] In the pending case C-634/21 [SCHUFA Holding and Others (Scoring)], the CJEU has finally the opportunity to assess the existence of legal remedies to challenge operations that result in automated inferences that are not reasonably justified.[5] Thus, in this text we intend to clarify whether the GDPR adequately protects inferred data, in the light of the fundamental right to the protection of personal data provided in Article 8 of the CFREU.

As is apparent from the case law of the CJEU, and as is now laid down in Article 51 of the CFREU, the fundamental rights protected in the EU can be invoked when the claim (or the contested measure) comes within the scope of EU law. It follows from this that defining the range of protection ensured by EU fundamental rights is intimately related to the delimitation of competences. Indeed, the entry into force of

---

[1] Data Protection Working Party (WP29) (2017), Guidelines on Automated individual decision-making and Profiling for the purposes of Regulation 2016/679 (last revised and adopted on 6 February 2018). The WP29 guidelines are not binding, but they represent the shared opinion of the various data protection supervisory authorities in the EU and are persuasive before the courts and even the CJEU. The WP29 (so called because it was established under the then Article 29 of Directive 95/46 that preceded the GDPR) ceased to function on May 25, 2018, with the start of the implementation of the GDPR. It was functionally succeeded by the current European Data Protection Board—whose main task is to ensure the effective and consistent application of the GDPR and other Union data protection legislation.

[2] Id., where it recognizes as personal data also the data obtained or inferred, such as a profile of the person, to infer a credit score from it, for example.

[3] Incidentally, some scholars claim the "right on how to be seen". Wachter and Mittelstadt (2019).

[4] For the purposes of this text, the current designation of this European institution [see Article 13(1) of the Treaty on European Union (TEU)] is adopted, irrespective of the actual judicial mechanism and body competent within that Court.

[5] See Opinion of Advocate General Priit Pikamäe, submitted on 16 March 2023, ECLI:EU:C:2023:220.

the CFREU was accompanied by the definition, in the Treaties, of a catalogue of EU competences.[6]

The EU's competence to regulate personal data protection can be found in Article 16 of the Treaty on the Functioning of the European Union (TFEU) and is related to the proper functioning of the internal market—it stems from the need to circulate personal information among the Member States, accompanying the free movement of persons, goods, services, and capital.[7] Pursuant to Article 16(1) TFUE everyone has the right to the protection of personal data concerning them, and it also stems from Article 16(2) TFUE that the European Parliament and the Council are to establish rules to ensure the protection of individuals with regard to the processing of personal data by the Union institutions, bodies, offices and agencies, as well as by Member States when carrying out activities involving the implementation of Union law, and the free movement of such data.

This is a competence shared with the Member States in the sphere of the internal market [Article 4(2)(a) TFEU], the exercise of which by the EU, as follows from Article 2(2) TFEU, inhibits the legislative initiative of the Member States. Thus, under competences shared between the EU and its Member States, both can legislate and adopt legally binding acts in that area. However, Member States make use of their competence to the extent that the EU has not exercised its competence, and they will only be called into it play again to the extent that the EU decides to cease exerting its power. Now, as the EU has put to use its competence, and increasingly does so, in the area of the processing of personal data and its movement, data protection in the EU area is governed by EU law—and in particular, for the purposes of this text, by the GDPR.

With regard to the EU's competence in the field of personal data protection, there is a further important element to consider—which is, precisely, the CFREU—legally binding since the Treaty of Lisbon entered into force on December 1, 2009, as follows from Article 6(1) TEU. The provisions of the CFREU, which constitute primary EU law, do not extend the competences of the EU as defined in the Treaties [Article 6(1), (2) TEU]. However, they do oblige the EU institutions and the Member States to respect and promote the application of the fundamental rights contained therein [Article 51(1) CFREU], becoming quite clear that the entry into force of the CFREU affects the exercise of the EU's competences. Therefore, as the EU has

[6] Vilaça and Silveira (2017).

[7] This is reflected in Recital 7 of the GDPR which states that "[t]hose developments require a strong and more coherent data protection framework in the Union, backed by strong enforcement, given the importance of creating the trust that will allow the digital economy to develop across the internal market", as well as in the Recital 10 of the GDPR, according to which "[i]n order to ensure a consistent and high level of protection of natural persons and to remove the obstacles to flows of personal data within the Union, the level of protection of the rights and freedoms of natural persons with regard to the processing of such data should be equivalent in all Member States", and, also, in Recital 13 of the GDPR: "[i]n order to ensure a consistent level of protection for natural persons throughout the Union and to prevent divergences hampering the free movement of personal data within the internal market, a Regulation is necessary to provide legal certainty and transparency for economic operators."

exercised its competences in the field of data protection, the standard of fundamental rights protection applicable to concrete situations will be the one resulting from the CFREU. Moreover, what's relevant in this context is that the CFREU autonomizes the right to the protection of personal data (Article 8) from the right to the protection of privacy (Article 7), because not all personal data are by nature likely to cause harm to the data subject's privacy, but they must also be protected as they allow the data subject to be identified.

In this sense, the protection of personal data has developed with the impulse of the EU, as an autonomous fundamental right with its own normative recognition. This has been the case, otherwise the protection of personal data would occupy a hierarchically inferior position in comparison with other rights and interests protected by the EU. This reflects the relevance attributed by the Union to the fundamental right to the protection of personal data, one which differs from the right to the protection of private life. The right to privacy, originally recognized as the right to be let alone, has undergone considerable developments since its first doctrinal references in the United States in the nineteenth century[8]—and it is no longer fully compatible with the protection needs of internet users who definitely do not want to be alone. Therefore, the CFREU enshrines a fundamental right that protects data that does not have to be private—or, perhaps, intimate—the only requirement is that it is personal.

Taking into consideration the main theme in this text, it is relevant to bear in mind that Article 8(1) CFREU not only reproduces the content of Article 16(1) TFEU—in the sense that "everyone has the right to the protection of personal data concerning him or her"—but Article 8(2) CFREU also adds that "such data must be processed fairly for specified purposes and on the basis of the consent of the person concerned or some other legitimate basis laid down by law" and that "everyone has the right of access to data which has been collected concerning him or her, and the right to have it rectified." For the interpretation of this provision, it is important to emphasize that the meaning of collect is, precisely, "to gather into a collection what is scattered, to infer, to deduce"—and regarding the data thus collected, the legal basis highlighted by the CFREU is related to the fairness, purpose, consent, and lawfulness of its processing, in addition to the holder's access to personal data to obtain their rectification.

It therefore follows from Articles 16 TFEU and 8 CFREU that personal data is subject to protection when subject to any operation or processing, whether carried out with or without automated means, and Article 4(1) and (2) GDPR defines both personal data and the processing thereof. Personal data is defined as any information relating to an identified or identifiable individual (the data subject), and the term identifiable concerns a subject which can be identified directly or indirectly. To this extent, personal data are not only those data that directly enable the identification of a person (the personal identification number, name, and address), but also those data that enable such identification by association of concepts, characteristics, or content

[8] Warren and Brandeis (1890).

(a location data, electronic identifiers, elements of physical, physiological, genetic, mental, economic, cultural or social identity of an individual).

By way of example, the doctrine identifies as personal data the customer number of a commercial establishment, the amount of a payment, the sound of the voice recorded to allow access to a bank account, school grades, curriculum vitae, medical history, debts and credits, the record of purchases made by someone, the record of the means of payment used, the IP (Internet Protocol)[9] address of the computer with which one accesses the internet, the license plate number of a vehicle, etc.—as long as they are associated with a person and allow that person to be identified.[10]

Personal data are, as already stated, to be protected when they are subject to processing, this is, "any operation or set of operations which is performed on personal data or on sets of personal data, whether or not by automated means, such as collection, recording, organization, structuring, storage, adaptation or alteration, retrieval, consultation, use, disclosure by transmission, dissemination or otherwise making available, alignment or combination, restriction, erasure or destruction" [Article 4(2) GPDR].

The obligation to respect and ensure the exercise of the various dimensions that make up the right to the protection of personal data rests on the data controller—the natural or legal person, public authority, agency, or other body which alone or jointly with others determines the purposes and means of the processing of personal data [Article 4(7) GDPR]. The controller and the processor, someone who processes personal data on behalf of the controller, are liable for any breach of data security leading to the accidental or unlawful destruction, loss, alteration, unauthorized disclosure of, or access to personal data transmitted, stored, or otherwise processed [Article 4(12) GDPR].

Bearing this in mind, to what extent do these introductory definitions allow us to direct our concerns regarding automated inferences? Indeed, if such inferences identify or allow the identification of a natural person by association of concepts, characteristics, and contents, then they would be inferred personal data worthy of protection. Therefore, what is being called into question in this regard is the automated processing of such inferences—roughly speaking, the operation consisting in the automated exploration of information indicating relations of personal interest, and on which learning algorithms are used to predict individualized behavior. Thus, it is important to (i) assess whether such an operation would

[9]Breyer judgment of 19 October 2016, C-582/14, ECLI:EU:C:2016:779, recital 15: "IP addresses are series of digits assigned to networked computers to facilitate their communication over the internet. When a website is accessed, the IP address of the computer seeking access is communicated to the server on which the website consulted is stored. That connection is necessary so that the data accessed maybe transferred to the correct recipient"; La Quadrature du Net judgment of 6 October 2020, C-511/18, C-512/18 and C-520/18, ECLI:EU:C:2020:791, recital 153: "IP addresses may be used, among other things, to track an Internet user's complete clickstream and, therefore, his or her entire online activity, that data enables a detailed profile of the user to be produced."

[10]Castro (2013).

correspond to the processing of personal data within the meaning of the fundamental right to data protection enshrined in the GDPR, and (ii) assess the existence of legal remedies to challenge the operation resulting in automated inferences that are not reasonably justified.

Throughout this text the fundamental legal dimensions of personal data protection implemented by the GDPR will be addressed, as well as some of the rights of those whose data is subject to automated processing. The scope of protection of some of these rights has been developed by the case law of the CJEU in preliminary rulings, notwithstanding the essential issue of the intelligibility of exploration and exploitation techniques affecting personal data subjects has not yet been addressed by CJEU case law.

In a chronological perspective, the first CJEU judgment applying Directive 95/46 to automated data processing was the *Lindqvist* judgment of 2003.[11] The preliminary questions were asked in the context of criminal proceedings against a catechist who was accused of violating the Swedish legislation transposing Directive 95/46 by publishing personal data on the Internet without proper consent, relating to colleagues who worked with her in a Protestant parish. The CJEU considered that the scope of the Directive was not limited to the exercise of an economic activity, since it also regulated the circulation of personal data in the exercise of social activities, in the broader context of a European integration guided by the protection of fundamental rights.[12] To this extent, the CJEU ruled that the creation of a webpage and its installation on a server—as well as the input of personal information available to anyone connecting to the internet—constituted processing of personal data by automated means within the meaning of the Directive.

Following the *Lindqvist* ruling, the CJEU has been assembling the puzzle of automated data processing from mainly three relevant material areas: (i) de-indexing of data, (ii) retention of data, (iii) transfer of data. The first domain includes the judgments concerning the disassociation of results relating to personal data appearing on third-party websites but accessible by search engines through the name of the data subject (from the *Google Spain* judgment of 2014[13]); the second one includes the judgments concerning the retention of traffic and location data by providers of electronic communications services with a view to making them available for the purposes of fighting crime and safeguarding security (from the *Digital Rights* judgment of 2014[14]); the third material area includes the judgments concerning the transfer of personal data to a third country where the law and practices in force do not ensure an adequate level of protection under EU law (from the *Schrems* judgment of 2015 onwards[15]).

[11] Lindqvist judgment of 6 November 2003, C-101/01, ECLI:EU:C:2003:596.
[12] Ib., recitals 35 and 36.
[13] Google Spain judgment of 13 May 2014, C-131/12, ECLI:EU:C:2014:317.
[14] Digital Rights judgment of 8 April 2014, C-293/12 and C-594/12, ECLI:EU:C:2014:238.
[15] Schrems judgment of 6 October 2015, C-362/14, ECLI:EU:C:2015:650.

In addition to these three broad categories, the CJEU is occasionally faced with preliminary rulings that provide food for thought on the problem of inferred data. For example, in the judgments *Wirtschaftsakademie* 2018,[16] *Fashion ID* 2019,[17] and *Planet49* 2019,[18] the CJEU admitted that the collection of data through cookies amounts to the processing of personal data.[19] The *Planet49* case is of particular interest because the CJEU was faced with the question of whether the consent referred to in Article 6(1)(a) GDPR is validly given when the storage of information through cookies (or the access to information already stored in the terminal equipment of a website user) is allowed by means of a pre-validated option that the user must uncheck in order to refuse consent.

One should note that "the data subject's consent" is expressly referred to in Article 8 CFREU and defined in Article 4(11) GDPR as a "freely given, specific, informed and unambiguous indication of his or her wishes", by which the data subject agrees, by a positive and clear statement or act—which rules out the acceptance of deduced consents—to the processing of personal data relating to him or her. To this extent, the CJEU held that consent is not validly given when

---

[16] Wirtschaftsakademie judgment of 5 June 2018, C-210/16, ECLI:EU:C:2018:388, recital 33: "According to the documents before the Court, the data processing at issue in the main proceedings is essentially carried out by Facebook placing cookies on the computer or other device of persons visiting the fan page, whose purpose is to store information on the browsers, those cookies remaining active for 2 years if not deleted. It also appears that in practice Facebook receives, registers and processes the information stored in the cookies in particular when a person visits the Facebook services, services provided by other members of the Facebook family of companies, and services provided by other companies that use the Facebook services." At issue in this case was whether the concept of 'controller' encompasses the administrator of a fan page hosted on the Facebook social network in the event of a breach of the rules on personal data protection—which was confirmed by the CJEU. However, the existence of joint liability does not necessarily translate into equivalent liability of the different operators concerned for a processing of personal data. On the contrary, they may be involved at different stages of the processing and to different degrees, so that in order to assess the level of responsibility of each one, all relevant circumstances of the case must be considered. Wirtschaftsakademie judgment, cit., recital 43.

[17] Fashion ID judgment of 29 July 2019, C-40/17, ECLI:EU:C:2019:629. This case concerned the question, also in relation to the liability for processing, who is responsible for providing information and obtaining consent from the data subject when the administrator of a website incorporates a social module "like" from the Facebook social network—which allows the transmission of the personal data of the visitor to that website, but the administrator has no influence on the processing of the transmitted data. The CJEU held that consent must be obtained by the administrator only in respect of the personal data processing operation or set of operations the purposes and means of which are actually determined by the administrator. Fashion ID judgment, cit., recital 106.

[18] Planet49 judgment of 1 October 2019, C-673/17, ECLI:EU:C:2019:801, recitals 45 and 67.

[19] A cookie is a means of collecting information generated by a website and stored by the user's browser; websites use cookies for user identification purposes, allowing the website to "remember" certain actions, characteristics or preferences of the user over time. Cookies can also be used to collect information to tailor advertising and marketing to online behaviors. Several companies use software to track users' behavior and build personal profiles that allow them to serve ads relevant to users from their previous searches. Opinion of Advocate General Szpunar, submitted on 21 March 2019, C-673/17, ECLI:EU:C:2019:246, recitals 36–39.

access to information through cookies is allowed by means of a pre-validated option that the user must uncheck in order to refuse consent.[20]

The referring court in *Planet49* further asked whether the answer to consent would be different depending on whether information stored or consulted in the terminal equipment of a website user constituted personal data or not. The CJEU held that all information stored in the terminal equipment of the user of electronic communications networks—regardless of whether it is personal data or not—is protected against the risk of hidden identifiers or other similar devices entering those terminals without the user's knowledge.[21] Consent applies to any information, regardless of the nature of the data that is stored or accessed, this is, consent is not limited to personal data, the concept of "information" includes all types of data stored on the device.[22]

The CJEU adhered to such a broad understanding of the expressions "storage of information" and "access to information already stored" in Article 5(3) of Directive 2002/58 on privacy protection in the electronic communications sector that it led it to dispense with the qualification of such information as personal data,[23] despite the Advocate General's view that such information would undoubtedly be personal data.[24] In any event, for both the Advocate General and the CJEU, there was no difference as to whether consent was required if information stored or accessed through cookies constituted personal data or not.

This implies an inclination of the CJEU to protect individuals against "any intrusion into their private sphere",[25] regardless of whether or not such intrusion concerns personal data within the meaning of EU law. This is relevant in view of the

[20] However, the referring court did not ask the most relevant question for a preliminary ruling, namely whether the fact that consent to the use of cookies is conditional on participation in a promotional game would be compatible with the requirement of free consent under the GDPR. In other words, if access to the game is conditional on consent, would we be facing a manifestation of free will? The CJEU itself draws attention to the absence of this question—Planet49 judgment, cit., recital 64. In this regard, it is worth noting WP29 position, according to which consent is only valid if the data subject is able to exercise real choice without risk of intimidation, coercion or negative consequences if one chooses not to consent: "The consent mechanism should present the user with a real and meaningful choice regarding cookies on the entry page. The user should have an opportunity to freely choose between the option to accept some or all cookies or to decline all or some cookies and to retain the possibility to change the cookie settings in the future"—WP29 (2013), Working Document 02/2013 providing guidance on obtaining consent for cookies.

[21] Planet49 judgment, cit., para 69–71.

[22] The Advocate General suggested that the CJEU adhere to the understanding of WP29 that the consent requirement would apply to storage of and/or access to "information" of any kind. Opinion of Advocate General Szpunar, cit., recital 108 and footnote 60.

[23] On 10 February 2021 the Council of the EU agreed on a proposal for the new "e-Privacy" Regulation that intends to replace Directive 2002/58 and establish a coherent framework between the *lex specialis* for the electronic communications sector and the general data protection rules now embodied in the GDPR. For a critical reading of the proposal, Cabral (2021).

[24] The Advocate General was in no doubt that the information referred to in Article 5(3) of Directive 2002/58 constitutes personal data. Opinion of Advocate General Maciej Szpunar, cit., recital 105.

[25] Planet49 judgment, cit., recital 69.

increasing identifiability of data subjects, with less effort and cost, even if identification may not seem possible in the first place. Moreover, the purpose of cookies is precisely to identify or, at the very least, to individualize a user: to reach a specific individual in order to provide that person with personalized advertising, based on the analysis of their preferences/interests/desires/aversions, allowing the monitoring of their behavior over time.[26]

On the other hand, the CJEU's decision reduces the expectations regarding the recognition of rights exercisable over inferred data, since the issue of information stored or accessed through cookies was finally settled by reference to the protection of privacy: information entailing any interference with one's private sphere, "regardless of whether or not that interference involves personal data."[27] This raises some perplexity because it does not seem to fit with the reason why data protection was autonomized from privacy, that is, to protect data that does not have to be private, as the only requirement is that they are personal. Is the scope of protection of personal data not broader than the scope of protection of privacy? The decision of the CJEU may indicate some recognition of the weaknesses of the legal regime for the protection of personal data—as "identified or identifiable information"—in the face of the opacity of automated processing.

It is quite unfortunate that the CJEU has not yet been directly confronted with the question to what extent personal data protection is fully exercisable over automated inferences. A recent case discussing who would be the competent supervisory authority in the face of cross-border data processing—whether the Belgian authority or the Irish authority, given that the entity that carried out the data processing was Facebook Ireland—would have been particularly well suited to explore this possibility if the CJEU had been confronted with the matter. In any case, the case highlights the topicality of the issue that must be dealt with.[28]

The questions referred originated precisely in cases concerning alleged violations of data protection by Facebook, consisting in the unlawful collection and use of information about the browsing behavior of internet users. The Belgian supervisory authority alleged that Facebook uses various technologies to monitor and track users as they navigate from one website to another—and that it uses the information collected to create patterns of their browsing behaviors and present them with targeted advertising based on those patterns. The company would do this without properly informing Internet users and without obtaining their valid consent and would develop such practices regardless of whether or not the person concerned had signed up on Facebook. Indeed, the illegal collection of data without information and consent of the data subject for profiling and targeting advertisements was the issue at stake, and the Belgian authority asked the courts to order Facebook to (i) stop

[26]Guerra (2019).

[27]Planet49 judgment, cit., recital 69–70.

[28]Gegevensbeschermingsautoriteit judgment of 15 June 2021, C-645/19, ECLI:EU:C:2021:483. Opinion of Advocate General Michal Bobek, submitted on 13 January 2021, ECLI:EU:C:2021:5, recitals 19–21.

placing non-consented cookies that remain active for 2 years on all Internet users established on Belgian territory, (ii) stop collecting data through technologies that retrieve it from third-party websites, and (iii) destroy all personal data obtained on each user established on Belgian territory.

And in a pending case [C-634/21, SCHUFA Holding and Others (Scoring)], the right not to be subject to automated decisions (Article 22 GDPR) is finally being considered for the first time before the CJEU.[29] This case concerns proceedings between a citizen (the applicant OQ, data subject) and the Land Hessen (Germany), regarding the protection of personal data. The Land is represented by the Hesse Commissioner for Data Protection and Freedom of Information (HBDI) and the joined party SCHUFA Holding AG (SCHUFA)—a private German credit information agency that provides its contractual partners with information on the creditworthiness of consumers. SCHUFA establishes credit scores—where the probability of a person's future behaviour is predicted on the basis of certain characteristics of that person using mathematical statistical methods. SCHUFA provided a financial entity with a score for the applicant OQ, which served as the basis for refusing to grant the credit for which the latter had applied. That citizen subsequently requested SCHUFA to erase the entry concerning her and to grant her access to the corresponding data. However, SCHUFA merely informed her of the relevant score and, in general terms, of the principles underlying the method of calculating the score, without informing her of the specific data included in that calculation, or of the relevance attributed to them in that context, arguing that the method of calculation was a trade secret.

According to the referring court, it is ultimately the credit score established by credit information agencies that actually decides whether and how a financial entity/bank enters into a contract with the data subject. The referring court proceeds on the assumption that the establishment of a score by a credit information agency does not merely serve to prepare that bank's decision, but constitutes an independent "decision" within the meaning of Article 22(1) of the GDPR. Thus, by providing that a data subject has the right "not to be subject to a decision based solely on automated processing, including profiling", Article 22(1) GDPR expressly establishes a causal link and a chronologically fixed sequence between automated processing (including profiling) and then the decision based on it.[30]

In so far as the citizen concerned claims that SCHUFA's refusal is contrary to data protection norms, the Advocate General Priit Pikamäe is of the opinion that the CJEU is called upon to rule (i) on the restrictions that the GDPR imposes on the economic activity of credit information agencies in the financial sector (in particular in data management), and (ii) on the effect to be conferred to trade secrets. Similarly, the CJEU would have to clarify the scope of the regulatory powers that certain provisions of the GDPR bestow on the national legislature, namely the exception to the prohibition in Article 22(2)(b) GDPR—according to which such prohibition does

[29] See Silveira (2023).

[30] See Request for a preliminary ruling of 1 October 2021, Case C-634/21, recital 23.

not apply if the decision is authorized by European Union or Member State law to which the controller is subject.[31]

2 Contextualizing the Object: AI Systems and Automated Inferences

The evolution of AI systems in recent years has been facilitated by the availability of huge amounts of digital data (big data), as well as major advances in processing and storage capacity for that data. When addressing the issue of AI, one is faced with "systems that exhibit intelligent behavior"—intelligent to the extent that they are able to analyze their environment and make autonomous decisions in order to achieve specific goals. The central issue in defining this intelligence has to do with the understanding of learning. Alan Turing argued that to be considered intelligent, a machine would need to have the ability to learn and evolve.[32] That is, not only to process data or compute large amounts of information, but also determine what to do next, similar to a digital brain.

For the inventor of the "Turing machine", the question of whether a machine could think was vague and irrelevant in the past, because machines could not think like human beings. Insofar as they are different from a human being, machines also function differently, but just because they think differently from humans, this does not mean that they do not "think". However, Turing was rather concerned with how a machine could simulate a person, through computer programs that were good at imitating human intelligence (the "imitation game"). Computers are made up of billions of tiny switches called transistors, and algorithms turn them on and off millions of times a second. Claude Shannon, known as the father of information theory, was the first to grasp that what transistors are doing, by switching on and off in response to other transistors, is, precisely, reasoning.[33]

Today AI-based systems can be confined to software and act in the virtual world (e.g., voice assistants, image analysis programs, search engines, facial and speech recognition systems), or they can be integrated into physical devices (e.g., advanced robots, autonomous cars, unmanned aerial vehicles, or Internet apps).[34] Indeed,

---

[31] See Opinion of Advocate General Priit Pikamäe, cit., recital 3.

[32] Turing (1950).

[33] Domingos (2017).

[34] Bearing in mind AI inherent characteristics, its concept is dynamic. The European Commission provided a definition in 2018, according to which "(artificial intelligence) refers to systems that display intelligent behavior by analyzing their environment and taking actions—with some degree of autonomy—to achieve specific goals." European Commission (2018a), The concept has been further developed, already in 2019, through the intervention of experts organized within the High-Level Expert Group on Artificial Intelligence (HLEG AI), established by the European Commission in June 2018: "Artificial intelligence (AI) refers to systems designed by humans that, given a complex goal, act in the physical or digital world by perceiving their environment, interpreting the

people rely on AI on a daily basis to translate, generate subtitles in videos, or block spam.

As a scientific discipline, AI includes many approaches and techniques—robotics is perhaps the most famous one. However, the one which raises higher concern, insofar as it programs itself, is machine learning—a technology that builds itself, and requires data to improve its performance. This would be a method of transforming data into knowledge, whereby algorithms learn by simulating reasoning by analogy.[35] In fact, Google, Facebook, Amazon, Apple, and other companies, have learning algorithms which evolve from the data they are given. That means they learn what to do on their own, based on inferences made from data, and the result of this operation applies to our everyday lives. This is why data is said to underlie not only a revolution, but a metamorphosis that is reconfiguring science, economics, politics,[36] and, consequently, law.

An algorithm can be understood as a set of instructions that defines a sequence of operations for various purposes—that is, a sequence of commands intended to transform an input into an output.[37] All algorithms have an input and an output: data enters the computer, the algorithm acts on it, and this operation generates a result. Machine learning, however, reverses this situation: the data and the desired result enter the system, and what comes out is the algorithm (which transforms the former into the latter). Learning algorithms are those that create other algorithms, that is, mathematical models that can be fed new data to produce new results and allow computers to design their own programs.[38] In fact, the relationship between AI and big data is bidirectional: AI needs large volumes of information to learn, while big data needs AI to extract values from large data sets.[39]

Thus, through machine learning techniques, algorithms are trained to infer certain patterns based on a dataset. The increasing availability of data (including personal data) has driven the implementation of automated exploration techniques (data mining) and prospection (machine learning). To this extent, a learning algorithm would not be a mere "cake recipe", as one could put it in a more colloquial way, since it is capable of analyzing old recipes (what worked and what failed), as well as designing new recipes that which deem more effective (and doing it autonomously).

---

collected structured or unstructured data, reasoning on the knowledge derived from this data and deciding the best action(s) to take (according to pre-defined parameters) to achieve the given goal. AI systems can also be designed to learn to adapt their behaviour by analysing how the environment is affected by their previous actions.", HLEG AI (2019a).

[35] Automated learning takes many forms and is known by several names: pattern recognition, statistical modeling, data mining, predictive analytics, adaptive systems, etc. On the subject, Domingos (2017).

[36] On the digital metamorphosis, Beck (2017). The author explains that while the digital revolution still implies the clear distinction between online and offline, digital metamorphosis has to do with the essential entanglement of online and offline.

[37] FRA - European Union Agency for Fundamental Rights (2018).

[38] Domingos (2017).

[39] Buttarelli (2017).

Provided it is equipped with appropriate learning algorithms, a computer can learn to drive a vehicle, for example, simply by analyzing the behavior of a human driver. This approach to learning by analogy is inspired by natural living organisms, most notably the functioning of the human brain.

Even though the human brain has inspired learning mechanisms—particularly neural networks[40]—the algorithms are trained to solve a specific problem and are unable to tackle distinct problems. In other words, learning algorithms are far from using the mechanisms that the human brain uses to process information. Moreover, the way the human brain is organized, the way it pursues different goals, the way memories are stored throughout life, etc., it all depends on mechanisms that are only now beginning to be unraveled.[41] However, from a conceptual point of view, it may be possible to simulate the electrical and biochemical behavior of the complex network of neuronal cells that constitute the brain, i.e., to simulate a nervous system on a computer, a process that raises certain issues that will not be addressed in this text.[42]

[40] Neural networks are one of the most flexible and powerful approaches currently in use in automated learning. They reproduce in the computer the essentials of the information processing mechanism used by the human brain. In a human brain, neurons are connected through synapses. In neural networks used in automated learning, mathematical methods determine the values of these connections in order to maximize the accuracy of the match computed by the neural network—which can be used to process images, sounds, and videos. When they are used to process images, for example, each neuron in one of these networks eventually learns to recognize a certain feature of the image. Oliveira (2019).

[41] New digital technologies have helped unravel how the brain works, how it stores and triggers memories, how it makes decisions—and thus have helped unravel how Evolution sculpted who we are. This decoding of the brain has become a global priority (as was once the mapping of the human genome), so much so that the EU has launched the "Human Brain Project" to understand the inner workings of cognition and consciousness. How much longer will it take to map the human brain? The answer to this question depends on the desired mapping accuracy—perhaps still in the 2020s. It is already possible to record memories—and not long ago it was not even known where they were stored, let alone record them and send them over the Internet. Michio Kaku, theoretical physicist at the City College New York, explains the procedure succinctly: in the center of the brain is the hippocampus, where short-term memories are stored. You can place two electrodes on either side of the hippocampus, measure the impulses traveling back and forth, and record them on a recorder. Months later, it is possible to take this record and put it back into the brain of an animal, which will remember what happened to it. The idea is to apply such technology to Alzheimer's patients, so that in the future they will have a memory chip, which they activate simply by pushing a button, so that memories flood the hippocampus. Kaku (2018). Since it is possible to measure/sequence brain activity, and analyze someone's thoughts in real time, how can we protect thoughts and emotions of human beings from brain manipulation? On the issue of "neuro-rights", Debasa (2021).

[42] On the subject Oliveira (2019). The author explains the hypothesis of emulation of the operation of a human brain, i.e., the complete simulation of a specific system (a brain) by another system (a computer), tending to discover treatments for many, if not all, the degenerative diseases that affect it. However, such a hypothesis would not be without problems, since the program doing the emulation can be duplicated and copied an arbitrary number of times, can be sent to a distant computer and be executed there, can confer virtual immortality to the emulated person, etc. In any event, the insights of António Damásio are pertinent in this context, according to which the content of the human mind depends on the organic substrate that sustains it—that is, the brain is not

For the purpose of this article, it should be noted that scientists are searching for the "master algorithm," based on the hypothesis that all knowledge—past, present and future—can be deduced from data by a single universal learning algorithm. In practice, and for the time being, each learning algorithm works well for a few things, but not for others. The current goal consists in achieving a single algorithm that combines every algorithm's key feature, and that is capable of deriving all the knowledge in the world: in other words, a general-purpose learning algorithm that could learn everything there is to learn from data. Its invention would be one of the greatest advances in the history of science, as it would be the gateway to solving the most difficult problems facing humanity.[43]

Learning algorithms already control the digital world, they are everywhere, they shape the world around us. They have acquired a relevance in our daily lives that simply did not exist a few years ago, affecting our relationships with the world and with others, as well as how we build and what we build. Increasingly, intelligent algorithms decide who gets credit, who buys what, who gets which job, who gets which raise, which stocks go up and down in the stock market, how much insurance costs, where police officers are located, who has romantic dates with whom, etc. Machine learning automates automation itself, because computers design their own programs, they do, in fact, learn and develop programs that programmers cannot design.

However, in the face of such self-governance of automated systems, several law-related problems arise, e.g., how do we prevent learning algorithms from perpetuating the discrimination underlying the data from which they learn and develop (whether on the basis of gender, age, ethnic origin, sexual orientation, religious/philosophical/political convictions, etc.)? Certainly, human decision-making processes are not immune to errors and possible prejudice, but the same bias within an AI system can have an effect on a much larger scale, affecting and discriminating against many people without the social control mechanisms that govern human behavior.

In any case, the main concern discussed in this article is certainly broader than the one related to algorithmic discrimination. Indeed, to challenge the differentiations of treatment without material basis or reasonable justification, we have anti discriminatory legal standards minimally stabilized, although the effectiveness of its application to automated situations can be questioned.[44] Automated discrimination is part

---

independent from the living organism of which it is a part. The narratives we create and the emotions we experience are not at all independent from their organic substrate. Damásio (2020).

[43] Domingos (2017).

[44] The legal protection offered by anti-discrimination legislation is challenged when AI systems, not humans, discriminate. Humans discriminate on the basis of negative attitudes (prejudices) sometimes unintentional (stereotypes) which signal victims when discrimination occurs. Compared to traditional forms of discrimination, the automated one is more abstract, subtle, intangible, and non-intuitive—it is harder to detect. The increasing use of learning algorithms disrupts the effectiveness of traditional legal procedures and remedies, designed for discriminations predominantly based on intuition—and for which the impact produced in the legal sphere of the person being

of another problem which must be addressed, namely, how to protect individuals against inferences or predictions about themselves produced in an automated way, and the consequences of their application to everyday situations, since legal tools are required to allow control over when, how, and under what conditions data subjects are evaluated by automated systems. And, as in a Russian doll, the question that moves us could be integrated in an even broader one: would it be possible to legally regulate the operation and application of automated exploration and prospection techniques, with a view to the development of a digital environment that tends to be safe, fair, and open?[45]

There are no doubts about the positive impact that data processing already has, and will continue to have, on the development of the global society. Moreover, the free movement of data is indispensable for the development of a European digital economy. [46] The technological solutions that enable the smarter use of resources like energy and water, the reduction of pesticides in agriculture, the competitiveness of the manufacturing industry, as well as the reduction of accidents on the roads, etc., all depend on data processing.[47] Likewise, it is quite clear that AI can bring about great opportunities to address the challenges we, as a society, are facing—be it the aging population, degenerative diseases, or environmental pollution. Hence the implementation of a European AI Strategy to address these and other challenges.[48]

However, it is paramount to ensure that the risks and negative impacts associated with digital technologies are properly managed, especially since AI systems can cause unintended harm. In truth, such risks can result from the use of personal data, for which possible distortions have not yet been anticipated. In cases where the result could not have been avoided or foreseen at the program design stage, the risks will result from the practical impact of the correlations or patterns that the system identifies in a large set of data, either in terms of (i) the quality of the information collected and stored—which influences the accuracy of the inference; (ii) the neutrality/objectivity of data processing—which, when obeying partial/fallacious criteria, leads to discriminatory results; (iii) the decontextualized effect on profiling—which leads to the standardization of individuals.[49]

Additionally, the specific characteristics of some AI technologies—including opacity, complexity, unpredictability, autonomy—may make it difficult to enforce

---

discriminated is relevant. Therefore, the doctrine has revealed the need for the definition of a common standard of statistical evidence, aimed at detecting automated discrimination, as well as supporting legal operators, data controllers, and data subjects. Wachter et al. (2020).

45 Council of Europe – Committee of Experts on Internet Intermediaries (MSI-NET) (2018).

46 European Commission (2020a)

47 European Parliament (2017). In this Resolution, the European Parliament called on the European Commission to submit, on the basis of Article 114 TFEU, a legislative proposal on legal issues relating to the development and use of robotics and artificial intelligence foreseeable over the next 10–15 years. The European Parliament identified the need for efficient and up-to-date rules that correspond to technological development and to newly emerging innovations used in the market.

48 European Commission (2018b).

49 Analide and Rebelo (2019).

and verify compliance with standards designed to protect fundamental rights (most notably personal data, privacy, non-discrimination). Such characteristics make it an arduous task to trace potentially problematic decisions made with the involvement of AI systems.[50] In particular, explaining how information is correlated and weighed to achieve a specific result becomes more demanding due to opacity.[51]

For all these reasons, the protection of personal data has become the main identity issue of our times, so that the project of humanism does not become irrelevant. As the Israeli historian Yuval Harari explains,[52] if the association between big data and AI is not properly regulated, this may result in the loss of what is most genuine in humanity, as human experiences may be reduced to data patterns. Until recently, we took for granted that experiences happened inside of us, and we would look inside to understand the reason why something happened to us, individually, but that is not the case anymore. Now, when we connect our experience to the great flow of digital data, allowing algorithms to discover the meaning of what happens to us, we no longer make free choices based on rational judgments and, consequently, we lose human dignity—this is because value no longer resides in everyday experiences, but in the ability to transform them into freely circulating data. Learning algorithms are capable of holding information on our desires, tastes, and inclinations and will soon be able to know exactly who we are. The question that must be posed is: will we have models to deal with such a life?[53]

And here the weaknesses of legal protection are related to a general problem, which in fact pervades all regulation in the Internet field, namely, legal intervention tends to be more efficient in a repressive (*ex post*) than in a preventive (*ex ante*)

---

[50] European Commission (2020b).

[51] Datatilsynet - The Norwegian Data Protection Authority (2018).

[52] Harari (2017).

[53] Explaining how "surveillance capitalism" exploits sensitivities revealed by behavioral data—that is, how it is possible to know what a certain individual in a certain time and place thinks, feels and does—Shoshana Zuboff explains that Google's user profile, for example, does not depend on the user voluntarily giving up information, but is inferred from analyzing their search patterns, documents and websites visited, advertisements previously selected, purchases made after viewing, and a host of other signs of online behavior. This means that the information can be provided by the user, by an authorized third-party, or it can derive from the user's actions—which hinders curbing this market through the exercise of rights by reluctant users. The first stage of the expropriation of the behavioral surplus begins with the unilateral incursion of our defenseless space: our laptop, our cell phone, our web page, the street we live in, an e-mail to a friend, the online search for a birthday present, sharing pictures of our children, our interests and tastes, our feelings, our face. In the second stage the purpose is habituation—individuals get used to the incursion in a mixture of agreement, helplessness, and resignation; here the sense of wonder and outrage dissipates because everything seems to be inevitable. While parliamentary inquiries and court cases proceed at the slow pace of the democratic rule of law, the surveillance capitalists continue to develop their sometimes contested practices at great speed. In a third stage of the cycle, when any of the Internet giants are occasionally forced to change their practices, their executives and technicians produce superficial but tactically effective adaptations, satisfying the immediate demands of the authorities and public opinion. Then surveillance capitalism redirects the contested supply operations with new rhetoric, methods, and concepts—and everything stays just the same. Zuboff (2020).

mode. The Law usually acts in a deferred time, not exactly in real time, and even less preventively. However, legal treatment of AI systems shows weaknesses if it is enforceable only after the production and identification of harm (*ex post*). This requires a combination of *ex ante* and *ex post* controls from the legal, ethical, and technical dimensions of the operation of AI systems, allowing for reasonable measures to be taken to minimize the damage caused, above all, by high-risk AI applications—"the main risks related to the use of AI concern the application of rules designed to protect fundamental rights (including personal data and privacy protection and non-discrimination), as well as safety and liability-related issues."[54]

Ethics plays a relevant role in the context of AI because a balance needs to be struck between what should and what could be done in this domain, and particular care should be taken about what definitely should not be done.[55] Even in circumstances where compliance with legal requirements is demonstrable, legal rules may not cover all ethical concerns about AI, not least because the understanding of what might be ethically appropriate invariably evolves, and may change over time.[56] Taking this into consideration, it is possible to grasp the EU's efforts to consolidate an ethical paradigm and a positive influence in setting technical rules, in line with the respect for the fundamental rights of citizens.

In any case, machine learning is just a technology and what matters is what we decide to do with it and how we regulate its use. Technology is not, and cannot be, an end in itself, isolated from society, economy, and law—it is always a means.[57] In this

[54] European Commission (2020), White Paper on Artificial Intelligence – a European approach to excellence and trust, cit.

[55] HLEG AI (2019b). Neuroscientific studies are unveiling a path to AI from the technologies of "soft robotics," that is, a new generation of machines that feel. According to Antonio Damásio, the universe of affection was crucial for the emergence of creativity in human beings—it is the foundation for the intelligence that conscious minds have gradually developed. In this sense, if machines function according to "homeostatic feelings," then they will be able to process and react to the conditions around them, improving the quality and efficiency of intelligent reaction. Such machines with feelings will eventually develop functional elements related to consciousness—since feelings are part of the path to consciousness—into a kind of hybrid of natural and artificial creatures that could result as effective assistants to humans. Damásio (2020).

[56] Ethics is an academic discipline that constitutes a subdomain of philosophy. Broadly speaking, it deals with questions such as "What is a good action?", "What is the value of a human life?", "What is justice?" or "What is a good life?" In academic ethics, there are several areas of inquiry, among which applied ethics concerns what we are obliged (or allowed) to do in a specific (sometimes unprecedented or historically new) situation. Applied ethics deals with real-life situations, where decisions have to be made under time pressure and often with limited rationality. AI ethics is generally seen as an example of applied ethics, and focuses on the issues raised by the design, development, deployment, and use of AI. European Commission (2019).

[57] As Shoshana Zuboff clarifies, one of the first challenges to understanding and regulating AI systems has to do precisely with the confusion between what the author understands as "surveillance capitalism" and the digital technologies it uses. Surveillance capitalism would not be the technology itself—but rather a dynamic that permeates the technology and controls its use. In other words, surveillance capitalism would be a type of marketplace unthinkable outside the digital medium, but it would not represent the digital. This distinction is important to measure the extent to which some perplexities associated with the digital market are not challengeable simply through the protection of personal data. Zuboff (2020).

vein, and while the legal regime for AI is being built in the EU, it is important to look at the legal solutions that regulate the raw material used by learning algorithms: digital data (including personal data). Furthermore, it is crucial to observe whether existing EU rules on personal data, especially those on profiling and automated decisions, are adequate to address the risks introduced by AI systems.

However, the doctrine is not unanimous, as some theorists have insisted on the need to adjust certain legal instruments currently in force.[58] Researchers from the Oxford Internet Institute at Oxford University and the Alan Turing Institute at the British Library, for example, postulate the need to construct a "right to reasonable inferences".[59] The British scholars understand inferences to mean information relating to an identified or identifiable person that results from automated reasoning,[60] and they argue that the protection based on the GDPR would not be sufficient to assess the reasonableness of processes from which inferences produced by learning algorithms result in. To this extent, the legal protection of the GDPR would need to be expanded to unambiguously consider inferred data as personal data, and the Article 29 Working Party (WP29) acknowledges this argument, something we will be able to observe further in this article.

3 Identifying the Object: Profiling and Automated Decisions in the GDPR

The widespread availability of personal data from Internet of Things devices[61]—and more recently the Internet of Bodies[62]—as well as technologies to find correlations from such data, all make it possible to determine, analyze and predict aspects of a

[58] Mendoza and Bygrave (2017). The authors are researchers at the University of Oslo and they raise many questions as to whether Article 22 GDPR (right not to be subject to uniquely automated decisions) will have a relevant practical impact on profiling.

[59] Wachter and Mittelstadt (2019).

[60] The authors define inferences as "[i]nformation relating to an identified or identifiable natural person created through deduction or reasoning rather than mere observation or collection from the data subject (. . .) which are created or used by data controllers or third parties, are privacy-invasive or harmful to reputation—or have a high likelihood of being so in the future—or have low verifiability in the sense of being predictive or opinion-based while being used for important decisions". Wachter and Mittelstadt (2019), A right to reasonable inferences: re-thinking data protection law in the age of big data and AI, cit.

[61] In 2017 the European Commission estimated that, until 2020, around 6 billion household devices (televisions, refrigerators, washing machines, etc.) would be connected to the Internet in the EU. European Commission (2017). In February of that year, the European Parliament had already alerted that these devices constituted a significant threat to privacy, due to the placement of connected devices in traditionally protected and intimate spaces, as well as their ability to extract information regarding sensitive personal data and transmit it. European Parliament (2017), European Parliament resolution with recommendations to the Commission on Civil Law Rules on Robotics, cit.

[62] On the process of transforming bodily experiences into behavioral data, Zuboff (2020).

person's personality, behavior, interests, and habits. The process of profiling is frequently used to make predictions about individuals, based on data from various sources to deduce something about someone, considering the characteristics of other people which are statistically similar. Such technologies have diverse commercial applications, and can be used, for example, to segment markets and tailor services and products to individual needs. This is why profiling and automated decisions are used in more and more areas of both the private and public sector: banking and finance, healthcare, taxation, insurance, marketing, and advertising are just a few examples of the domains where profiling is most frequently used to support decision-making.

Exploration (data mining) and prospection (machine learning) operations serve auxiliary or substitutive purposes in the evaluation and automated decision processes based on functionalities that are (i) descriptive, i.e., they translate statements that narrate what happened and the preceding motivation (descriptive analysis), (ii) predictive, i.e., they anticipate events or actions in the probable conjecture of what may happen (predictive analysis), and (iii) prescriptive, i.e., they project the answer to questions on what will or may happen (prescriptive analysis). In the current "state of the art" of big data, the process of achieving a predictive result begins with the exploration of datasets to trap the correlations detected in the stored data. Hence, (i) the recognition of the problem to be answered is followed by (ii) the identification of the data to be considered, and the consequent (iii) detection of patterns or regularities in the information that may be relevant to the solution of the problem. And it is from this process that results/conclusions are extracted, that is, affinities/trends/prediction models are inferred.[63]

Nevertheless, profiling, and automated decisions are susceptible to generating significant risks for the rights and freedoms of individuals, meaning that requires adequate safeguards. The operations which result in profiling tend to be nontransparent, and the data owners usually do not quite understand that their being profiled, neither do they grasp what is at stake. Indeed, profiling tends to perpetuate existing stereotypes and promote social segregation. It can also tie the individual to a specific category and limit their suggested preferences, putting their freedom of choice at risk, regarding products and services. In certain cases, profiling may lead to imprecise predictions, and, in others, it is likely to result in a denial of goods and services and unjustified discrimination.[64]

---

[63] Analide and Rebelo (2019).

[64] Shoshana Zuboff argues that "surveillance capitalism" claims human experience as free raw material and turns it into behavioral data. The processing of personal data tending to improve the supply of goods and services would lead to a behavioral surplus—which would be transformed in predictive products capable of anticipating our current and future actions. Such predictive products or inferences would be sold in a new kind of market for behavioral predictions—which the author refers to as behavioral futures markets—that would only incidentally deal with the less lucrative targeting of advertisements. The surveillance capitalists would be getting rich from this new business model, as numerous companies would be eager to bet on our future behavior. In this market, personal data would not be traded—because raw materials are not sold, but rather

Article 4(4) GDPR defines profiling as "any form of automated processing of personal data consisting of the use of personal data to evaluate certain personal aspects relating to a natural person, in particular to analyse or predict aspects concerning that natural person's performance at work, economic situation, health, personal preferences, interests, reliability, behaviour, location or movements". This definition refers to "any form of automated processing", and not "exclusively" automated, as embodied in article 22 GDPR. It follows that the issue of profiling is not exhausted in Article 22 GDPR, as this provision only concerns exclusively automated decisions, i.e., decisions adopted through technological means without relevant human intervention.[65] Thus, there may be decisions based on profiling that are not exclusively automated.

Moreover, automated decisions may be performed with or without profiling, and profiling may occur without automated decisions. Thus, there is profiling which does not lead to an exclusively automated decision disputable under Article 22 GDPR—and deserves equal protection. An example provided by WP29 helps to understand the distinction between profiling and automated decisions. The imposition of speeding fines based solely on speed camera evidence is an automated decision process that does not necessarily involve profiling. However, it would become a profiling decision if the individual's driving habits were monitored over time and, for example, if the amount of the fine imposed were the result of an assessment considering other factors, such as whether the speeding was repeated or not, or whether the driver had recently committed a traffic related offence.

The protection of individuals from automated inferences or predictions is still under development in the EU. According to the WP29, the GDPR introduces provisions intended to ensure that profiling and automated decisions (regardless of whether they include profiling or not) do not produce an unjustified impact on individuals' rights. In this sense, for the WP29, the GDPR would not only apply to dada collection but also to the application of profiling to individuals. It follows that profiling would involve three distinct phases: (i) data collection; (ii) automated analysis to identify correlations; and (iii) applying the correlations to an individual to identify present or future behavioral characteristics. If there were perhaps automated

predictions resulting from the behavioral surplus. The competitive dynamics of these new markets would have encouraged the search for progressively more predictable sources of behavioral surplus: our voices/personalities/emotions. Until the surveillance capitalists discovered that they got more predictive data if they intervened in the behaviors themselves, trying to adjust, persuade, tune, and steer them to more profitable outcomes. Any agent interested in buying probabilistic information about our behavior (and/or influencing future behavior) would be able to pay to intervene in markets where individuals' behavior is guessed at and sold. Protected by the opacity of automated processes and the sense of inevitability that emanates from them, the project of surveillance capitalism would entrench our dependence on an effective life, creating a psychic torpor that habituates us to the reality of being tracked, analyzed, and modified. Therefore, the elementary rights associated with individual autonomy, essential to the mere viability of a democratic society, would be nullified. Zuboff (2020).

[65] WP29 (2017), Guidelines on Automated individual decision-making and Profiling for the purposes of Regulation 2016/679, cit.

individual decisions based on profiling, these would also be subject to the GDPR—whether exclusively automated or not. That is, for WP29, profiling is not limited to the mere categorization of the individual, but it also includes inferences and predictions about the individual.

An example provided by WP29 helps to understand the operation: a data broker collects data from different public and private sources, either on behalf of its clients or for its own interests. The data broker compiles the data to develop profiles concerning people and inserts them into various segments, and it then sells this information to companies that wish to improve the suitability of their goods and services for the target audience. The data broker performs profiling, placing a person in a certain category according to their interests. Whether or not exclusively automated decisions within the meaning of Article 22 GDPR are made will depend on the subsequent circumstances and purposes. In any case, decisions that are not exclusively automated may also include profiling and, therefore, are worthy of protection.

Thus, according to the WP29, the scope of the GDPR would include (i) general profiling, (ii) decision-making based on profiling, and (iii) purely automated decisions, including profiling, which produce legal effects or significantly affect the data subject in a similar manner [Article 22(1)]. In other words, all profiling and automated individual decisions would be protected, including decision-making processes that are not exclusively automated. The difference between (ii) and (iii) becomes more understandable through an example: (ii) an individual decides whether a loan should be granted, based on a profile drawn up by purely automated means (this would be a decision based on profiling); (iii) an algorithm decides whether the loan is granted and the decision is automatically communicated to the individual, without any prior and relevant assessment by a human being (this would be a purely automated decision).

In any case, according to the WP29, automated decisions can be based on any kind of data, be it (i) data provided directly by the individual (such as answers to a questionnaire concerning name, postal address, e-mail address, etc.); (ii) observed data about the individual (such as location data collected through an application accessed by the individual); (iii) data obtained or inferred (such as a profile of the individual created for the purposes of a credit score). This is relevant to the argument made at the beginning of this article, according to which inferences and predictions resulting from data analysis through learning algorithms, i.e., inferences whose application to everyday situations determine how each of us, as personal data subjects, are perceived and evaluated by others, deserve protection as inferred personal data.

To this extent, the WP29 guidance seeks to explain the provisions of the GDPR that, according to them, would pertain to all profiling and automated individual decisions. The WP29 starts from the premise that controllers may engage in profiling and automated decisions involving personal data, as long as (i) these respect all principles laid out in Article 5 GDPR (lawfulness, fairness, transparency, purpose limitation, data minimization, accuracy, limitation of storage, integrity, confidentiality, accountability), and (ii) have a lawful basis for processing among those referred to in Article 6 GDPR (i.e., they may do so if processing is necessary for the performance of a contract, in order to comply with a legal obligation, to protect the vital interests of the data subject or a third party, in the performance of a task carried out in the public interest, or in the legitimate interests of the controller—or otherwise with the data subject's consent), and additional safeguards would apply in the case of purely automated decisions within the meaning of Article 22 GDPR. In addition, there would be a general prohibition on automated decisions only, in order to repel potential risks to the rights and freedoms of individuals—and the safeguards in Article 22 would apply to situations where the general prohibition does not apply.

Despite the praiseworthy exegetical effort carried out by the WP29—according to which the GDPR would apply to all profiling and automated individual decisions, whether they are based on provided data, observed data, or inferred data—what appears to be true is that the effectiveness of the application of the GDPR to inferred data faces several obstacles. This has to do with fact that the GDPR was designed for data provided directly by the data subject and not for data inferred by AI systems.

The WP29 starts by listing the principle that personal data shall be processed lawfully, fairly, and transparently in relation to the data subject [Article 5(1) (a) GDPR]. Here, profiling and automated decisions stumble upon transparency of processing as a fundamental requirement of the GDPR. As the WP29 itself admits, the profiling process tends to be invisible to the eyes of the data subject, as it works on the basis of creating data obtained or inferred about individuals (new data which has not been sent directly by the dada subjects). Furthermore, individuals have different levels of reasoning, and may find it difficult to understand the opaque techniques involved in the processes of profiling and automated decisions. Meanwhile, under the Article 12(21) GDPR, the person responsible for handling the data must provide the data subject with transparent, comprehensible, and concise information, and easily accessible, about their personal data processing. However, one must ask in this context: how can this be done with regard to inferred data, resulting from algorithmic operations which are unpredictable and counterintuitive?

Moreover, according to Article 5(1) GDPR, processing must be fair and transparent. Nevertheless, as the WP29 underlines, profiling risks being abusive and creating discrimination, preventing people from accessing employment/credit/insurance opportunities, or offering financial products with excessive risks or costs. WP29 exemplifies a situation potentially violating the GDPR: a data broker sells consumer profiles to financial entities, without the consent or knowledge of the underlying data by the consumers. Profiles define consumers through categories (for example, "small town resident and ethnic difficulties", "rough start in life: young single parents", etc.) or assign them scores based on the consumers' financial vulnerability. The financial entity then offer these consumers high-cost loans and other financially risky products that make it impossible for them to access the resources they want. Here is where the perplexity lies: would it be possible to properly challenge such an automated operation on the basis of the GDPR?

Moreover, contrary to the purpose limitation principle, profiling tends to cover the use of personal data collected for other purposes. This is the business model of free mobile applications on the Internet, which serve to create profiles used in targeted advertising.[66] And the business opportunities generated by profiling encourage more data collection of personal information than what is strictly necessary in case they show to be useful in the future. For profiling to be compatible with the GDPR, controllers should be able to clearly explain and justify the need to collect and retain personal data; they should ensure that they respect the principle of data minimization, as well as the principles of purpose limitation and retention limitation. Yet, how can this be achieved if learning algorithms are designed precisely to handle large volumes of data (the more data, the more they learn) and establish correlations that allow for detailed and exhaustive profiling?

It should also be noted that data controllers must take into account the principle of accuracy at all stages of the profiling process, including when they (i) collect the data, (ii) analyze the data, (iii) profile an individual, or (iv) apply a profile to make a decision concerning them. If the data used in an automated operation is inaccurate or dated, any profiling, inference or decision resulting from that will be imprecise/incorrect. Inaccurate data can lead to inadequate inferences about, for example, health status or the credit or insurance risk of a person. Even if input data is accurately recorded, the dataset involved may not be fully representative or analyses may contain hidden biases. It is necessary for controllers to introduce robust measures to verify and ensure on an ongoing basis that re-used or indirectly obtained data is accurate and up to date. This reinforces the importance of providing clear information regarding the personal data being processed, so as to allow the data subject to rectify any inaccuracies and improve data quality. This can definitely be achieved when the data is provided by the subject, but when it comes to inferred data from other data, it becomes an issue how to effectively ensure its adequate protection.

In any case, controllers wishing to rely on consent as a ground for profiling [Article 6(1)(a) GDPR] will have to demonstrate that data subjects (i) understand exactly what they are consenting to, and (ii) have sufficient and relevant information about the use and envisaged consequences of the processing—to ensure that any consent represents an informed choice. In this sense, profiling is also allowed in case it is deemed necessary for the purposes of the legitimate interests pursued by the controller or by a third party [Article 6(1)(f) GDPR], but according to the WP29, this ground of lawfulness requires a balancing exercise to assess whether the interests of the controller override the interests or rights of the data subject. For this assessment, the following aspects would be particularly relevant: (i) the level of detail of the profile (whether the profile is integrated into a generic description, or whether it is segmented in detail); (ii) the completeness of the profile (whether the profile describes only some aspects of the data subject, or whether it draws a comprehensive picture); (iii) the impact of the profile (the effects on the data subject).

[66] The Apps available online collect huge amounts of data daily from mobile devices—and process it to provide more up-to-date and appealing services to the user. However, such data may be further processed, usually to generate revenue, in ways not known or desired by the data subject. On the subject, WP29 (2013), Opinion 02/2013 on apps on smart devices, 00461/13/EN, adopted on 27 February 2013.

The WP29 also considers important including, in terms of this assessment, "the safeguards aimed at ensuring fairness, non-discrimination and accuracy in the profiling process". Nonetheless, we believe that such guarantees result from an obligation incumbent on the controller and are not mobilizable for the purposes of a balancing of interests. Moreover, the WP29 admits that it would be difficult to justify the exercise of legitimate interests as a lawful ground for profiling practices aimed at marketing or advertising, particularly when they involve the intrusive tracking of individuals across multiple websites, locations, devices, services, or data brokering—and the WP29 cautions the controller to consider the use of profiling in the future when assessing the validity of processing under Article 6(1) (f) GDPR, particularly in view of the difficulties of controlling algorithmic operations.

Particular caution is required in special categories of data—so-called "sensitive data"—i.e., data which reveal racial or ethnic origin, political opinions, religious or philosophical beliefs, trade union membership, as well as the processing of genetic data, biometric data to uniquely identify a person, data concerning health or data concerning sexual life or sexual orientation.[67] The processing of sensitive data is, in principle, forbidden by the Article 9(1) GDPR; to this extent, controllers may process special category personal data only if they can meet one of the conditions set out in Article 9(2) GDPR.[68] However, profiling can create sensitive data by inference from data that is not special category data per se but becomes so when combined with other data. It is possible to infer a person's health status, for example,

[67] It is important to note that categories such as sex and age, for example, traditionally protected by EU law [Articles 8 and 10 TFEU, and Article 21(1) CFREU], are not included in this list. Nevertheless, even though they are not considered sensitive data, they do matter for the protection of inferred data, because if the AI system is trained using only or mostly male data, for example, this can lead to skewed/biased results regarding women.

[68] According to Article 9(2) GDPR, the prohibition of processing of special categories of personal data does not apply: (a) if the data subject has given explicit consent; (b) if processing is necessary for the purposes of carrying out the obligations and exercising specific rights of the controller or of the data subject in the field of employment and social security and social protection law; (c) if processing is necessary to protect the vital interests of the data subject or of another natural person where the data subject is physically or legally incapable of giving consent; (d) if processing is carried out in the course of its legitimate activities with appropriate safeguards by a foundation, association or any other not-for-profit body with a political, philosophical, religious or trade union aim; (e) if processing relates to personal data which are manifestly made public by the data subject; (f) if processing is necessary for the establishment, exercise or defence of legal claims or whenever courts are acting in their judicial capacity; (g) if processing is necessary for reasons of substantial public interest; (h) processing is necessary for the purposes of preventive or occupational medicine (...) or pursuant to contract with a health professional; (i) if processing is necessary for reasons of public interest in the area of public health; (j) if processing is necessary for archiving purposes in the public interest, scientific or historical research purposes or statistical purposes (...).

from records of their food purchases in combination with data on the quality and energy value of foods.[69]

The WP29 warns that in case preferences and sensitive characteristics are inferred from profiling, the controllers must ensure that (i) the processing is not incompatible with the original purpose; (ii) they have identified a lawful ground for processing the special categories of data; and (iii) they inform the data subject about the processing. At this point of the analysis, we come to the biggest challenge of all regarding data inferred from AI systems: the entity implementing them may not be in a position to exercise its obligations as a controller. The absence of an adequate level of insight into the operation of the AI system makes it impossible to ascertain whether the processing operation complies with the basic principles enshrined in the GDPR. Therefore, a controller who is not in a factual position to fulfill its obligations as such should not assume such a position for the purposes of the GDPR.[70]

4 Equating the Problem: The Rights of the Inferred Personal Data Holders

In light of the above, the crux of the matter is to understand *if* and *what* rights would the holders of inferred data benefit from under the GDPR. The WP29 makes an interpretative effort to adapt provisions conceived for (i) provided data (directly provided by the data subject to the controller), and (ii) observed data (indirectly provided by the data subject to the controller) and apply these provisions to (iii) data

[69] Examples abound of sensitive data inferred from opinions/preferences voluntarily provided on social networks. WP29 refers to a U.S. study published in 2012 [Kosinski et al. (2012), Private traits and attributes are predictable from digital records of human behaviour], according to which it would be possible, from Facebook "likes", to infer the sexual orientation of a male user in 88% of cases, the ethnic origin of a user in 95% of cases, and whether a user is Christian or Muslim in 82% of cases.

[70] According to Recital 78 GDPR, "[i]n order to be able to demonstrate compliance with this Regulation, the controller should adopt internal policies and implement measures which meet in particular the principles of data protection by design and data protection by default." In this sense, "the controller shall, both at the time of the determination of the means for processing and at the time of the processing itself, implement appropriate technical and organisational measures, (...)" [Article 25(1) GDPR] to ensure "that, by default, only personal data which are necessary for each specific purpose of the processing are processed. That obligation applies to the amount of personal data collected, the extent of their processing, the period of their storage and their accessibility. In particular, such measures shall ensure that by default personal data are not made accessible without the individual's intervention to an indefinite number of natural persons" [Article 25(2) GPDR]. Faced with the vicissitudes of explainability under the GDPR ("meaningful information about the logic involved"), some are relying on the principles of data protection by design and data protection by default as the feasible solution for more explainable and responsible algorithms. Edwards and Veale (2017). Underlying this is the idea that the development of AI requires that all those involved in the development and marketing of such systems take legal responsibility for the quality of the technology they produce at all stages of the process.

inferred via automated operations. According to the WP29, automated decisions are based on data processing—provided data, observed data or inferred data—and, in this sense, data processing would fall under the application of the GDPR, despite WP29's broad interpretation of the GDPR provisions—according to which any profile or automated decision would be protected by the GDPR—only exclusively automated decisions are expressly mentioned in article 22 GDPR.

Thus, the GDPR applies to all exclusively automated decisions (Article 22 GDPR), however, this disposition is limited to (i) decisions adopted without human intervention that (ii) produce effects in the legal sphere of the data subject or that (iii) significantly affect them in a similar manner. However, considering what we have contemplated so far, it is quite clear to understand that this would only be the tip of the iceberg, since the problem of inferred data is not restricted to exclusively automated decisions—which, in principle, are prohibited, a matter we will be discussing further. First, and aligning with WP29's interpretation, it is crucial to grasp what rights would the holders of inferred data benefit from under the GDPR.

An example put forward by WP29 helps to clarify some dimensions of the problem we are dealing with. Assuming that a data broker performs profiling with personal data, in accordance with its obligations under Articles 13 and 14 GDPR [information to be provided when data is collected (or not) from the data subject], the data broker must inform the data subject of the processing in question, including whether it intends to share, or not, the profile with any other organization, as well as provide information on the data subject's right to object to the processing under Article 21(1) GDPR. The controllers are specifically obliged to ensure the right to object in all cases where the lawfulness of the processing is based on Article 6(1) (e) or (f) (i.e., public interest or legitimate interests of the controller), unless they can provide compelling and legitimate reasons that outweigh the rights of the data subject (an issue the GDPR does not clarify). In any case, if the data subject exercises the right to object, the controller must discontinue, or prevent from initiating, the profiling process, and it may have to remove the personal data concerned [Article 17(1)(c) GDPR]. It is important to emphasize that letting the data subject know its rights is not enough (Article 13, 14 GDPR), because in view of the fundamental principle of transparency that underlies data protection, it is necessary to explain to data subjects, in a clear and simple way, how the profiling or automated decision-making process works. The perplexity regarding inferred data lies precisely in explaining how the AI system produced a given inference.[71]

In the same vein, assuming that a controller shares the profile with another company, and the latter uses it to send direct marketing material to the person

[71] As the Articles of the GDPR provide for a right to information and not exactly a right to explanation (as stated in Recital 71: "to obtain an explanation of the decision reached"), the doctrine is divided as to whether there is a right to explanation under the GDPR. On the subject, Wachter et al. (2017); Cabral (2020). The author concludes that several Articles of the GDPR would underpin the right to explanation, i.e., not only the right to information (Articles 13 and 14), but also the right of access (Article 15 GDPR) and the right not to be subject to exclusively automated decisions (Article 22 GDPR).

concerned, the rights under the GDPR apply both against the controller creating the profile and against the controller applying the profile to draw an inference or prediction from it, if those entities are not the same. In this sense, the company must inform the data subject of the purposes for which profiling is used [Article 14(1)(c)] and the source from which the information was obtained [Article 14(2)(f)], as well as inform the data subject of their unconditional right to object to processing for the purposes of direct marketing [Article 21(2) GDPR]. Both the broker and the company must give the data subject the right to access the information used about them (Article 15 GDPR), to rectify any erroneous information (Article 16 GDPR), and to delete the profile or the personal data used to create it (Article 17 GDPR).

Translating these provisions into practical terms: under Article 15 GDPR (right of access), the data subject has the right to access his/her personal data used for profiling, including the categories of data used to create a profile. The controller is obliged to make the input data to create the profile available, as well as to provide access to information about the profiling and the categories where the data subject has been included.[72] Furthermore, this categorization may lead to an inaccurate prediction if the input data leading to inferred data is inaccurate, irrelevant, or out of context—regardless of a possible flaw in the algorithm itself used to identify correlations. In this case, Article 16 GDPR (right of rectification) could be applied to challenge the accuracy of the input data used, as well as the category into which a person has been entered and which indicates their ability to perform a task. For the WP29, the rights to rectification (Article 16 GDPR) and erasure of data (Article 17 GDPR) would apply to both (i) input personal data (the personal data used to create the profile) and (ii) output data (the profile itself or the score assigned to the person). Still, in any event, it is crucial to unravel how one reaches such a score, as inferred data resulting from automated processing, and to what extent such processing would be questionable on the basis of the GDP, especially when there are no inaccuracies relating to the input data to be rectified.

[72] Recital 63 of the GDPR specifies that, where possible, the controller should provide access to a secure electronic system that enables the data subject to directly access their personal data. Recital 63 further ensures a certain level of protection for controllers who may be concerned about the possibility of revealing commercial secrets or intellectual property, which may be relevant to profiling. According to this recital, the right of access "(. . .) should not adversely affect the rights or freedoms of others, including trade secrets or intellectual property and in particular the copyright protecting the software." However, the WP29 warns that controllers cannot invoke the protection of their trade secrets as a pretext to deny access or refuse to provide information to the data subject. WP29 (2017), Guidelines on automated individual decision-making and profiling for the purposes of Regulation 2016/679, cit. Additionally, the doctrine has been advocating that the high levels of precision of the data mining and machine learning techniques have nothing to with the software, because it is the raw data and not the software that drives operation. Analide and Rebelo (2019). In any event, and bearing in mind the intellectual property rights dimension included in Article 17 CFREU, a resulting concrete conflict must be dealt with using the method of Article 52(1) CFREU—which establishes a general clause restricting the exercise of fundamental rights—considering the essential content of the fundamental right in question as well as the principle of proportionality. On the subject, FRA - European Union Agency for Fundamental Rights (2020).

One could also question whether Article 22 GDPR provides adequate protection for inferred data that is the basis of automated decisions only. According to Article 22(1) GDPR, the "data subject shall have the right not to be subject to a decision based solely on automated processing, including profiling, which produces legal effects concerning him or her or similarly significantly affects him or her". We would therefore be facing a prohibition that only applies when the processing is exclusively automated and produces legal or significantly similar effects. And even in these cases, there are exceptions that allow the processing to be performed.

The provisions of Article 22 GRPD will only apply when there is no relevant human intervention is the decision-making process. It is in this sense that one must interpret the expression "without human intervention" advanced by the WP29. Indeed, if a human being examines and weighs other factors when making the final decision, it will not be "made solely on the basis of" the automated processing—and the prohibition in Article 22(1) GDPR will not apply. Therefore, the controller cannot evade the provisions of Article 22 GDPR by artificially fabricating a human intervention. For example, if someone systematically applies automatically generated profiles without any actual influence on the outcome, it is still considered a decision made solely on the basis of the automated treatment. In order to be considered human intervention, the controller must ensure that any oversight of the decision is relevant, and not a mere token gesture—that is, the oversight must be able to consider all relevant data and change the decision.

WP29 interprets the provision of Article 22(1) GDPR as a prohibition. In this sense, it would establish a general prohibition on decision-making based solely on automated processing—and being a general prohibition, it would apply regardless of whether the data subject takes a measure concerning the processing of their data. One can understand the effort of the WP29 to prevent Article 22(1) GDPR from being applicable only when actively invoked by the data subject, which would reduce the margin of protection in the face of exclusively automated decisions. The interpretation of Article 22(1) GDPR as a general prohibition, instead of a right that can be invoked by the data subject, means that people are automatically protected from possible effects of that kind of processing.

Meanwhile, according to Article 22(2) GDPR, such prohibition does not apply if the decision (i) is necessary for the conclusion or performance of a contract between the data subject and a controller;[73] (ii) is authorized by Union or Member State law to which the controller is subject;[74] (iii) is based on the data subject's explicit

---

[73] As for the first exception to the prohibition in Article 22(1) GDPR for contractual (including pre-contractual) reasons, the controller must be able to demonstrate the necessity of the processing [Article 22(2)(a)] by assessing whether another equally effective and less intrusive method of achieving the same purpose could be adopted—if any, the automated processing alone would not be necessary.

[74] Recital 71 GDPR contextualizes such a possibility [provided for in Article 22(2)(b) GDPR] and explains that the automated operation: "(...) should be allowed where expressly authorised by Union or Member State law to which the controller is subject, including for fraud and tax-evasion monitoring and prevention purposes conducted in accordance with the regulations, standards and

consent. It should be noted that the exceptions of contractual necessity and explicit consent carry substantial data protection risks, requiring a high level of individual control over personal data—the effectiveness of which is highly questionable. The prohibition of Article 22(1) GDPR runs the risk of becoming blurred in the exceptions of Article 22(2) GDPR (especially contract and consent), based on clauses that subvert the meaning of the autonomy of the will, to which individuals adhere out of ignorance or lack of alternative.

In any way, in situations where such a general prohibition does not apply, the data controller must take appropriate measures to safeguard the rights and interests of the data subject, in particular the right to (i) obtain human intervention from the controller, (ii) express his/her point of view and (iii) challenge the decision [Article 22(3) GDPR]. To this extent, any review of the automated inference must be carried out by someone with the appropriate authority and competence to change the result. According to Recital 71 GDPR—which serves as an interpretative benchmark for the provisions of the GDPR—the suitable safeguards should include the right to obtain "an explanation of the decision reached after such assessment and to challenge the decision." This entails guaranteeing the data owner—who has been the subject of an exclusively automated decision—the possibility of exercising a right to contradict and reviewing the decision with someone who has the power to reverse it.[75]

---

recommendations of Union institutions or national oversight bodies and to ensure the security and reliability of a service provided by the controller."

[75] Strictly speaking, Article 22(3) GDPR provides that in the cases referred to in Article 22(2)(a) and (c), i.e., contractual necessity and explicit consent, the controller shall implement suitable measures to safeguard the data subject's rights, namely to obtain human intervention on the part of the controller, to express its point of view and to contest the decision. The exclusion of Article 22(2)(b) GDPR—i.e., the exception according to which such prohibition does not apply if the decision is authorized by Union or Member State law to which the controller is subject—could indicate a willingness of the legislator not to provide for appropriate measures when legal authorization is involved. This would be a solution of very doubtful compatibility with the fundamental right to the protection of personal data in Article 8 CFREU. Moreover, recital 71 GDPR suggests a general application: "[i]n any case, such processing should be subject to suitable safeguards". So, not being that recital contradictory to the spirit of Article 22 GDPR—i.e., to protect the data subject from the dangers of decision-making based purely on automation—there does not seem to be a compelling reason to exempt processing based on legal authorization from the appropriate measures of Article 22(3) (obtain human intervention, express view, and challenge the decision). Thus, the aim of the legislature is (can only be) to prevent decision-making from taking place without individual assessment and evaluation by a human being. So, it is worth recalling the case law of the CJEU according recitals: (i) even if recitals are not mandatory and cannot be invoked to derogate from the very provisions of the legal act in question (Nilsson judgment of 19 November 1998, C-162/97, ECLI:EU:C:1998:554, recital 54); (ii) recitals have legal force and clarify the scope and purpose of legislative provisions (Lindqvist judgment of 6 November 2003, C-101/01, ECLI:EU:C:2003:596, recital 79, and C judgment of 27 November 2007, C-435/06, ECLI:EU:C:2007:714, recitals 31, 48 and 52); (iii) recitals are powerful interpretative tools that allow to clarify the meaning of binding provisions of an EU legal act (Casa Fleischhandels-GmbH judgment of 13 July 1989, 215/88, ECLI:EU:C:1989:331, recital 31).

In summary, Article 22 GDPR implies (i) a general prohibition of exclusively automated individual decisions, however (ii) there are exceptions to this prohibition, and (iii) where such exceptions apply, the rights provided for in Article 22(3) GDPR must be protected. Thus, for WP29, Article 22(1) GDPR does not provide a right but a prohibition; and there would be a right applicable to situations where exclusively automated decisions are permitted—namely, the right to obtain human intervention, express a view, and challenge the decision. Additionally, exclusively automated decisions concerning special categories of personal data are allowed only if they meet the following cumulative conditions [Article 22(4) GDPR]: (i) an exception to Article 22(2) GDPR applies; and (ii) Article 9(2)(a) or (g) GDPR applies (i.e., upon the data subject's explicit consent; or if the processing is necessary for reasons of substantial public interest).

Despite the provision of such safeguards, it remains that the prohibition in Article 22(1) GDPR applies only in specific circumstances, i.e., when a decision taken solely on the basis of automated processing (i) produces effects on the legal sphere of the data subject, or (ii) significantly affects him or her in a similar manner. The content of the latter provision is not quite clear, considering what is already stated in the former: "produces effects on the legal sphere of the data subject". To this extent, the effectiveness of Article 22 GDPR may be very limited until European case law clarifies (i) what a decision taken solely on the basis of automated processing would be, and (ii) to what extent this decision produces legal effects or significantly affects the data subject in a similar manner.

For WP29, although it does not imply changes on the legal rights and duties, the similar effect could (i) significantly affect the circumstances, behavior or choices of data subjects; (ii) have a lasting or permanent impact on the data subject; or (iii) result in the exclusion of or discrimination against individuals. On this matter, it gives the following examples: decisions that affect a person's financial situation, including his or her eligibility for credit; decisions that prevent a person from accessing a job opportunity or place him or her at a serious disadvantage; decisions that affect a person's access to education, such as admission to higher education institutions.

In any case and considering the potential risks of profiling within the meaning of Article 22 GDPR, the transparency obligations of the controller are of particular importance. Article 13(2)(f) and Article 14(2)(g) require controllers to provide specific and easily accessible information about exclusively automated decisions, including profiling, which produce legal or similarly significant effects. This means that the controller would have to (i) let the data subject know that such activity is being held; (ii) provide meaningful information regarding the rationale behind the treatment;[76] and (iii) explain the importance and anticipated consequences of the treatment.

[76]Regarding significant information on the logic applied, the Spanish Data Protection Agency clarifies that it allows to understand or know something precisely, or that it should be interpreted as information that, provided to the data subject, makes them aware of the type of processing that is

This is the case, as the data subject can only manifest their point of view on an automated decision or evaluation—and eventually challenge the content of a result they disagree with—if one fully understands how the decision was taken and on which grounds. WP29 suggests that the data subject should be provided with: (i) the categories of data that have been or will be used in the profiling or decision-making process; (ii) why these categories are considered relevant; (iii) how any profile used in the automated decision process is developed, including any statistics used in the analysis; (iv) why this profile is relevant to the automated decision process; and (v) how it is used for a decision concerning the data subject.[77]

Thus, in any automated decision or evaluation, providing enough information makes data processing fair,[78] as the opacity of automated learning hinders the perception of the process, which involves profiling and automated decisions. Therefore, the information given should be complete, so that the data subject fully grasps the reasons for the outcome that affects him/her. In this vein, the controller must find simple ways to inform the data holder about the logic behind the process, to clarify the criteria applied, and above all justify the result. In order to clarify the consequences of the treatment, the responsible party should use real and tangible examples of possible effects, possibly using additional tools to support the illustration of such effects. In other words, it is not enough to inform, one must explain and also justify.[79]

being carried out with their data and provides them with certainty and confidence about its results. Agencia Española Protección Datos (2020).

[77] A more exhaustive array is provided by the Spanish Data Protection Agency, which explains that fulfilling this obligation by providing a technical reference to the implementation of the algorithm can be opaque, confusing, and even lead to information fatigue. Information should be provided to enable understanding of the processing behavior. Although it will depend on the type of AI component used, an example of information that could be relevant to the data subject would be: the detail of the data used for decision making, beyond the category, and in particular information on the time frame of use of the data; the relative importance of each data in decision making; the quality of the training data and the type of patterns used; the profiling performed and its implications; accuracy or error values according to the appropriate metric to measure the soundness of the inference; the existence or not of qualified human supervision; the reference to audits, especially on possible deviations of the results of the inferences, as well as the certification or certifications performed on the AI system. In the case of adaptive or evolutionary systems, the last audit performed; in the case that the AI system contains information of identifiable third parties, the prohibition to treat such information without legitimacy and the consequences of doing so. Id.

[78] According to Recital 60 GDPR, "[t]he controller should provide the data subject with any further information necessary to ensure fair and transparent processing taking into account the specific circumstances and context in which the personal data are processed. Furthermore, the data subject should be informed of the existence of profiling and the consequences of such profiling."

[79] The guidelines conceived within the Council of Europe on the subject are particularly fortunate: "Data subjects should be entitled to know the reasoning underlying the processing of data, including the consequences of such a reasoning, which led to any resulting conclusions, in particular in cases involving the use of algorithms for automated-decision making including profiling. For instance in the case of credit scoring, they should be entitled to know the logic underpinning the processing of their data and resulting in a "yes" or "no" decision, and not simply information on the decision itself. Having an understanding of these elements contributes to the effective exercise of other

Thus, the responsible entity of the decision should be identifiable, and the decision-making process must be justifiable, so that one can challenge and seek effective redress against decisions made by AI systems. In order to give a proper explanation (i) the processes must be transparent, (ii) the capabilities and purpose of AI systems must be openly communicated, and (iii) automated assessments or decisions should be comprehensible by those affected by them—for only then can an outcome based on judgments driven by AI systems be questioned and challenged.[80]

5 Unravelling the Enigma: Weaknesses Regarding the Protection of Inferred Data

Despite the broad interpretation of the GDPR provisions by the WP29—according to which any profile or automated decision would be protected under that Regulation—only decisions taken "exclusively" on the basis of automated processing are expressly referred to in Article 22(1) GDPR, and such provision is limited to (i) decisions taken without relevant human intervention that (ii) produce effects in the legal sphere of the data subject or that (iii) significantly affect him/her in a similar manner.

As long as there is no judicial decision as to the material scope of application of the GDPR with respect to automated profiling and decisions, the question remains as to whether or not the WP29's broad interpretation of the GDPR would be upheld by the CJEU. In the same vein, while the CJEU does not rule on the operative concepts of Article 22(1) GDPR, the scope of protection of that provision remains unknown (what it protects, what it prohibits), i. e., whether or not we are facing a general prohibition (as advocated by WP29) and what its effective extent is (especially with regard to similarly significant effects).

In any event, the issue with inferred data is not limited to exclusively automated decisions within the meaning of Article 22 GDPR. Automated decisions can be performed with or without profiling, and profiling may occur without automated decisions. Thus, there are profiles that do not give rise to an exclusively automated decision challengeable under Article 22(3) GDPR, and they are worthy of protection. In this sense, CJUE's interpretation of Article 22 GDPR provisions would still be far from solving the issue of inferences produced by AI systems.

As already explained by computer engineers, in the processes of exploration and mining of large data sets via data mining and machine learning, any decision that

essential safeguards such as the right to object and the right to complain to a competent authority.". Council of Europe (2018), Explanatory Report to the Protocol amending the Convention for the Protection of Individuals with regard to Automatic Processing of Personal Data (the Explanatory Report of Convention 108).

[80] On the subject, HLEG AI (2019b).

does not require any human control to extract the outputs inferred by a learning agent is considered to be exclusively automated. This is why the GDPR requires that the effects on the legal sphere of the data subject be more than trivial, otherwise the learning algorithms would be left without the raw material to evolve—and technological development would be compromised. To this extent, some computer engineers raise many doubts about the feasibility of the provisions of the GDPR, because the fuzzy logic that underlies AI systems would not allow the average person to understand the inference process.[81]

Somewhere in between the interpretation of legal experts and the interpretation of computer engineers, what does the GDPR mentions about the logic and functionality of AI systems, as well as the criteria and weightings used in operations that generate inferences? Very little. The GDPR imposes that the controller provides information about the personal data collected (or not) from the data subject, in particular the existence of automated decisions referred to in Article 22(1) and (4) [obligation provided for in Article 13(2)(f) and Article 14(2)(g) respectively]. It turns out that the provisions of Article 22(1) and (4) relate to situations where purely automated decisions would, in principle, be prohibited—and it is perplexing that the GDPR requires the provision of meaningful information on decisions whose existence it prohibits. The doubt remains if these are not actually prohibitions, or if it's forbidden but it can be done...

Apparently, this removes the obligation to provide information in situations where the prohibition of exclusively automated decisions does not apply [provided for in Article 22(2)], be it contractual necessity, authorization by Union or Member State law, explicit consent of the data subject. Or else the legislator wanted to refer to those situations in which the prohibition of exclusively automated processing does not apply, but did so by prohibiting that such exceptions are based on sensitive data—a rocky solution, to say the least, which does not indicate satisfactory legislative technique.

Overcoming this perplexity that would void the obligation to inform about automated decisions of practical relevance—and adhering to the systematic interpretation advocated by the WP29 and more favorable to the protection of personal data—it follows from Articles 13 and 14 of the GDPR that the obligation imposed on the controller would include meaningful information about the logic involved, as well as the significance and the envisaged consequences of such processing for the data subject. Thus, the same obligation to include meaningful information is laid down as to the data subject's right of access to his or her data [Article 15(1)(h)], whereby the information provided under the right of access (Article 15 GDPR) may evolve from that under the right to information (Articles 13 and 14 GDPR). This is because when exercising the right of access, the data subject accesses their data in

[81] Analide and Rebelo (2019). The authors explain that the processing operations within AI make use of analytical models whose approximate predictions externalize fuzzy arguments that accept different degrees of truth (almost, maybe, somewhat) and not just the distinction between truth and falsehood.

order to have the processing operations confirmed, and it is already possible at this point to be clarified about the exclusively automated decision in question.

It happens that, even when the information is significant, substantial and relevant, it is not sufficient to inform the data subject about the logic, the importance and consequences of automated processing. Thus, given the fundamental principle of transparency that underlies data protection, it is crucial to explain to the data subject, in a way that is desirable and understandable to the average person, how the profiling or automated decision-making process works. Although the Articles of the GDPR do not expressly refer to an obligation of explainability, this is what is required in light of the systematic interpretation of that Regulation, taking into account in particular recital 71 GDPR (which refers to the right "to obtain an explanation of the decision reached after such assessment"), Article 5(1)(a) GDPR (lawfulness, fairness and transparency in relation to the data subject) and Article 12(1) GDPR (to provide the data subject with information in a concise, transparent, intelligible and easily accessible form).

Most importantly, this is the interpretation of the secondary law compatible with the primary EU law, insofar as Article 8 CFREU recognizes the right of access of the data subject to his/her collected data, precisely so that he/she may, by exercising their right, obtain its rectification.[82] To rectify means to make straight, align, correct, amend—and, in a broader sense, to respond to a less true assertion in order to restore the truth of the facts. When applied to automated inferences, this dimension of rectification cannot be interpreted restrictively, as it is not enough to ensure the accuracy of the input data. If Article 16 GDPR provides for the rectification of inaccurate data—because the legislator had in mind the data provided by the data subject—it does not follow that the lack of objectivity of inferred data prevents its rectification.

Thus, the cornerstone as regards inferred data lies in the intelligibility/explainability/reasonableness of the operation from which digital technologies as AI systems have produced a given inference. Ultimately, it lies in justification—without which it is impossible to effectively challenge the outcome of the processing of personal data, be it profiling or the automated decision resulting thereof. This may depend on the reconsideration of exploitation and profiling technologies, in order to make them more intelligible to the data subject of the inferred data. Because in the legal sphere, it is not enough to inform, it is necessary to explain; and it is also not enough to explain, it is necessary to justify.

[82]The right of access is materialized by Article 15 GDPR, so that the data subjects have access to their data in order to be clarified about: "(a) the purposes of the processing; (b) the categories of personal data concerned; (c) the recipients or categories of recipient to whom the personal data have been or will be disclosed (. . .); (d) (. . .) the envisaged period for which the personal data will be stored (. . .); (e) the existence of the right to request from the controller rectification or erasure of personal data (. . .); (f) the right to lodge a complaint with a supervisory authority; (g) where the personal data are not collected from the data subject, any available information as to their source; (h) (. . .) meaningful information about the logic involved, as well as the significance and the envisaged consequences of such processing for the data subject."

6 Conclusion

The main concern that moved us in this text was to know how to protect individuals against automated inferences, and the consequences of their application to everyday situations, in order to allow control over *when, how, and under what conditions* data subjects are evaluated by learning algorithms. In this vein, we have sought to assess whether the inferences resulting from data processing by AI systems—the application of which to everyday situations determines how we are perceived and evaluated—are adequately protected under the GDPR, in the light of the fundamental right to data protection. And the conclusion is that the provisions of the GDPR are geared to the protection of data provided by the data subject, but not quite to the protection of inferred data—that is, they are particularly geared to the protection of input data, not to the protection of output data from an automated operation.

This finding is mirrored in the CJEU's data protection jurisprudence to date. The CJEU has not yet been confronted on the rights exercisable over inferred data; it has only ruled on automated collection of information indicating personal preferences/interests/desires/aversions (i. e., cookies). It so happens that on such information, learning algorithms act to predict individualizable behaviors—and therefore it is no longer sufficient to focus on the lawfulness of the collection of input data. To this extent and considering the trilogy adopted by the WP29 (personal data provided, observed, inferred), one can conclude that the GDPR does not adequately protect data subjects regarding automated inferences. The CJEU can (partially) fill in the gaps left by the EU legislator through an interpretative route, and it can do so in the light of the fundamental right to the protection of personal data. Nevertheless, it is crucial this is not only prompted by the national judge but also made aware by European doctrine.

Until then, it remains to be seen whether the right to data protection set by the GDPR lets uncover whether the justification on which automated assessments and decisions are based is reasonable or not. Or, in a less ambitious perspective, the protection of personal data only serves to test (i) whether input data are lawfully collected, and (ii) whether their processing serves the purpose for which they were collected—and, in which case, the reasonableness of the justification for an automated inference would have to be pursued outside the scope of data protection. In the face of the constraints revealed by the inferred data protection, did the CJEU take the view that data protection is only one dimension of privacy, in order to protect internet users against "any intrusion into their private sphere"? (*Planet49* judgment). Did the CJEU realize that legal categories originally designed for the protection of provided data tend to be innocuous for the protection of inferred data?

These are important questions because when it comes to the inferred data issue, that is where individuals need more protection nowadays: (i) to know why it is acceptable that certain input data produces certain results; (ii) to know why it is justifiable that certain inferences lead to a given decision; (iii) to know why the logic used to convert an inference into a decision is reliable.[83] In any case, there is only a violation of a right that can be recognized and invoked, and the scope of protection of the inferred data from the Articles of the GDPR is still incomplete. Even if in the future the CJEU does not acknowledge that automated inferences are personal data, the most relevant question on the matter is the following: what effective rights and guarantees do individuals have to control how they are evaluated by others—and, eventually, to challenge the operation from which automated inferences result and whose justification not turn out reasonable?

Individuals are more and more subject to assessments and decisions taken by or with the assistance of AI systems—which are extremely difficult or practically impossible to understand and possibly challenge. In the current "state of the art" of inferred data, individuals affected by automated assessments and decisions do not have the necessary means to check how they have been adopted, nor whether the applicable standards for processing personal data have been properly respected. Furthermore, they have fewer effective resources to challenge these automated evaluations and decisions affecting them, compared to situations where harm is caused by traditional technology—and this undermines the fundamental right to effective judicial protection enshrined in Article 47 CFREU.[84]

In this sense, the right to informational self-determination—which would give people the right to control the information available about them—is currently a long way from protecting individuals before AI systems that produce data from data. No one can control the myriad of information incessantly produced about them anymore. But it is incumbent upon legal experts to demand that automated inferences resulting from the processing of personal data be based on reasonable justification. Indeed, when it is not evident why a result was achieved, it is not possible to assess the changes needed to arrive at a different solution, nor is it possible to challenge an unfavorable outcome adequately and consistently.

References

Agencia Española Protección Datos (2020) Adecuación al RGPD de tratamientos que incorporan Inteligencia Artificial. Una introducción, Report

Analide C, Rebelo D (2019) Inteligência artificial na era data-driven, a lógica fuzzy das aproximações soft computing e a proibição de sujeição a decisões tomadas exclusivamente com base na exploração e prospeção de dados pessoais, Fórum de proteção de dados, No. 6. Comissão Nacional de Proteção de Dados, Lisbon

Beck U (2017) A metamorfose do mundo 70. Edições, Lisbon

[83] Wachter and Mittelstadt (2019).

[84] On the subject, FRA - European Union Agency for Fundamental Rights (2020), in which the Agency identifies the main challenges posed to the fundamental right to effective judicial protection by operations based on AI systems. The report concludes that only the explainability of such operations guarantees the injured party the possibility of appearing before a court, alleging the facts that effectively embody the violation of a right.

Buttarelli G (2017) Inteligência artificial, robótica, privacidade e proteção de dados, Fórum de proteção de dados, No. 4. Comissão Nacional de Proteção de Dados, Lisbon

Cabral T (2020) AI and the right to explanation: three legal bases under the GDPR. Computers, privacy & data protection. Hart Publishing, Oxford

Cabral T (2021) The Council's position regarding the proposal for the e-Privacy Regulation: out of the frying pan and into the fire?, The official blog of UNIO (https://officialblogofunio.com/)

Castro C (2013) Artigo 8.° - Proteção de dados pessoais. In: Silveira A, Canotilho M (eds) Carta dos Direitos Fundamentais da União Europeia Comentada. Almedina, Coimbra

Council of Europe – Committee of Experts on Internet Intermediaries (MSI-NET) (2018) Algorithms and human rights – Study on the human rights dimensions of automated data processing techniques (in particular algorithms) and possible regulatory implications, DGI(2017)12, Strasburg

Damásio A (2020) Sentir e saber – a caminho da consciência. Temas & Debates, Círculo de Leitores, Lisbon

Datatilsynet - The Norwegian Data Protection Authority (2018) Artificial intelligence and privacy, Report, Oslo

Debasa F (2021) Neuro-rights, The official blog of UNIO (https://officialblogofunio.com/)

Domingos P (2017) A revolução do algoritmo mestre. Como a aprendizagem automática está a mudar o mundo. Letras & Diálogos, Lisbon

Edwards L, Veale M (2017) Slave to the algorithm? Why a 'right to an explanation' is probably not the remedy you are looking for. Duke Law Technol Rev 16:18

European Commission (2017) Communication from the Commission to the European Parliament, the European Council, the Council, the European Economic and Social Committee and the Committee of Regions on the mid-term review on the implementation of the Digital Single Market Strategy—a connected Digital Single Market for all, [COM(2017) 228 final], Brussels, 10 May 2017

European Commission (2018a) Communication from the Commission to the European Parliament, the European Council, the Council, the European Economic and Social Committee and the Committee of Regions—Artificial Intelligence for Europe, Brussels, 25 April 2018, COM (2018) 237 final

European Commission (2018b) Communication from the Commission – Artificial intelligence for Europe, COM/2018/237 final, Brussels, 25 April 2018

European Commission (2019) Communication from the Commission to the European Parliament, the Council, the European Economic and Social Committee and the Committee of the Regions – Building Trust in Human Centric Artificial Intelligence, COM(2019)168, Brussels, 8 April 2019

European Commission (2020a) Communication from the Commission to the European Parliament, the Council, the European Economic and Social Committee and the Committee of the Regions – Shaping Europe's digital future, COM(2020) 67 final, Brussels

European Commission (2020b) White Paper on Artificial Intelligence – a European approach to excellence and trust, COM(2020) 65 final, Brussels, 19 February 2020

European Parliament (2017) European Parliament resolution with recommendations to the Commission on Civil Law Rules on Robotics [2015/2103(INL)], 16 February 2017

FRA - European Union Agency for Fundamental Rights (2018) #BigData: discrimination in data-supported decision making, FRA Focus

FRA - European Union Agency for Fundamental Rights (2020) Getting the future right – Artificial intelligence and fundamental rights, Report

Guerra C (2019) Consequências do caso 'Planet49' na atividade de marketing, Fórum de proteção de dados, No. 6. Comissão Nacional de Proteção de Dados, Lisbon

Harari Y (2017) Homo Deus. História breve do amanhã. Elsinore, Amadora

HLEG AI (2019a) A definition of AI: main capabilities and scientific disciplines. European Commission, Brussels

HLEG AI (2019b) Ethics guidelines for trustworthy AI. European Commission, Brussels

Kaku M (2018) O futuro da humanidade. Editorial Bizâncio, Lisbon

Mendoza I, Bygrave L (2017) The right not to be subject to automated decisions based on profiling, SSRN [Preprint]
Oliveira A (2019) Inteligência artificial. Fundação Francisco Manuel dos Santos, Lisbon
Silveira A (2023) Finally, the ECJ is interpreting Article 22 GDPR (on individual decisions based solely on automated processing, including profiling). The official blog of UNIO (https://officialblogofunio.com/)
Turing A (1950) Computer machinery and intelligence. Mind Q Rev Psychol Philos 59:236
Vilaça JC, Silveira A (2017) The European federalisation process and the dynamics of fundamental rights. In: Kochenov D (ed) EU citizenship and federalism – the role of rights. Cambridge University Press
Wachter S, Mittelstadt B (2019) A right to reasonable inferences: re-thinking data protection law in the age of big data and AI. Colum Bus Law Rev 2:494
Wachter S et al (2017) Why a right to explanation of automated decision-making does not exist in the general data protection regulation. Int Data Priv Law 7(2):76
Wachter S et al (2020) Why fairness cannot be automated: bridging the gap between EU non-discrimination law and AI, SSRN [Preprint]
Warren S, Brandeis L (1890) The right to privacy. Harv Law Rev 193:5
Zuboff S (2020) A era do capitalismo da vigilância – a disputa por um futuro humano na nova fronteira do poder. Relógio d'Água, Lisbon

Alessandra Silveira is Associate Professor (with Aggregation in Law), University of Minho, Portugal. Director of the Master's Degree in EU Law, University of Minho. Jean Monnet Chair Holder in European Union Law. Director of the "UNIO - EU Law Journal" (https://revistas.uminho.pt/index.php/unio/issue/archive) and its official blog "Thinking & Debating Europe" (https://officialblogofunio.com/about/). PhD in Law (Legal and Political Sciences), University of Coimbra, Portugal.

Legal Developments on Smart Public Governance and Fundamental Rights in the Digital Age

Isabel Celeste Fonseca and Joel A. Alves

Abstract As the title itself suggests, this chapter proposes to reflect on two of the most important challenges which are being faced by public governance over the last years: (i) at one hand, the call for public administrations to explore digital tools in the performance of their administrative functions, contributing to the smartification of public governance; (ii) at the other hand, the need for the State and other public legal persons to strictly respect the fundamental rights and freedoms of individual citizens, assuring that the introduction of new technologies in the administrative action is not at the expense of their legal guarantees. Even though they seem irreconcilable, this text tries to prove the opposite, confirming the idea put forward by the European Commission, according to which it is possible to find legal—and technical—solutions capable of "balancing the flow and wide use of data, while preserving high privacy, security, safety and ethical standards".

1 Legal Developments on Smart Public Governance: The Acceleration of Digital Transition is an (European and) Portuguese Priority

The digital transition is a priority for Europe and Portugal.[1] It is in this framework that this text proposes to think about how the digital transition should be reconciled with the protection of fundamental rights in the digital age.

"Imagine for a moment what life would be like in this pandemic without the digital in our lives": Ursula von der Leyen, President of the European Commission, began by saying when she addressed the topic of technology and digital in her speech on September 16, 2020 (Building the world we want to live in: A Union of

[1] Fonseca (2021a), pp. 27–56.

I. C. Fonseca (✉) · J. A. Alves
JusGov – Research Centre for Justice and Governance, Braga, Portugal
e-mail: ifonseca@direito.uminho.pt

F. A. Carneiro Pacheco de Andrade et al. (eds.), *Legal Developments on Cybersecurity and Related Fields*, Law, Governance and Technology Series 60,
https://doi.org/10.1007/978-3-031-41820-4_16

vitality in a world of fragility).[2] Assuming that we are reaching the limit of what we can do in an analog way, "it is necessary to create" a common plan for digital Europe with clearly defined goals for 2030, she said. These goals include connectivity, digital public services, following "clear principles", such as "the right to privacy and connectivity, freedom of expression, free movement of data, and cyber security". The President of the European Commission identifies 3 areas that need focus: data, artificial intelligence and finally infrastructure.

In Europe, the Digital Single Market was conceived as an absolute priority and there are several strategies adopted.[3] As part of the Digital Single Market objective, the European Commission has presented a series of measures including the European Action Plan (2016–2020) for e-government: accelerating the digital transformation of public administration (eGovernment & Digital Public Services), designing the unique digital platform and implementing the European cloud, as part of the NextGenerationEU model. And multiple are the benefits to be achieved, it is said.[4]

In the European context, there has been strong investment in the digital field: (i) in the creation of programmes and strategies to boost the digital and economic competitiveness of businesses; (ii) supporting initiatives aimed at empowering citizens with the necessary skills for the digital world and labour market and promoting the closing of the gap in participation between women and men; (iii) the institutionalization of a regulatory and economic environment conducive to the use and creation of new technologies, with particular focus on the well-being and prosperity of citizens; (iv) the development of a digital infrastructure that allows citizens to take advantage of the new opportunities offered by technologies. And in particular in initiatives to promote e-Government, responsible State innovation based on new technologies, the co-creation and experimentation of digital public services, the implementation of Open Administration principles and the creation of partnerships between innovation actors.

The acceleration of the digital transition process is also a commitment of the Portuguese authorities. The Action Plan for the Digital Transition (Resolution of the Council of Ministers no. 30/2020, of 21.04:2020) was approved, with the purpose of accelerating Portugal, without leaving anyone behind, and projecting the country in the world, aiming at convergence with Europe, in the digital domain. This Action Plan for the digital transition is based on 3 pillars: empowerment and digital

---

[2] State of the Union Address by President von der Leyen at the European Parliament Plenary. https://ec.europa.eu/commission/presscorner/detail/en/SPEECH_20_1655. Accessed 25 November 2021.

[3] Fonseca (2021b), pp. 9–33.

[4] Von der Leyen said: "We must make this Europe's Digital Decade. We need a common plan for digital Europe with clearly defined goals for 2030, such as for connectivity, skills and digital public services. And we need to follow clear principles: the right to privacy and connectivity, freedom of speech, free flow of data and cybersecurity. But Europe must now lead the way on digital—or it will have to follow the way of others, who are setting these standards for us. This is why we must move fast". https://ec.europa.eu/commission/presscorner/detail/en/SPEECH_20_1655. Accessed 25 November 2021.

inclusion, the digital transformation of the business fabric and the digitalization of the State (and central and local public administrations). And it translates, in fact, another stage in the journey of administrative modernization and simplification, the strengthening of digital public services and the achievement of connectivity and openness of data held by Public Administrations.[5]

Precisely, the digitalization of the Public Governance is the third pillar of the Action Plan for the Digital Transition of Portugal. At this level, the Plan includes three measures, among which instituting a connected and open Regional and Local Administration is only briefly listed.

Scanning is a priority for Portugal. And this is proven by the Digital Transition Plan for the Nation, which is in line with the European strategy. The Portuguese Digital Transition Plan presupposes strategic action on three main focuses: people,[6] companies[7] and Public Government.

With regard to the digital transformation strategy of Public Governance, it goes through the digital public services, it goes through the whole Public Administration of the State, seeking to achieve, an agile and open central administration, and includes the Regional and Local Public Administration. This has to be connected and open. Therefore, the digitalization of the State is the third level of action for the digital transition. And it translates, on one hand, the continuity of programs for simplification and dematerialization of procedures (continuing the Simplex and TIC 2020 programs) and aims at instituting connected and open Public Administration (to include Local Governance).

Thus, as for public services, the Digital Transition Plan considers that facilitating citizens' access to public services and simplifying and dematerializing

[5]The Strategy for Innovation and Modernization of the State and Public Administration 2020–2023 (Resolution of the Council of Ministers No. 55/2020 of 31.07.2020) develops around 4 axes and 14 strategic objectives: Investing in people, with three strategic objectives: (i) developing and renewing leadership; (ii) mobilizing and training workers, and (iii) involving workers in cultural change; Develop management, with four strategic objectives: (i) strengthen performance management to improve the quality of public services; (ii) plan human resources in an integrated manner; (iii) invest in administrative simplification, and (iv) promote innovation in public management; To exploit technology, with three strategic objectives: (i) to strengthen the global governance of technology; (ii) to improve interoperability and service integration, and (iii) to manage the data ecosystem with security and transparency; (iv) Strengthen proximity, with four strategic objectives: (i) promote integration and inclusion in the service; (ii) encourage citizen participation; (iii) deepen the decentralization of competencies to local authorities, and (iv) strengthen proximity public services, namely through the decentralization of public services to the regional level.

[6]Naturally, at the level of people's empowerment, the strategy goes through Digital Education, Professional Training, requalification and inclusion and digital literacy. The Plan aims to develop and implement the INCoDe.2030 program, as an inter-ministerial initiative that aims to respond to three major challenges: ensuring digital literacy and inclusion for the exercise of citizenship; stimulating specialization in digital technologies and applications for the qualification of employment and producing new knowledge in international cooperation.

[7]From the point of view of the transformation of companies, the national strategy involves entrepreneurship and investment attraction, focuses on the business fabric, focusing on SMEs, and the transfer of scientific and technological knowledge to the economy.

administrative procedures continue to be identified as ways for the State to better serve citizens, thus ensuring the reconversion of processes to the digital universe, their multi-lingual translation, as well as investing in training and valuing workers in information technology and digitalization.

The Digital Transition Plan aims to expand the supply of digitized public services, with 25 online procedures and the promotion of public services connected to each other and open, in the sense that they have reusable information. The Cloud Measure for Public Administration is one of the most measured measures, following the proposal of the Cloud Strategy for Public Administration, in 2019, by the Council for Information and Communication Technologies in Public Administration.

All measures, included in the XXII Constitutional Government Program, aim to ensure simplification and online access to at least the 25 most used administrative services, ensuring their dematerialization and that everyone has access to public digital services.

Hoping to achieve several benefits, this measure will actively contribute to the reduction of bureaucratic obstacles in public services, optimize other channels of contact at a distance with the Public Administration and contribute to the decarbonization and significant improvement of the environment.

Finally, regarding the connected and open regional and local Administration, the strategy to which the Digital Transfer Plan summarily refers is the definition and implementation of the National Strategy of Smart Cities (From Smart Cities to Smart Nation).

For years now, the public sector in Portugal has been changing its operating model, adapting to new technological realities and the challenges of the so-called e-government.[8] For example, the Simplex+ Program, launched in 2006, already includes more than a thousand administrative and legislative simplification measures to make life easier for citizens and companies in their relationship with the Administration, as well as to contribute to increase the internal efficiency of public services.

[8]The ICT2020 Strategy, Strategy for Digital Transformation in Public Administration, published in 2017 by the Resolution of the Council of Ministers No. 108/2017, has contributed to strengthen the transparency of the public sector and the participation of citizens, consolidating the use of ICT as a central tool for the process of modernization of the State, presenting a series of measures grouped into three axes of action: integration and interoperability; innovation and competitiveness; sharing of resources. Know The Agency for Administrative Modernization, which is the public institution responsible for the promotion and development of administrative modernization in Portugal, promoted, in May 2018, the creation of the National Open Administration Network. With regard to the circular economy of data, the First Action Plan of the National Open Administration Network (RNAA) is structured on four main axes, namely: Open Data, promoting the availability and reuse of information generated by the Public Administration; Transparency, promoting access to public information and administrative documents from the public sector; Use of Information and Communication Technologies and Digital Inclusion, disseminating new relationship channels between the Public Administration and citizens/companies and standards of accessibility and assisted access to public services; and Public Participation, stimulating the use of processes of public consultation and participatory democracy.

Reinforced in 2016, the Program includes 255 measures of administrative and legislative simplification and modernization of public services.

The entry into force of the Public Procurement Code in 2008, which placed Portugal at the forefront of public procurement through exclusively electronic means, it is also possible to consult online all contracts resulting from the public procurement process through the Public Procurement Portal (Portal BASE), managed by the Institute for Public Markets and Construction (IMPIC). Subsequently, in 2009, it was established the obligation of electronic public procurement as well as the creation of a private market of certified service providers of public procurement platforms, two pioneering and innovative solutions worldwide.

The e-procurement system adopted by the Portuguese Government is based on the promotion of a private market for e-procurement services, by companies under a regulated competition regime, managing the corresponding electronic platforms.[9] In 2015, Law no. 96/2015 of 17.08.2015 updated the legal regime for electronic procurement platforms in Portugal, having transposed article 29 of Directive 2014/23/EU, article 22 and Annex IV of Directive 2014/24/EU and article 40 and Annex V of Directive 2014/25/EU. This diploma contains, namely, the rules regarding the use and availability of electronic platforms, as well as all the conditions to which they must be subject, including the obligation of interoperability with the Public Procurement Portal and also with other systems of public entities. In general terms, the new legal framework has brought three major innovations: (1) licensing requirements for the activity of management and operation of electronic platforms and other requirements to the managing entities, namely greater duties and functional, technical and security requirements; (2) Interoperability and compatibility requirements; (3) introduction of a penalty system.

The electronic public procurement platforms thus constitute a fundamental and indispensable instrument in the dematerialization of public procurement procedures, and the contracting entity must make available there the following elements: the procedure notice: tender notice or invitation; the tender documents, of which the tender specifications are an example; the clarifications and rectifications of the procedure documents, lists of errors and omissions identified by the competitors in those documents, as well as the decision that will fall on them; the competitors' proposals; the qualification documents of the successful bidder; the list of competitors and the list of candidates; the preliminary and final reports and the drafts and the respective contracts.

The creation of the National Public Administration Open Data Portal, launched in 2011 and reformulated in 2018, which aggregates, references and hosts open data from different bodies and sectors of the Public Administration, being the central

[9] Currently, and according to the information available on the BASE portal, five electronic platforms are licensed: ACINGOV (Academia de Informática, Lda.), ANOGOV (ano—Sistemas de Informática e Serviços, Lda.), Electronic Platform for Public Procurement COMPRASPT (Miroma—Serviços e Gestão de Participações, Lda.), SAPHETYGOV (Saphety Level—Trusted Services, S.A.) and VORTALGOV (Vortal, Comércio Electrónico Consultadoria e Multimédia, S. A.).

catalog of open data in Portugal. This portal allows citizens and companies to access, study and (re)use the data produced by the State. The data.gov is an open portal, i.e. any user can create an account and upload data to be shared with the community under open licenses.

Reference should also be made to the recent amendment to the Administrative Procedure Code (approved by Decree-Law No. 4/2015 of January 7), which introduced important novelties in this field, consecrating, from the outset, the principle of "electronic administration", with a view to reinforcing procedural simplification and respective digitalization, including in procedures in which local authorities are involved. There is also the recent amendment of 2021 (approved by Law No. 72/2020 of November 16), that allows collegiate bodies of Public Administration to function normally online, through telematic channels.[10]

The digital transition is not only bringing about the fourth Industrial Revolution, or also known as Industry 4.0, corresponding to the automation and exchange of data in production processes through the implementation of cyberphysical systems ("CPS"), it is also being requested by citizens or consumers.

Thus, from a technocratic perspective of Smart Public Governance (although without forgetting the Rights), Smart Public Governance must offer itself to its citizens on digital platforms, so that, much like commercial platforms—Apple Itunes or Google Play, which allow immediate contact between applications and their respective consumers—be able to provide information, allow connection with other National and European digital platforms, offer digital tools for the exercise of participatory citizenship, allow the most widely used procedures to be activated online to reach quick decisions in certain specific areas of the exercise of public powers, according to their own conditions of use, within the privacy and security rules of their infrastructures.

The Smart governance concept must take into account the evolution towards an increasingly inclusive and democratic digital society, endowed with public services that better serve communication accessibilities, providing everyone, and in particular people with disabilities, conditions to access the opportunities that are created by new digital technologies.[11]

At the heart of the scientific issue is the need to address connectivity and openness of data in local governments, to prepare public officials for the application of Open

---

[10] A new legal precept was introduced, article 24-A, which postulates the preference for the use of telematic means in the context of procedural meetings, which is understood in view of the pandemic context caused by the disease COVID19. The measure under consideration takes another step along the path of electronic administration, whose regulatory principles are found in article 14. Consistently, paragraph 1 of article 23 now requires the president of the body to indicate the telematic means for the participation of members; n.° 4 of the same article determines that, in the convocation, the indication of those means must be mentioned; paragraph 2 of article 64 establishes the preference for the dematerialization of the administrative process and paragraph 6 of article 113 determines that the notification made in an electronic account or electronic mailbox, in cases of absence in the face of these are considered to be carried out on the fifth business day following the dispatch or on the first business day following that, when it is not a business day.

[11] For further developments, Caporale and Moreno (2019), pp. 391–411.

Data and Data Protection law, in particular with regard to the protection of personal data and Cyber Security. In this scenario, the new IoT products, the current Information and Communication Technology tools and the access to Big Data (or set of data and information of great volume and variety that the Local Government may have in its possession) demand the Ethics and Law regulation of the administrative structure that will make the appropriate use of its functionalities and procedures foreseen or yet to be conceived for this purpose.

Considering this panorama, we understand that it is the University's role to foster ethical reflection and debate on current and challenging topics, with an impact on several branches of knowledge, especially in the legal universe, promoting economic and social development, with consequent improvement in the quality of life in cities, through knowledge.[12]

It is a fact that the first demands and challenges that public e.governance and the digital transition have been calling for concern the law, and are focused on solving three types of problems: (1) The adoption of digital technologies in the management of public organizations; (2) The promotion of smart public governance and smart cities, that is cities where technologies are an integral part of the urban fabric and social practices, including matters concerning public bodies and labour relations between them and their employees;[13] (3) The solution of problems related to the treatment of data, in a logic of difficult balance between the opening (or circular economy of data) and the protection of citizens' privacy and secrets.[14]

2 Legal Developments on Fundamental Rights in the Digital Age

2.1 The Risks of Digital Transformation

Despite its undeniable advantages, it should, however, be born in mind that the aforementioned digital transformation process also entails risks, introducing a series of new threats to citizens' fundamental rights and freedoms, whose consequences cannot be underestimated.[15]

In this regard, one of the main concerns raised by the doctrine is related to the fact that *electronic administration* implies an increase of the amount of personal data likely to be processed by the State and other public legal persons, wholly or partially by *automatic means.*[16]

[12]By following Schuurman et al. (2012), pp.49–62; Veeckman and van der Graaf (2015), pp. 6–17; Gil-Garcia et al. (2015) pp. 61–87.

[13]López-Folgués et al. (2017, 24), pp. 23–42.

[14]Fonseca (2020a), pp. 45–50.

[15]Mañas (2011), p. 148.

[16]Reigada (2008), p. 61.

The problem is quite simple to explain. After all, if it is true that the managing of large sets of information regarding identified or identifiable persons—including information of particularly sensitive nature—is far from being a novelty, in the context of the administrative action,[17] it does not seem hard to realize that performing operations on *computerized information* is substantially different than performing operations on *manual files*[18]—especially, in the era of *data mining, artificial intelligence* and other disruptive technologies.[19]

It could be said that *public administrations are intended to pursue the public interest*.[20] So, being the solely objective of this institutions to *serve the community*,[21] granting the satisfaction of the *collective needs* that the legislator qualifies as instrumental for the promotion of the *common good*,[22] the likelihood of abuses arising from their activity—particularly, with respect to the processing of personal data—would be no more than residual.

It happens that, as already stressed by the Agencia Española de Protección de Datos, even though all the personal data processing operations carried out by such institutions are supposed to be guided by a "spirit of public service", that does not mean that exceptions cannot occur (namely, in the case of *breaches of the rule of law*; *emergency situations* that are out of control; *corruption* episodes implicating public officials; etc.).[23] Also, reality has shown that *personal data breaches*[24] may take place, even when personal data are transmitted, stored or otherwise processed by data controllers in a fairly and legitimate way.

Thus, the dangers are real. Worst still: if not addressed in an adequate and timely manner, they may result in physical, material or non material damages to data subjects, "such as loss of control over their personal data or limitation of their rights, discrimination, identity theft or fraud, financial loss, unauthorised reversal of pseudonymization, damage to reputation, loss of confidentiality of personal data protected by professional secrecy, or any other significant economic or social disadvantage to the natural person[s] concerned".[25]

---

[17] Auby (2021), p. 7.

[18] Otero (2016), pp. 491 f, note 1643; Reigada (2008), p. 61.

[19] An overview of the modern challenges in personal data protection, brought by the advent of some of this technologies—and many other—can be found at European Agency of Fundamental Rights (2018), pp. 347 ff.

[20] Among others, Antunes (2001), p. 15; Amaral (2020), pp. 32 and 38; Gonçalves (2019), p. 51; Almeida (2020), p. 108; Correia and Marques (2021), p. 31.

[21] See Morón (2020), p. 41.

[22] For further developments, Fonseca (2020b), pp. 21 ff.

[23] Agencia Española de Protección de Datos (2020), p. 8.

[24] According to article 4 (12) of the GPDR, a "personal data breach" means "a breach of security leading to the accidental or unlawful destruction, loss, alteration, unauthorised disclosure of, or access to, personal data transmitted, stored or otherwise processed".

[25] Recital 85 of the GDPR.

2.2 The Importance of the Right to Personal Data Protection

Considering this, the first conclusion to be drawn seems quite clear: *digital transformation makes it necessary to process personal data in a responsible manner.*[26] This is because, just like *asbestos*—"a mineral that can be cheaply mined and is unusually durable and fire resistant"[27]—*personal data* can be *useful*, but also tremendously *toxic.*[28] Hence, the importance of legal safeguards that can prevent their exploitation from poisoning individual lives, institutions, and societies. Safeguards that, ultimately, ensure that the amazing opportunities brought by the *fourth industrial revolution* are properly harnessed to improve the performance of public functions, but not at the expense of the legal guarantees offered to citizens whose positions are affected by the administrative action.[29]

In this vein, it is important to recall that the protection of natural persons in relation to the processing of personal data is a fundamental right. The same steams from article 8(1) of the Charter of Fundamental Rights of the European Union, which unambiguously provides that "everyone has the right to the protection of personal data concerning him or her".

Moreover, an explicit reference to such *right to the protection of personal data* is also formally incorporated into the Treaty on the Functioning of the European Union,[30] followed by a mandate to the European Parliament and the Council to lay down rules relating to the protection of individuals with regard to the processing of personal data by Union institutions, bodies, offices and agencies, and by the Member States when carrying out activities which fall within the scope of Union law.[31] Circumstance that leaves no room for doubts regarding the importance accorded to this institute into the Union legal system.

That is to say, under the European Union, the aforementioned necessity of processing personal data responsibly is not just an *ethical duty*, but rather a *legal*

---

[26] Fonseca (2021c), p. 56.

[27] Véliz (2020), p. 91.

[28] Idem, ibidem.

[29] Orofino (2020), p. 141.

[30] Article 16(1) of the Treaty on the Functioning of the European Union.

[31] Article 16(2) of the Treaty on the Functioning of the European Union. Having regard that mandate, the European Parliament and the Council have adopted the so-called "data protection reform package composed of the following legislative acts: (i) the GDPR; (ii) the Directive (EU) 2016/680 of the European Parliament and of the Council of 27 April 2016 on the protection of natural persons with regard to the processing of personal data by competent authorities for the purposes of the prevention, investigation, detection or prosecution of criminal offences or the execution of criminal penalties, and on the free movement of such data, and repealing Council Framework Decision 2008/977/JHA; and (iii) the Regulation (EU) 2018/1725 of the European Parliament and of the Council of 23 October 2018 on the protection of natural persons with regard to the processing of personal data by the Union institutions, bodies, offices and agencies and on the free movement of such data, and repealing Regulation (EC) No 45/2001 and Decision No 1247/2002/EC.

obligation. So that, in the development of the *4.0. public administration*, attention should be paid to the rules laid down in the GDPR and other relevant legislation regarding the processing of personal data.

2.3 The Role of Public Administrations as Data Controllers

In the view of the above, a few clarifications must be done, in order to avoid some common misunderstandings that tend to jeopardize both the prosecution of the public interest by public administrations and the rights and legitimate interests of citizens as data subjects.

2.3.1 The GDPR and the Public Sector: The Myth of Exemption

Thus, it is appropriate to begin by pointing out that the GDPR does not establishes any systematic distinction between the processing of personal data by public or private entities. Accordingly, the idea that public administrations are covered by a *rule of exception*, with respect to the legal provisions laid down by that Regulation, is entirely incorrect.[32]

In fact, the reality is quite clear: "the GDPR applies to anyone *processing* or *controlling* the processing of personal data",[33] being the decision about what is within or out of its material scope merely dependent of the definition and interpretation of two key terms: the notion of *personal data*, on the one hand, and the notion of *processing*, on the other hand.[34]

This is confirmed by article 2(1) of the Regulation; provision which limits itself to state that such legislative act "applies to the processing of personal data wholly or partly by automated means and to the processing other than by automated means of personal data which form part of a filing system or are intended to form part of a filing system". Therefore, as with the former Directive 95/46/EC,[35] the question of who performs such operations remains irrelevant:[36] the focus is on the *activity*, not in the *entity* that develops it.

[32] For further developments, see Alves (2020), pp. 179 ff.

[33] Voigt and von den Bussche (2017), p. 17.

[34] Rücker (2018), p. 9.

[35] Directive 95/46/EC of the European Parliament and of the Council of 24 October 1995 on the protection of individuals with regard to the processing of personal data and on the free movement of such data, which was recently repealed by the GDPR.

[36] In fact, article 2(1) of the GDPR is nearly identical to the former article 3(1) of the Directive, which stated: "This Directive shall apply to the processing of personal data wholly or partly by automatic means, and to the processing otherwise than by automatic means of personal data which form part of a filing system or are intended to form part of a filing system".

In other words: for the GDPR it does not matter if personal data is processed by a legal or natural person, a public authority, an agency or any other body; as long as the processing of personal data takes place it should, in principle, be subject to that Regulation.

Excluded from this general rule are, exclusively, the processing of personal data: (i) in the course of activities which falls outside the scope of Union law, such as those concerning public security;[37] (ii) by the Member States when carrying out activities in relation to the common foreign and security policy of the Union;[38] (iii) by a natural person in the course of a purely personal or household activity, and thus, with no connection to a professional or commercial activity;[39] (iv) by competent authorities for the purposes of the prevention, investigation, detection or prosecution of criminal offences or the execution of criminal penalties, including the safeguarding against and the prevention of threats to public security.[40] Conversely, there is no such a thing as a *general clause of exemption*, applicable to all the personal data processing operations performed by the State and other public legal persons.[41] If there could be any doubts in this respect, the Court of Justice of the European Union seems to have dispelled in the case *VQ v Land Hessen*.[42]

Hence, faced with the question if the GDPR—and in particular, its article 15—should be applicable to the committee of a parliament of a Federated Stated of a Member State that is responsible for dealing with the petitions of citizens, the Court has been unequivocal. So, stated this jurisdictional institution that, while the activities carried out by such an entity are incontestably political as much as administrative, it is not clear that they correspond, in this instance, to the activities exempted from the material scope of the Regulation, under article 2(2) thereof.[43] Thus, in so far as the committee determines, alone or with others, the purposes and means of the

[37] Article 2(2)(a) of the GDPR, read in conjunction with recital 16 thereof.

[38] Article 2(2)(b) of the GDPR, read in conjunction with recital 16 thereof.

[39] Article 2(2)(c) of the GDPR, read in conjunction with recital 18 thereof.

[40] Article 2(2)(d) of the GDPR, read in conjunction with recital 18 thereof.

[41] It is true that restrictions concerning *specific provisions* of the Regulation may be imposed, in order to meet certain *objectives of general public interest* of the Union or of a Member State, such as the safeguard of public security; the prevention, investigation and prosecution of criminal offences or the execution of criminal penalties; the promotion of important economic or financial interests, including monetary, budgetary and taxation matters, public health and social security; etc.. However, both article 23 and recital 73 of the GDPR makes clear that those restrictions should be in accordance with the requirements set out in the Charter of Fundamental Rights of the European Union and in the European Convention for the Protection of Human Rights and Fundamental Freedoms. That is to say, (i) such restrictions must be provided by law of the Union or of a Member State; (ii) respect the essence of the fundamental rights and freedoms of the data subjects; (iii) and constitute a necessary and proportionate measure in a democratic society to safeguard the objectives of general public interest concretely pursued with its adoption. Therefore, it is not correct to qualify the merely possibility of implementing *specific restrictions* as a *general clause of exemption*. After all, such restrictions will not be the *rule*, but rather themselves the *exception*.

[42] Court of Justice of the European Union (2020) Case C-272/19.

[43] Idem, §71.

processing of personal data, it must be categorised as a "controller" within the meaning of article 4(7) of the GDPR.[44] Consequently, the processing of personal data carried out by that committee should be considered as falling within the scope of the Regulation—and, particularly, of article 15 thereof.[45]

2.3.2 Principles Relating to Processing of Personal Data

That said, a second misconception must be undone: the idea that the GDPR *liminary prohibits* the processing of information relating to identified or identifiable natural persons.

Actually, while article 6(1)(a) of the Regulation stipulates that any operation which is performed upon personal data shall only take place if and to the extent that at least one of the conditions listed in that article applies,[46] such provision must not be misinterpreted. After all, it does not impose a *general ban* on the processing of personal data, but rather requires such processing, in order to be lawful, to be developed on the basis of (i) the consent of the data subject concerned or (ii) some other legitimate basis laid down by law.[47]

In this regard, the logic underlying to the abovementioned article can be summed up as follow: *any activity involving the processing of personal data is forbidden, unless it is legitimated by a legal ground.*[48] That is, what is commonly known in some jurisdictions (for example, in Germany) as the basic concept of a "general prohibition with exceptions";[49] notion that, still, cannot be confused with a formula of *total* and *absolute prohibition*.

Accordingly, *personal data can be lawfully processed by public administrations*, particularly, if the operations concerned are necessary (i) for compliance with a legal obligation to which the controller is subject;[50] or (ii) for the performance of a task carried out in the public interest or in the exercise of official authority vested in the controller.[51] Furthermore, under specific situations, such institutions may also rely

---

44 Idem, §73.

45 Idem, §74.

46 The introductory part of the aforesaid provision states the following: "Processing shall be lawful *only if and to the extent that at least one of the following applies*" (emphasis added).

47 Recital 40 of the GDPR.

48 Dienst (2018), p. 51.

49 Idem, ibidem.

50 Article 6(1)(c) of the GDPR.

51 Article 6(1)(e) of the GDPR.

on one of the other four legal grounds contemplated in the Regulation,[52] including, the consent of the data subjects.[53]

As for the processing of personal data which are, by their nature, specifically sensitive with relation to fundamental rights and freedoms (read, "special categories of data"[54]), the GDPR is, understandably, stricter.[55] Nevertheless, even in that case, the Regulation sets out several conditions in which public administrations can legitimately process personal data.[56] If this were not so, the performance of public tasks in areas as crucial as *public health* or *social security* (to name just two examples) would be impossible—scenario whose negative impact on numerous economic, social and cultural rights granted to individual citizens, both at European[57] and at national level,[58] seems to be self-explanatory.

Without prejudice to the foregoing, it must, however, be emphasized that, as data controllers, public administrations are still subject to the further provisions of the GDPR. Therefore, even if the processing of personal data by these institutions are considered to be compatible with the articles 6(1) and 9(2) of the Regulation (*principle of lawfulness*),[59] pursuant to the *principle of accountability*, they shall be responsible for, and be able to demonstrate compliance, with all the other general

---

[52] Apparently, the only exception to this rule appears to be related with the legal basis of legitimate interests. This is because, according to second paragraph of article 6(1) of the GDPR, read in conjunction with recital 47 thereof, this legal ground should not apply to the processing by public authorities in the performance of their tasks. However, as opportunely noted by the Irish supervisory authority, "this does leave open the possibility for public authorities to rely on this legal basis for a legitimate reason other than performing their tasks as a public authority". Therefore, such provisions have to be interpreted restrictively. See Data Protection Commission (2019), p. 21.

[53] In line with the recital 43 of the GDPR, the European Data Protection Board has recently recall that "it is unlikely that public authorities can rely on consent for processing as whenever the controller is a public authority, there is often a clear imbalance of power in the relationship between the controller and the data subject". Nevertheless, despite considering that "there are other lawful bases that are, in principle, more appropriate to the activity of public authorities", the Board has equally made it clear that "the use of consent as a lawful basis for data processing by public authorities is not totally excluded under the legal framework of the GDPR". For further developments, see European Data Protection Board (2020), pp. 8 f.

[54] Article 9(1) of the GDPR qualifies as such: (i) personal data revealing racial or ethnic origin, political opinions, religious or philosophical beliefs, or trade union membership; (ii) genetic data; (iii) biometric data for the purpose of uniquely identifying a natural person; and (iv) data concerning health or data concerning a natural person's sex life or sexual orientation.

[55] Pursuant to article 9(1) of the Regulation, read in conjunction with recital 51 thereof, the processing of such personal data is prohibited—even if based on one of the legal grounds laid down by article 6(1)—unless one of the derogations in article 9(2) is fulfilled. For further developments, see Alves (2021), pp. 53 ff.

[56] Inter alia, articles 9(2)(g), 9(2)(i) and 9(2)(j) of the GDPR.

[57] Take by example the *right to healthcare* and the *right to social security and social assistance*, enshrined respectively in articles 35 and 34 of the Charter of Fundamental Rights of the European Union.

[58] See, for instance, the *right to the protection of health* and *the right to social security*, enshrined respectively in articles 64 and 63 of the Constitution of the Portuguese Republic.

[59] Article 5(1)(a) of the GDPR.

principles set forth in article 5(1),[60] concretely: (i) fairness;[61] (ii) transparency;[62] (iii) purpose limitation;[63] (iv) data minimization;[64] (v) accuracy;[65] (vi) storage limitation;[66] and (vii) integrity and confidentiality.[67]

2.3.3 General Obligations

In this vein, the GDPR establishes, as a general rule, that taking into account the specificities of each processing operation (nature, scope, context and purposes), as well as the risks for the rights and freedoms of the natural persons concerned, data controllers shall implement appropriate technical and organisational measures to ensure and to be able to demonstrate that their activities are in accordance with the said requirements.[68] This means that, when processing personal data, public administrations should adopt internal policies and put in place mechanisms, which meet, in particular, the principles of *data protection by design* and *data protection by default.*[69] Mechanisms that, as clarified in recital 78 of the Regulation, could consist, inter alia, "of minimising the processing of personal data, pseudonymising personal data as soon as possible, transparency with regard to the functions and processing of personal data, enabling the data subject to monitor the data processing, enabling the controller to create and improve security features".

In addiction, it is worth mention that the GDPR imposes some general obligations which could be regarded as a "specific implementation of the principle of accountability".[70] Thus, the introduction of new technologies in the administrative action may require, among other things, the carrying out of a Data Protection Impact Assessment,[71] in order to (i) better understand the potential data protection operations concerned; (ii) access the necessity and proportionality of such operations; and

[60] Article 5(2) of the GDPR.

[61] Article 5(1)(a) of the GDPR.

[62] Article 5(1)(a) of the GDPR.

[63] Article 5(1)(b) of the GDPR.

[64] Article 5(1)(c) of the GDPR.

[65] Article 5(1)(d) of the GDPR.

[66] Article 5(1)(e) of the GDPR.

[67] Article 5(1)(f) of the GDPR.

[68] Article 24(1) of the GDPR.

[69] Recital 78 of the GDPR, read in conjunction with article 25 thereof.

[70] Dienst (2018), p. 74. Such obligations are laid out on in articles 25–31 of the GDPR.

[71] Pursuant to article 35(1) of the GDPR, the carrying out of a Data Protection Impact Assessment is mandatory "where a type of processing *in particular using new technologies*, and taking into account the nature, scope, context and purposes of the processing, is likely to result in a high risk to the rights and freedoms of natural persons" (emphasis added). Nevertheless, the former Article 29 Data Protection Working Party has recommended, in a document endorsed by the European Data Protection Board, that in the cases where it is not clear whether a Data Protection Impact Assessment is required, data controllers should still conduct one, as a Data Protection Impact

(iii) manage the risks that their performance may implicate for the fundamental rights and freedoms of individual citizens.[72]

Moreover, it is equally vital that public administrations comply with their obligation to designate a Data Protection Officer;[73] as it is to ensure that such Data Protection Officers are (i) involved, from the earliest stage possible, in all issues which relate to the protection of personal data;[74] (ii) provided with all the necessary resources to perform their tasks;[75] and (iii) covered by adequate safeguards of independence and autonomy.[76] Otherwise, the design of solutions which are capable of reconcile the smartification of public governance with the respect for citizens fundamental rights and freedoms will become a mirage.

3 Final Remarks

Whether we like it or not, digital transition is underway and there is no way to stop it. Therefore, it is absolutely vital that the State and other public legal persons do not miss that train, making the most of all the opportunities brought by the so-called fourth industrial revolution.

In fact, with regard to the implementation of new technologies in the administrative action, the benefits are clear: from the improvement of public services to the better use of resources; from the increasing of transparency to the promotion of citizens engagement; etc.[77]

However, the path is not strewn with roses: digital transformation also entails risks. That is why this phenomena should not be perspective as a merely technically. After all, the use of digital tools to perform public functions is not an *end* in itself,[78] but rather a *mean* to better pursue the public interest serving the interests of the community and all its members.[79]

In any case, one thing is clear: citizens should not have to choose between a smarter performance of public functions and the protection of their fundamental

Assessment "is a useful tool to help controllers comply with data protection law". For further developments, Article 29 Data Protection Working Party (2017), pp. 8 ff.

[72] Article 35(7) of the GDPR.

[73] According to article 37(1)(a) of the GDPR, the designation of a Data Protection Officer is mandatory where the processing is carried out by a public authority or body, except for courts acting in their judicial capacity.

[74] Article 38(1) of the GDPR.

[75] Article 38(2) of the GDPR.

[76] Article 38(2) of the GDPR.

[77] European Commission (2020), p. 3.

[78] Reigada (2008), pp. 36 f.

[79] Idem, ibidem.

rights. It is possible to achieve both,[80] finding a European way, which are capable of "balancing the flow and wide use of data, while preserving high privacy, security, safety and ethical standards".[81]

Accordingly, the compliance with the relevant provisions governing data protection could not be regarded by public administrations as an *obstacle to innovation*, or even as a *legal burden*, the violation of which may lead to the imposition of undesirable sanctions. This is because, the European Commission has already remembered that "citizens will trust and embrace data-driven innovations only if they are confident that any personal data sharing in the EU will be subject to full compliance with the EU's strict data protection rules".[82]

In other words: the trust of citizens in a data-driven society, as well as the very success of the European strategy for data, will be dependent on how data controllers manage the personal data they are responsible for. After all, the Commission has equally stressed that to "have legal certainty and trust in the processing of data is essential for EU's ability to use data to its fullest potential, where value chains can develop across sectors and borders".[83]

References

Agencia Española de Protección de Datos (2020) Tecnologías y Protección de Datos en las AA.PP. https://www.aepd.es/sites/default/files/2020-11/guia-tecnologias-admin-digital.pdf

Almeida MA (2020) Teoria Geral do Direito Administrativo. Almedina, Coimbra

Alves JA (2020) The general data protection regulation and its application to the public sector. Portuguese Law Rev 4(2):175–190

Alves JA (2021) O novo modelo de proteção de dados pessoais europeu. Da heterorregulação à autorregulação publicamente regulada. Almedina, Coimbra

Amaral DF (2020) Curso de Direito Administrativo, vol II. Almedina, Coimbra

Antunes LFC (2001) O Direito Administrativo e a sua justiça no início do século XXI. Almedina, Coimbra

Article 29 Data Protection Working Party (2017) Guidelines on data protection impact assessment (DPIA) and determining whether processing is "likely to result in a high risk" for the purposes of Regulation 2016/679. https://ec.europa.eu/newsroom/just/document.cfm?doc_id=47711

Auby J (2021) Administrative Law facing digital challenges. Eur Rev Digit Adm Law 1–2:7–16

Caporale M, Moreno JM (2019) Smart cities and disability: digital accessibility as a precondition. In: Auby J-B (ed) Le Futur du Droit Administratif/The future of administrative law. LexNexis, Paris, pp 391–411

Correia JMS, Marques FP (2021) Noções de Direito Administrativo, vol I. Almedina, Coimbra

Data Protection Commission (2019) Guidance note: legal bases for processing personal data. https://www.dataprotection.ie/sites/default/files/uploads/202004/Guidance%20on%20Legal%20Bases.pdf

[80] Idem, pp. 60 f.

[81] European Commission (2020), p. 3.

[82] Idem, p. 1.

[83] European Commission (2020), p. 21.

Dienst S (2018) Lawful processing of personal data in companies under the General Data Protection Regulation. In: Kugler T, Rücker D (eds) New general data protection regulation. A practitioner's guide. Nomos, Baden-Baden, pp 49–104
European Agency of Fundamental Rights (2018) Handbook on European data protection law, https://fra.europa.eu/sites/default/files/fra_uploads/fra-coe-edps-2018-handbook-data-protection_en.pdf
European Commission (2020) A European strategy for data. https://eur-lex.europa.eu/legal-content/EN/TXT/PDF/?uri=CELEX:52020DC0066&from=EN
European Data Protection Board (2020) Guidelines 05/2020 on consent under Regulation 2016/679. https://edpb.europa.eu/sites/default/files/files/file1/edpb_guidelines_202005_consent_en.pdf
Fonseca IC (2020a) E.governação, transparência e protecção de dados: a caótica perspectiva portuguesa (rectius europeia). In: Pires LRGM (ed) Cidades Inteligentes, humanas e sustentáveis: II Encontro de Direito Administrativo Contemporâneo e os Desafios de Sustentabilidade. Arraes Editores, Belo Horizonte, pp 45–60
Fonseca IC (2020b) Curso de Direito Administrativo. Gestlegal, Coimbra
Fonseca IC (2021a) Governação Pública (Local) Digital: notas breves sobre a aceleração da transição digital. In: Flamínio A (ed) Direito Administrativo e Tecnologia. Almedina, Coimbra, pp 27–56
Fonseca IC (2021b) Governação Pública Digital e a Proteção de Dados Pessoais: notas breves sobre as dificuldades de harmonização. In: Fonseca IC (ed) Estudos de E. Governação, Transparência e Proteção de Dados. Almedina, Coimbra, pp 9–33
Fonseca IC (2021c) Smart Cities and Law, E. Government and Rights: do we need a global digital transition strategy for smart cities? Eur Rev Digit Adm Law 2(1):47–56
Gil-Garcia JR et al (2015) What makes a city smart? Identifying core components and proposing an integrative and comprehensive conceptualization. Inf Polity 20(1):61–87
Gonçalves P (2019) Manual de Direito Administrativo. Almedina, Coimbra
López-Folgués A et al (2017) La innovación social digital colectiva y la administración en el entorno de la Ciudad Inteligente. GAPP Nueva Época 18:23–42
Mañas JLP (2011) Administración Electrónica y Protección de Datos Personales. Dereito. Revista xurídica da Universidade de Santiago de Compostela. Estudios sobre la modernización administrativa XX, Monográfico, pp 145–175
Morón MS (2020) Derecho Administrativo. Parte General. Tecnos, Madrid
Orofino AG (2020) The implementation of the transparency principle in the development of electronic administration. Eur Rev Digit Adm Law 1–2:123–142
Otero P (2016) Manual de Direito Administrativo, vol I. Almedina, Coimbra
Reigada AT (2008) La administración electrónica y la protección de datos personales. Revista Jurídica de Castilla y León 16:31–111
Rücker D (2018) Scope of application of the GDPR. In: Kugler T, Rücker D (eds) New general data protection regulation. A practitioner's guide. Nomos, Baden-Baden, pp 9–48
Schuurman D et al (2012) Smart ideas for smart cities: investigating crowdsourcing for generating and selecting ideas for ICT innovation in a city context. J Theor Appl Electron Commer Res 7(3):49–62
State of the Union Address. by President von der Leyen at the European Parliament Plenary, https://ec.europa.eu/commission/presscorner/detail/en/SPEECH_20_1655
Veeckman C, van der Graaf S (2015) The city as living laboratory: empowering citizens with the citadel toolkit. Technol Innov Manag Rev 5(3):6–17
Véliz C (2020) Privacy is power. Bantam Press, London
Voigt P, von den Bussche A (2017) The EU general data protection regulation. Springer, Cham

Isabel Celeste Fonseca is Principal Investigator on the Research Project "Smart Cities and Law, E.Governance and Rights: Contributing to the definition and implementation of a Global Strategy for Smart Cities", NORTE-01-0145-FEDER-00006. She is Associate Professor of Administrative Law at University of Minho Law School and Integrated Researcher at JUSGOV – Research Centre for Justice and Governance at University of Minho Law School.

Joel A. Alves is a Research Fellow at the Research Centre for Justice and Governance, under the project «Smart Cities and Law, E. Governance and Rights: Contributing to the definition and implementation of a Global Strategy for Smart Cities». He is also an Invited Assistant at the Law School of the University of Minho, as well as a PhD student at the same university. He graduated in Law at the Law School of the University of Minho (2017). Furthermore, he concluded his Master's in Law – Legal and Administrative Sciences at the Faculty of Law of the University of Porto (2020). He still completed a Post-Graduation in Data Protection Law at the Faculty of Law of the Catholic University of Portugal (2019) and the ECPC-B Data Protection Officer (DPO) Certification Course at the European Centre on Privacy and Cybersecurity of the Maastricht University (2020).

Biometric Signatures in the Context of Regulation (EU) nr. 910/2014 and the General Data Protection Regulation: The Evidential Value and Anonymization of Biometric Data

Francisco António Carneiro Pacheco de Andrade, Ana Silva, and Ricardo Guimarães

Abstract In this chapter, we intend to analyze the importance of the biometric signature in the context of the dematerialization of legal business, given its proximity to the handwritten signature. Currently, despite the existence of Portuguese and European legislation regarding the legal framework of electronic signatures, there is no autonomous provision regarding biometric signatures. For this reason, we will analyze whether or not there is a need for legislative autonomy regarding this type of signatures, considering their idiosyncrasies in the context of electronic signatures, especially regarding their evidential value. Furthermore, we will frame biometric signatures within the General Data Protection Regulation, since biometric signatures presuppose the processing of sensitive—biometric—data. It is precisely within this framework that one of the central issues of this text arises, namely, the use of biometric signatures to formalize legal transactions, paying attention to the importance of using appropriate measures to protect biometric data when affixing this type of signature. Thus, we intend to present a solution to this issue, namely, through encryption techniques capable of anonymizing biometric data at the moment the biometric signature is affixed by the signer.

F. A. Carneiro Pacheco de Andrade (✉) · R. Guimarães
School of Law, University of Minho, Braga, Portugal
e-mail: fandrade@direito.uminho.pt; rguimaraes@digitalsign.pt

A. Silva
University of Minho, Braga, Portugal
e-mail: PG41403@alunos.uminho.pt

F. A. Carneiro Pacheco de Andrade et al. (eds.), *Legal Developments on Cybersecurity and Related Fields*, Law, Governance and Technology Series 60,
https://doi.org/10.1007/978-3-031-41820-4_17

1 Typology of Electronic Signatures According to Regulation (EU) No. 910/2014 of the European Parliament and of the Council of 23 July 2014

Before we densify the concept of biometric signature, its legal framework, its identifying capacity and its level of security in the digital context, it is essential to first inquire about the concept of signature and then the different types of electronic signatures allowed by Regulation (EU) No. 910/2014 of the European Parliament and of the Council of July 23, 2014 (hereinafter, Regulation No. 910/2014), in order to understand what path the legislation can take in relation to greater assurance and evidential effectiveness of biometric signatures.

Observing the traditional concept of signature, we conclude that the electronic signature should respect three essential functions of the signature, [1] namely, the identifying function, the person who affixed the signature is the holder of the signature, offering guarantees with regard to his/her real identity; the finalizing function, demonstration of the declaration of negotiating will with regard to authorship, or binding, with regard to the content, of an electronic document, i.e., the signature was made with the intention of signing the electronic document; and, finally, the inalterability function, the electronic document has not been altered since the signature was affixed.

Thus, the fulfillment of these requirements by the type of electronic signature used will determine its level of legal and technological security and, consequently, its level of effectiveness for evidential purposes. According to the principle of symmetry, which is the basis of the discipline of evidence, the greater the security of a piece of evidence—in this case technological—the greater its evidential effectiveness will be. [2]

One of the main problems of electronic communication and, consequently, of electronic signatures, consisted in the identification function, since, after their regulation, there was little—if any—possibility for the receiver to verify, as well as to be sure of the sender's identity. This problem jeopardized the legal security of this type of transaction, [3]so the Qualified Trust Service Provider functionality proved to be essential to provide the identifier element to electronic signatures, without jeopardizing their evidential value.

In this context, Regulation No. 910/2014 established three types of electronic signatures, namely simple electronic signature, advanced electronic signature and qualified electronic signature, each of them with different levels of legal security.

According to Article 3(10) of Regulation No. 910/2014, a simple electronic signature is defined as "data in electronic form which is attached to or logically associated with other data in electronic form and which is used by the signatory to

[1] Sousa (2013), p. 88.

[2] Sousa (2017), p. 63.

[3] Correia (2006), p. 1.

sign". Looking at this definition, it is clear that the European legislator has left out the use of a particular technology, respecting the principle of technological neutrality, as set out in recital 27 of Regulation No. 910/2014, since it does not define its implementation. Furthermore, the simple electronic signature, through the definition above, in the final part, "*to sign*", underlines the signatory's identifying function [4] as well as his declarative will.

However, this technological neutrality enshrined in the simple electronic signature leads us to procedural vagueness and, therefore, to a lack of technical accuracy, as well as a lack of legal security, since this type of signature may be materialized by a mere digitalization of a handwritten signature, i.e., a mechanical reproduction, as enshrined in Article 368 of the Portuguese Civil Code (hereinafter, Civil Code).

According to Article 10(3) of Portuguese Decree-Law No. 12/2021, February 9, the evidential value of the simple electronic signature will be assessed under the general terms of the law, since it is not a qualified trust service. Nevertheless, this type of signature has a fragile evidential value, due to the existing difficulty in ensuring the identifier element, as well as ensuring the declarative will of the signatory. In this context, the Lisbon Court of Appeal ruling of June 21, 2011 stated that "in the case of a weak or simple (non-secure) signature, the evidential value of documents is subject to the general terms, and in particular to the free appraisal of the court", emphasizing that "without a secure electronic signature, we do not believe that the enforcement order, as the typical document that it is, will fully fulfill its function". [5]

In turn, the advanced electronic signature guarantees a higher level of legal security than the simple electronic signature, since it contains additional security requirements. This signature is legally defined in Article 3(11) and Article 26 of Regulation No. 910/2014. Thus, advanced electronic signatures are those that meet the following requirements: [6] "it is uniquely linked to the signatory; it is capable of identifying the signatory; it is created using electronic signature creation data that the signatory can, with a high level of confidence, use under his sole control; and it is linked to the data signed therewith in such a way that any subsequent change in the data is detectable".

Despite these additional security requirements, this type of signature also respects the principle of technological neutrality, since here too there is no imposition of a certain type of technical instrument to be used. [7] Only the procedures to be followed to be considered an advanced electronic signature are defined. Just like the simple electronic signature, which is not implemented by qualified trust services, it also falls under Article 3(10) of Portuguese Decree-Law No. 12/2021 and, therefore, is

[4] Delfini et al. (2017), pp. 39–40.

[5] Judgment of the Lisbon Court of Appeal, Case no. 10693/10.5YYLSB.L1-1. http://www.dgsi.pt/jtrl.nsf/-/8E497D46D599C183802578E80054CC79 [access: 17.2.2022].

[6] In accordance with article 26 of Regulation (EU) No. 910/2014 of the European Parliament and of the Council of July 23, 2014.

[7] Sousa (2017) op. cit., p. 65.

assessed under the general terms of the law. However, due to the additional requirements mentioned above, this type of signature has a higher evidential value than a simple electronic signature, since it has to guarantee that the signature is uniquely associated to the signatory, thus providing a greater guarantee in relation to the signatory's identifier, besides also guaranteeing the integrity of the electronic document.

However, due to its technological neutrality, it is precisely in this category of electronic signatures that we fit the biometric signature, and we will elaborate on it later in this text.

Finally, we have the qualified electronic signature, located in the spectrum of electronic signatures as the one with a higher level of technological security and, consequently, legal security. In the current context, taking into account the legislation in force, it has been presented as the electronic signature to be used in e-commerce. As stated in Article 3(12) of Regulation No. 910/2014, it is a subspecies of the advanced electronic signature.

According to Article 25(2) of Regulation No. 910/2014, the qualified electronic signature has a legal effect equivalent to that of a handwritten signature. Thus, the Portuguese national transposition law, Decree-Law No. 12/2021, established, in its Article 3(5), that the qualified electronic signature has the probative force of a signed private document, pursuant to Article 376 of the Civil Code. This being the case, it provides full proof of the statements attributed to its author, without prejudice to the argument and proof of the document's falsity, [8] which "can only be challenged by alleging and proving". [9]

In addition, Article 25(3) of Regulation No. 910/2014 states that qualified electronic signatures based on qualified certificates issued in a Member State are recognized as qualified electronic signatures in all other Member States.

Therefore, the qualified electronic signature represents the pinnacle of security, largely due to the fact that it is created from a qualified device, allowing the data necessary for the creation of the qualified signature to be kept under the sole control of the signatory and, furthermore, because it is based on a digital certificate, uniquely guaranteeing the signatory's identity.

1.1 The Concept of Biometric Signature

There is no definition of handwritten or traditional signature in Portuguese law. However, "in general terms, signature is a way to identify someone and to show his/her agreement with a fact, an object or a content [10]". Thus, the signature has the

[8] In accordance with article 376(1) of the Portuguese Civil Code.

[9] Prata (2019), p. 499.

[10] Andrade (2018), pp. 90–98.

function of associating the author of the signature and the facts he subscribes to. It aims to guarantee the authenticity and genuineness of a document, ensuring the coincidence between the "real author and the apparent author [11]". Therefore, the signature is a fundamental aspect of the legal transaction between the parties. According to Article 374 of the Civil Code, the handwriting and signature, or the signature alone, of a private document are considered true when recognized or not contested by the party against whom the document is presented. In addition, Article 376 of the same law states that a private document whose authorship is recognized under the terms of Article 374, or even through a notary's acknowledgment, provides full proof of the statements attributed to its author, without prejudice to the argument and proof of the document's falsity. In these terms, there is a reversal of the burden of proof, since the party that imputes a signed document to another party is implicitly guaranteeing the authenticity of that signature and, thus, the latter party will have the burden of challenging the handwriting or signature on that document, [12] as provided in Articles 444 and 445 of the Code of Civil Procedure.

This introduction regarding the handwritten signature is fundamental for the way in which, according to the idea we will defend throughout this text, the biometric signature should be understood, as well as a possible legislative development that would ensure greater legal security for this type of signature.

First, we can consider that the biometric signature is the natural descendant of the handwritten signature, [13] since it has the same purpose, in addition to the same signature methodology, and is the electronic signature that is most similar, or even familiar, to the handwritten signature.

Biometric signature is, as the name implies, based on biometric technologies, using the same behavioral characteristics that are used in handwritten signatures, since the human behavior performed in a handwritten signature is transferred to the digital world through the use of a sensitive screen and a digital pen. [14] Therefore, we can consider the biometric signature a subtype of handwritten signature. However, it differs in the method used to capture the idiosyncrasies of the signer's writing and, unlike the handwritten signature, the biometric signature is captured through a chronological presentation made by the signer during the signing, considering that the sensitive screens show the movement signal made by the digital pen. [15] In this way, the biometric signature describes the complete signature creation process, by capturing the signature duration, pressure exerted, digital pen inclination, loops, among others, [16] allowing the signer's unique identification.

By capturing the biometric behaviors performed during the realization of the signature by the signer, it allows us to ensure a high level of technical security, with

[11] Prata (2019) op. cit., p. 497.

[12] Geraldes et al. (2020), p. 512.

[13] Wright (1996).

[14] Gaudreau (1999).

[15] Linden et al. (2018), pp. 216–229.

[16] Kurowski et al. (2021).

respect to the identification of the signer, [17] with an estimated probability of error of less than 5%, [18] thus constituting a small margin of error and, therefore, we consider these techniques reliable for the identification of the individual who affixes his signature. [19]

Moreover, after the capture of biometric data by the device, a biometric file is created in relation to the signature of the signer, and these data are encrypted and associated with an electronic document in PDF format. [20] In other words, a unique association of the biometric signature to an electronic document in PDF format is created, since these data are encrypted, not allowing them to be modified again,[21] ensuring the authenticity and integrity of the document signed electronically with a biometric signature, allowing the unique identification of the signer.

1.2 Biometric Signature and Regulation (EU) No. 910/2014 of the European Parliament and of the Council of July 23, 2014

Regarding biometric signature under Regulation No. 910/2014, we can see that there is no reference to biometric signature in it. Like the Regulation, Portuguese legislation also chose to leave biometric signature aside, not creating a special legal regime for it.

Instead, as mentioned above, biometric signature may be framed in the spectrum of advanced signature, since it meets in its technical characteristics the requirements enshrined in Article 26 of Regulation No. 910/2014, namely being uniquely associated with the signatory; allowing the identification of the signatory; being created using data for the creation of an electronic signature that the signatory may, with a high level of confidence, use under his exclusive control and being linked to the data signed by it in such a way that any subsequent alteration of the data is detectable. Given that the legislator has foreseen a technologically neutral approach, the advanced electronic signature thus allows for the creation of biometric signatures. [22]

Biometric signatures allow for the creation of an electronic signature through the signer's behavioral characteristics. Therefore, the collection of these data allows for the unique identification of the individual who created the biometric signature and, since these behavioral characteristics can only be done by the signer himself, they are under the signer's exclusive control. Moreover, since the biometric signature is

[17] Andrade (2012).

[18] Idem.

[19] Ibidem.

[20] Ibidem.

[21] Gaudreau (1999).

[22] Andrade (2018), pp. 90–98.

encrypted, it is bound to the document to which it is attached, not allowing any change in the document after the biometric signature is affixed.

However, it is necessary to inquire about the possibility of creating a special legislative regime for biometric signatures, namely by comparing them with handwritten signatures at the level of Regulation No. 910/2014, as exists for qualified electronic signatures, since, as mentioned above, it is possible to carry out expert evidence with a high degree of technical and therefore legal certainty as to the identification of the signatory, as is presumed in the case of handwritten signatures.

1.3 The Assimilation, in Evidential Terms, of Biometric Signatures to Handwritten Signatures

Handwritten signature, as the name implies, comes from handwriting, a motor behavior that we learn and develop over time that naturally materializes into a biometric behavior. Handwriting is considered a "complex neuromuscular task" [23] (Pereira, Artur 2010), since the act of controlling the object that we use to write consists of a manual mechanism, coming from our neurological control, involving acquired and other innate skills. [24] Now, as mentioned before, we can consider the biometric signature as a subtype of the handwritten signature, since both come from the same biometric behaviors that allow us to univocally identify the signer.

According to the study "Individuality of Handwriting", [25] it is possible to identify the author of a handwritten document with about 98% certainty, and for this reason, it is a probative means used by the courts to establish a certain fact. However, it is an aid to the judge's decision, and does not guarantee full proof, as stated in Article 389 of the Civil Code. In this way, the expert opinion is only a means of proof that must be analyzed and considered sufficient for the judge in question, who is "the expert of experts" at the moment of free appraisal of the evidence, that is, the expert opinion presented does not become imperative before the judge's decision, and is not recognized as having full evidential force. [26]

As stated in the Guimarães Appeal ruling of February 19, 2015: "evidence does not necessarily have to create in the mind of the judge an absolute certainty about the facts to be proved, a certainty that would be impossible or generally impossible: what it should do is determine a degree of probability so high as to be sufficient for the needs of life". [27] It is in this spirit that expert evidence is used by Portuguese courts, both in expert evidence concerning the collection of handwritten autographs

---

[23] Pereira (2010).

[24] Idem.

[25] Srihari et al. (2021).

[26] In accordance with the decision of the Coimbra Court of Appeal of February 10th, 2015, Case No. 927/03.8TBFND-A.C2. http://www.dgsi.pt/jtrc.nsf/8fe0e606d8f56b22802576c0005637dc/cd2a8aa7818edff180257df5004d4180?OpenDocument. [access: 23. 2.2022].

and in expert evidence concerning the collection of biometric autographs, using the technology described above.

Expert reports regarding handwritten signatures proceed to morphological examinations, where the handwriting of the disputed signature and the documents suitable for comparison are compared, using means suitable for carrying out expert evidence. Describes the ruling of the Guimarães Court of Appeal of June 7, 2018: "using specific and appropriate methods and equipment for the purpose, and the observation of the writing of the genuine signatures and that of the contested one, in its general elements, revealed similarities, namely" in the degree of evolution, in the fluency and speed of writing, in the degree of inclination, in spacing, in the relative size of writing and in the degree of angularity and curvature resulting from the type of writing, "also mentioning that the detailed comparative analysis of all the letters and connections also reveals similarities" [28].

Considering what has been explained, we can see that the handwritten signature is a fundamental aid in proving facts that are not within the immediate reach of the judge. Without expert evidence, the exercise of proving the signer's declarative will would be a Herculean exercise. Thus, we can state that, in certain cases, expert evidence proves to be indispensable for the correct establishment of facts.

Having said this, observing what was described above, regarding the capture of biometric signatures, we conclude that the general elements that may be analyzed in expert evidence of handwritten signatures are very similar to the general elements that could be analyzed in expert evidence regarding biometric signatures, since the behavioral idiosyncrasies would be the same.

Therefore, it becomes pertinent to question why there is not a special regime regarding biometric signatures, making it independent from the advanced signature, since, due to the possibility of being assessed through expert evidence—like the handwritten signature—with a high degree of certainty and legal security, it presents a more reliable way of identifying the signatory and, for this reason, a greater evidential strength than the advanced signature.

[27] See Judgment of the Guimarães Court of Appeal of february 19th, 2015, Case No. 165/10.3TBMUR-A. http://www.dgsi.pt/jtrg.nsf/-/D3DD88EAE72AADFE80257E130049DBFF. [access: 23. 2.2022].

[28] Judgment of the Guimarães Court of Appeal of June 7th, 2018, case no. 3/14.8TJVNF.G2. http://www.dgsi.pt/jtrg.nsf/86c25a698e4e7cb7802579ec004d3832/7f4f9ddd0bfbac8c802582b800313a27?OpenDocument. [access: 27. 2.2022].

2 Biometric Signature Under the General Data Protection Regulation

2.1 Legal Framework for Biometric Signatures Within Special Data Categories

In general terms, and within what has already been mentioned above, biometrics corresponds to a technique in which the verification of the identity of an individual is carried out by measuring his physical characteristics and/or his behavioral characteristics. Particularly in what concerns biometric signatures, identity verification is performed through the interaction of the signer with the computerized system, with the speed and rhythm of writing or the inclination and pressure applied when signing as key factors in this type of authentication.

In this part of the text, the aim is to understand whether the data contained in a biometric signature should be included in the category of personal data and, if so, to analyze its framework in light of the special categories of data. In this regard, it is necessary to analyze the entire legal framework relating to data protection, with special focus on Regulation (EU) No. 2016/679 of the European Parliament and of the Council of 27 April 2016 on the protection of natural persons with regard to the processing of personal data and on the free movement of such data, commonly referred to as the General Data Protection Regulation (hereinafter, GDPR) and its Portuguese implementing law, Law No. 58/2019, of August 8.

First, under Article 4(1) of the GDPR, personal data is defined as any information relating to an identified or identifiable natural person ('data subject'). In other words, information will be categorized as personal data if it relates to a specific natural person and allows his or her identification. An aspect that must be taken into account in the context of the topic under analysis is that this identification may be direct, allowing the individual to be recognized by itself, that is, unequivocally and without the aid of any other information, or indirect, if it is possible to predict the identification of a particular person through the combination of this information with other data. [29]

At this point, it should be noted that the European legislator has decided not to proceed with a conclusive enumeration of personal data, with the intention of encompassing the greatest number of pieces of information, regardless of their nature or support. [30]

Therefore, it is easy to see that this concept does not materialize only in names and identification numbers, but is capable of encompassing a multiplicity of other data, whether factual or subjective, concerning private, social or professional life. [31]

---

[29] Cordeiro (2020), pp. 120–126.

[30] Magalhães and Pereira (2020), pp. 20–22.

[31] Cordeiro (2020) op. cit., pp. 107–112. In accordance with Nowak ruling, Court of Justice of the European Union, December 20th, 2017. https://eur-lex.europa.eu/legal-content/PT/TXT/PDF/?uri=CELEX:62016CJ0434&from=PT. [access: 10.3.2022].

And note that this conceptual breadth has been corroborated by European jurisprudence and by the various national control authorities. As an example, in the Breyer ruling, the Court of Justice of the European Union (CJEU) considered that dynamic IP addresses should be categorized as personal data, as it considered that online media service providers have legal means to identify the person in question, due to the additional information held by the Internet access provider. [32] Although this CJEU decision does not meet with a consensus within the academic community, it is certain that we can extract from it the widely protectionist vision that has been adopted in relation to personal information.

After this brief introduction, we will move on, without further delay, to the analysis of the actual case. As mentioned in the previous chapter, the biometric signature allows us to identify someone through something that only that person knows how to do, at least in a unique way, being one of the paradigmatic examples when we talk about genetic or inheritance authentication factors.

It turns out that the methodology adopted by the signer to sign biometrically corresponds exactly to the one used to sign handwritten. Following an analogous reasoning, a priori, the data contained in a biometric signature will coincide with those resulting from a handwritten signature. We are clearly referring to the signer's name and his particular way of signing. There is no doubt that the name of a physical person is personal information as defined in the GDPR, and is one of the reference identifiers when referring to natural persons. In turn, we believe that the particular way of signing also makes it possible to recognize a person, at least indirectly. After all, although there are cases of forged signatures and identity theft, we cannot forget the uniqueness that is intrinsically associated with it—no other person will be able to write exactly the same way.

Now that we have answered affirmatively to the initial question, it is now important to analyze the situation from the point of view of data sensitivity. As we know, the GDPR has created a category of data that, by its nature, is worthy of increased protection, given the potential collision with fundamental rights and freedoms. Contrary to what happens with the notion of personal data, here the legislator has chosen not to provide a definition of "sensitive data" or "special data", listing alternatively and exhaustively the categories of data worthy of this designation in its Article 9(1). [33]

From the outset, the category "biometric data for identification" stands out—after all, we find ourselves using the term "biometric" in both realities, which would appear to show a clear correspondence between them. Let's see.

According to the provisions of Article 4 (14) of the GDPR, biometric data correspond to personal data resulting from specific technical processing relating to the physical, physiological or behavioural characteristics of a natural person, which

[32] Cordeiro (2020) op. cit., p. 129. In accordance with Breyer ruling, Court of Justice of the European Union, October 19th, 2016. https://eur-lex.europa.eu/legal-content/PT/TXT/PDF/?uri=CELEX:62014CJ0582&from=PT. [access: 14.3.2022].

[33] Cordeiro (2020) op. cit., pp. 132–135. Saldanha (2018), pp. 35–36.

allow or confirm the unique identification of that natural person, such as facial images or dactyloscopic data. From reading this provision, we quickly identify three distinct requirements:

- The data needs to relate to the physical, physiological or behavioral characteristics of a natural person—requirement concerning the nature of the data;
- The data must derive from a specific technical processing—requirement relating to the means and manner of processing;
- The data must be used to identify an individual unambiguously [34]—a requirement relating to the purpose of processing.

Let us elaborate on these requirements.

First of all, it should be noted that biometric data may refer to physical characteristics as well as to behavioral characteristics of a person, as long as they are clearly measurable. Thus, biometric techniques can include the verification of fingerprints, face or iris recognition, or the analysis of a person's particular typing or signing, way of walk, or subconscious intentions. This is, undoubtedly, an open requirement, aggregating a substantial amount of parameterizable realities, which, considering the expected technological advances, seems more than convenient.

In turn, the second requirement refers to the need for a specific technical processing—in order to explain the meaning of this assumption, we will use a practical example: the processing of photographs or videos. In the light of the precept under analysis, the mere processing of photographs or videos of individuals, even if used for identification purposes, will not be sufficient to claim the existence of a biometric data processing. Even if a photograph makes it possible to recognize someone through their physical properties, this recognition is only biometric if it is performed through specific technical means. [35] This usually involves using the image to create a template or individual digital profile (commonly called a reference template) for later comparison and automated identification, from which the matching decision will result.

It is therefore plausible to conclude that a biometric data processing must be based on a system composed of at least the following components: a sensor, which captures and interprets the information; a database/device, which stores it; and software, which converts the information into code and compares the commonalities. Each of these elements will therefore correspond to three distinct phases: collection/ registration phase, storage, and comparison:

- Enrollment Phase: corresponds to the first contact with the biometric system, and can be defined as the process of extracting data from the biometric source and associating it with the natural person to whom they relate;

[34] European Data Protection Board (2020b).

[35] Information Comissionare's Office (ICO) What is special category data? https://ico.org.uk/for-organisations/guide-to-data-protection/guide-to-the-general-data-protection-regulation-gdpr/special-category-data/what-is-special-category-data/#scd4. [access: 16.3.2022].

- Storage phase: refers to the process of storing the data obtained in the enrollment phase. This storage can occur either locally at the enrollment operations center (for example, biometric reader), on a device brought by the individual (smartcard or token), or centrally in a database;
- Comparison phase: this is the comparison of the biometric data/model (obtained during enrollment) with biometric data/models collected from a new sample.

With regard to the third requirement, and in accordance with what has been said above, the ultimate purpose of the biometric processing must necessarily converge with the unambiguous identification of the data subject. Indeed, imagine that a given system detects certain physical characteristics of a person (such as gender and age) for the sole purpose of classifying him/her for the purpose of personalizing advertisements. According to the understanding of the European Data Protection Board (EDPB), [36] the data processing performed would never fall within the scope of Article 9 of the GDPR, since the system only aims at detecting certain specific properties of the individual and not at identifying him/her. The same would not be true if the system performed facial measurements, creating and storing biometric templates in order to recognize the data subject. As it is possible to verify, only a detailed analysis of the specific purposes of the controller will allow a correct assessment of whether this requirement is met or not.

In view of this exposition, we conclude that the GDPR has positivized a restricted concept of biometric data, making the application of the rules contained in Articles 4(14) and 9(1) dependent on the cumulative fulfillment of these three assumptions.

A biometric signature recognition system operates by registering the signer's behavior, expressed by the dynamics of the handwritten signature. We explained above that, from the outset, the data contained in a biometric signature will correspond, mutatis mutandis, to that resulting from an autograph signature. Although this reasoning is not completely incorrect, the fact is that there is a crucial aspect that cannot be disregarded—in a traditional recognition system, only the static or geometrical characteristics of the visual image of the signature are analyzed, which is different from the methodology adopted in a biometric recognition process. In this case, besides the visual reproduction of the signature, its unique dynamic properties are appreciated and registered, such as pressure, writing angle, pen speed and acceleration, letter formation, and line direction. [37] Since a measurement of all these properties and their association to the respective signer is carried out, the first two requirements of Article 4(14) of the Regulation are fulfilled. Finally, the identifying function inherent to any type of signature, whether traditional or electronic, is, from the outset, demonstrative of the fulfillment of the last requirement. After all, what is intended is to demonstrate that the person who affixed the signature effectively corresponds to its holder.

[36] European Data Protection Board (2020b).

[37] Article 29 Data Protection Working Party (2012).

Furthermore, even if we consider that the particular way of signing is inferable in both situations, the biometric recognition system provides a multiplicity of additional identifying elements. If, on the one hand, this addition of elements is advantageous in terms of the evidential value conferred to the electronic signature under analysis, [38] on the other hand, there is a clear disadvantage in terms of the collision with the right to privacy.

In fact, if we "opt" to reconduct biometric signature data to the special categories of data, in the sense advanced by the GDPR, there is no doubt that its processing will be substantially limited.

If we compare the common regime for the processing of personal data—contained in Article 6 of the GDPR—with the specific regime for the processing of special categories of data—recommended in Article 9 of the same European diploma—we easily notice a worsening of the existing legal limits. First of all, a general prohibition of processing is enshrined, which is clearly not the case with regard to the processing of other data, said to be non-sensitive.

Without disrespect, the European legislator has decided, even so, to advocate some exceptions, legitimating, under certain circumstances, the processing of these special categories of data. For example, if the controller obtains the explicit consent of the data subject or has at its disposal a law which expressly provides for and permits such processing, it is safeguarded against this general prohibition. However, even here the European legislator has been stricter.

Under the provisions of Article 4 (11) of the Regulation, consent must, in any event, correspond to a free, specific, informed and unambiguous expression of will. However, in situations where the processing involves special categories of data, in addition to complying with all these conditions, consent must, in addition, be explicit. It is considered that, because of the high risk to the rights and freedoms of the data subjects, a higher level of individual control over personal data must be achieved. Thus, here the data subject must expressly give his or her consent, which may occur not only through the traditional written declaration, but also by filling out an electronic form, by sending an email or by using an electronic signature. [39]

At the same time, the GDPR has chosen to make room for the prescription of further restrictions by establishing an open clause, stipulating in its Article 9(4) that "Member States may maintain or introduce further conditions, including limitations, with regard to the processing of genetic data, biometric data or data concerning health."

---

[38] For more information about the evidentiary value of the biometric signature, see Sect. 1.2 of this article.

[39] European Data Protection Board (2020a).

2.2 *Anonymization and Pseudonymization of Personal Data*

In the previous section, we concluded about the insertion of biometric signature data in the scope of special categories of data. At this stage of the paper, we intend to put forward legally relevant solutions, given the existing legal framework, in order to reduce the risks of processing this type of sensitive data. This will involve an analysis of the anonymization and pseudonymization of data.

First of all, it should be noted that the General Data Protection Regulation does not clarify, in any of its articles, what is meant by anonymization. However, it is possible to extract its notion from Recital 26. In view of what is stated in this precept, anonymous data must be understood as information that previously concerned an identified or identifiable natural person, but whose identification is no longer possible, in an irreversible way. Irreversibility is, of course, the basic characteristic of anonymization, since it is understood that anonymization must be equivalent to the permanent deletion of personal data, thus making it impossible to process it. [40]

Because of this equivalence, the Regulation is not considered applicable to the processing of a truly anonymized set of data, since it is assumed that if the information becomes anonymized, not even the controller himself will be able to associate it with any individual.

In turn, according to Article 4(5) of the GDPR, pseudonymization means the processing of personal data in such a manner that the personal data can no longer be attributed to a specific data subject without the use of additional information, provided that such additional information is kept separately and is subject to technical and organizational measures to ensure that the personal data are not attributed to an identified or identifiable natural person.

In other words, pseudonymization refers to the set of techniques that aim at replacing, removing or transforming the identifying information of an individual (example: replacing a name with a reference number). It begins with a single input—the so-called original personal data—and culminates with two outputs—the pseudonymized set of personal data and the additional information—and, if aggregated, these two outputs allow the reconstruction of the original personal data. [41]

Unlike anonymized data, pseudonymized information is susceptible to indirect re-identification with reasonable computational effort—susceptibility that dictates it falls within the scope of the Regulation. Thus, while the use of pseudonyms effectively reduces the possibility of a link between a set of data and the original identity of a data subject, it should not be understood as a method of data anonymization. Indeed, even if individuals cannot be identified by the pseudonyms themselves, they can be recognized through the additional information, even if stored separately.

In practice, and in order to operate the distinction between these two techniques, a judgment of reasonableness has, imperatively, to be called upon. According to

[40] Article 29 Data Protection Working Party (2014), p. 6.

[41] Information Comissionare's Office (2022).

Recital 26, all means likely to be reasonably used, whether by the controller or by a third party, must be taken into account, considering all objective factors (such as costs and time needed for the identification of the natural person), the available technology at the time of the data processing and the expected technological developments (evolution of computational capacity and available mechanisms).

Therefore, the idea to retain is that if, for any reason, it is possible to associate the data with the data subject, such data will be considered personal, and the application of the Regulation will be observed. [42]

2.3 *Cryptography and Encryption Techniques*

Cryptography aims to ensure the confidentiality of communications between different agents, by encrypting the messages exchanged between them, and this is achieved through the use of a secret key known to both parties and the corresponding encryption algorithm. [43] Thus, cryptography is based on a mathematical perspective and complex computational models, based on the confidentiality of the communications exchanged, namely, through encryption techniques (algorithms), the integrity of the messages, namely, with the use of hashes and, finally, through the authentication of these communications. [44]

Having said this, there are two relevant types of cryptography, namely, symmetric cryptography and asymmetric cryptography. Thus, some general aspects about these two types of cryptography should be enunciated.

Regarding symmetric cryptography or secret-key cryptography, this type of cryptography uses only one cryptographic key for encryption and decryption operations, and this key must be kept secret. [45] In fact, the strength of symmetric cryptography depends on two things: the algorithm must be robust enough not to be broken and the cryptographic key must be kept secret. The main challenge facing symmetric cryptography stems from the need to distribute keys securely, given the fact that there are now a very large number of users and that establishing secure channels is costly.

Asymmetric cryptography, also known as public key cryptography, is characterized by the use of two cryptographic keys: a public key and a private key. Simply put, in this type of cryptography, one of the keys is used to encrypt, that is, to transform the original information ("clear text") into information unreadable by third parties, and the other to decrypt, that is, to do the reverse operation. [46] While the public key is accessible to all users and can be freely distributed, the private key must

[42] Information Comissionare's Office (2021).

[43] Boavida and Bernardes (2019), pp. 10–12.

[44] Ahmed et al. (2021).

[45] Katz and Lindell (2014).

[46] IBM (2021).

be kept secret and can never be shared. In this context, it should be noted that these two keys are related through mathematical functions, but it is computationally impossible to discover a key through its pair, thus preventing the message from being deciphered by any user other than the recipient. Because the public key can be shared, it is necessary to guarantee its authenticity, so that the identity of the user to whom the key belongs can be identified. This is precisely why digital certificates are used—so that a user can verify the digital signature and validity period, find out if the digital document was issued by a trusted certification authority, and find out if this document contains the desired information, i.e. if the author is indeed who he says he is.

Furthermore, as mentioned earlier, cryptographic hash functions are critical to ensure the integrity of the data contained in encrypted messages. Simply put, a hash function transforms a randomly sized data set into a fixed size of bits. [47] Since it is a unique function, this means that it is impossible, from a computational perspective, to produce two identical hash codes. In fact, if a change is made to the original data set, this will necessarily cause a change in the corresponding hash code, so that two different messages will not lead to the same hash function—this is one of the main properties of the hash function, called "collision resistance". [48] Thus, the hash function must satisfy the pseudo-randomness requirements. Thus, the hash function can guarantee the integrity of the message in question. [49] However, these functions only guarantee the integrity of messages, not guaranteeing their authenticity.

Asymmetric cryptography and hash functions allow the production of digital signatures, which can guarantee the authenticity of the message or document. The creation of this digital signature corresponds to two moments: first, it will be necessary to create the hash value of the message that will be signed. Secondly, there is the encryption of the hash value by the signer of the message through his private key. Thus, a digital signature reflects the combination of this hash encryption with the private key to the message in question, making it possible to verify who created this message—its author—and, in this way, the corresponding authenticity of the message. [50]

We can conclude that the combination of asymmetric cryptography, hash functions and digital signatures guarantees us secure and reliable communication, as well as message confidentiality, integrity and authenticity.

[47] Karpman et al. (2015).

[48] Liu et al. (2019).

[49] Boavida and Bernardes (2019) Op. cit., p. 138.

[50] Martins (2018), pp. 28–29.

2.4 Biometric Signature: Encryption Techniques While Anonymizing Data Using Qualified Trust Service Providers

In opinion 05/2014 on anonymization techniques, Working Party 29 has reconducted the generality of encryption techniques to pseudonymization and not anonymization. According to Working Party 29, encryption techniques only reduce the risk of re-identification, but do not irreversibly eliminate it, since there will always be a theoretical way to decipher encrypted personal data. [51]

However, it seems to us that Working Group 29 has not taken into consideration the evolution of the state of the art of encryption techniques, nor the scenarios where the cryptographic key is stored in a third party, such as a Qualified Trust Service Provider.

In fact, we believe that the reconduction of encryption techniques to anonymization or, conversely, to pseudonymization is dependent on the storage location of the cryptographic key, which would make data decryption possible. As argued by the United Kingdom's Information Commission Office (ICO), pseudonymized data may no longer be identifiable if the key that decrypts the data is stored in an organization other than the one that holds the encrypted personal data itself. [52] In the same vein, Gerald Spindler and Philipp Schmechel state that if the data controller does not have access to the cryptographic key capable of decrypting the original personal data, this means that he will not have access to this data either and, for this very reason, we should consider it to be anonymized. [53]

Imagine a situation where an entity decides to start dematerializing its internal processes and decides to adopt biometric signatures to sign its contracts in electronic document format. In this case, the entity uses a third party entity, namely a Qualified Trust Service Provider, to supply specialized devices for the collection and storage of biometric signatures.

In a system of this type, the signatory goes to the place where the contract will be formalized, where he will find a sensitive screen responsible for collecting the biometric signature, known as a signature pad, connected to an electronic signature management platform of that organization. Once the signatory signs on the touch screen, the visual reproduction of his biometric signature is applied to the electronic document provided by the entity for this purpose, and his biometric data, resulting from the biometric signature verification process, are encrypted in less than a second, using the public key of the Qualified Trust Service Provider, and stored in the same way in the document itself (PDF). When the document is signed, and in order to ensure its integrity, a cryptographic hash function is also generated using the private key of the trusted third party, which will ensure the inalterability of the biometric

[51] Article 29 Data Protection Working Party (2014), p. 6.

[52] Information Comissionare's Office (2022).

[53] Spindler and Philipp (2016).

data contained in the PDF document and verify its correspondence with the electronic document signed by the signatory—a document that is in the possession of the Organization and the signatory.

Furthermore, the corresponding private key, responsible for decrypting the biometric data, is stored with the trusted third party and is never shared with the Organization or any other entity.

Having said this, since the entity does not have access to the private key capable of decrypting the biometric data resulting from the biometric signature and, in turn, the Qualified Trust Service Provider does not have access to the electronic document nor, consequently, to any personal data of the signatory, it can be concluded that the biometric data are anonymized for both parties.

Given the reasonability criterion, already mentioned above, and the likelihood of re-identification, we believe that a specific encryption technique such as this should in any case be envisaged as anonymization of data. [54] As recital 26 of the GDPR tells us, the cost and time needed to break such a cryptographic solution should be taken into account—exploiting a vulnerability of an asymmetric cryptographic system would involve unreasonable efforts.

In fact, in the event of a cyber attack on either party, the biometric data of the holder would be subject to little risk from a data protection point of view, since the information stored is complementary and therefore unintelligible when analyzed separately. [55]

Furthermore, so as not to impede the identifying function of the biometric signature, this solution should presuppose the existence of a contractually established relationship between the Organization and the Qualified Trust Service Provider. In this contract, it should be stipulated that the decryption process of the biometric data will only occur in two specific situations:

- If the processing is necessary for the declaration, exercise or defense of a right in legal proceedings or where the courts are acting in the exercise of their jurisdictional function, in accordance with the provisions of Article 9(2)(f) of the GDPR;
- Upon the express request of the signatory (data subjects). Only in these situations would the document containing the encrypted biometric data be linked to the key that decrypts it. Otherwise, the data would always be anonymised for both parties.

2.5 *Moment of Collection of Biometric Data and the Absence of Further Processing*

In the same opinion, the Working Party 29 also considered that anonymization constitutes a subsequent processing of personal data and not an initial processing,

[54] Spindler and Philipp (2016).

[55] Gresham (2019).

since it will always occur at a time subsequent to the collection. This means that, even if the GDPR is not deemed applicable to anonymized information, it will apply until the anonymization process is completed. In fact, if we look at the definition of processing, set forth in Article 4(2) of the aforementioned law, its undeniable scope stands out: the notion encompasses a wide range of operations performed on personal data, by manual or automated means, including its alteration.

The mention of the term "alteration" in the aforementioned definition brings anonymization within the scope of the GDPR. In addition, since it consists in further processing, it is essential that it meets the requirement of compatibility with the initial processing. In fact, if we consider that the anonymization process corresponds to a processing operation subsequent to the collection, it is readily understood that all the principles and other rules contained in the General Data Protection Regulation and its implementing law (Portuguese Law No. 58/2019) must be respected.

At this point, the question is whether this understanding has a logical basis in a situation where the data collected is anonymized in less than a second.

We understand that this view of the Working Party makes logical sense in situations where the data collected is anonymized after a certain time lag has elapsed. However, in the case under consideration, the data is encrypted after it is generated, and, considering the reasonability principle, it is not possible for any party to access the biometric data itself.

Thus, it is our understanding that, in this particular case, anonymization cannot be perceived as post-processing, but rather as processing simultaneous to collection.

3 Conclusion

The need for a world without physical paper is increasingly evident, not only for making commercial and legal methodology more sustainable, but also for creating a more simplified and faster communication between the parties. However, we can still see that the understanding of these new procedures by the legal world is still very weak, especially from a technical perspective, where the knowledge on which these new technologies are based, by jurists, is obviously fragile. Naturally, this lack of knowledge, as well as the lack of existing training in the spectrum that encompasses law and technology, makes it difficult to draw up legislative projects capable of keeping up with technological evolution and understanding.

It is precisely for these reasons that there is an urgent need to recast Regulation No. 910/2014, creating a separate legal regime for biometric signatures—in relation to advanced electronic signatures—which, along with qualified electronic signatures, appear to be a subtype of electronic signature capable of providing an evidential value equivalent—or even greater—than the evidential value of handwritten signatures.

Moreover, it is also imperative to understand encryption techniques—in light of the current state of the art—so that we can consider them as an option for anonymizing biometric data, allowing for a safe and effective adoption of biometric signatures. It is essential that the legislator understands the reasonability principle according to the technical specificities of the different encryption methods, not creating purely theoretical limitations, far away from what is possible to accomplish in practice, taking into consideration, not only the evolution of the state of the art, but also the role of trusted third parties, namely Qualified Trust Service Providers.

References

Ahmed AA, Paruchuri H, Vadlamudi S, Ganapathy A (2021) Cryptography in financial markets: potential channels for future financial stability. Acad Account Financ Stud J 25(4):1–9. https://www.proquest.com/scholarly-journals/cryptography-financial-markets-potential-channels/docview/2543524908/se-2?accountid=192066. Accessed 24 Mar 2022

Andrade F (2012) Consideração Jurídica das Assinaturas Dinâmicas no Ordenamento Jurídico Português, Atas do XVI Congresso IberoAmericano de Derecho e Informática, Tomo II. Ministerio de Justicia, Derechos Humanos y Cultos, Quito

Andrade F (2018) Electronic identification, signature and trust services. UNIO EU Law J 4(2): 90–98. https://doi.org/10.21814/unio.4.2.9

Article 29 Data Protection Working Party (2012) Opinion 3/2012 on developments in biometric technologies, adopted on April 27th, 2012. https://ec.europa.eu/justice/article-29/documentation/opinion-recommendation/files/2012/wp193_en.pdf. Accessed 17 Mar 2022

Article 29 Data Protection Working Party (2014) Opinion 05/2014 on anonymization techniques, adopted on April 10th, 2014, p 6. https://ec.europa.eu/justice/article-29/documentation/opinion-recommendation/files/2014/wp216_en.pdf. Accessed 21 Mar 2022

Boavida F, Bernardes M (2019) Introdução à Criptografia (Introduction to encryption). In: FCA – Editora de Informática, 1st edn, Lisbon

Breyer ruling, Court of Justice of the European Union, October 19th, 2016. https://eur-lex.europa.eu/legal-content/PT/TXT/PDF/?uri=CELEX:62014CJ0582&from=PT. Accessed 14 Mar 2022

Cordeiro ABM (2020) Direito da proteção de dados: à luz do RGPD e da lei n°58/2019 (Data protection law: in light of the GDPR and Law No. 58/2019), Coimbra, Almedina

Correia MP (2006) Assinatura Eletrónica e Certificação Digital (Electronic signature and digital certification). In: Direito da Sociedade da Informação, vol VI. Coimbra Editora, Coimbra, p 1; (Portuguese Association of Intellectual Law (ed), Information Society Law)

Decision of the Coimbra Court of Appeal of February 10th, 2015, Case No. 927/03.8TBFND-A.C2. http://www.dgsi.pt/jtrc.nsf/8fe0e606d8f56b22802576c0005637dc/cd2a8aa7818edff180257df5004d4180?OpenDocument. Accessed 23 Feb 2022

Delfini F et al (2017) Electronic identification and trust services for electronic transactions in the internal market - commentary on EU Regulation 910/2014. Giappichelli

European Data Protection Board (2020a) Guidelines 05/2020 on consent under Regulation 2016/679, version 1.1, adopted on May 4th, 2020. https://edpb.europa.eu/sites/default/files/files/file1/edpb_guidelines_202005_consent_pt.pdf. Accessed 18 Mar 2022

European Data Protection Board (2020b) Guidelines 3/2019 on processing of personal data through video devices, version 2.0, adopted on 29th January 2020. https://edpb.europa.eu/sites/default/files/files/file1/edpb_guidelines_201903_video_devices_pt.pdf. Accessed 16 Mar 2022

Gaudreau M (1999) On the distinction between biometrics and digital signatures. CIC Enterprise Solutions. http://www.penop.com/enterprise/whitepapers/whitepaper5.asp. Accessed 21 Feb 2022

Geraldes AA, Pimenta P, Pires de Sousa LF (2020) Código de Processo Civil Anotado Vol I - Parte Geral e Ação Declarativa, 2nd edn. Almedina, Coimbra, p 512. (Annotated code of civil procedure Vol I - general part and declarative action, 2nd ed. Coimbra, Almedina)

Gresham J (2019) Is encrypted data personal data under the GDPR? IAPP. https://iapp.org/news/a/is-encrypted-data-personal-data-under-the-gdpr/. Accessed 6 Apr 2022

IBM (2021) Cryptography concepts. https://www.ibm.com/docs/en/i/7.4?topic=cryptography-concepts. Accessed 24 Mar 2022

Information Comissionare's Office (2021) Chapter 2: How do we ensure anonymisation is effective? Draft anonymisation, pseudonymisation and privacy enhancing technologies guidance. https://ico.org.uk/media/about-the-ico/documents/4018606/chapter-2-anonymisation-draft.pdf. Accessed 23 Mar 2022

Information Comissionare's Office (2022) Chapter 3: pseudonymisation - draft anonymisation, pseudonymisation and privacy enhancing technologies guidance. https://ico.org.uk/media/about-the-ico/consultations/4019579/chapter-3-anonymisation-guidance.pdf. Accessed 21 Mar 2022

Information Comissionare's Office (ICO). What is special category data? https://ico.org.uk/for-organisations/guide-to-data-protection/guide-to-the-general-data-protection-regulation-gdpr/special-category-data/what-is-special-category-data/#scd4. Accessed 16 Mar 2022

Judgment of the Guimarães Court of Appeal of February 19th, 2015, Case No. 165/10.3TBMUR-A. http://www.dgsi.pt/jtrg.nsf/-/D3DD88EAE72AADFE80257E130049DBFF. Accessed 23 Feb 2022

Judgment of the Guimarães Court of Appeal of June 7th, 2018, case no. 3/14.8TJVNF.G2. http://www.dgsi.pt/jtrg.nsf/86c25a698e4e7cb7802579ec004d3832/7f4f9ddd0bfbac8c802582b800313a27?OpenDocument. Accessed 27 Feb 2022

Judgment of the Lisbon Court of Appeal, Case no. 10693/10.5YYLSB.L1-1. http://www.dgsi.pt/jtrl.nsf/-/8E497D46D599C183802578E80054CC79. Accessed 17 Feb 2022

Karpman P, Peyrin T, Stevens M (2015) Practical free-start collision attacks on 76-step SHA-1. https://eprint.iacr.org/2015/530. Accessed 25 Mar 2022

Katz J, Lindell Y (2014) Introduction to modern cryptography, 2nd edn. CRC Press, Boca Raton

Kurowski M, Sroczyński A, Bogdanis G, Czyżewski A (2021) An automated method for biometric handwritten signature authentication employing neural networks. Electronics 10(4):456. https://doi.org/10.3390/electronics10040456

Linden J, Marquisa R, Bozzaab S, Taronia F (2018) Dynamic signatures: a review of dynamic feature variation and forensic methodology. Forensic Sci Int 291:216–229. https://doi.org/10.1016/j.forsciint.2018.08.021

Liu H, Kadir A, Liu J (2019) Keyed hash function using hyper chaotic system with time-varying parameters perturbation. IEEE Access 7:37211–37219. https://ieeexplore.ieee.org/stamp/stamp.jsp?arnumber=8631029. Accessed 25 Mar 2022

Magalhães FM, Pereira ML (2020) Regulamento Geral de Proteção de Dados – Manual Prático, 3rd edn. Vida Económica, Porto, pp 20–22. (General data protection regulation – practical manual, 3rd ed. Porto)

Martins P (2018) Introdução à Blockchain, 1st edn. Editora de Informática, Lisboa, pp 28–29. (Introduction to blockchain, 1st ed. Lisbon)

Nowak ruling, Court of Justice of the European Union, December 20th, 2017. https://eur-lex.europa.eu/legal-content/PT/TXT/PDF/?uri=CELEX:62016CJ0434&from=PT. Accessed 10 Mar 2022

Pereira A (2010) As perícias na Polícia Judiciária (Investigations in the Judiciary Police). http://www3.bio.ua.pt/Forense/As%20Pericias%20na%20Pol%C3%ADcia%20Judiciaria%20ArturPereira.pdf. Accessed 22 Feb 2022

Prata A (2019) Código Civil Anotado - Volume I, 2nd edn. Almedina, Coimbra. (Annotated Civil Code - Volume I, 2nd ed. Almedina, Coimbra)

Saldanha N (2018) Novo Regulamento Geral de Proteção de Dados – O que é? A quem se aplica? Como implementar? (New General Data Protection Regulation – What is it? Who does it apply to? How to implement?), Lisbon. FCA – Editora de Informática

Sousa LV (2013) Alguns Problemas Colocados Pela Assinatura Electrónica das Propostas. Revista de Contratos Públicos, n.° 9, p. 88 (Some problems posed by the electronic signature of proposals. In Public contracts magazine, no. 9)

Sousa LFP d (2017) O Valor Probatório do Documento Eletrónico no Processo Civil, 2nd edn. Almedina, Coimbra. (The evidential value of the electronic document in civil procedure, 2nd edn. Almedina, Coimbra)

Spindler G, Philipp S (2016) Personal data and encryption in the European General Data Protection Regulation. J Intellect Prop Inform Technol E-Comm Law 7:163. https://www.jipitec.eu/issues/jipitec-7-2-2016/4440. Accessed 23 Mar 2022

Srihari SN, Cha S-H, Arora H, Lee S (2021) Individuality of handwriting. Center of Excellence for Document Analysis and Recognition (CEDAR) University at Buffalo, State University of New York. https://www.ojp.gov/pdffiles1/nij/grants/190133.pdf. Accessed 23 Feb 2022

Wright B (1996) Signing electronic tax returns with PenOp. https://www.icommercecentral.com/open-access/signing-electronic-tax-returns-with-penop.pdf. Accessed 20 Feb 2022

Francisco António Carneiro Pacheco de Andrade holds a PhD in Law (Legal Privatistic Sciences) from University of Minho and a MSc in Electronic Information Management from the University of Sheffield (United Kingdom). He is auxiliary professor at Universidade do Minho Law School and he has been, for 11 years, the Director of the Master Course in Law and Informatics. He is also lecturer in the same Master in the Units of "Cryptography, Electronic Identification and Documents", "Privacy and Data Protection", "Electronic Commerce and Electronic Contracting". He is an integrated member of JUSGOV – Research Center on Justice and Governation at University of Minho Law School.

Ana Silva worked as a Privacy & Legal consultant and currently is a Legal & Compliance Officer at DigitalSign - Qualified Trust Service Provider, accredited under the European Regulation eIDAS. Graduated in Law and with a postgraduate degree in Law and Informatics at the School of Law, University of Minho.

Ricardo Guimarães is Legal & Compliance Officer at DigitalSign - Qualified Trust Service Provider, accredited under the European Regulation eIDAS -, specialized in law and technology, namely, GDPR and eIDAS regulation. Graduated in Law and with a postgraduate degree in Law and Informatics at the School of Law, University of Minho.

Cybersecurity Issues in Electronic Communications and Some Insights on Digital Literacy and Technological Infrastructures' Demands: Anticipations of the European Digital Decade Through the Lens of a Declaration on Digital Rights and Principles

Joana Covelo de Abreu

Abstract European Union is living its Digital Decade until 2030, where digital technologies are changing the way people relate, work, and behave, with the emergence of great opportunities but also threats, which can also lead to digital poverty and divide. This digital divide is caused by lower digital literacy and the lack of (understandable) technological infrastructures. This also impacts on cybersecurity demands: as people cannot understand digital transformation, they cannot dimension security issues and how these can impact in their rights' exercise. To overcome it, two major goals were set under electronic communications: to have digitally skilled people and highly digitally skilled professionals and to have secure and performant sustainable digital infrastructures. This contribution aims at understanding these goals' accomplishment and at critically perceiving if a European Union Declaration on digital rights and principles is able to deploy and foster this digital decade.

> A Europe that innovates. A Europe that protects. A Europe that illuminates through its democratic model. These are the three pillars on which we can build a new European project. A new project of hope.
>
> David Sassoli (16th December 2021)

J. C. de Abreu (✉)
School of Law, University of Minho, Braga, Portugal
e-mail: jabreu@direito.uminho.pt

F. A. Carneiro Pacheco de Andrade et al. (eds.), *Legal Developments on Cybersecurity and Related Fields*, Law, Governance and Technology Series 60,
https://doi.org/10.1007/978-3-031-41820-4_18

1 Electronic Communications: Brief Introduction and State of the Art

The European Commission, facing the changes COVID-19 pandemic brought, understood how it "radically changed the role and perception of digitalization in our societies and economies, and accelerated its pace". In fact, digital technologies are nowadays indispensable for many social, economic and ludic purposes as they continue to represent an effective "disruptive innovation"; but, at the same time, they expose previous vulnerabilities and shortcomings the digital environment was able to enhance.[1] In this sense, the European institutions—but, mostly, the European Commission—understood there was a need to "pursue digital policies that empower people and businesses to seize a human centred, sustainable and more prosperous digital future", in order to "secure digital sovereignty with a common vision of the EU in 2030", which led to the presentation of a "Digital Compass by March 2021, setting out digital ambitions for 2030".[2]

In fact, the pandemic and its isolation periods have shown that "[d]igital infrastructure and rapid connectivity bring people new opportunities": "geographical distance matters less" but there was the emergence of a new "digital poverty" with more people set aside from online environment because of lower literacy, lacking infrastructures, difficult and / or incomprehensible public services... Therefore, it is "imperative to ensure that all citizens and businesses in Europe can leverage the digital transformation for a better and more prosperous life".[3]

In order to do so, "four cardinal points for mapping the EU's trajectory" were established: (i) "[a] digitally skilled population and highly skilled digital professionals"; (ii) "[s]ecure and performant sustainable digital infrastructures"; (iii) "[d]igital transformation of businesses"; and (iv) "[d]igitalisation of public services".[4]

In this sense, development on electronic communications focuses on two main features: (a) population—and professionals, in particular—have to further develop basic digital skills and to absorb and enhance advanced digital skills as the European Union needs "digitally empowered and capable citizens, a digitally skilled workforce and way more digital experts than today"[5]; and (b) technological infrastructures must meet a new development, where public and private sectors are equally evolved in the evolution.

Concerning people's aptitude to the Digital Decade, there is a need to invest "in skills and education to unlock new opportunities for all" as "[t]he green and digital transitions further amplify the need for continuous investment in education and

[1] European Commission (2021c), p. 1.

[2] Idem.

[3] Ibidem, p. 2.

[4] Ibidem, pp. 4–12.

[5] Ibidem, p. 4.

training systems"[6]: and one aim of the European Union is to support "the development of a high-performing digital education ecosystem in Europe and [to enhance] digital skills and competences to address digital transformation for all", demanding higher education institutions to ensure future workforce will have the needed skills, which also includes providing training for people of working age.[7] This goal will be met if "public and private investment" is made:

- On one hand, with the combination of the European Social Fund Plus (ESF+)[8] and Erasmus+[9] funding alongside with European Regional Development Fund (ERDF), funding opportunities are provided for "up- and re-skilling of adults, to design certification and validation systems are well as to foster learning continuity and mobility",[10] on a public domain;
- On the other hand, through the Pact for Skills,[11] "[n]ew private investments from both big and small companies also need to be encouraged", so "a shared engagement model across regions, sectors and value chains, for companies committed to skilling their workforce"[12] can be developed.

In fact, accordingly to Digital Economy and Society Index (DESI) Report, published in 2021, on the key area concerning "Human Capital",[13] much more has to be done: divided between "internet user skills" and "advanced skills and development", this key area is going to also address main goals to be achieved in the Digital Decade such as (i) "[a]t least basic digital skills"; (ii) "ICT specialists"; and (iii) "[f]emale ICT specialists".[14]

In this sense, despite "84% of people used the internet regularly in 2019, only 56% possessed at least basic digital skills" which means that "[a] large part of the EU population [. . .] still lacks basic digital skills, even though most jobs require such skills", also meaning much has to be done to meet the 2030 target of "at least 80% of citizens hav[ing] [. . .] basic digital skills".[15] Furthermore, concerning an increase on ICT specialists, although the "steady growth since 2013, an acceleration is needed to reach the target" as "[t]here remains a general shortage of ICT specialists on the EU labour market, and the number vacancies keeps growing as new jobs emerge".[16] Nowadays, "[m]ore than 70% of businesses report a lack of staff with adequate (digital) skills as an obstacle to investment", which appears as a factor that might be

[6]European Commission (2021d), p. 22.

[7]Idem, p. 23.

[8]European Commission (2021b).

[9]European Commission (2020a).

[10]European Commission (2021d), p. 23.

[11]European Commission (2020c).

[12]European Commission (2021d), p. 23.

[13]European Commission (2021f).

[14]European Commission (2021g), p. 14.

[15]Idem, p. 15.

[16]Ibidem, pp. 15 and 16.

aligned with another shortcoming: "[t]here is also a severe gender balance issue, with only 19% of ICT specialists [. . .] being women".[17]

Although "skills indicators are strongly influenced by socio-demographic aspects", "youth is not a determinant of digital skills and growing up in a digital world does not automatically make one digitally competent".[18] Insofar, DESI 2021 on Human Capital, relying on the International Computer and Information Literacy Study (ICILS) 2018,[19] stressed that, evaluating "digital skills of 8th-graders based on a competence test, rather than self-reporting, young people do not develop sophisticated digital skills just by growing up using digital devices"; in fact, "more than one third of the pupils achieved scores below the threshold for underachievement in digital competence".[20] However, when analysing Special Eurobarometer's Report concerning the "Future of Europe", only 8% of the respondents understood "digital transformation of the economy and of society" as one of EU's main challenges in its future,[21] which poses difficulties on advancing solutions concerning digital environment and, particularly, on electronic communications and cybersecurity scalable solutions that have to be adopted and densified in this decade.

Concerning digital and technological infrastructures, during this Digital Decade it is aimed at promoting "[e]xcellent and secure connectivity for everybody and everywhere in Europe" since it "is a prerequisite for a society in which every business and citizen can fully participate",[22] through a "more sustainable next generation fixed, mobile and satellite connectivity, with Very High Capacity Networks including 5G being rolled out, based on swift and efficient allocation of spectrum and respect of the 5G cybersecurity toolbox, and with 6G being developed in the years to come".[23] These demands on connectivity will be closely connected to the technological development (for instance, to achieve "real-time data processing") that will be met during the decade.[24]

In this sense, DESI 2021 stresses that "[w]hile the EU has full coverage of basic broadband infrastructure, only 59% of households can benefit from fixed very high capacity network (VHCN) connectivity with the potential of offering gigabit connectivity".[25] On mobile technologies, "while 4G is almost universal reaching 99,7% of populated areas, 5G commercial services were launched in about half of the member states by mid-2020 covering 14% of populated areas".[26] Even though, rural

[17] Ibidem, p. 16.

[18] European Commission (2021f), p. 4.

[19] For further development, IEA – International Association for the Evaluation of Educational Achievement (2018).

[20] European Commission (2021f), p. 4.

[21] European Parliament and European Commission (2022).

[22] European Commission (2021c), p. 5.

[23] Idem, p. 5.

[24] Ibidem, pp. 6 and 7.

[25] European Commission (2021g), p. 16.

[26] European Commission (2021e), p. 5.

areas still pose some difficulties, "as 10% of households are not covered by any fixed network, and 40% are not served by any NGA technology"; insofar, "4G is widely available also in rural areas (98,6%)".[27]

Therefore, "[f]ixed coverage is close to universal in the majority of the EU with less than 3% uncovered households in 19 Member States".[28]

Having established these concerns and objectives, electronic communications path must be developed taking some cybersecurity issues into account. New European Electronic Communications Code[29] will be analysed to understand its cybersecurity solutions, without forgetting the role Cybersecurity Strategy[30] can play on these approaches.

In fact, only a secure online environment based on reliable electronic communications is able to meet both worries of the European Digital Decade: (i) people to further develop digital skills and (ii) digital and electronic infrastructures being sufficiently scalable to new technological developments, so a "digital citizenship"[31] is reached.

2 Cybersecurity Worries on Electronic Communications' Regime

As the Joint Communication on the Cybersecurity Strategy for the Digital Decade was adopted and the European Commission and the High Representative of the Union for Foreign and Security Policy, it started by recognizing "[c]ybersecurity is an integral part of Europeans' security" since "[t]he EU's economy, democracy and society depend more than ever on secure and reliable digital tools and connectivity" and "[c]ybersecurity is [...] essential for building a resilient, green and digital Europe".[32] Digital decade will reach its goals if main areas of public and private action continue to rely on "network and information systems [...] increasingly interconnected". To this purpose, the COVID-19 pandemic had an important impact: "during [it,] 40% of EU workers switched to telework, with likely permanent effects on everyday life", leading to an increase to cyberattacks' vulnerabilities.[33]

---

[27] Idem, p. 6.

[28] Ibidem, p. 7.

[29] Directive (EU) 2018/1972 of the European Parliament and of the Council, of 11 December 2018, establishing the European Electronic Communications Code (recast).

[30] European Commission and High Representative of the Union for Foreign Affairs and Security Policy (2020).

[31] European Commission (2021c), p. 12.

[32] European Commission and High Representative of the Union for Foreign Affairs and Security Policy (2020), p. 1.

[33] Idem, p. 1.

In fact, "[c]yberspace is increasingly exploited for political and ideological purposes, and increased polarization at international level is hindering effective multilateralism" as "[h]ybrid threats combine disinformation campaigns with cyberattacks on infrastructure, economic processes and democratic institutions, with the potential for causing physical damage, obtaining unlawful access to personal data, stealing industrial and state secrets, sowing mistrust and weakening social cohesion".[34] These challenges demand Digital Decade to bear in mind cybersecurity issues when electronic communications are being addressed, so digital literacy can be highlighted, enhancing general population and specialists' digital skills, and a more secure online environment can be created, with electronic infrastructures being able to overcome any kind of digital divide.

In fact, concerning the creation of a secure online environment through infrastructural settings, the Cybersecurity Strategy points out the need of "[s]ecuring the next generation of broadband mobile networks"; insofar, "EU citizens and companies [are expected to use] advanced and innovative applications enabled by 5G and future generations of networks should benefit from the highest security standard".[35] As this new generation of telecommunication networks is able to impact in all aspects of EU citizens, "[t]he cybersecurity of 5G networks is therefore essential not only to protect our economies, societies and democratic processes but also to ensure a trustful digital transformation for the benefit of all EU citizens".[36]

As the European Union is one of the most advanced place in the world concerning the "commercial launch of 5G services", and these services are mainly provided to the general public, there is a need to promote further secure mechanisms, where the European Electronic Communications Code is perceived as "an important basis to create an investment friendly environment for 5G networks and beyond" alongside with "European structural and investment funds" that are "essential to support future deployment of 5G networks, in particular by connecting communities to 5G-enabled services like schools, hospitals, cities and local administrations".[37] Therefore, a toolbox was presented, where some measures have been identified:

- strategic measures (i) "concerning increased regulatory powers for authorities to scrutinise network procurement and deployment"; (ii) "to address risks related to non-technical vulnerabilities"; and (iii) "possible initiatives to promote a sustainable and diverse 5G supply and value chain in order to avoid systemic, long-term dependency risks";

[34] Ibidem, p. 2.

[35] Ididem, p. 8.

[36] European Commission (2020b), p. 1.

[37] Idem, p. 2.

- technical measures "to strengthen the security of 5G networks and equipment by addressing the risks arising from technologies, processes, human and physical factors";
- risk mitigation plans "based on the highest effectiveness measures".[38]

In this sense, the path focuses on "[s]afeguarding the cybersecurity of 5G networks and a diverse 5G value chain" through "telecoms and cybersecurity rules [...], notably with regard to relevant provisions under European rules on electronic communications, and consider the added value of possible implementing acts detailing technical and organisational security measures in order to complement national rules and enhance the effectiveness and consistency of security measures imposed on the operators".[39]

Concerning human developments, the Joint Communication aimed at establishing "[a] cyber-skilled EU workforce" as "an important component of protecting against cyber threats generally", especially if the European Union is capable of "attracting and retaining more diverse talent" and of encouraging "women's participation in science, technology, engineering and mathematics ('STEM') education and ICT jobs upskilling and reskilling in digital skills".[40]

Cybersecurity sensitivity increased social regulation on electronic communications: insofar, concerning two main vectors leading these communications—people's literacy and infrastructures' scalability—the promotion of a universal service continues to be a need to be observed in all Member States. In fact, it demands, in a geographical ubiquity's perspective, making available some services that are deemed as essential, to mitigate population's asymmetries. In this sense, the universal service's concept must be dynamic, demanding its adequacy to technological progress, market's development and users' shifts on services' supply. But it also includes the need to provide safe networks and services.

Cybersecurity worries were particularly taken into consideration under the new European Electronic Communications Code, which demanded its transposition—as it stems from a Directive—until 21st December 2020.

In several Member States, that has not yet happened—as it is the case of Portugal. This country, through Despacho No. 303/2020, of ninth January 2020,[41] established a working group (i) to make a study and to analyse new legislation concerning electronic communications and (ii) to elaborate a legislative preparatory project concerning the transposition of the European Electronic Communications Code. This group, through Autoridade Nacional de Comunicações (ANACOM)—the Portuguese regulatory body on communications—has already fulfilled its task as

[38] Ibidem, p. 5.

[39] European Commission and High Representative of the Union for Foreign Affairs and Security Policy (2020), p. 9.

[40] Idem, p. 12.

[41] Cabinet of the State Secretary of Communications – Infrastructures and Habitation (2020) Despacho No. 303/2020: ninth January 2020. https://dre.pt/dre/detalhe/despacho/303-2020-127910190 [access: 22.2.2022].

ANACOM issued a Decision, on 31st July 2020, which approved the legislative preparatory project to be submitted to the Portuguese Parliament and to the State Secretary of Communications, that also included a sort of proposals concerning specific alterations in other legislative acts still in force in the Portuguese legal order.[42] However, legislative changes have not yet been adopted by the Portuguese legislative authorities. This determined European Commission to start an infringement procedure (under Articles 258–260 TFEU) against Portugal—and other 23 Member States—on fourth February 2021.[43] Nowadays, infringement procedure is still pending before the European Commission, following its prelitigation phase.[44]

However, the Electronic Communications Code's transposition reveals itself of outstanding importance since it aims at implementing "an internal market in electronic communications networks and services that results in the deployment and take-up of very high capacity networks, sustainable competition, interoperability of electronic communications services, accessibility, security of networks and services and end-user benefits [Article 1 (2) (a)]; therefore, security demands are already underlined in its goals and further developed when European legislator establishes, under Article 3 (2) (d), that "national regulatory and other competent authorities as well as BEREC, the Commission and the Member States shall [. . .] promote the interests of the citizens of the Union, [. . .], by maintaining the security of networks and services" and "by ensuring a high and common level of protection for end-users through the necessary sector-specific rules". In the same line, Articles 40 and 41 of this European Code deal with security of networks and services, namely establishing parameters taken into account in the determination of the impact of a security incident—Article 40 (2).

Furthermore, whereas 94 set the interpretative path to understand the role of cybersecurity in electronic communications: "[p]roviders of public electronic communications networks or publicly available electronic communications services, or of both, should be required to take measures to safeguard the security of their networks and services, respectively, and to prevent or minimise the impact of security incidents". Therefore, it is up to them to adopt capable measures to "ensure a level of security of networks and services appropriate to the risks posed". Security measures must fulfil, at least, a set of aspects:

1. Concerning security of networks and facilities, these should observe patterns of "physical and environmental security", "security of supply", "access control to networks" and "integrity of networks";
2. Concerning handling of security incidents, it demands the establishment of "handling procedures", "security incident detection capability", "security incident reporting and communication";

[42] ANACOM (2020).

[43] European Commission (2021a).

[44] For further development concerning infringement procedure in electronic communications' field and BEREC's evolutions, Covelo de Abreu (2018a, b).

3. Concerning business continuity management, the European legislator enhances that the adoption of a "service continuity strategy and contingency plans" along with "disaster recovery capabilities" can enhance cybersecurity;
4. Concerning monitoring, auditing and testing, it is highlighted the need of undertaking "monitoring and logging policies", "networking and service testing" along with providing security assessment and complying with "international standards".

In the same sense, whereas 264 enlightens that it is imposed to the services' providers, in terms of security, the specification, in contracts with users, of which measures will be adopted in case of security incidents, of threats and vulnerabilities. In fact, it will be also up to the provider to clarify applicable compensatory and reimbursement regimes when an inadequate answer is given to a security incident, including those cases when a security incident is caused by vulnerabilities already known and the provider was not able to adopt adequate countermeasures to avoid / surpass the incident.

In line with these objectives, the Portuguese legislative preparatory project also tackles cybersecurity issues. In Article 3 (1) (o) of that ANACOM's project, a "security incident" is defined as "an event with real adverse effect in the security of networks or services of electronic communications".

Furthermore, Article 59, under the theme "Security incidents", determines the emergence of two essential duties to suppliers that intervene in public networks of electronic communications or services of online communications available to the general public: i) the one of notifying ANACOM, as the national regulatory body [Articles 3 (1) (c) and 5], of any security incident with significant impact on the functioning of networks and services; ii) and the one of informing general public, by resorting to adequate means, about security incidents, when it is deemed, by ANACOM, of being of public interest. Article 59 (2) enshrines a specific duty to providers: the one of informing, free of charge, potentially affected users by a specific and significant security threat and, even, of advising a possible prevention measure or a hypothetical response to adopt. In this case, Article 60 (3) identifies the parameters ANACOM will consider to classify a security incident as of having "significant impact".

Annex III of this preparatory project identifies information requirements that companies have to provide to users, where especially it is detailed the need of the user to be informed of "eventual regimes of liability and reimbursement, including, if possible, explicit references to consumers' rights applicable to the infringement of quality levels or if the company gives an inadequate answer to a security incident, to a threat or to a vulnerability".

In this sense, cybersecurity worries in electronic communications are strictly intertwined with achieving a digital citizenship in this decade. In fact, "[r]estrictions of and on the Internet threaten global and open cyberspace, as well as the rule of law, fundamental rights, freedom and democracy—the core values of the EU"[45] and people need to trust online environment so true development can be achieved and digital divide and poverty can be, firstly, addressed and then eradicated.

In fact, nowadays, "[b]eing digitally connected and competent enables active participation in society"; however, the problem remains since "not everyone is online" which "can affect people in the exercise of their rights".[46] "Digital divide" aims at expressing the phenomenon concerning the emerging difficulties posed to those that are not able to express themselves online: "[t]hose who lack regular access to the internet, the necessary skills to make use of these services, or cannot access a digital product or service due to physical or cognitive disability, increasingly risk being excluded and face difficulties in making use of their rights".[47]

In order to overcome this phenomenon, in Portugal there is a mobilization of young volunteers, through a digital inclusion programme, "to help educate adults about the digital transition, based on a national network of 1500 training centre and a number of free tools and resources"—it is estimated to reach one million people.[48]

Furthermore, the impact digital divide can have on fundamental rights also tackles public administration services: since 2017, through interoperable efforts, there is a path of public services' digitalisation, particularly to promote better, cheaper, easier and effective cross-border services, achieving a e-Government paradigm. However, there is a need to promote a sort of general principles so the tonic set by the Lisbon Declaration of June 2021 that "no one is left behind" is observed.[49]

3 Cybersecurity on Electronic Communications: A Means at the Service of the Digital Decade Through the Lens of a European Union Declaration on the Digital Rights and Principles

In the past years, "[a]n increasing number of essential activities are moving to the online sphere, ranging from looking for a job, performing work by means of teleworking, pursuing an education, to interacting with a public administration or making a doctor's appointment".[50] The problem emerges as "not everyone is online"

---

[45] European Commission and High Representative of the Union for Foreign Affairs and Security Policy (2020), p. 2.

[46] European Commission (2021i), p. 21.

[47] Idem, p. 21.

[48] Ibidem, p. 21. For further development, Portuguese Ministers' Council (2020) Resolution No. 30/2020: 21.4.2020. https://dre.pt/dre/detalhe/resolucao-conselho-ministros/30-2020-132133788 [access: 31.1.2022].

[49] Council of the European Union – Portuguese Presidency Digital Democracy with a purpose – Lisbon Declaration: 1.6.2021. https://www.lisbondeclaration.eu/learn-more/ [access: 2.2.2022].

[50] European Commission (2021i), p. 21.

and, even for those that have online expression, almost half of the European population do not congregate "basic digital skills".[51] This creates the digital divide because one of two reasons: or by (i) lacking regular access to the internet; or by (ii) lacking needed skills to use these services (or to use them with a wider knowledge of its threats and opportunities). Therefore, the first is related to infrastructural limitations; the latter concerns population literacy. Both cases—which can also appear in combined scenarios—can lead people to "increasingly risk being excluded and [facing] difficulties in [making] use of their rights". For instance:

- If digital administrative proceedings can only be finished online (without alternative means of access are not maintained), that can jeopardise equal access to public services;
- If economic activities more and more advance to digital environment, "the right of access to services of general economic interest [can] become increasingly conditional on internet access"[52];
- And if regular access to internet is lacking, students can experience difficulties on participating in online activities connected to school, affecting their right to education.

Some solutions are being implemented both on an infrastructural level and on literacy worries: on connectivity, the goal is that "every European household to have access to high-speed internet coverage by 2025 and gigabit connectivity by 2030" while facilitating "access to the 5G spectrum" and "enabling access to fast internet connectivity, 5G [...] and digital technology, as well as strengthening digital competences" in rural areas.[53] On literacy, "[s]everal Member States have policies and programmes to foster access to technology and strengthen digital competencies in the context of formal education"[54] and the European Union adopted the Digital Education Action Plan (2021–2027), bringing a "long-term strategic vision for a sustainable and inclusive digital transformation in education and training", since "[i]t promotes the right of access to high-quality digital education for all and equal access to infrastructure, with a particular focus on encouraging the participation of girls and women" in subjects such as science, technology, engineering and mathematics.[55]

Therefore, these actions will enhance fundamental rights' protection in the digital age as long as they are combined with the presentation of a structured "set of digital principles in an inter-institutional solemn declaration between the European

[51] Idem, p. 21.

[52] Ibidem, p. 21.

[53] Ibidem, p. 23.

[54] Ibidem, p. 23. Greeks are tackling digital divide steaming from social and economic conditions (by providing pupils vouchers to purchase equipment like tablets and computers) and by providing relevant educational programmes through a virtual "Digital Skills Academy", which was launched in 2020.

[55] Ibidem, p. 23.

Commission, the European Parliament and the Council" as it "will inform users and guide policy makers and digital operators about the European way to the digital transformation".[56]

Concerning this set of general principles, its aim is at defining "a European way for the digital transition, launching a broad consultation and engagement exercise" to promote "a values-based European digital landscape to help nurture more democratic and inclusive societies, ensuring a level playing field for all EU citizens to access and leverage the full potential of an increasingly digital world",[57] showcasing European citizenship already has an online expression, as a digital citizenship.

Concerning digital divide and population unawareness concerning basic digital skills, "[a] large number of EU citizens surveyed is not aware that rights such as the freedom of expression, privacy, or non-discrimination should also be respected online"[58]—for instance, in Portugal, 61% of the enquired stated they were aware those rights should be both respected offline and online but 33% thought they ought not to be protected in the online environment. Consubstantiating the need of further digital literacy, "[a] large majority of respondents would consider it useful to know more about their rights in the online environment", as "[m]ore than three quarters (76%) of respondents indicate they would find it useful".[59] Taking the Portuguese example, 22% thought it would be "very useful", 52% "fairly useful" and only 7% and 6% find it "not very useful" or "not at all useful", respectively. Notwithstanding, 11% still replied they do not use the internet, which makes Digital Decade ambitions a more demanding reality to the Portuguese population as this Member State presented the highest percentage in this indicator,[60] which demands, from it, also a campaign to sensitize population to internet use.

This survey reveals there is still a portion of the European society that is not open to digital transformation and, therefore, to the opportunity to be heard both offline and online. It also reveals a resistance to cybersecurity approaches as the general public still have not developed a complete comprehension of their rights and the opportunities and threats they can experience online; therefore, they cannot grasp which online affections and restrictions they can be submitted to and, furthermore, which security incidents can impact on their effectiveness. This undermines cybersecurity demands on people's eyes as they are not able to understand its true impact on protecting their fundamental rights and freedoms.

In order to overcome this reality, a set of general principles of EU law particularly designed to the digital environment is needed, which is also a common sensitivity: "[a] large majority of respondents considers it useful for the European Commission to define and promote a common European vision on digital rights and principles".[61]

[56] Ibidem, p. 35.

[57] European Commission (2021h), p. 5.

[58] Idem, p. 19.

[59] Ibidem, p. 8.

[60] Ibidem, p. 23.

[61] Ibidem, p. 26.

In the special Eurobarometer "Digital rights and principles", respondents faced some given situations that could influence and inspire principles' proclamation in order for them to categorize which could be important to secure.

In the overall scenario, 90% of the respondents understood, as (very or fairly) important that "everyone, including people with disabilities or at risk of exclusion, should benefit from easily accessible and user-friendly digital public services",[62] setting empirical grounding to the proclamation, as general principles of EU law, particularly in the digital context, user-friendly and user-focused principles. In the same diapason, for 90% of respondents, "everyone should be clearly informed about the terms and conditions that apply to their internet connection", while 89% understood there was a need of promoting a right to internet access in a technological approach ("everyone needs to be able to access the internet through an affordable and high speed connection").[63]

On cybersecurity matters, 90% of the respondents also understood the principle of secure and trustworthy environment is important since "a safe and trusted online environment where people are protected from cybercrime and illegal content and goods" is necessary.[64] Respondents also shown concerns about how they are digitally portrayed: 85% understood "everyone should be able to use a secure and trustworthy digital identity that can be used to access a broad range of public and private online services". To ease and haste their relations with public services, 42% still understood once-only principle as "very important" while 35% saw it as "fairly important".[65]

On digital literacy and education, around 84% still understood digital literacy a priority by standing that it is (very/fairly) important to promote the "understanding of digital technologies", while 90% perceived as vital the "access to education and training enabling everyone to acquire the necessary digital skills to take an active part in society, the labour market and democratic processes".[66] Bridging technological and educational approaches to overcome digital divide, 88% of the respondents also underlined "high-quality digital education" based on the availability of equipment and courses as relevant, since 87% perceived education as a means to "encourage critical thinking while navigating the internet, including online social networks",[67] which is aligned with the digital decade goal of enhancing population at general basic digital skills and promoting high-level digital skills in related fields, making them more desirable to women.

In January 2022, the European Commission made available a Communication where it established the grounding for a future joint solemn declaration on digital

[62] Ibidem, p. 28.
[63] Ibidem, p. 28.
[64] Ibidem, p. 34.
[65] Ibidem, p. 28.
[66] Ibidem, p. 34.
[67] Ibidem, p. 42.

rights and principles for the Digital Decade,[68] to be signed by the European Parliament, the Council and the Commission. By reinforcing a human centric approach to the digital transition, Commission understood "digital transformation should be shaped according to our European values and law", which can be assessed with "an effective monitoring of the principles enshrined in the Declaration" presented annually, "together with a yearly Eurobarometer on the European citizens' perception of the actions and measures taken".[69] This Declaration is also sensitive to security demands: "the burgeoning availability of new digital technologies and data also comes with undesirable risks that can have far-reaching effects for citizens, our democratic values, our security, or the fundaments of our societies" since "[t]hese risks have grown significantly, including with regard to privacy and personal data breaches, the spread of illegal and harmful content and unsafe products as well as disinformation, cybercrime and cyberattacks, exploitation and abuse of human beings, [. . .] mass surveillance, algorithmic biases hindering fair and non-discriminatory access to information and democratic debate and even outright censorship". In fact, if cybersecurity measures are not addressed, these issues "go to the heart of the fundamental rights and undermine the hard-fought progress made in this filed both in the European Union and internationally".[70]

In the proposal of the European joint Declaration on Digital Rights and Principles for the Digital Decade[71] major worries on electronic communications' field are the ones concerning technological availability and population literacy, where some relevant achievements that can be found:

- On Chap. I, it is said that people will be "at the centre of the digital transformation" since "[t]echnology should serve and benefit all Europeans and empower them to pursue their aspirations, in full security and respect of their fundamental rights". Therefore, only by "fostering responsible and diligent action by all digital actors, public and private, for a safe and secure digital environment" will allow to strength "the democratic framework" and to ensure "that the values of the Union and the rights of individuals [. . .] are respected online as well as offline"[72];
- On Chap. II, particularly on the "inclusion" dimension, there is a commitment path of not leaving "nobody behind", by "making sure that technological solutions respect people's rights, enable their exercise and promote inclusion" which calls the attention both to technological and literacy demands. In this Chapter, there is a literal mention to "connectivity": "[e]veryone, everywhere in the EU, should have access to affordable and high-speed digital connectivity", "wherever they live and whatever their income"[73]; while it also addresses "Digital education

[68] European Commission (2022b).
[69] Idem, p. 2.
[70] Ibidem, p. 3.
[71] European Commission (2022a).
[72] Idem, p. 2.
[73] Ibidem, p. 3.

and skills" since "everyone has the right to education, training and lifelong learning and should be able to acquire all basic and advanced digital skills": in this sense, trying to address it by inception, the Declaration proposal aims at promoting and supporting equipment needs on "digital connectivity, infrastructure and tools" while making efforts so teachers and students have the needed "digital skills and competences to take an active part in economy, society, and in democratic processes" but also on work environment, by allowing up-skilling and re-skilling of the working population[74];

– On Chap. V, focus is on "Safety, security and empowerment". In this sense, "access to digital technologies, products and services [have to be] safe, secure, and privacy-protective by design".

All these public interests have to be pursued under electronic communications framework, relying on the Electronic Communications Code solutions—engaging national regulatory authorities in close relations with BEREC (Body of European Regulators for Electornic Communications). In fact, as these digital rights and principles will steam from a political declaration, they will appear as primary public interests that have to be executed by administrative authorities within the European Union law scope of application. Insofar, both national public administrations—hereby represented by national regulatory authorities—and European agencies—as BEREC—will take a vital role on legally activating these rights and principles, so fundamental rights' protection can be both promote online and offline and a true felling of European digital citizenship can emerge in this digital decade.

References

ANACOM (2020) Decision of 31st July 2020 - Anteprojeto de diploma de transposição da Diretiva (UE) 2018/1972 (Legislative preparatory transposition Project): 4.8.2021. https://anacom.pt/render.jsp?contentId=1555005. Accessed 15 Feb 2022

Covelo de Abreu J (2018a) Digital Single Market as the new world to the European Union: repercussions in the social and institutional regulatory structure – the universal service and the Body of European Regulators for Electronic Communications' (BEREC) redefinition. UNIO EU Law Journal 4(2):48–60. https://doi.org/10.21814/unio.4.2

Covelo de Abreu J (2018b) New European Framework relating to the making available on the market of radio equipment (Directive 2014/53/UE): national legislator and ANACOM's role – inadequate pursue of the accused? Perspectives under EU procedure. In: Canedo MDP (ed) La competencia como motor de desarrollo económico. Thomson Reuters – Aranzadi, pp 351–374

European Commission (2020a) Commission welcomes political agreement on Erasmus+ programme. Press release: 11.12.2020 Brussels. https://ec.europa.eu/commission/presscorner/detail/en/IP_20_2317. Accessed 19 Jan 2022

European Commission (2020b) Communication to the European Parliament, the Council, the European Economic and Social Committee and the Committee of the Regions "Secure 5G

[74]Ibidem.

deployment in the EU – Implementing the EU toolbox", Brussels: 29.1.2020, COM(2020) 50 final
European Commission (2020c) Pact for skills, employment, social affairs & inclusion Website: 10.11.2020 Brussels. https://ec.europa.eu/social/main.jsp?catId=1517&langId=en. Accessed 19 Jan 2022
European Commission (2021a) Commission opens infringement procedures against 24 Member States for not transposing new EU telecom rules. Press release: 4.2.2021 Brussels. https://ec.europa.eu/commission/presscorner/detail/en/IP_21_206. Accessed 23 Feb 2022
European Commission (2021b) Commission welcomes political agreement on the ESF+. Press Release: 29.1.2021 Brussels. https://ec.europa.eu/commission/presscorner/detail/en/IP_21_225. Accessed 19 Jan 2022
European Commission (2021c) Communication to the European Parliament, the Council, the European Economic and Social Committee and the Committee of the Regions "2030 Digital Compass: the European way for the Digital Decade". Brussels: 9.3.2021, COM(2021) 118 final
European Commission (2021d) Communication to the European Parliament, the Council, the European Economic and Social Committee and the Committee of the Regions, "The European Pillar of Social Rights Action Plan", Brussels: 4.3.2021, COM(2021) 102 final
European Commission (2021e) Digital Economy and Society Index (DESI) 2021 – Digital infrastructures: 12.11.2021
European Commission (2021f) Digital Economy and Society Index (DESI) 2021 – Human Capital: 12.11.2021
European Commission (2021g) Digital Economy and Society Index (DESI) 2021 – Thematic chapters: 12.11.2021
European Commission (2021h) Digital Rights and Principles, Special Eurobarometer 518 Report: September–October 2021
European Commission (2021i) Report to the European Parliament, the Council, the European Economic and Social Committee and the Committee of the Regions "Protecting fundamental rights in the digital age – 2021 Annual Report on the Application of the EU Charter of Fundamental Rights", Brussels: 10.12. 2021, COM(2021) 819 final
European Commission (2022a) European Declaration on Digital Rights and Principles for the Digital Decade, Brussels: 26.1.2022, COM(2022) 28 final
European Commission (2022b) Communication to the European Parliament, the Council, the European Economic and Social Committee and the Committee of Regions "Establishing a European Declaration on digital rights and principles for the Digital Decade", Brussels: 26.1.2022, COM(2022) 27 final
European Commission and High Representative of the Union for Foreign Affairs and Security Policy (2020) Joint Communication to the European Parliament and the Council "The EU's cybersecurity strategy for the digital decade", Brussels: 16.12.2020, JOIN(2020) 18 final
European Parliament and European Commission (2022) Future of Europe, Special Eurobarometer 517 Report: September–October 2021
IEA – International Association for the Evaluation of Educational Achievement (2018) ICILS 2018. https://www.iea.nl/studies/iea/icils/2018. Accessed 19 Jan 2022

Joana Covelo de Abreu is a Professor of European Union law at the University of Minho – School of Law, Portugal. She acts within the European Union Law, namely devoting her attention to EU Procedure, Data Transfer and Interoperability within European e-Government and e-Justice paradigms. She was, until August 2022, the Coordinator of the Jean Monnet Module eUjust – "EU Procedure and credits' claims: approaching electronic solutions under e-Justice paradigm". She was an appointed expert to the modernization of judicial cooperation in civil matters (DG Justice and Consumers – European Commission), in 2018, namely concerning discussing Commission's proposals on taking of evidence and service of documents' Regulations. Editor of UNIO – EU Law Journal and its official blog "Thinking & Debating Europe – The official blog of UNIO".

Printed in the USA
CPSIA information can be obtained
at www.ICGtesting.com
LVHW011235110224
771537LV00003B/156

9 783031 418198